THE COLORADO RIVER
YESTERDAY, TO-DAY AND TO-MORROW

HERMIT RAPIDS.

THE COLORADO RIVER
YESTERDAY, TO-DAY AND TO-MORROW

BY

LEWIS R. FREEMAN

AUTHOR OF

"DOWN THE YELLOWSTONE," "DOWN THE COLUMBIA,"
"IN THE TRACKS OF THE TRADES," ETC., ETC.

WITH ILLUSTRATIONS

NEW YORK
DODD, MEAD AND COMPANY
1923

PRINTED IN THE U. S. A. By
The Quinn & Boden Company
BOOK MANUFACTURERS
RAHWAY   NEW JERSEY

TO
FREDERICK S. DELLENBAUGH,
DEAN OF COLORADO RIVER EXPLORERS,
ARTISTS AND HISTORIANS

FOREWORD

THERE is only one worse thing that a river-rat can do than turn turtle, and that is to turn historian.

I'll make that little joke right here at the outset on the chance that it will head some one else off from making it later on. I already have considerable first-hand knowledge of what happens to a river-rat when he turns turtle, and have no doubt that I shall broaden my experience not a little along that line before these pages appear in print. *After* that event I may expect to learn something of the sort of justice that is dealt out to the river-rat that turns historian.

Some are born historians, some achieve history and others have history thrust upon them. I am of these last, and—since it seems that history had to impinge anyhow—rather glad that it came by thrust rather than by birth or by achievement. Somehow that fact leaves me feeling just a shade less guilty over what has happened. No book was ever written with less malice aforethought than was the present volume. I hope the circumstances will be interpreted extenuatingly. I really didn't mean to do the thing I have done at all. I was going to do something quite different. Here is about the way it befell:

The early summer of 1922 found me finished with only one of the three volumes my publishers had announced to cover my previous seasons' voyage down the Yellowstone, Missouri and Mississippi. With work for another year or two ahead, further material was the last thing in the world of which I was in search. Then came a chance to handle one of the boats for a party of Government engineers who were studying the middle canyons of the Colorado in connection with plans for reclamation and flood-control. At the end of three weeks— in company with a half dozen engineers who will influence profoundly all but the political destinies of Colorado Basin development for many years to come—I had visited practically every important dam and reservoir site on the middle and lower river. Then I boated alone down to Yuma, picked up two more engineers, and followed the newly-diverted Colorado from the Pescadero Cut to the head of the Gulf of California. Finally I journeyed back to Yuma and boated by the Alamo Canal and River to the ancient mouth of the Colorado in Salton Sea.

In rather less than two months I had been given practical demonstration of the menace and the might of the Colorado, and of how, by binding the might, the menace could be removed. Men had spent years, even decades, on the river without gaining so comprehensive a first-hand survey of its problems as a fortunate combination of circumstances had made possible to me in those few full weeks at the end of the summer. With the development of this great arid basin becoming of increasing national interest, my publishers and I were agreed that we ought to defer the publication of the volumes covering my Missouri and Mississippi voyages and rush into print with a right-down-to-the-minute work on "Binding the Colorado."

Assuring myself that I had the whole subject at my fingertips, I settled down at my desk along about the first of the year and prepared to write. It was a real comfort to know that I had in mind just what I wanted to say. Then came an insidious idea that had to do with a brief historical introduction—just a few pages about how the river was found by way of leading up to how it was to be bound. And, so, as an overconfident boatman allows himself to be drawn into the grip of an unreconnoitred rapid, I found myself swept into the resistless current of Colorado River history. At the foot of the first pitch I was wallowing hard but unswamped—also unchastened. The thrill of the colourful panorama unwinding ahead drew me on. I had known a similar sensation times without number in real rapids. I had to see the adventure through to the finish whatever there was at the end of it. Stowing my mooring lines, I pulled out into the middle of the current and turned loose. Signalling often for guidance but never for aid to reach the bank, I ran the full course—four centuries of Colorado River history passed in swift review.

A few days ago I eased down to quiet water, pulled into an eddy and beached my battered shallop upon a strip of friendly beach. The run had been a breathless, a memorable one; but it was over. My task was finished, though hardly along the lines of that timely, right-down-to-the-minute work on "Binding the Colorado" as originally planned. On the binding of the river I had written but three chapters; on the finding of the river there were sixteen. Perhaps that is about as it should be after all. They have been finding the Colorado for nearly four hundred years; binding is just beginning to be discussed. Finding is all but complete; binding has barely begun. Indeed, what may well be considered as the final act of exploration— the surveying of the gorge of the Grand Canyon—might also stand in a sense as the opening act of exploitation.

If all goes well, the work of the Geological Survey party in the Grand Canyon should be completed by some time in October. The date will be one of unique significance in Colorado River history, as marking the end of the finding and the beginning of the binding. Thereafter there will be little to be learned of the river but much to be gained from it. At just about the same time as that historic survey is finished this volume should be coming from the press. There will never again be so fitting a moment for the publication of a book bearing the title: "The Colorado River: Yesterday, To-day and To-morrow." Whether that fitness extends beyond the cover of this particular book is quite another matter.

Whatever the worth (or the worthlessness) of the result of the effort, the writing of this record has been an outstanding personal experience, and for two reasons. For one, because of

the sheer thrill of the adventure of following the Finders; for
the other, because of the profound gratification of discovering
myself the object of as hearty and kindly a spirit of co-
operation, as prompt and willing a showing of beacon and a
buoying of channel, as navigator of strange waters can ever
have known.

Concerning the Great Adventure of following the Finders:
I only hope that Alarçon and Escalante, Ashley, Manly and
Hardy, Ives and Wheeler, Powell, Dellenbaugh and Stanton,
Stone and the Kolbs, had half the fun in showing the way in
fact that I have had out of following it in fancy. They have
all been very real characters to me—those whose story I have
had to glean from the printed page scarcely less than those
who have told me of their voyages by word of mouth. The
thing I have striven to do above all others is to preserve and
transfer to my own pages as much as possible of the flesh-and-
blood humanness of the pioneer explorers and navigators, a
humanness of which I have personally never failed to be con-
scious from the first.

Not the least of the Finders has been a shadow to me; every
figure in the moving pageant has been three-dimensional and
full of good red blood. If I shall have helped others to a similar
sense of reality something will have been done toward compensating for shortcomings hardly avoidable in the work of a
novice who has had perforce to complete in four months a task
to which an honest-to-goodness historian would have given the
painstaking research of as many years.

As for the Helping Hands: Perhaps the most abiding impressions of my own voyages down the Columbia, Yellowstone and
many other rivers have had to do with the simple, unpretentious
kindliness of those who dwelt along the way. My voyage
in fancy down the wakes of the Finders of the Colorado seems
destined to leave corresponding memories no less pleasant to
dwell upon. There was none who tried to dissuade me from
the presumptuous enterprise, many who lent willing hands to

fend me from the rocks. Wherever possible in my record I
have endeavoured to indicate my obligations as I went along.
There are a number, however, for whose friendly aid my especial thanks are due. First among these are those veterans of
notable Colorado canyon voyages, Frederick S. Dellenbaugh,
Julius F. Stone, and the Kolb brothers, Ellsworth and Emery.

Mr. Dellenbaugh, first among Colorado River historians,
wrote at the very beginning of my effort to say that all the
original material of his personal collection was at my disposal.
Unable to avail myself of this generous offer, I am still indebted to that distinguished artist and explorer for many letters
discussing earlier and later Colorado canyon voyages and clarifying numerous obscurities with testimony and opinion that
none but himself is in a position to give.

To Julius F. Stone I am indebted for material which has enabled me to write what I believe is the first account to be published of his notably successful voyage down the whole Colorado canyon series with that most resourceful of rough-water
navigators, Nathan Galloway. Mr. Stone's keen comment—
in conversation and in correspondence—on several moot questions of Colorado River exploration has been invaluable.

To Ellsworth Kolb I owe the privilege of condensing to an
all-too-short chapter the fine, modest story of river adventure
he told in his "Through the Grand Canyon from Wyoming to
Mexico" (The Macmillan Company, New York, 1920). For
much illuminative discussion of practical navigational problems
of the Colorado I am indebted to both Ellsworth and Emery
Kolb, with whom, as fellow river-rats, I have yarned for many
hours.

Material for my chapter on the Brown-Stanton voyages,
which the untimely death of Robert Brewster Stanton prevented my securing at first-hand from that courageous navigator, has been furnished me by his daughter, Mrs. Lewis S.
(Anna Stanton) Burchard.

My account of Father Escalante's great *entrada* of 1775 is

largely based upon the translation of his diary published in "The Catholic Church in Utah," by Dean Harris. The extracts I have quoted from the condensation of the diary kept by General Ashley during his voyage through the canyons of the upper Green are from "The Ashley-Smith Explorations," ably edited by Professor Harrison Clifford Dale. The original document is in the Library of the Missouri Historical Society.

To the Munk Library of Arizoniana of the Southwest Museum, Los Angeles, I am under great obligation for books, pamphlets, magazine articles and reports bearing on Colorado River subjects. Much of this material could hardly have been obtained in any library west of New York. For the kindness of Miss Cora Hatch, Librarian, in searching out this matter, and for the courtesy of Dr. Munk in allowing me to pack it home to go over in my own time, I am especially grateful.

For data bearing upon the material development of the Basin of the Colorado I am indebted in general to the U. S. Reclamation Service and the U. S. Geological Survey, and in particular to five members of the Glen Canyon survey party of last summer. These latter are: The Honourable Arthur Powell Davis, Director of the Reclamation Service; Dr. John A. Widtsoe, Commissioner of Education of the Church of Jesus Christ of the Latter Day Saints; Herman Stabler, Chief of the Land Classification Branch of the U. S. Geological Survey; E. C. La Rue, Hydraulic Engineer of the U. S. Geological Survey; and Clarence C. Stetson, Secretary of the Colorado River Commission. What I did not garner from these amiable companions of the river-road by dam-site and camp-fire, I have since gathered in through correspondence.

Mr. Davis furnished me with information covering the reclamation work already complete in the Basin of the Colorado and with outlines of the comprehensive plans of the future. Mr. Stabler and Mr. La Rue kept me advised concerning the work and the plans of the Geological Survey. Dr. Widtsoe put at

my disposal several volumes having a bearing on the settlement
of the Basin of the Colorado by the Mormons. Mr. Stetson,
besides keeping me informed on the work of the Colorado
River Commission, exhumed for my use from Washington
archives several reports long out of print and otherwise un-
obtainable.

Mr. Ray S. Carberry, Chief Engineer of the Imperial Irrigation District, gave me material assistance in my attempt to follow the diverted Colorado from the Pescadero Dam to tide-
water, as did also Frank Higley, Superintendent for the Imperial Irrigation District at Andrade, and Ray Priest, Chief
Engineer of the Yuma Reclamation Project, who accompanied
me on this novel voyage. To Mr. Higley my thanks are also
due for the boat which I subsequently broke in two while trying to run down to the Salton Sea by the drainage ditch that
was once the channel of the Alamo River.

Except those taken by myself, all photographs of which I
could trace the origin have been credited to the photographer
or owner of the negative. My greatest obligation on this score
is to the U. S. Geological Survey, which has given me the use
of photographs taken in the Colorado River Basin from the
time of the second Powell Expedition to the present year. By
far the largest number of these views were taken by E. C. La
Rue and Ralf R. Woolley, Hydraulic Engineers of the Water
Resources Branch, N. C. Grover, Chief Engineer. To the Kolb
Brothers and to Julius F. Stone I am indebted for the photographs which illustrate their respective chapters, and to the
Chief of Engineers of the U. S. War Department for the views
taken by the Wheeler Expedition. A number of especially
striking photographs of the Grand Canyon are used through
the courtesy of Fred Harvey.

This list of obligations, incomplete as it is, is a formidable
one; but if anything I have written brings even a few of my
readers to a realization of what was involved in the Finding

of the Colorado, and of what may eventuate through the Binding of the Colorado, it will not have been incurred entirely in vain.

PASADENA,
   June, 1923.

CONTENTS

PART I: FINDING THE RIVER

PART II: BINDING THE RIVER

PART III: AFTERWORD

ILLUSTRATIONS

xvii

ILLUSTRATIONS

Part I

FINDING THE RIVER

THE COLORADO RIVER

CHAPTER I

THE CONQUISTADORES

FOR our earliest knowledge of the river we now call the Colorado we are about equally indebted to the Spanish *conquistadores* and the Spanish *padres*. As commerce follows the flag in world expansion of the present day, in the fifteenth and sixteenth centuries it was the Cross that followed the Sword. It fell to the *conquistador* to find and to establish temporal power, to the *padre* to consolidate spiritually. Possibly because the priest received and set down his impressions under conditions more nearly normal than did the soldier, it was he who left us rather the more dependable records.

The fanciful stories told to Cortez by Alvar Nunez Cabeza de Vaca of the incalculable wealth of the region covered by his wanderings on the head waters of the Rio Grande were responsible for the first expedition to the vicinity of the mouth of the Colorado. In July, 1536, three years after Alvar Nunez and his glib-tongued negro, Estavan, had electrified Mexico with their tales of the gold of Cibola, Cortez dispatched three ships from Acapulco for the purpose of approaching as near as possible to the supposed El Dorado by water. The plan, doubtless, was to proceed northward along the coast of what was then called the Sea of Cortez to the approximate latitude of the fabulous Seven Cities, and then make an endeavour to reach them by an overland journey from the west.

Francisco de Ulloa navigated his clumsy caravels to a point where shoaling water, heavy tides and converging shores told him that he was at the head of a long gulf rather than the open

3

strait which at that time was believed to separate what we
now know as the peninsula of Baja California from the mainland. Although, because of the extensive building southward
of the delta which cannot but have taken place in the intervening centuries, Ulloa must have reached a point far inland
of the present mouth of the Colorado, he seems to have observed nothing to lead him more than to surmise that there
was any considerable drainage to the gulf whose head he had
so plainly attained. Yet the following description of the conditions in the immediate vicinity of his sorely beset little fleet
might well have been taken from the log of the packet that
anchored last night at La Bomba, after its run to the mouth
of the Colorado from Guaymas with peons for the cotton fields
of the Imperial Valley.

"We always found more shallow water" [he wrote] "and the sea
thick, black, and very muddy. . . . We rode all night in five fathom
of water, and we perceived the sea to run with so great a rage into
the land that it was a thing much to be marvelled at; and with
the like fury it returned back again with the ebb, during which time
we found eleven fathom water, and the flood and ebb continued from
five to six hours."

From the lookout the pilot reported:

". . . all the land full of sand in a great round compass and
joining itself with the other shore; and it was so low that whereas
we were a league from the same we could not discern it, and it
seemed there was an inlet of the mouths of certain lakes, whereby
the sea went in and out. There were diverse opinions amongst
us, and some thought that that current entered into these lakes,
and also that some great river there might be the cause
thereof."

A wall of water running with "a great rage into the land,"
and that baffling blending of shore-line and overflowed tidal
flats so graphically sketched in Ulloa's description, are the
high-lights in the mental picture formed on a visit I made to

the head of the Gulf of California but a few months ago. The thirty-six feet of tidal rise indicated by a low-water sounding of five fathoms and a high-water one of eleven, is perhaps fifty per cent. greater than the maximum of the present day, though it is by no means improbable that the "bore" ran more fiercely before the head of the Gulf was broadened by the accumulated silt of later centuries.

Greatly as Ulloa failed to take advantage of his opportunity by pushing farther north on land or in small boats, he is hardly open to the charge of pusillanimity in refusing to risk his ships in penetrating the shallows swept by the tidal bore of the Gulf. A skipper who, without power to fall back upon, would risk a schooner of over fifty tons in those waters to-day would certainly be putting himself in line for loss of his license if not for an examination for sanity. Indeed, with a fairly comprehensive knowledge of the voyages of Captain James Cook, I am inclined to the opinion that this greatest of all navigators of uncharted seas never deliberately put a ship into so treacherous a corner as that infernal neck of mud and sand where the Colorado breaks the strength of the tide of the Gulf of California.

Dellenbaugh, telling how Cortez had pawned his wife's jewels and made a gambler's final fling of the expedition of Francisco de Ulloa picturesquely characterizes the failure of that voyage as the expiring ray of the setting sun of the conqueror of Mexico. A journey to Spain, undertaken in 1540 in the hope of rehabilitating his declining fortunes, was barren of results, and he never recrossed the Atlantic. Ulloa, after sending back one ship to Acapulco to bear the news of his failure, doubled the cape of Baja California and sailed away into the Unknown, never to return.

The killing of the negro, Estavan, on his attempted return to the Seven Cities of Cibola only served to fan the flame of the desire of the Spaniards to open a road to riches which were described as incomparably greater than the treasures of the

Aztecs of Mexico. To make assurance doubly sure, Mendoza, viceregal successor to Cortez, decided to equip two expeditions of exploration and conquest. One was to go by land under Francisco Vasquez de Coronado, and the other, under Hernando de Alarcón, by way of the Gulf. Perhaps nothing could give a better idea of the faulty geographic conceptions of the time than the fact that Mendoza expected that the two expeditions would pursue almost parallel courses, and so keep in constant touch throughout their operations. As was inevitable, of course, neither leader heard aught but the most indirect and fragmentary reports of the other until after all opportunity for co-operation was long past. That each expedition, moving independently, accomplished notable feats of exploration, was due to the remarkable courage and energy of its leader and the unusually staunch stuff of the rank-and-file.

Coronado, marching in May, reached Cibola in July to discover just about what we find in that region to-day—picturesque mud villages inhabited by an unwarlike agricultural people, possessed of almost nothing at all in the way of gold, silver or precious stones. The subsequent explorations of neither Coronado nor his indefatigable lieutenants pointed the way to treasure for the enrichment of the coffers of New Spain, but they added greaty to the knowledge of a region hitherto completely unknown to the outer world. Perhaps the salient feature of their geographic contribution was the establishment of the fact that the extensive plateau land over which they had wandered was completely cut off from the region to the north by a gorge of a profundity undreamed of outside the Stygian depths of the Inferno. Of the march of Cárdenas to the brink of the Grand Canyon I shall write in its due chronological sequence; the real discoverer of the Colorado River claims prior notice.

Alarcón, after riding out a severe storm, provisioning at Santiago, and adding a third ship to his squadron at Aguaiauall, arrived at the head of the Gulf on the 26th of August, 1540.

On his own statement it was only the sense of his responsibility to Coronado, whom he had been ordered to support with supplies, that nerved him to risking his ships among the tide-swept bars at the mouth of the half-guessed river. So treacherous appeared "the flats and shoals from which the aforesaid fleet" had turned, that Alarcón's pilots advised against venturing farther. "But because your Lordship commanded me that I should bring you the secret of that gulf," he wrote, "I resolved that although I had known that I should have lost the ships, I would not have ceased for anything to have seen the head thereof."

Sending his Pilot Major to sound out a channel from a small boat, the intrepid Captain followed close with his Flagship, which in turn gave the course to the remaining units of the little fleet. What followed was approximately what would happen to-day to an equal number of fishing sloops or trading schooners venturing under sail into the same waters, although I am inclined to doubt if once in a hundred times the percentage of salvage would be as high as in the case of the brave and fortunate Alarcón. I fear there is not much in his account that may be taken as "Sailing Directions" by the skipper who would follow in the wake of the Discoverer.

". . . within a short while after we found ourselves fast on the sands with all our three ships, in such sort that one could not help another, neither could the boats succor us because the current was so great that it was impossible for one of us to come to another. Whereupon we were in such great jeopardy that the deck of the *Admiral* was oftentimes under water; and if a great surge of the sea had not come and driven our ship right up and given her leave, as it were, to breathe awhile, we had there been drowned; and likewise the other two ships found themselves in very great hazard, yet because they were lesser and drew less water their danger was not so great as ours. Now it pleased God upon the return of the flood that the ships came on float, and so went forward, and though the company would have returned back, yet for all this I was determined to go forward and to pursue our attempted voyage. And we passed forward with much ado, turning our stems now this way, now that way, to seek and find the channel. And it pleased God that after this sort we came to the very bottom of the bay, where we found a very mighty river, which ran with so great a fury of a stream, that we could hardly sail against it."

It would be extremely interesting, especially if one were sure of being able to make the necessary calendar adjustments correctly, to endeavour to figure out if Alarcón crossed the bar of the Colorado within a day or two one way or the other of either the full or the new moon. The August tides of these moons would have been but slightly less than those of the September equinox, so that if his passage coincided with either of the phases mentioned it would have been the great bore in all its strength that buffeted the ships stranded upon the bar. On the other hand, the materially less savage tides of the " 'tween-new-and-full" phases would have made the passage, although still dangerous, much easier.

From Alarcón's description I am inclined to believe his passage was made at a tide somewhere between the worst and the most favourable stages. Although they built ships wondrous stout in those days, and sailed them wondrous well, I cannot conceive it possible that any sort of a sea-craft, once solidly stranded, could feel the full force of the August bore and fail to be capsized, if not torn to pieces. The fact that none of Alarcón's fleet lost so much as a rudder makes it almost certain that they were called to withstand the force of a bore of only moderate strength.

The recent loss of the *Topolobampo* on a bar below La Bomba is an example of the way of the bore with a stranded ship. Although the captain of this thirty-six-ton steamer, which was plying up and down the Gulf with peons for the cotton-fields near Calexico, was fully cognizant of the character of the currents and the channels, he was unable to prevent it from grounding and being rolled before the advancing wave of the tide. The loss of something like fourscore of the passengers and crew of the *Topolobampo* made that disaster the most serious in the history of Gulf of California navigation.

No sooner was the worst of the danger zone passed than Alarcón, mooring his ships at the first point where protection from the onslaught of the bore was offered, armed and provisioned two of his small boats and pushed off up the river. His force consisted of twenty men and included two important functionaries listed respectively as Treasurer and Comptroller. On paper the official roster conveys rather the suggestion of a modern debt-collecting commission on a punitive visit to a South American republic, or the board of directors of a get-rich-quick organization of frenzied financiers. And as a matter of fact, glamorous as were his doings, probably no better characterization than "Frenzied Get-Rich-Quickster" could be applied to the Spanish *conquistador*. Nor, if we substitute souls for gold as the medium in which wealth was sought, would that name prove unduly or unjustly inapt if applied to the fanatically zealous proselyting *padre* of the same period.

The current of the river proving too swift to be breasted with oars, Alarcón was compelled almost immediately to land his men and resort to towing from the bank. Cordelling upstream, rather a heart- and back-breaking task on any sort of a river, is pretty nearly at its worst on one flanked by alternate mud-bars and undermining and caving banks. I write both feelingly and authoritatively on that point, for it has fallen to my lot to muddle through many miles of Colorado delta mud in the course of the last decade and a half, some of the muddiest of the muddling dating back no more than a few months. Totally lacking in the fine technique of cordelling, and doubtless soft from long weeks of inaction on shipboard, the Spaniards might have gone on floundering impotently in the tidal flats for many days had not the genius of their resourceful leader intervened to provide more effective power.

Alarcón evidently was generously blessed with that quick adaptability to circumstance that enables its possessor to fly

to success on the wings of defeat. He had rated hostile Indians as the main menace to his advance, and it was to provide against attack that small cannon were mounted in what
must have been already badly overloaded boats. Yet when
an increasingly formidable array of hideously masked and
painted Indians began to gather upon the bank the keen-witted
Captain received them, not with a salvo from his guns, but with
the confident announcement that he had been sent as an emissary to them from their sovereign lord, the sun. As not even the
most roundabout liaison of Indian interpreters had been effected
at this time, doubtless pantomime figured extensively in the
passing of the glad word. No doubt, also, this "Son-of-the-
Sun" rôle had already been found effective in winning over the
Mexican Indians, for it transpired later—even to Alarcón's
temporary embarrassment—that some of Coronado's Captains
had claimed the same celestial relationship in knocking at the
doors of certain of the Cibolan citadels.

Although the Cocopah inhabiting the Colorado delta to-day
exhibits nothing more deep-seated than sun-burn to proclaim
him a worshipper of the celestial orb, there appears no question that his progenitor of four centuries back could not but
attribute divinity to a force sufficiently potent to sickly over
with even a pale cast of crust the all-pervading mud of the
overflow area. Alarcón's crusty claim of kinship to the Chief
Crust-Maker was the signal for the instant crumbling of crustiness on the part of the ever augmenting horde of Indians. If
they did not exactly bend their knees to His Sunship, they did
something that served him far more practically in bending their
backs to his tow-ropes. Somewhat diffident and jumpy at
first, the willing slaves warmed to their task as the Sun God
beamed beneficent approval. By afternoon they were jostling
each other for a place on the sacred cordelle, which they relinquished at evening only under protest. Rising next morning
long before either their Lord of the Sky or his ambassador, they
swam off to the anchored boats and begged for priority of place

on the tow-lines. One can picture the divinely condescending gesture with which the mud-smeared hemp was tossed from Alarcón's remark that "we gave it to them with a good will, thanking God for the good provision which He gave us to go up the river."

In the gentle art of breaking enemies the doughty Alarcón can have had few equals. The delicate finesse with which he made those who came to scalp remain to tow has had few authentic historical parallels. Offhand, Tom Sawyer, making his scoffing playmates pay him for the privilege of white-washing the fence, is the only one I can think of; and possibly that was somewhat fictionized.

Faring on up river, increased intercourse effected a better comprehension of signs and tongues. Vague descriptions of white men far to the East were given by the Indians, who also told of a very distant river swarming with an animal Alarcón chronicled as a crocodile. The slight differentiations of the Mississippi alligator from the Nile crocodile are such as would have puzzled a more erudite naturalist than the Spanish *conquistador* to recognize from the far-passed descriptions of Indians. Finally came a visitor who claimed to have heard of the killing of the adventurous but mendacious Estavan, slain, so the stranger said, to prevent his showing the Spaniards the way to Cibola.

Fifteen days of towing brought the boats to what was probably the vicinity of present-day Yuma. Here the first word of Coronado came as a consequence of a summons from the local natives for Alarcón to come ashore and show cause why he and his party should not be executed as Christians. The Indians had received word, they said, that bearded white men, known to be Christians, had been murdering and pillaging about Cibola. As these white men from the river answered the same description, they must also be Christians, and therefore potential murderers and pillagers. To prevent the two bands from uniting and operating on an enlarged scale, the Indians were considering wiping out the lesser one while it was at their mercy. Evidently reluctant to do an injustice to any one, the simple souls decided to put up to Alarcón himself the momentous question of his Christianity. That simplified matters materially, for a *conquistador* who would have hesitated over a simple bit of apostasy would not have been worthy of the name. Those little crosses, made of sticks and paper, with which he had been paying off his towing Cocopahs must have taken a bit of explaining, and just how the wily Captain managed it he does not make clear. At any rate, however, when the session was over another tribe of Colorado River Indians had been added to the number hailing him as Minister Plenipotentiary and Envoy Extraordinary from the Court of the Sun.

How completely Alarcón won over these Indians may be judged from the fact that they agreed to furnish him an escort to join his Sun-brothers at Cibola, stipulating as a precedent condition, however, that he should help them defeat their enemies, the Cumanas. Whether he had this punitive expedition in mind in returning to his ships for provisions and reinforcements is not made clear. He arrived again in the vicinity of the mouth of the Gila in due course, but the fact that he lists on his bill of lading "wares of exchange, with corn and other seeds, with hens and cocks of Castile," hardly smacks of grim-visaged War. As one of his ships, the *San Gabriel*, was laden with supplies intended for Coronado, it is possible that it was planned to transport the peaceful staples enumerated overland to Cibola.

Since the Cumanas, hereditary enemies of the Yumas, are probably identifiable with the Mojaves, it is still quite possible that in pushing on up the Colorado from the mouth of Gila Alarcón was embarking upon the punitive expedition that was to win him an escort to Cibola. As the river is considerably swifter above the Gila than it is below, and as there is no evidence that further towing help was had from the Indians, it

SUNRISE WHERE THE LOWER COLORADO MEETS THE GULF OF CALIFORNIA.

COCOPAH OF THE COLORADO DELTA WITH BOAT MADE OF TULE
OR REED.

COCOPAH SQUAW.

is probable that the progress of the three boats that now constituted the flotilla was very slow. The party turned back at a point where the Colorado "entered between very high mountains, through which this river passeth with a straight channel, and the boats went up against the stream very hardly for want of men to draw the same."

That complaint about the lack of men for towing is absolutely conclusive evidence that the Spanish soldiers, brave fighters though they were, had no stomach at all for the hard grind of working a boat up flowing water. Any boat carried by Alarcón's comparatively small West-Coast-built ships would have been more likely to be under twenty feet in length than over. From the fact that twenty men were distributed between the two boats with which the first start up-river was made, these must have been broad of beam and stoutly built. Even so, there is no water between the foot of the Grand Canyon and the mouth of the Colorado through which two good river-men could not work a laden boat of this character with comparative ease. This would apply even to Black Canyon, where the water is somewhat swifter than at any point Alarcón could have possibly attained. If those Spaniards—averaging ten to a boat, or twenty and even thirty by relaying—funked the task of working up over the hard bottoms of what we now call Bill Williams' Canyon, it goes to show that the lolling ease they had been able to enjoy as "Sons of the Sun" while the Cocopahs plodded at the tow-lines had utterly prevented the development of their river-legs and river-sense. This, it seems to me, is a point of which by no means sufficient cognizance has been taken in the several attempts that have been made to determine Alarcón's head of navigation.

The basic evidence bearing on the points reached by Alarcón in pushing up the Colorado is too conflicting to permit of building upon it with much profit. For that reason I shall not endeavour to elaborate a complete thesis here, but merely to make a few passing comments on the conclusions reached by slow and erratic. There was also some trouble with the Indians, notably that arising from the efforts of a Cumana medicine-man to wreck the whole expedition by setting magic reeds in the river.

The best check we have upon the distance covered by Alarcón on this second trip is his statement that he arrived back at his original base on the second day after starting down from the highest point to which he attained. This would make the time of descent somewhere between one and two days. The day and a half which Mr. Dellenbaugh assumes may be taken as a fair estimate. The fifty-five miles a day average of travel this would have entailed is a good deal more speed than a light skiff manned by experienced men would make in the comparatively slow current of September, and very much more than I can conceive that Alarcón's men could have made with their awkward and overloaded sea boats. Ellsworth Kolb, riding the abnormally swift current of the June floods, averaged about fifty miles a day from the Needles to the Gulf. In the shorter days and slacker water of the first week in October I found thirty-five miles the best I could do between sunrise and sunset. In the somewhat faster water between Boulder Canyon and Needles, six of us, rowing a twenty-foot boat in relays of two each, averaged rather less than thirty miles to a late September day. Yet I am sure that any one of the three light units mentioned made much better speed than the best that could have been expected from the combination of boats and men at Alarcón's disposal.

Mr. Dellenbaugh, in endeavouring to arrive at a speed that would work out to check with Alarcón's estimate of eighty-five leagues, mentions "six miles an hour for twelve hours" as a rate of progress that could fairly have been expected. I think if Mr. Dellenbaugh will turn back to his own notes on the second Powell expedition which he has so brilliantly put on record in "A Canyon Voyage," he will be the first to concede that this estimate is far too high for even light boats trying to make time, to say nothing of Alarcón's heavy outfit. I should say that the average speed of the current of the Colorado over the stretch between Blythe and Yuma is somewhat less than that of Glen Canyon; yet I doubt if any of the outfits going down the latter without power have averaged over thirty miles a day.

To allow Alarcón over thirty-five miles a day—or fifty-three miles for a day and a half—would bring him out to the open reaches of the Cibola and Palo Verde valleys. From the foot of the Cibola Valley—say five miles above Lighthouse Rock—to the nearest point above where the mountains encroach closely upon the river, Bill Williams' Canyon, is about a hundred miles. As it is utterly beyond the range of possibility that he could have come from so distant a point to the Gila in twice a day and a half, it would seem nothing is left but to ease down stream and locate Alarcón's "farthest north" somewhere between Lighthouse Rock, fifty miles above the Gila, and the vicinity of Picacho, fifteen miles below the "Lighthouse." There are several mountainous stretches along here that might answer the explorer's description, from any one of which he would have had a very busy day and a half reaching the Gila.

When Alarcón returned to his squadron for the second time it was with no intention of giving up his attempts to establish contact with Coronado. Just why he set sail without making further effort to carry out the mission on which he had primarily been dispatched is not quite clear, though it is believed that the ravages wrought by the torredo upon the wood of his ships caused him to doubt their ability to withstand longer the onslaughts of the raging tidal waves. While it might not be literally correct to say that the men who had remained with the ships had suffered from boredom, it cannot be denied that the marine bore-worm and the tidal bore had been at the bottom of most of their troubles.

Of the two officers sent by Coronado to scout for news of Alarcón one, Don Rodrigo Maldonado, returned bootless from a long search to the south, and the other, Melchior Díaz, reached the mouth of the Colorado only after the ships had departed. That Díaz, though a brave and resolute officer, was somewhat inclined to flights of fancy when it came to recording his observations is attested by the following spirited description of the gigantic Indians whom he encountered at the point where he first came upon the Colorado:

"More than one hundred persons, old and young, sleep in one cabin. When they carry anything they can take a load of three or four hundred-weight on their heads. Once when our men wished to fetch a log for their fire, and six men were unable to carry it, one of these men is reported to have come and raised it in his arms, put it on his head alone and carried it very easily. . . . On account of the great cold they carry a firebrand [tison] in the hand when they go from place to place, with which they warm the other hand and the body as well, and in this way they keep shifting it every now and then." [1]

Díaz was even more impressed with what he assumed to have been a sort of peripatetic furnace than by the Samsonian feats of the giants, for he gave the name of *"Rio del Tison"* to a river the more spiritually inclined Alarcón had already christened *"El Buena Guia"*—"Good Guidance." To a stream that was destined to have half a dozen names before it settled to one, two or three more or less at the discovery stage made little difference.

In the matter of those firebrands carried against "the great cold" of early October in the lower Mojave or Chemehuevis valleys, I am inclined to believe that the brave Captain made a faulty diagnosis. In that very season I have seen the river Indians, stripped to the breech-clout for relief from the sweltering end-of-the-afternoon heat of the humid bottoms, carrying firebrands to protect their hides from mosquitoes. There is just a nip of chill in the air for the hour or two before dawn at this time of year, but the days of glaring sunlight are still

[1] The Casteñada narrative of Coronado's journey.

intensely hot, and the evenings balmy until well along toward midnight. Indeed, in boating alone from Needles to Yuma last October, I always took a dip in the river after landing at dusk, and then proceeded to the business of cooking supper in a costume not more elaborate sartorially than that of the primitive *tison*-bearers for whom the sympathetic Díaz felt so sorry. Firebrands I did brandish occasionally, but only when my green grass and rotten wood smudges ceased to function.

As for the gigantic stature of Indians reported to have been seen by both Díaz and Maldonado, there was either considerable exaggeration or else the present-day Indian of the lower Colorado River valleys has been shrunken by the heat of the passing centuries. The average Mojave, Yuma or Cocopah is a stout, husky physical specimen, but will still be topped in stature by the average white man that he jostles on the platform of the Needles or Yuma station. Men of abnormal size and strength will occasionally be found among all three tribes, but by no means so often as among the labourers of—say—an Arizona copper camp.

There is much confusion of testimony as to whether Díaz first came to the river above or below the highest point reached by Alarcón. One account has it that the Indians told him that boats had come up the river to a point three days below; another that Díaz came to the river at a place thirty leagues from its mouth, and that Alarcón had gone an equal distance above. In any event, Díaz never found the large cross which Alarcón states he erected to mark the point at which he turned back. He did find, however, but fifteen leagues up stream from the Gulf, a tree bearing the inscription:

"Alarcón reached this place—there are letters under this tree."

Díaz dug up the letters and learned how Alarcón, failing in his efforts to get in touch with Coronado, had sailed away for New Spain but a few weeks previously. He also learned "how that sea was a bay, which was formed by the Isle of the Marquis, which is called California, and it was explained how California was not an island, but a part of the mainland forming the other side of the Gulf."

Knowing what we now do of the geography of this region it is not difficult to make out what Alarcón was trying to say; to poor Díaz, however, that statement about the island that was not an island after all must have been just about as clear as the Colorado mud. If the worthy Captain could only have lived long enough to hear about the elucidating wire of the Irish section-boss to the Superintendent stating that "them horses what we killed was mules," surely he would have exclaimed, "That reminds me!"

Realizing that there was little that Alarcón would not already have learned of the river country, Díaz fared westerly, probably in the hope of establishing the coast-line of the mainland. At the end of a couple of days they came to some "sandbanks of hot ashes which it was impossible to cross without being drowned as in the sea. The ground they were standing on trembled like a sheet of paper, so that it seemed as if there were lakes under them. It seemed wonderful and like something infernal, for the ashes to bubble up here in several places."

By this description it seems probable that Díaz reached the field of hot mud springs that give the name to Volcano Lake. There are also some mud volcanoes and so-called "paint-pots" close to what is now Mullet Island, on the rim of Salton Sink. These latter, however, would hardly have been extensive enough to create an obstacle to travel, and it is even possible they were submerged at that time by the great inland sea.

A remarkable accident which befell Díaz not long after his party turned back from the mud springs robbed him of the honour of reporting in person to Coronado the results of his valuable exploration. Trying to spear from horseback a dog that was chasing some sheep belonging to the camp, he was impaled upon the butt of the weapon when it missed its mark and stuck

THE PLATEAU OF THE COLORADO.

Photo. by Fred. Harvey.

FOREST ON NORTH RIM OF GRAND CANYON.

in the ground. Carried by his men for twenty days in spite
of incessant fighting with Indians, he died some time before
Coronado's camp was reached.

To the swashbuckling Don López de Cárdenas fell the distinction of the most spectacular discovery resulting from the
Coronado expedition. Hearing at a somewhat indefinitely located place called Tusayan of a great river, "and that several
miles down that river there was a people with very large bodies,"
Coronado dispatched Cárdenas to investigate. At the end of
twenty days' travel from Tusayan they were led by their Indian guides to the brink of a great gorge. The region is described in the Castañeda narrative of Coronado as

" . . . elevated and full of low twisted pines, very cold and
lying open toward the north, so that [even though] this being the
warm season, no one could live there on account of the cold. They
spent three days on this bank looking for a passage down to the
river, which looked from above as if the water was three feet across,
although the Indians said it was half a league."

What Dr. Coues calls the "pretty rocky old Spanish" of parts
of the Coronado narrative is so ambiguous at this point that
it is difficult to decide whether Cárdenas thought the gorge
was three or four leagues deep or only that wide. As the estimate would be about correct for width between the outer rims
of the Grand Canyon at the section it is most likely Cárdenas
reached, and as it is not conceivable that his well-trained eye
for distance and perspective would have deceived him on a ten-
to-one scale, it would seem reasonable to lay that leagues-long
measuring stick down horizontally rather than to stand it up
perpendicularly.

The point popularly believed to be that from which Cárdenas
first saw the Grand Canyon is the vicinity of the mouth of the
Little Colorado, a belief which has doubtless been fostered by
reason of the fact that Desert View is also conveniently reached
by auto from the hotels. Mr. Dellenbaugh, by a careful de-

duction drawn from the fact that Cárdenas described the river as coming from the northeast and turning to the south-south-west, identifies the place with a point about midway between the mouths of Diamond Creek and Kanab Canyon. As this is the only place that comes near to satisfying the description of Cárdenas there is good reason to believe that the soldier-explorer sounded his "View Halloo!" from somewhere in that vicinity, though his three days of wandering along the rim may well have taken him considerable distances above and below. Until there is a further westerly extension of the rim road, however, it is probable that the exigencies of transportation will force the tourist to continue "seeing the Canyon as Cárdenas saw it" from a bit nearer the orbit of auto busses.

After the best of his climbers had striven vainly for three days to descend more than a third of the way to the river, Cárdenas started on his return. His guide told him that to reach the land of the big-bodied people it would be necessary to cross a broad belt of dry country, in traversing which it was always the custom to take along women to carry *ollas* of water. No females being available for this menial labour, they advised against the attempt. "On the way home," writes Castañeda, "they saw some water falling over a rock and learned from the guides that some bunches of crystals hanging there were salt."

Both a waterfall and crystals might have been found in Cataract Canyon, the home of the Havasupai, but this remote retreat would have been more likely to be reached in the course of the wandering along the rim than on any probable "homeward" course. Just where was "home"—in this case Tusayan—must always remain somewhat in doubt. Those who have identified it with the Moqui towns have been unable to account for the twenty days Cárdenas took to reach the Canyon save by suggesting that his guides followed a roundabout course to confuse him. No satisfactory motive has been suggested as to why they should have desired to practise this deception.

Moreover, Cárdenas carried a compass as well as a gun. Undue circling on those comparatively open plateaus would have been detected by the one and—judging by our rough-and-ready Captain's treatment of the Indians on the Rio Grande—punished by the other. Mr. Dellenbaugh advances a much sounder theory to account for that twenty-day march by locating Tusayan some three hundred miles to the south-east, "near Four Peaks on the New Mexican line."

CHAPTER II

THE PADRES

A LTHOUGH the *conquistador* has often been spoken of as fighting with the Sword in one hand and the Cross in the other, and although he never failed to number zealous members of the Church Militant in his company, yet the finer type of *padre* never came to his own until the period of bloody conquest was over and he was free to seek converts in his own gentle way. It is a far cry from Melchior Díaz's naïvely contemptuous description of certain Indians as "good for nothing but to make into Christians," to Garcés complaining of a sickness of heart at the contemplation of the souls that must inevitably be lost because he had failed to sprinkle the necessary three drops of water on the dark skins of their owners. Yet that may be said to represent fairly the comparative attitudes of conqueror and priest.

The century and a half following the expeditions of Coronado and Alarcón roughly corresponds to what may be called the period of the *padres* in the basin of the lower Colorado. Its comparatively scant records inform us somewhat of the peoples and the general geography of this region, but of the river itself little beyond what had already been observed and chronicled by Alarcón, Cárdenas and Díaz. Don Juan de Oñate, Governor of New Mexico, and Eusibo Francisco Kino, an Austrian Jesuit, crossed and skirted the Colorado, but their records amplify nomenclature rather than knowledge. Oñate called it the *Rio Grande de Buena Esperanza*, while Padre Kino, perhaps in gloomier mood on naming-day, expressed his feelings with *Rio de los Martires*. There is something to be said for both names. Perhaps, in view of the visions conjured by the present plans for Colorado River development, "Good

24

Hope" would be even more appropriate to-day than in the time of Oñate. Yet a failure to hasten the consummation of the particular one of those plans that has to do with flood control would undoubtedly result in the polling of many votes for "The River of the Martyrs," especially down Imperial Valley way.

By and large, explorers seem to have exercised a good deal of restraint in refraining from perpetuating mood in nomenclature. Powell stumbled only once—when he called the present Frémont River the "Dirty Devil"—but took the first occasion to back up. There have been days on the lower Colorado—days replete with mud, mosquitoes and misery—when I have called the Colorado names which would make "Dirty Devil" sound like an excerpt from a roster of the saints. The stout-hearted Alarcón must have known just such days, and so the measure of his restraint is expressed in the fact that— on paper at least—he called the fount of his troubles nothing worse than "Good Guidance."

It is not until we come almost to the end of the period of the *padres* that we find in the records of the two Franciscan contemporaries, Garcés and Escalante, evidences of a somewhat further extension of knowledge of the Colorado. Both were keen observers, though Escalante was perhaps the more careful recorder of the two. Garcés, a most human and lovable character, is spoken of by Dr. Coues as literally living the life of Christ. From his headquarters at the mission of San Xavier del Bac, near the present site of Tucson, he departed upon successive *entradas* that ultimately criss-crossed a major portion of what is now the southwestern corner of the United States.

Garcés was the first to make regular use of the name Colorado in writing of the great river that was so indissolubly linked to his life and fate. He applied it, he explains, because the river, draining a red country, is tinged with red in the month of April, when the water is high from the melting snows. High water on the lower Colorado reaches its peak in late May or early June rather than April, and the reddish tinge, though most pronounced in flood-time, is almost perennial. Yet Garcés shows that he had a very good idea of the character of the drainage basin of the river.

"This much is certain [he writes], that from the Yutas, who are on the north of the Moqui, unto its disemboguement into the Golfo de California, it gathers to itself no notable body of water; wherefore it is likely that the greater part of its abundance comes from far beyond."

Although Alarcón and Díaz may have seen migratory members of the tribe, Garcés was undoubtedly the first white man to visit the Mojaves in their home valley. After the light-fingered but heavy-handed bullies of the lower river he found them comparatively pleasant to live with. He records:

"I can say with great truth that these Indians have great advantages over the Yumas and the rest of the natives of the Colorado; they are less molestful, and none are thieves; they seem valiant and nowhere have I been better served. I showed them the picture of the Virgin, but they did not like to look at that of the Lost Soul. . . . The female sex is the most comely on the river; the male is healthy and robust. The women wear petticoats. The men go entirely naked, and in a country so cold this is well worthy of compassion."

Either the good Father was carried away by the kindness of his hosts, or else the passing centuries have brought material changes, both ethnological, meteorological and moral. The present-day denizen of Needles, with its not infrequent summer temperature of a hundred and twenty-five in the shade, undoubtedly rates himself as a proper object for compassion, but not because of lack of clothes to protect him from the cold. On the contrary, his principal grudge is against the law that prevents his going round in the very state that stirred good old Father Garcés to pity when he first came upon the undraped Mojave. On the score of moral changes, I can testify from my

own experience that certain prowling river-bottom bucks of
the Mojave tribe are both molestful and thievish. As for the
comeliness of the female of the species, Garcés qualified his
comparison somewhat by confining it to ladies of the upper
river. Yet on a 1923 rating I would take issue with him even
at the risk of touching a subject that no male of properly
chastened spirit would allow himself to be drawn into. Neither
the pixie nor the sylph has nested in the Mojave family-tree
of the last hundred and fifty years, as a possible consequence
of which the twentieth century squaw of that tribe is one of
the most unlovely bumps of bulk and bulbosity in semi-cap-
tivity. Nor does the tribal modiste appear to have cultivated
the art ("those lengthening effects, my dear!") of avoiding
the accentuation of the defects of what is at best a very trying
figure. I had best not enlarge further on a subject which is
quite expansive enough already. But no—the Mojave lady is
not the belle of the Colorado. The beauty of the banged-
browed Yuma maid is hardly of the sort that would rise up
and hit a man between the eyes, and yet she is many a degree
less hard to look upon than the descendant of those "comely
females" that first intercepted the kindling glance of the lifted
weather-eye of the good old Garcés.

And the Cocopah maid is a shade less unlovely than the
Yuma. The farther south you go . . . But before we are
hopelessly aground let us back off into the main current from
an eddy of digression that we should never have been drawn
into in the first place.

The print of the "Lost Soul" before which the Mojaves re-
coiled was exhibited by way of giving potential converts a
pictorial foretaste of what would happen in the event they refused the *padre's* proffered sprinkle of "three drops of water."
Garcés does not describe the picture in detail, but if the sight
of it struck horror to the progenitors of a race to whom the
burning of emigrants at the stake became a popular outdoor

sport, the pitch-forking fiends must have been giving that luck-less "Lost Soul" a very merry time of it.

But whereas Father Garcés' big heart had rather the better of his head in writing of these people whom he loved, when it came to recording his observations of natural features he was the keen, careful topographer. Nearly every step of his fa-mous fifth *entrada*, from Mojave to the Moqui towns, can be traced from his descriptions. Following a trail that appears to have been identical throughout its length with that of the present time, he descended to the depths of Cataract Canyon, the first white man to visit the Havasupai in their secure re-treat. Climbing back to the plateau, he pushed on to reach the rim of the Grand Canyon at a point probably not far from the El Tovar of to-day. Like Cárdenas, he at once identified the stream at the bottom of the gorge as the same that flowed through the lowlands to the Gulf, for he writes of "the most profound caxones that ever onward continue, and within these flows the Rio Colorado." The rim of the Kaibab looming to the north he describes as "a great Sierra," plainly under the impression that he was looking across to the side of a moun-tain. He writes further:

"I named the singular pass Puerto de Bucareli [after the Viceroy of New Spain], and though to all appearances would not seem to be great the difficulty of reaching thereunto, I consider this to be im-possible in consequence of the difficult caxones which intervene. From this position this pass bore east-north-east."

In adding that the Indians "took down the beasts to give water in these caxones," Garcés evidently meant to refer to a descent to some small side canyon, not to the bottom of the main gorge. Pushing on to clamber into and out of the canyon of the Little Colorado, the tireless traveller fared across the Painted Desert to a very unfriendly reception in the Moqui villages.

On a day of an *entrada* that carried Garcés to a certain little

© Fred. Harvey.

A STREET IN WALPI.

© Fred. Harvey.

THE PLAZA AT WALPI.

ANCIENT PICTURE WRITING IN UPPER GLEN CANYON.

A HOPI VILLAGE.

Much the same to-day as when visited by Coronado and Garces.

Indian farm on the lower Colorado he made this entry in his journal: "To this *rancheria* and to all those contiguous I gave the name of *Lagrimas de San Pedro.*" To which Dr. Coues appends the elucidative if somewhat irreverent note that "the Tears of St. Peter were shed on the California side of the river, nearly opposite La Paz, and thence downward opposite Ehrenburg and Mineral City." Yet the picturesque name was prophetic. In July, 1781, Garcés and all of his followers were killed at the culmination of an uprising of the Yuma Indians led by a chief called "Captain" Palma, once the favourite protégé of the saintly *padre.*

As relating to the Colorado, the great *entrada* of Father Francisco Silvestre Vélez de Escalante was important in recording the first definite facts concerning the nature of portions of the gorges to which we now apply the names of Marble Canyon and Glen Canyon. Setting out from Santa Fé on the 29th of July, 1776, Escalante headed westward in the hope of discovering a northerly route to the missions of California that would lead through regions less arid and difficult to traverse than those hitherto followed across the southern deserts. Crossing in turn the Grand and the Green at points considerably above their junction, he pursued a wandering and circuitous route without making any material progress toward his particular destination, Monterey. Early in October, after reaching at one time a point not many miles south of Great Salt Lake, fear of having to winter on the high, barren plateaus made him decide to turn back on what he believed was the easiest and most direct route to Santa Fé. At this time he must have been not far north of the comparatively favourable route to California that later came to be known as the "Old Spanish Trail." There can be no question, indeed, that he would have had to endure far less hardship in pushing on to the Coast than fell to his lot as a consequence of attempting a traverse that was blocked by the all but impassable gorges of the Colorado canyon series.

As a careful and intelligent account of travel and observation Father Escalante's journal, as published in Dean Harris's "The Catholic Church in Utah," is the most illuminative geographic record that has come down to us from the period of the *entradas* of the *Padres*. No more prolific field of research is open to the southwestern historian of to-day than the study of this amazing fifteen-hundred-mile journey in the light of the excellent translation presented by Dean Harris. He, unfortunately, was compelled to limit his comments on the journal to a brief though highly interesting chapter based, I think, largely on map study. It is a matter of the greatest regret that Dr. Coues, who placed the world so much in his debt for his works on Garcés, Lewis and Clark, and other early western travellers, could not have lived to realize his ambition of publishing a volume on the Escalante *entrada*. In his faculty for clothing with real flesh and blood the dry bones of a day-to-day record of travel Dr. Coues stood without a rival in the world of historical research. I welcome the opportunity to pay this passing tribute to a historian whose humour and inimitable human touch were responsible for conjuring up the all but living and breathing reincarnations of William Clark and Meriwether Lewis to voyage with me down the Columbia, Yellowstone and Missouri.

Fascinating as it would be to follow the footsteps of Father Escalante and his companions from day to day in their historic circuit of the Great Basin, too much of the route lies outside of our special zone of interest to make the complete excursion practicable. Where he crossed or skirted the Colorado, however, he was in territory that makes a closer examination of his record well in point.

Of Father Escalante's talent for expressing much in a few words we have a foretaste in the pompous but amazingly comprehensive opening sentence of his diary. Here it is verbatim:

"On the 29th of July, in the year 1776, under the protection of our Lady the Virgin Mary, conceived without original sin, and under that of the most holy Patriarch Joseph, her honoured spouse, Fray Francisco Atanasio Dominguez, the present visiting delegate of this district of the conversion of St. Paul of New Mexico, and Fray Francisco Silvestre Vélez de Escalante, teacher of Christian Doctrine in the mission of Our Lady of Guadalupe of Zuni; accompanied by Don Juan Pedro Cisneros, the mayor of the town of Zuni; Don Bernardo Miera y Pacheo, a retired captain, and citizen of the town of Santa Fé; Don Joaquin Laon, citizen of the same town; Lorenzo Olivares, of the town of Paso; Lucretio Muniz, Andres Muniz, Juan de Aguilar and Simon Lucero, having invoked the protection of the most holy saints, and having received the Holy Eucharist, we departed from the town of Santa Fé, capital of New Mexico, and after nine leagues of travel we arrived at the town of Santa Clara, where we passed the night."

Here are covered the matters of personnel, protection, patronage, departure and the first day's travel and camp; also a brief statement as to who the several members of the party were, as well as two or three of the saints. The good *padre* follows this same *multum in parvo* style all the way through, and save for what appears at this distance a somewhat over-stressing of the saints, manages to convey an astonishing lot of information without blackening a great amount of white paper.

The earlier part of Escalante's journey was across a region already explored by two of his contemporaries. Don Juan Maria de Rivera had gone as far as the Grand and Gunnison in 1761, crossing the divide at a point to which the expressive name of "Purgatory" was applied. Escalante records that "it was this river that they judged at that time to be the great river Tizon." This is probably the first conjecture as to the identity of the clear and torrential Grand with the muddy and comparatively quiet-flowing lowland stream Díaz had called *El Rio Tizon*. Slowly as knowledge came to the *padres*, their geographical sense was extremely sound.

Fray Alonso de Posadas, penetrating farther than Rivera, had reached the other great branch of the Colorado, naming

San Buenaventura the river we now call the Green. Knowledge gained by both of his predecessors made Escalante's progress up to reaching the San Buenaventura much easier than it would have been had he had to cross this rough and difficult region unguided. He reached this river on September 13th and made camp at a point Harris believes to have been about opposite to the present site of Jensen.

In writing of the San Buenaventura "as the largest [river] we have crossed," Escalante was only recording an impression shared by Powell and, indeed, every one else up to within very recent years. It is only since accurate measurements have been made by the Water Resources Branch of the Geological Survey that it has become known that the Grand has a somewhat larger mean flow than the longer Green. It was this fact that had the most weight in bringing about the recent decision to change the name of the Grand to Colorado, definitely establishing it as the main river and the Green as a branch.

Escalante describes the place where he camped on the river as

" . . . a fine plain abounding in pasturage, and fertile, arable land, provided it were irrigated, which might be, perhaps, a little more than a league in length, entering in between two mountains; the space taking the form of a corral; and the mountains coming so close together that one can hardly distinguish the opening through which the river flows."

This is an excellent example of Escalante's undeniable gift for sketching topography in a few brief, telling words. His reference to irrigation is probably the first forerunning suggestion of the possibility of reclaiming a valley of the Colorado. The vision of future settlement must have been ever in the back of his mind, for two small rivers seen the day he pushed westward into the Unknown conjured it up again and prompted the entry: "From both of these rivers the land on the bank could be irrigated, making them very good for planting, but water could not be carried from the larger river."

Of the ford he says: "The river can be crossed only at one fording place. . . . The bottom is full of small stones, and the river so deep that the mules could not cross it except by swimming."

The actual crossing was made three days later, and in recording it Escalante does not state whether or not the mules were forced to swim. That point is one on which it would be very interesting to have assurance. If they did succeed in crossing a comparatively deep ford at this point, I cannot understand why Escalante should have been unwilling to attempt to swim the mules across the main Colorado at the mouth of the Paria a month and a half later. Had this latter crossing been made some of the most punishing days of the return trip would have been avoided.

A buffalo was killed during the three-day rest-halt at the San Buenaventura, and a Laguna Indian called Joaquin furnished diversion one morning when, "from mischief," he attempted to ride a very vicious horse, which fell, throwing the fellow some distance. It is recorded that they were all "much frightened, thinking that the fall had injured the Laguna, who, recovering from his fright, began to shed tears and cry aloud; but God permitted that the horse received all the wounds, injuring his neck, and so being useless."

Which entry shows the kindly father's saintliness of soul. I am inclined to think that a present-day packer would attribute to infernal rather than celestial intervention an accident which rendered a sound horse useless and spared a smart-Aleck Indian.

Three weeks of hard travel after leaving the Green found the party facing the first snows of an early winter and but little advanced toward its destination. Under date of October 6th appears this entry:

"It was still snowing at daybreak, and continued to snow all day, so that we could not resume our journey. The night came on, and seeing conditions were no better, we implored the intercession of our mother and patron, reciting in chorus the three parts of the rosary, and singing the litanies. It pleased God that at nine o'clock at night the snow, hail and rain ceased."

The propitious intervention was of short duration. They continued snowbound in camp the following day, and on the next the miriness of the ground held progress down to a scant three leagues and a half. It was on this day, October 8th, that the decision to turn back was made, Escalante stating his reasons for the action as follows:

"The winter had now set in with great rigor, and all the mountain ranges that we could see were covered with snow; the weather was very changeable and long before we could reach them [in Monterey] the mountain passes would be closed up, and we would be obliged to remain two or three months on some mountain, where there were no people and where we would not be able to provide necessary food. The provisions we had brought were now nearly exhausted, and if we continued to go on we would be liable to perish with hunger if not with cold."

The entry of October 9th is preceded by the heading, *"New Route, and the Beginning of Our Return. . . ."* In the course of the next three or four days it appears that there was dissension in the party, and the leaders conferred as to the most expedient means to adopt to dispel from the minds of certain of their companions, mentioned by name,

". . . the disgust which they felt on account of our abandoning the route to Monterey to follow this one, that we now understood to be expedient, and according to the Holy Will of God, for Whom only we desired the journey, for Whom we were willing to suffer, and if necessary, even to die."

After reciting at considerable length the somewhat personal matters entering into their differences, Father Escalante states that it was decided to propose to the disgruntled ones that the trouble be settled by casting lots. To this, he continues, "they all agreed like Christians, and with fervent devotion recited the third part of the rosary, while we recited the Penitential Psalms with the litanies and the other prayers which follow. Concluding our prayers, we cast lots and it came out in favour of Cosnina. We all accepted this, thanks be to God, willingly and joyfully."

Escalante used the name Cosnina occasionally for the Colorado, and, rather more specifically, to designate a tribe of Indians—probably the Havasupai—living south of that river. "*Rio del Cosnina*" adds still another to the long list of names applied to the Colorado since Alarcón first designated it "*Buena Guia.*" Escalante referred to it once or twice in his correspondence as the "River of Mystery," perhaps the most appropriate name of the lot.

In spite of the extremely severe hardships endured on the remainder of the journey, it would appear that the decision as to course balloted for in the snows of the upper Beaver River was accepted by all quite as sportingly as it was arrived at piously. In all of the succeeding days of disappointment, fatigue and near-starvation there is no further record of complaints or lack of co-operation from the original dissenters.

Doubtless due to anxieties about food and the uncertainties of the route, the record of the earlier portion of the journey southward toward the Colorado was less carefully kept than the rest of the journal, making it difficult to recognize the occasional topographical features described en route. There is no doubt that it paralleled the Virgin for a considerable distance, on a south-westerly course that would have brought them to the Colorado below the foot of the Grand Canyon. An abrupt turning to the north-eastward at a point probably not over fifty miles from the main river was due to assurances from the Indians that the latter was not fordable anywhere in that region. Had Escalante pushed on and made the by no means impossible crossing in the vicinity of the Grand Wash or the mouth of the Virgin, a short southerly journey would have led him onto the trail already followed by Garcés on his *entrada* from Mojave to the Moqui towns. This would have been an easy route compared to the one he did follow, but taking it would have deferred exploration of the extensive plateau region north of the Grand, Marble and Glen canyons for nearly a hundred years. Since the complete translation of Escalante's diary only became available during the first decade of the present century, long after the explorations of Wheeler and Powell, this loss would have been more apparent than real.

The painfully slow journey southward was marked by repeated attempts to secure food and information from the badly scared and highly suspicious Indians encountered on the way. Neither weariness nor the pangs of hunger dulled the kindly *padre's* compassion for the primitive state of these savages, nor his pious horror over the fact that the costumes of some of the ladies were not all that decorum demanded. That even personal safety, rather than mere decorum, was menaced on one occasion is evident from a delicious entry describing the meeting with twenty Indian women surprised gathering seeds and herbs on a plain.

"These Indian women were poorly dressed [he recounts], and wore only a piece of deerskin hanging from the waist, which hardly covered what one could not see without danger. We took leave of them, asking them to tell their people that we came in peace, that we would injure none of them, and that we loved them all, and that the men who were able should come to where we were going to sleep, without imagining any evil would befall them."

Good old soul, what did he not owe to his protecting saint for not having allowed him to be exposed to the dangers of the South Sea islands! And yet, when grim necessity stalked, Father Escalante did not prove lacking in the high moral or physical courage to take grave risks. A little farther along, when doubt arose as to the proper course to pursue, he records the providential chancing upon "other Indian women who fled from us."

"We sent the interpreter with Joaquin and another companion [he continues] to try to bring one of them to where we were to halt near by, in order to inquire of them if the Rio Grande was as near as the other Indian women had assured us it was, and to see if some of them did not wish to accompany us as guides as far as Cosnina. They ran with such swiftness that our men could hardly overtake even one."

Presently Don Joaquin was descried returning, bearing one of the captured fugitives behind him on his horse. Can one imagine the dear old *padre's* relief on discovering that the spoil of this Sabine pursuit was a *man?* He does not record that any rosaries or litanies were chanted in celebration of this miraculous deliverance, yet profound relief is plainly in evidence in the entry: "We quieted him a little by giving him something to eat and a ribbon that we ourselves put on him." One wonders if the decoration would have thus been bestowed in person had the captive proved really to have been one of the dangerous sex. We can at least be sure that the award would have taken the form of something broader than a ribbon.

The original stock of provisions ran out completely within a few days after starting on the return trip, and from that time on the party subsisted on pine-nuts, roots, herbs, squashes and the like, such as could be foraged along the way or traded from the Indians. Hardly more than eight or ten miles a day were averaged over this stage, and the linear progression, owing to much zigzagging and circling, amounted even to less. Such guidance as was had from the Indians was provided only under compulsion, and so proved erratic and undependable. All of the aboriginals, however, spoke of an easy ford across the Colorado some days' travel to the eastward, and toward this crossing as a goal the course was laid.

For a number of days Escalante must have been aware that the gorge of the Colorado ran but a few miles to the south, but, doubtless because the Indians had impressed upon him the fact that the river could not be reached in that section, he held to a parallel course far enough back from the outer rim to avoid the worst of the steep-walled side canyons. On October 24th he notes:

"The River Colorado flows along here from north-north-east to south-south-east, very deep, with high banks, so that if one should cultivate the land on the banks of the river, although the soil might be good, the stream would be of no service to him. We caught sight this afternoon of the precipices lining the sides of the river, and seen from the western side they resembled a long ridge of houses."

Hunger, fatigue and uncertainty could not prevent visions of the future forming in the back of Father Escalante's mind, and even on the arid heights of the Paria Plateau he was thinking of men who would come to build homes and cultivate the land. But his passing comment on the difficulties of irrigation proved that the widest stretch of his imagination faltered and failed far short of compassing the ultimate wonders that the time must see wrought almost within eye-scope of the camp— piously called St. Bartholomew—at which he penned the lines I have quoted. The precipice he describes as resembling a long ridge of houses was the towering wall to which Powell subsequently gave the name of Echo Cliffs, and not far above the point where that wall closes in upon the river is the site of the great Glen Canyon dam, which shares with that of Boulder Canyon the distinction of being the most favoured location for the erection of the keystone work of the whole lower Colorado reclamation, flood-control and power plan.

Dellenbaugh, who had read only a condensed version of the Escalante diary at the time he wrote his most carefully compiled "Romance of the Colorado River," believed that the party reached "the brink of Marble Canyon, perhaps half-way between the Paria and the Little Colorado, and followed upstream first north and then (beyond the Paria) north-east, hunting for a ford." This appears to be the correct conclusion as regards the latter portion of this part of the *entrada*, but I can find nothing in the diary to indicate that any member of the party came within sight of the main gorge until October 25th, the day preceding that upon which they all descended to the banks of the river by the canyon and valley which we now call the Paria. The concluding entry for this day—the 25th— reads:

"In the afternoon, Don Juan Pedro Cisneros left camp to examine the northern point of the valley, to see if he could find an outlet, or could get sight of the river and its crossing. He returned after midnight with the news that he had arrived at the river; but he did not know if we could pass over some mesas and lofty peaks that he saw on the other side. Nevertheless, because he thought the river afforded a crossing at that point, we determined to travel in that direction."

The record of the 26th opens with a description which no one who has ever noted the distinctive scenic features of that doubly historic point can fail to recognize as the mouth of the Paria and Lee's Ferry.

"We pushed ahead for three leagues and a half, and arrived at the spot that we thought might be the outlet of the valley. It is a corner entirely surrounded by mountains and peaks, very lofty, of coloured red earth of different formations, and as the soil underneath the surface is of the same colour, it has an agreeable aspect. We continued in the same direction, travelling with great difficulty, for the horses sank to their knees in the soft earth, when the surface was broken through. Having covered another league and a half, we reached the great river of the Cosninas. Another smaller one unites with it at this point, and we called this the Santa Teresa. We crossed this one, and pitched our camp on the larger one close to a precipice of gray stone."

That "coloured red earth of different formations" is beyond doubt the striking *chinle* outcropping to the north of the mouth of the Paria, Escalante's Santa Teresa. That last league and a half of soft going was probably over the powdered silt of the valley floor. I have trudged through foot-deep dust there myself. The "precipice of grey stone" at the foot of which the party made camp is the dominating feature of the valley. Presenting a sheer wall many hundred feet high where the Paria undermines its base, the ascent from the Colorado River side is comparatively easy. At the summit one finds the low circular wall of piled rock, which is all that remains of the "four-ways" lookout where the renegade, John D. Lee, kept lonely vigil against the appearance of his pursuers during the years following the Mountain Meadows Massacre.

From the lofty vantage of Lee's Lookout the route of Escalante's approach to the Colorado appears readily identifiable with that of the present road along the base of the Vermilion Cliffs. This would give the northerly direction of the last day's march, where coming any distance down the canyon and valley of the Paria would have necessitated travelling south-easterly. It is just possible that the spring at which camp was made the night preceding the arrival at the mouth of the Paria may have been the halting-place now called Jacob's Pools, though the fourteen miles which the march works out to on that day would not be enough to bridge the distance. Neither is mention made of the crossing of the side canyons of Badger and Soap creeks. Escalante's description of this camp is hardly full enough to make a definite conclusion possible. He says:

" . . . we descried poplar trees at the foot of the mesa. We pushed on toward them and found a spring of good water. On the edges of the spring we found evidences of the presence of saline matter; but upon tasting it we found it sweet."

The location at the foot of the mesa corresponds to that of Jacob's Pools; but that, of course, is also the place where any spring or seepage would be most likely to be in evidence. It is unfortunate that Escalante did not add the few words of further description necessary to make identification of this camp site possible. That at the foot of the great grey cliff at the mouth of the Paria is perhaps the most definitely fixable of any on the whole *entrada*, not excepting the one at the Crossing-of-the-Fathers itself. Jacob's Pools would locate another quite as certainly, but the description is too general to make assurance possible.

Father Escalante describes at some length the efforts made to cross the river and seek for a way out to the plateau on the other side. On the afternoon of their arrival he states that:

"We determined to make a reconnoitre . . . to ascertain whether, if we crossed the river, we could continue our way here to the east or south-east. On all sides we were surrounded by mesas and lofty mountains. For which reason two of our people who knew how to swim entered the water of the river with their clothing tied above their heads. They found the current so deep and swift that it was with great difficulty they reached the opposite bank, having left their bundle in the middle of the stream, without seeing it again. As they had got over with great fatigue, and because they were naked and bare-footed, they found it impossible to make the desired examination, and when they partook of some nourishment they returned."

Nothing could have been more ill-advised in attempting a crossing of this kind than to carry the clothes, and especially the foot-gear, in a bundle. The way to do it is to go into the stream with the minimum of clothes one needs for whatever he is going to undertake on the other side, and trust to the high, dry air and brisk movement to get rid of surplus moisture soaked up in the swim. Ten minutes' hard walking will usually have a single layer of garments flapping in the breeze and shaking out their own dust. We lost large and varied assortments of shoes, shirts and breeches last summer in the hundred and twenty miles between Lee's Ferry and Hall's Crossing, but none of them as a consequence of the silver-platter form of presentation represented by a neatly tied bundle balanced on the head. The ravenous river gulped them all in time, to the last rag and shoestring, but we made it fight for every mouthful.

By the *padre's* own account his party displayed neither good water-sense nor water-courage in dealing with the problem of crossing the Colorado at the Paria. Yet when we consider that the whole *entrada* had been made through an arid country, with almost no opportunities to gain experience in fording pack-trains, this fact is hardly open to severe criticism. A seasoned Alaskan pack-train would ford rivers much colder, faster and deeper than the Colorado at Lee's Ferry a dozen times a day and think nothing of it. But the confidence to do that sort of thing comes only with experience; and lacking the experience, Escalante's men were also lacking in confidence.

In preparing for our trip through Glen Canyon last summer I pulled a boat up and down the mile of smooth-flowing water above the mouth of the Paria a good many times. This is the very stretch to which Escalante's fording efforts would necessarily have been confined. I do not recall that any of us crossed the river in our evening swims, but that was only because there was no occasion to do so. I have in mind a number of points where judicious wading down the bars and taking advantage of the cross-set of the current would have made it possible to go from one bank to the other with a comparatively short stretch of swimming. Crossing a pack-train would have been scarcely more difficult, as there is sufficiently solid bottom at a number of points on both sides to give good footing at the start and finish. I am writing now of the river as it was in the moderately high water of August. Fording would have been much easier when we came back down river to Lee's Ferry in the middle of September, as the water had fallen several feet. By the end of October—the time at which Escalante was at the mouth of the Paria—the river is near to its lowest stage of the year, at which time I am inclined to believe that places could be found where horses could be crossed with little or no swimming. But the matter of depth is not of great importance. As long as there is anything short of quicksand or bottomless mud for getting in and out, swimming a pack-train is attended with less risk either to horse or man than taking it up and down such cliffs as Escalante had been encountering for many weeks.

Discouraged by this first attempt to locate what they considered a suitable ford, the party spent all of the 27th and part of the 28th seeking for a more favourable crossing. The energetic Don Juan Cisneros reconnoitred

" . . . along the Santa Teresa, to see if he could find a way across the eastern mesa and return to the great river by a route more open, in which the river, finding more room, would be more fordable, or at least such that the horses might get across, for here at this point they would be drowned. He found one hill, by which it was thought we might surmount the mesa, but it appeared to him to be of great difficulty. Others went to reconnoitre in different directions, and they found nothing but insurmountable obstacles, preventing their finding a crossing unless they had gone great distances."

I can testify to the steepness of the hill Don Juan describes as one "of great difficulty." The thousand-foot climb is a hard pull even over the fairly good trail that now zigzags up to its crest. From here a few hundred yards over broken sandstone ledges would have taken him across the horse-shoe curve above Lee's Ferry to the brink of a sheer cliff, from which he could have tossed a pebble into the river at a point which is now distinguished as the great Glen Canyon dam-site. His climb would have been quite in vain, however. A half mile or so above is a slide down which it is just possible he could have scrambled without breaking bones, but which could never have been followed by horses. The opposite wall, moreover, presents an unbroken front for many miles in both directions.

On the 28th they "entered again upon the same search, but all in vain." Then, records the Father,

"We constructed a raft of poles, and with it Father Fray Silvestre, accompanied by the servants, attempted to cross the river. But as the poles which he employed in pushing the raft were too short to reach the bottom, although they were five yards in length, the waves thrown against the raft by a contrary wind forced him back three times to the same shore from which he started, without his having reached even the middle of the stream. Besides the great depth and swiftness of the current here, the banks of the stream on the other side are so muddy that we were afraid we would lose in them some, if not all, of our horses."

There are few things more difficult for even an experienced man to control than a raft in running water. It would not, therefore, be fair to criticize too sharply the failure of Father Silvestre's attempt. The lack of success was evidently due less to the unfavourable wind than to a failure to take advantage of the run of the bars and the cross-set of the current. The very considerable depth indicated by the impossibility of reaching bottom with five-yard poles makes it certain that the most difficult point was selected for the attempt.

For an inexperienced party of this kind probably the simplest solution of the rafting problem would have been arrived at through the use of a line made by knotting together a number of *riatas*. Men carrying an end of this could have swum across to the nearest point at which a footing was obtainable upon the farthest outreaching bar, when it would have been an easy matter to tow the raft over the short stretch where the poles were unusable. Such a means of getting the raft back and forth would have called for the exercise of no more common sense and resourcefulness than the party had repeatedly shown itself possessed of in meeting so many of the other crises which had been arising since the beginning of the *entrada*.

I have gone into this matter of the ford at the mouth of the Paria at what may seem undue length in an endeavour to show that Father Escalante took infinitely greater risks in venturing back into the Unknown of the lofty and broken plateaux with his starving men and dwindling pack-train than he would have faced in attempting what could not have been a difficult or dangerous crossing. I think that there are two facts that satisfactorily explain why he took the course he did. One of these (and perhaps the more important) is the fact that the Colorado at the mouth of the Paria failed in many respects to correspond to the description so many of the Indians had given him of an easy, shallow ford, where the horses could keep their feet all the way across. This being so he must have felt that continued exploration up-river would ultimately discover such a ford, and beyond it a practicable route to the Moqui towns.

The second reason influencing Escalante in not risking what he considered a dangerous crossing at the Paria would have been the fact that he could not be sure of finding a way out through the cliffs even if he did reach the opposite bank in safety. This is, by the way, conclusive additional proof that his route to the mouth of the Paria must have been along the foot, rather than the rim, of the Vermilion Cliffs. Had he been able to look southward and eastward from the altitudinous vantage of those heights he could not have failed to see the comparatively open going offered by a route along the base of the Echo Cliffs, the same, indeed, followed by the Lee's Ferry-Flagstaff road of to-day.

Following the unsuccessful attempts to get men across the river by swimming or by rafting, the party settled down in camp to await the return of Andres Muniz and his brother Lucero, who had been sent out with orders

" . . . to travel until they found a way by which they could get across the mesa, and that when they came again to the river, they should seek a good fording place, or at least a place where we might cross with a raft, while the horses swam."

After an absence of three days, the scouts returned on the afternoon of November 1st to announce that they had "found a way over the mesa, though exceedingly difficult, and a place where we could cross the river." No time was lost in breaking camp and travelling up the Santa Teresa a distance of a league to the foot of the ascent to the mesa. Provisions—mostly pine-nuts and horse-meat—having again become exhausted during the interval of waiting, another of the pack-animals had been slaughtered before leaving the river.

It is interesting to note that the record covering most of the route from the Paria over the mesas above Glen Canyon to the Crossing-of-the-Fathers is kept with much greater care and accuracy than that relating to the somewhat confused wanderings after turning back from California. The reason for this we can only conjecture, but it was quite possibly due to the heartening effect of coming close to a definite objective, just as the rather erratic entries preceding may have been due to the depression incident to being pretty well lost. The entry for November 2nd, the day after leaving the Colorado at the Paria, is a good example of the meticulous character of the record for this crucial stage of the *entrada*.

"We left camp on the Santa Teresa [it runs], climbed a hill, which we named Las Animas, and which may be a half league in length. We were more than three hours making the ascent, since it is a steep and rocky climb, and following it there is a stretch of shelving rocks that are very dangerous; till at last the way becomes almost impassable. We had, however, reached the top, and taking an easterly direction, we went down the other side at great risk, because of the broken character of the precipices, and then we turned to a northerly course, and after going a league, we turned in an oblique direction to the north-east along a red stony road that was very hard upon the horses. We ascended a low hill and pursuing our route for two and a half leagues to the north-east, we descended to a river bed in which we found water in places; and although it was of a saline nature, was drinkable. . . ."

From several glimpses of the mesa in the course of my boat trip up and down Glen Canyon last summer, supplemented by the two sheets (one of them appropriately called "Escalante") of the Reconnaissance Map of the Geological Survey covering this section, I have found it possible to trace this leg of the journey fairly closely. The so-called hill, named Las Animas, was clearly the backbone ridge of the great "U" which terminates Glen Canyon above the Paria, and I hope Father

Escalante had a bit cooler climb in November than we did last September. The ascent, being started from a point a league (two and three-quarters miles) up the Paria, would have been far enough back to miss the neck of the "U" by a good margin when they pushed on to the four thousand and five thousand-foot levels of the mesa. The contour lines of the map show good reason for the frequent changes of direction indicated in the record.

The river bed where camp was made could have been no other than that marked on the map as Sentinel Rock Creek, but commonly called by its Indian name of Wa-Weap. Powell gave the former name, from the remarkable sandstone pillar standing at the mouth of this creek in Glen Canyon. We made a noon-day halt at Sentinel Rock on our up-river trip, and in tasting the water of the stream a few yards above the backed-up flood of the Colorado I noticed a slight but unmistakable salinity. Escalante speaks of his camp of this night as "close to a number of gorges, mesas, and mountain peaks of a red colour; the whole resembling at first sight the ruins of a fortress." That description might well be applied to a very striking sandstone formation, crowning one of the cliffs of the west bank, against which we saw a terrific cloudburst expend its force the day after we pushed on from Sentinel Rock Creek.

The entry for November 3rd begins:

"We left San Diego [name of camp], and pursued our course to the east-south-east, and when we had journeyed two leagues we arrived for the second time at the river, that is to say, on the edge of the cañon, with its great banks and sides, from which the descent to the river is very long, very high, very precipitous and very rocky, and with such bad shelves of rock, that two of the beasts of burden that went down first were unable to return, although the packs had been removed from their saddles. We had not been advised about this cliff by those who had gone to reconnoitre, and we now discovered that they not only had not found the river crossing, but had not in the several days they were absent from us, made an examination of even so small a portion of the territory, since they had

spent their time in looking for the Indians who inhabit these re
gions, and they had accomplished nothing. The river was deep, although not quite so much so as in Salispuedes [name of camp at
mouth of Paria]; but for a long distance it was necessary that the
horses should swim. Fortunately they did not sink into the mire
either on entering the water or coming out of it."

These two concluding sentences do not make it quite clear
whether a complete crossing was made with the two horses
that were taken down the cliff, or whether they were brought
back to the bank from which they started.

The two leagues travelled to the east-south-east in reaching
the river would seem to locate the camp on Sentinel Rock
Creek three or four miles up from its mouth. One would have
to know whether Escalante's compass bearings were true or
magnetic to lay down his east-south-east course to the Colorado,
but the point at which the latter was reached was certainly
within sight of the mouth of Navajo Creek. Nothing else for
many miles corresponds to the "lofty and narrow cañon" entering through the opposite wall which suggested itself to him as
a possible channel of egress in the event crossing was made
to that side.

We stopped for lunch near the mouth of Navajo Creek the
day after camping above Sentinel Rock, and it was from that
point we watched the cloudburst dumping its countless thousands of tons of water upon the opposite pleateau—quite the
most stupendous natural phenomenon of which I have ever
made the acquaintance at such close range. Impaled on a
sharp pinnacle of sandstone, the savage cloud spilled the last
of its charge in tumbling cascades of white over the brink of
the cliff and dissolved into rags and tatters of flying nimbus.
The deluge from that thunder-storm must have wet down the
dust on the old Escalante trail.

For a mile above the point where we stopped the cliff wall
of the west bank was sheer or overhanging—quite impossible
to climb or descend. I remember that line of cliff particularly

because of the way my boat was bumped along the base of it by a cyclonic back-fire of the main storm. Above and below this cliff the side walls receded somewhat and became more broken; but the only place I can conceive it possible a horse could have been brought down uninjured was at least a half-mile down-stream from its lower end. Here, then, must have been the point where Escalante came a second time to the Colorado.

After some discussion Escalante decided to camp where he was on the cliff above the river and send "the half-breed, Juan Domingo," to cross over and explore the canyon opposite (Navajo Creek) for a possible outlet.

"We sent him off on foot [he writes], but Lucrecio Muniz told us that if we would grant him permission, he would accompany him on horseback, and take with him the materials to build a fire and raise a smoke, in case they found an outlet; and then we might go down on seeing that signal, so there would be less delay. We told him to go, but directed him to return that afternoon, whether he found an outlet or not. They did not come back, and we passed the night here, not being able to water the horses, although we were close to the river."

The following day horse-flesh again gave out and temporary recourse was had to "a few toasted cactus leaves and a por-ridge of some little fruit that was brought up from the edge of the river." Late in the afternoon the pack animals were taken down the cliff to the river, where another one was killed for meat. Several of the horses were severely bruised from rolling down the rocky bluff, but the risk of disabling them had to be taken on account of the impossibility of watering them above. A little before nightfall the half-breed, Domingo, returned, "saying no outlet had been found, and that his companion, having left his horse in the cañon, had followed fresh tracks left by Indians." On learning this, it was at once decided to push on up the river searching for the Indian ford.

As the missing Lucrecio Muniz had not turned up the next

morning his brother was left to await his possible coming. The
man evidently had a weakness for following Indian foot-steps
and forgetting the way travelled by his own. It was these two
sleuthing brothers, it will be remembered, who had been responsible for getting the party into its present difficulty by
searching for Indians instead of the ford they had been sent
to seek. After keeping the starving band waiting at the Paria
three days for their report, they returned to camp with what
turned out to be a false story of a practicable crossing they had
discovered. Now, after endangering the lives of the pack animals in taking them down a cliff, one of them was missing again
and the other left to search for him.

Father Escalante does not tell what difficulties were encountered in taking the pack-train back to the mesa, but merely
records that they "followed along the western bank over many
ravines and gorges, a league and a half to the north." This
particular day's route was one which I crossed at least twice
last summer in accompanying a Geological Survey party that
was studying the possibilities of a tentative dam-site in Glen
Canyon between the mouths of Navajo and Warm creeks. It
had been suggested that it might be practicable to use the comparatively low divide between the basins of Warm Creek
and Sentinel Rock Creek for a spillway for the projected reservoir, and in investigating this bold feature of the project the
engineers walked up the bottom of the canyon of the former,
climbed out over the southern wall at the first point possible,
and made a wide circle across the mesa to the drainage area
of the latter. We must have touched the Escalante trail of
November 5th at least twice, and probably—because of limiting
cliffs and ravines—even followed it for a considerable distance.

Since we were compelled to follow the windings of Warm
Creek for four miles before finding a place where it was possible
for a man to scramble out, it is certain that the *padre's* party
must have crossed that canyon at some point above. This must
have been a mile or more farther west, for the walls of the

canyon do not begin to open out any lower down. As no mention is made of running water, it appears likely that the crossing was made well toward the head of this short but steepwalled gorge. The record states:

"We descended into a dry ravine, and into a deep cañon, where we found much copperas. We came across a trail not much travelled, and followed it. By means of it we emerged from the cañon, passing along a shelf of white and difficult rock, but which afforded a road that could be easily improved."

Camp was made a league and quarter north-north-east, where water was found at the base of a lofty mesa. The next morning Andres Muniz came into camp to report no trace of his brother had been discovered. "This news," Father Escalante writes, "caused us great concern, as the absent man had gone now three days without anything to eat, and with no other covering than his tunic, for he did not wear trousers." Andres was sent back to continue the search for his brother, and the party pushed on three leagues in a north-easterly direction, when they were forced to stop and seek shelter from a violent storm of hail and thunder. "We recited the Litany of the Blessed Virgin," it is piously recorded, "that she might beg for us some relief, and God was pleased to cause the tempest to cease." The intervention must have been a brief one, for the next sentence states: "We continued our journey a half league to the east, and stopped near the river, as the rain continued to pour down, and a number of rocky bluffs impeded our progress."

Without knowing it, the party was almost at its long-striven-for goal. The impeding bluffs were a part of the westerly wall of the striking sandstone amphitheatre encircling what was thenceforth to be known as the Crossing of the Fathers. Sent out to scout, the reliable Don Juan Pedro Cisneros came back to report that the river appeared both wide and shallow—evidently a favourable ford. Two others, who pushed somewhat farther, threw cold water on this optimistic survey by stating that both approach and crossing were found very difficult. "We did not give much credit to the reports they brought us," observes the Father philosophically, "and determined to look it over on the following day in company with Don Juan Pedro Cisneros." The missing Muniz brothers came in together that night, but no further account is given of their wanderings. Doubtless every one was engrossed with the question of the ford.

Early on the morning of November 7th they started for the crossing. Steps had to be cut into the sandstone with a hatchet to get the horses down over one steep pitch of about three yards, and the rest of the distance "they were able to descend, but without pack or rider." A mile down the canyon took them to the river, and at two gun-shots down-stream the beginning of what looked like the most favourable fording place was reached. Here one of the men entered, "and found a foothold without being obliged to swim at any point."

"The rest of us [the record continues], followed him on horseback, going a little farther down the river. When half way across two of the horses that were in advance lost their footing and were carried into a narrow channel. We stopped, although at some risk, until the first man who had crossed could return from the farthest shore to lead and take us over with safety, without our horses having to swim."

The baggage was lowered over the bluff "with ropes and thongs, down to the vicinity of the ford," and the remainder of the horses were taken back to clamber down the stairway into the canyon. Then the crossing began, and

" . . . at about five o'clock in the afternoon we all accomplished the passage of the river, praising the Lord our God, and firing off a number of musket-shots to show the joy we felt on having triumphed over so great an obstacle, that had cost us so much labor and long delay . . . But it was without doubt the will of God that we were unable to secure a guide, partly in order to punish us for our sins, and partly that we might gain some knowledge of the people who inhabit this country."

Escalante speaks of the river as "a little more than a mile wide at this point," meaning, doubtless, the distance between the cliffs. There is a considerable strip of bottom land on the right bank, running back into the canyon down which the horses were brought, but even with this under encroachment by the spring overflow the river itself could never attain a width of a mile either there or anywhere else in Glen Canyon. We camped at the Crossing on our up-river trip of last August, and halted there again on the down-stream trip to pick up a cache of gasoline. Except for the continual cutting down and building up of the strip of bottom land, the river can have effected little change of channel here during the last hundred and fifty years, and the point one would unhesitatingly choose in crossing from the right bank to-day cannot vary by more than a few feet from that which Escalante followed in his historic passage of 1776. On the eastern bank one may readily recognize the "field of moderate size, containing good pasturage," and also the "small, round and high mountain" eight or ten leagues to the north-east. The latter was undoubtedly what we now call Navajo Mountain. It is close to 10,500 feet in height and quite the dominating landmark of the middle Glen Canyon region. Escalante took a sight on the polar star at the Crossing, but his reckoning of 36 degrees 55 minutes was something over ten minutes in error, probably through failure to make the proper corrections for time.

The second Powell expedition received supplies at the Crossing in October, 1871, camping there for several days. Dellenbaugh describes the ford as "half a mile down the middle of the river over a long bar or shoal to the opposite side, where the exit is made upon a rocky slope. It is a most difficult ford. The trail through the water at the low stage when, only, fording is possible, is marked by piles of large stones." We did not observe any evidences of these marking stones in the middle of September, though it is quite possible that the falling water of the next few weeks would have revealed them. On the other hand, of course, the fifty flood seasons that have come and gone since Dellenbaugh camped at the Crossing may either have carried away the rocks or have covered them with silt. The Indians have not used the ford for many years, so it is hardly to be wondered at that the marking cairns have suffered from lack of maintenance.

The rest of the way to Santa Fé was over a country already fairly well known to Escalante, and the journey was made by easy stages without any repetition of the privations that had marked the route north of the Colorado. He arrived in Santa Fé January 2, 1777, and set himself at once to the task of writing up his *diarios* from the notes taken during the progress of the *entrada*. These were completed and delivered to the Viceroy in Mexico City before the middle of the year. It is greatly to be regretted that the map known to have accompanied this report has been lost. It could not have but thrown much light upon a record which, even without it, is the most accurate and illuminative of all the early accounts of the exploration of the Colorado Basin.[1]

Escalante was as sincere and zealous a geographer as he was a priest—altogether one of the most admirable figures in Southwest history. Only the saintly, simple Garcés was worthy of comparison with him, and the passing of those two fine characters from the stage marked the end of the Twilight of the *Padres* and the fall of Night. The utterly empty four decades following the downfall of the Spanish Missions stands as a gulf definitely dividing the colourful early era of *conquistador* and *padre* on the Colorado from the years of brisk movement and action leading up to the era of material achievement upon the brink of which we stand at the end of this first quarter of the twentieth century.

[1] This map, with other material bearing upon the Escalante *entrada*, has recently been found in Mexico City and turned over to Frederick Dellenbaugh, who is contemplating editing a new edition of the journal.

CHAPTER III

THE TRAPPERS

IN writing the history of the Colorado Basin for the two score and more years following the time when the murder of Garcés brought the Mission period to a close, one might well borrow the language of the stereotyped military bulletin and record: "There is nothing to report." These words, literally true and comprehensive as far as events of even passing interest are concerned, tell practically the whole story. The period was a historical back-water. The spent tide of Spanish invasion was at the slack before the ebb; the onrushing American tide was gathering force for the flow that still augments.

The fore-running waves of the new tide did not begin to lap over into the Colorado basin until after the main current had been setting for some years along the Missouri River channel marked by Lewis and Clark. It was the discovery by the returning Astorians and by Fitzpatrick that the Rockies were more easily surmounted by the southerly than by the northerly passes used by the first explorers that brought the westward-swarming trappers to the headwaters of the Green. Barred by the all-but-impassable canyons of the Colorado from following the water to the Pacific as they had done by the Columbia, they spread fan-wise to the north and south of that series of obstacles and filtered on over the Great Basin and the Southwest. So completely did the trails of these intrepid nomads criss-cross the West that it may be said with truth that not one outstanding topographical feature beyond the Rockies was left to be discovered by the scientifically trained explorers who followed. Even Frémont was not a "Path-finder" in the sense that name might be applied to one who blazes a trail that has not been trodden before.

The trapper's courage and energy made him a wonderful discoverer, but his inability to record with accuracy what he saw robbed him of the laurels of the explorer. Even in the case of those who kept journals, ignorance and egotism conspired to render the records of little worth. More hopeless still were the results of the efforts of editors and collaborators to reconstruct so-called diaries, writing in dates and topography to lend verisimilitude to highly fanciful and fictionized stories of wanderings that were veritable Odysseys told as plain unvarnished tales. An instance of vicarious chronicling that was eminently justified by the result was that of Washington Irving's classic "Astoria." But there we have a complete and authentic record in the hands of a gifted chronicler. How utterly futile and banal the result when both of those prime *desiderata* are lacking is attested by practically every one of the averred personal narratives of the trapper pioneers, and by none more effectively than that of James O. Pattie.

Could the story of Pattie's wanderings in the middle twenties of the last century have been truthfully and intelligently told, the record would have constituted a contribution to Colorado River history second only to that of Powell. Indeed, in no single year was it given even to Powell to traverse so inclusive a strip of the Colorado Basin as that unfolded to Pattie when he rode from the mouth of the Gila—but a few miles above tide-water—to the uttermost sources of the river at the Continental Divide in Wyoming. A clear, sane story of that one ride, small part though it was of Pattie's sum total of amazing wanderings, would have advanced the world's knowledge of the River of Mystery more than a quarter of a century. It was misfortune enough that the brave but simple trapper was gifted with but scant powers of observation, and with still scanter powers to record even the little that he did observe. It was worse still that, returning from a series of wanderings perhaps without parallel in American history, he should fall into the hands of an editor who encouraged him to use his remarkable journeys as so many threads upon which to string an endless succession of Indian and bear fights and other blood-and-thunder clap-trap that would have curled the covers of a yellow-backed thriller. But worst of all was the effrontery of that editor who, by rationing this clap-trap out under exact dates as in a diary, and by what he describes as "the occasional interposition of a topographical illustration," endeavoured to give this astonishing hybrid the seeming of a regularly kept journal. Pattie's offence in supplying the colour for a stream of tragic relief in the form of Indian and bear by-play is negligible; the Reverend Timothy Flint, with his very evident interpositions of a number of things besides topographical illustrations, has more to answer for, especially as none but he could have been guilty of the tears-and-slushy-moralizing-obligato that runs through the whole story.

Pattie, penniless and discouraged at the end of his wanderings in the late twenties, was brought to the attention of the Reverend Flint, at that time editing a publication called the *Western Review* in Cincinnati. The "Personal Narrative of James O. Pattie," published in 1831 by John H. Wood, was the outcome of this meeting. In the Editor's Preface to this volume Flint protests at considerable length that the story was written entirely and solely by Pattie, and that his own efforts were exerted more in the way of suppression than embroidery. He says, in part:

"It has been my fortune to be known as a writer of works of the imagination. I am solicitous that this journal should lose none of its intrinsic interest, from its being supposed that in preparing it for the press, I have drawn from the imagination, either in regard to the incidents or their colouring. . . . My influence upon the narrative regards orthography, and punctuation and the occasional interposition of a topographical illustration, which my acquaintance with the accounts of travellers in New Mexico, and published views of the country have enabled me to furnish. The reader will award me the confidence of acting in good faith, in regard to drawing nothing from my own thoughts. . . . The very texture of the narrative precludes ornament and amplification. The simple record of events as they transpired, painted by the hungry, toil-worn hunter, in the midst of the desert, espying the footprint of the savage, or discerning him couched behind the tree or hillock, or hearing the distant howl of wild beasts, will naturally bear characteristics of stern disregard of embellishment. To alter it, to divest it of the peculiar impress of the narrator and his circumstances, would be to take from its keeping, the charm of its simplicity, and its internal marks of truth. . . ."

Flint thus flatly puts the responsibility for the facts of the narrative up to his protégé, but in that connection I cannot but recall the marginal annotation I found at this point of the Editor's Preface to the first rare and valuable volume of the original edition of Pattie of which I was permitted to turn the yellow leaves. "Methinks the lady doth protest too much," the astute commentator had quoted, and very much to the point beyond all doubt. The "very texture of the narrative" has certainly not precluded "ornament and amplification," and in deciding as to the responsibility for it one can hardly hesitate long between a very simple and illiterate trapper and a very live and enterprising editor "known as a writer of works of the imagination."

Almost if not quite valueless as was Pattie's contribution to Colorado Basin discovery and exploration, there are two reasons why his narrative cannot be fairly passed over in even so brief and superficial a survey of the early history of that region as I am attempting here. One of these is that Pattie was undoubtedly the first person ever to follow the river the whole distance from its mouth to its head-waters. Whether this record has since been duplicated I am not able to say, although it would have been comparatively easy for Powell to have done so once his Grand Canyon voyage was accomplished. This alone would certainly entitle the man if not his story to recognition. Since there is no other way of measuring the achievement of the man than through his story, we have to make use of that medium, however erratic and faulty it is.

Another reason why the Pattie narrative cannot be ignored is because of the extent to which it has been cited as authoritative by the most able and dependable of historians. Bancroft has quoted it in his histories of California and of New Mexico and Arizona, and Thwaites has enshrined it in a permanent place by reprinting it entire as a volume of his most excellent "Early Western Travels." Even Dellenbaugh, who could so easily have done so, did not go to the trouble of pointing out the interminable inconsistencies of the narrative in summarizing it in his "Romance of the Colorado River." It is the Thwaites reprint [1] to which I am referring in commenting on Pattie's account of his journeys up and down the Colorado.

Thwaites, while fully aware of what he describes as the "occasional discrepancies of dates, and the obvious confusion of events" in the narrative, believed it was worthy of reproduction in his series because of "the vast extent of country over which the author passed, the ethnological data which he presents . . . and his graphic picture of the contact between the two civilizations in the Southwest, with the inevitable encroachments of the more progressive race." While what Pattie had to tell of the meeting and merging Yankee and Mexican currents in New Mexico and California had a certain historical interest, the fact that his remarkable longitudinal traverse of the Colorado Basin was largely through an unpeopled desert necessarily confined the narrative covering that region to the crudely coloured Indian fight blood-and-thunder and the no less crude "topographical illustrations" interposed by the Reverend Flint. In this part of the narrative Dr. Thwaites was confronted with the altogether impossible task of trying to reconcile the hopelessly jumbled and inaccurate geographical

---

[1] "Early Western Travels—1748-1846," by Reuben Gold Thwaites, LL.D., Vol. XVIII. The Arthur H. Clark Company, Cleveland, 1905.

interpolations of the original editor with Pattie's dates and distances and the country as we know it to-day. That he failed to reduce these to any semblance of continuity is no reflection on the painstaking care lavished upon the effort by the brilliant editor of Lewis and Clark, Brackenridge, Pike and De Smet. It is unfortunate that geographical limitations of our subject confine us to this desert portion—both literally and figuratively speaking—of the Pattie narrative.

The Patties came of the best of Kentucky pioneering stock, and the elder had already made a considerable reputation in the Indian wars before coming to settle upon the banks of the Gasconade in Missouri. The death of his wife was responsible for the reawakening of the old wandering spirit, and in setting his face to the West to seek forgetfulness in action Sylvester Pattie was accompanied by his eldest son, James Ohio, who tells the story. Faring north-westward up the Missouri with the intention of becoming "free-trappers" on its upper tributaries, a failure to secure the necessary permits induced the pair and their companions to throw in their lot with a trading caravan bound for Santa Fé.

To judge from Pattie's account the road to the south-west ran all the way through a sort of Hindenburg Line manned by successive reserves of hostile Indians and belligerent grizzlies. Hacking their way through to Santa Fé in a little over three months, the Americans came onto the scene just in time to rescue the young and beautiful daughter of the ex-Governor from the spears of her Indian captors. Perhaps Pattie's account of the incident may be worth setting down as an example of his plain, blunt trapper's style and that "stern disregard of embellishment" which the Reverend Flint so vehemently disclaims. Ambushed behind a screen of rocks the avenging party awaited the coming of the Indians.

"The first object that came in sight [he writes] were women without any clothing, driving a large drove of sheep and horses.

NAVAJO BRAVE.

THE GILA, JUST ABOVE ITS JUNCTION WITH THE COLORADO.

A favorite halting-place for Conquistador, Padre, and Trapper.

SPILLWAY SITE FOR SENTINEL ROCK DAM.

Father Escalante passed very near to the foot of the big sand-stone butte.

These were immediately followed by the Indians. When the latter were within thirty to forty yards from us the order to fire was given. The women ran toward us the moment they heard the report of the guns. In doing this they encountered the Indians behind them, and three fell pierced by the spears of these savages. The cry among us now was, 'Save the women!' Another young man and myself ran forward to rescue the remaining two. My companion fell in the attempt. An Indian had raised his spear to inflict death upon another of these unfortunate captives, when he received a shot from one of our men, that rendered him incapable of another act of cruelty. The captives, one of whom was a beautiful young lady, the daughter of the governor before spoken of, both reached me. The gratitude of such captives, so delivered, may be imagined. Fears, thanks, and exclamations in Spanish were the natural expression of feelings in such a position. My companions aided me in wrapping blankets around them, for it was quite cold. . . ."

Not an especially exaggerated or improbable account of what would have happened given the conditions described, but most certainly not in the language of the rough and simple trapper. Somehow, from what one remembers of trappers' recitals, one knows that in at least Pattie's first verbal version of the affair he would have managed that blanket-wrapping alone and unaided. The co-operative effort was undoubtedly introduced by, or at the behest of, the Reverend Timothy on the score of propriety.

After the Indians had been put to flight the Spaniards, who Pattie says had remained out of the way until the fighting was over, were spurned and roundly rated by the Governor's daughter. "Nothing would induce her," she declared, "to leave her deliverers, and that when they were ready to go she would accompany them, adding that she would pray hourly for the salvation of those, who had resigned their lives in the preservation of hers." Then she "inquired for the individual, who first met her in her flight from the Indians, and so humanely and bravely conducted her out of danger, and provided for her comfort."

"I cannot describe [writes Pattie] the gratitude and loveliness, that appeared in her countenance, as she looked on me, when I was pointed out to her. Not attaching any merit to the act I had performed, and considering it merely as a duty, I did not know how to meet her acknowledgments, and was embarrassed."

Later, in the course of a two-day celebration of the rescue at the Governor's home, the beautiful Jacova brought out Pattie's old leather hunting shirt which he had taken off to aid in protecting her from the cold, and assured him that she intended to keep it as long as she lived. "She then put it on," he concludes touchingly, "to prove to me that she was not ashamed of it." The habit thus formed of giving shirts to unprotected ladies was one our hero was never quite able to shake off, as we shall see later upon the lower Colorado.

The golden thread of the Jacova romance glitters through all of the earlier narrative. According to Pattie, the beautiful daughter of the Governor must have spent the long hours of his absences longing for his return and mending his reserve wardrobe. On coming back from his first trapping trip he records that she received him "with the utmost affection; and shed tears on observing me so ill; as I was in fact reduced by starvation and fatigue, to skin and bone. . . . She had all my clothes prepared in perfect order." The anxieties awakened in the gentle breast during the long vigil incident to the extended trip up the Colorado and through the Rockies was almost too much for the fair señorita, for Pattie admits that on his return, after receiving the affectionate greetings of Jacova, she gave him "the most earnest counsels to quit this dangerous and rambling life, and settle myself down in a house of my own. I thanked her for her kindness and good counsel," he adds graciously, "and promised to follow it, after rambling another year in the wilderness."

Only once did this romantic friendship threaten to topple from the high moral plane on which it started, and Pattie's statement proves beyond doubt that the fault was entirely that of the impetuous Jacova rather than of himself. He arose one night to go home to his companions, but his enamoured *novia,*

" . . . showing me a bed, prepared for me, placed herself between me and the door. I showed her that my clothes were not clean. She immediately brought me others belonging to her brother-in-law. I wished to be excused from making use of them, but she seemed so much hurt, that I finally took them, and reseated myself."

Then followed the episode of the hunting shirt, already recorded—and Curtain. Pattie begins the next day with the discreet entry to the effect that he "went to bed early, and arose, and returned to my companions, before any of the family were visible." Something in the inconsequentiality of the narrative at this point makes one wonder if the piquant passage was one of those which the Reverend Flint had in mind when he said in his Preface, "I have found more call to suppress than to add, to soften, than to show in stronger relief any of the incidents." At any rate, no matter what happened, the blame for it did not rest upon the shoulders of our hero. His editor has seen to that.

I have touched somewhat in detail upon this first of Pattie's several romances not because it has any direct connection with our Colorado Basin (indeed, the gentle Jacova's tears, falling where they did, would mostly have drained to the Rio Grande), but to make clear at the outset that Editor Flint, in spite of all his protests to the contrary, told the story very much in his own way; that he did *not* leave it as he found it, and that it does *not* bear "characteristics of stern disregard of embellishment." One does not need to be deeply versed in the characteristic diction of either woodsman or romancer to know that this story is told, not in trapper-ese but in thriller-ese—that terribly trying soft, slushy, moralizing thriller-ese of a hundred years ago. One may dig into the narrative at almost any point and ages, started the fun by telling them in fluent pantomime that the river was his, and demanding a horse in payment for the furs they had taken from its denizens. When refused,

" . . . he raised himself erect, with a stern and fierce air, and discharged his arrow into the tree, at the same time raising his hand to his mouth, and making their peculiar yell. Our captain made no other reply, than by raising his gun and shooting the arrow, as it still stuck in the tree, in two. The chief seemed bewildered with this mark of close marksmanship, and started off with his men."

When the chief came back the next morning and again demanded the horse,

"The captain bade him be off, in a language and with a tone alike understood by all people. He started off on a full gallop, and as he passed one of our horses, that was tied a few yards from the camp, he fired a spear through the animal. He had not the pleasure to exult in his revenge for more than fifty yards, before he fell pierced by four bullets."

Travelling hard by day and watching behind log-built barricades at night, the party pushed on up river. Sixteen of the savages had been killed in a brush following the shooting of the chief, but the surviving braves had rallied and now hung on in relentless pursuit. Relaxing their vigilance on the fourth night the trappers exposed themselves to the long-deferred attack.

"At about 11 o'clock [Pattie writes] they poured upon us a shower of arrows, by which they killed two men and wounded two more; and what was most provoking, fled so rapidly that we could not even give them a round. One of the slain was in bed with me. My own hunting shirt had two arrows in it, and my blanket was pinned fast to the ground with arrows. There were sixteen arrows discharged into my bed."

At the end of an all-day pursuit the account was squared the following evening. Surprising the marauders at supper on the body of a horse, Pattie tells how he and his seventeen companions spurred up and overtook them just as they were entering a thicket, killing "a greater part of them. We suspended those we had killed upon the trees," he adds, "and left their bodies to dangle in terror to the rest, and as a proof, how we retaliated aggression."

At the "Shuena" village a little farther along the usual skirmish took place. Although a number of Indians were killed, the fight could not have been a serious one from the trappers' standpoint, for Pattie writes how, in the excitement of the attack, they "laughed heartily to see these sons of the desert dodge and skulk away half bent, as though the heavens were falling upon them."

The day after they arrived at the mouth of the Bill Williams two of the party were cut off and killed by Indians. Pattie does not identify the tribe of the latter, but that he believed them to have been cannibals is evident from his statement that they found "the bodies cut in pieces, and spitted before a great fire, after the manner of roasting beaver." I am unable to find reliable evidence convicting any of the Colorado Indians of eating human flesh. That impeachment has occasionally been made against the natives of the island of Tiburon, but it would have been a long stalk from fifty miles below the head of the Gulf of California to the Bill Williams.

Now comes Pattie's remarkable overnight jump from the mouth of the Bill Williams to the great plateau. It was at mid-day of March 27th that the dismembered bodies of his companions were found. He then records that "we gathered the fragments of the bodies together and buried them. With sadness in our hearts, and dejection on our countenances, we returned to our camp, struck our tents, and marched on." That would have made their departure well along toward the middle of the afternoon. Yet Pattie goes on to state that sometime the next day, the 28th, "we reached a point of the river where the mountains shut in so close upon its shores, that we were compelled to climb a mountain, and travel along the acclivity, "they would otherwise have met with the Havasupai in their Canyon, with the Little Colorado, and with the Moki." Assuming that a crossing—not mentioned in the narrative—was made somewhere above the mouth of the Bill Williams, this would seem to be the more likely side for the route, especially as the loftier Kanab and Kaibab plateaux have a heavier snowfall than the elevated regions to the south. Locating the route on the north side of the Grand Canyon would also assume another fording of the Colorado—likewise unmentioned in the narrative—somewhere in Glen Canyon to make possible the ascent of a certain "right-hand fork" recorded further on.

Dr. Thwaites, in an endeavour to keep the party on the south side of the river, is forced to a major surgical operation upon both the narrative and the topography of the canyon region. The cut into the narrative was made deliberately in an attempt to avoid a solution of its continuity; that into the topography was unintentional, and would hardly have occurred had Dr. Thwaites had a first-hand knowledge of the Marble and Glen Canyon regions, or had he even made a careful study of it upon a good relief map.

While there is really no point between the foot of the Grand Canyon and the headwaters of the Colorado that would even approximately correspond to Pattie's place "where the river emerges from these horrid mountains," there does occur, at just about the "100 leagues" he mentions travelling over the snowy plateau, a short stretch where there is a falling away of the cliff walls upon either side. This is at the mouth of the Paria, between the foot of Glen Canyon and the head of Marble Canyon, the point, it will be remembered, where Father Escalante camped in 1776 and made vain attempts at a crossing. As there is no other point within a couple of hundred miles in either direction that even remotely satisfies Pattie's description, we may assume that it was at the crossing we now call Lee's Ferry that he first descended from the plateau to the banks of the river.

How much time was spent in camp at this point is not stated, but on April 13th, three days after arriving, it is stated that they "reached another part of the river, emptying into the main river from the north," up which they trapped for two days, killing four of a band of attacking Indians. It is here that Dr. Thwaites, concerned over the continued absence of the Little Colorado in Pattie's story, starts shaking up both narrative and Nature in an attempt to locate it. He appends a footnote to the effect that "the river up which they trapped for two days was probably the Little Colorado, which comes in from the southeast. Pattie's 'north' is probably a misprint for 'south.' " Such a switching of Pattie's direction would doubtless be fully justified if only the Little Colorado were not something like a hundred miles too far up stream even when moved over to the south side. That river flows to the main Colorado in a deep gorge that divides Marble Canyon from the Grand Canyon proper. It is separated from the mouth of the Paria by the whole length of Marble Canyon, about sixty-five miles as "the river meanders." Dr. Thwaites' very considerable error—a most unusual one for that sincere and painstaking historian— was plainly due to the fact that he had not studied the topography of the region closely enough to know that Pattie could not have come to the Colorado in the manner he describes below the mouth of the Paria.

Unless we identify it with some such inconsiderable stream as the Paria or Escalante, there is no river below the Green itself even remotely answering to Pattie's description of this affluent that emptied "into the main river from the north." Four days more up the main river, which Pattie describes as a "clear, beautiful stream," brought them to a point "where it forked again, neither fork being more than from twenty-five to thirty yards wide." Dr. Thwaites concludes confidently that "This was the San Juan," when Pattie states they went up the right-hand fork, which pursues a N.E. course." The absurdity of describing the junction of the Colorado and San Juan as a fork-

There are many just as serious mistakes and hiatus in the record of the whole trip up the Colorado from the Gila, but as Dr. Thwaites had made a far less intensive study of that region than of the Northwest the palpable inconsistencies of the journal did not strike him with much force until they had to do with a section made thoroughly familiar to him from long and intimate research.

After more Indian battles the Pattie party arrived back in Santa Fé on the first of August, only to have the Governor, on the pretext that they had trapped without a license, rob them of all their furs. "We were excessively provoked," he writes, "and had it not been from a sense of duty to our beloved country, we would have redressed our wrongs, and retaken our furs with our own arms."

During the next eight or ten months Pattie, in spite of the admonition of the gentle Jacova to settle down in a house of his own and cease his dangerous and rambling way of life, fought bears and Indians pretty well all over northern Mexico. The elder Pattie also chided the adventurous youth for his wandering spirit, but when he found himself suddenly impoverished as a consequence of being robbed by a trusted clerk, "nothing seemed so feasible, and conformable to his pursuits, as a trapping expedition." It was this enterprise, embarked upon in the autumn of 1827, which took the Patties to the lower Colorado and finally to California.

After being reduced for some days to a diet of dog and horse, the party reached the Colorado at the mouth of the Gila on the first of December. That very night, under cover of a thunderstorm, the wily "Umeas" made off with all their horses. The elder Pattie, evidently quite as much of a fire-eater as the younger, proposed that they should follow the thieves in the morning and retake their horses or die in the attempt. It was further resolved that, failing to overtake the savages, they would return, "swim the river, attack their town, and kill as many of the inhabitants" as they could. "It was better to die by these Indians," Pattie elucidates, "after we had killed a good number of them, than to starve, or be killed by Indians who had not injured us, and when we could not defend ourselves."

The preference here expressed for being killed by Indians who had injured them, rather than by those who had not, suggests a subtle psychological discrimination one would hardly have expected in that rough-and-ready band of trappers. Whether the circumstance of being killed by Indians who had not previously injured them would not in itself have constituted an injury that would mitigate some of the wildness of regret at so dying is a still subtler point which Pattie fails to discuss.

According to the chronicle, that desperate band of trappers were as good as their word in the matter of wreaking their vengeance on the village. Losing the trail of the horse thieves, they came back to camp, ate heartily what they believed would be their last meal of beaver meat, swam across the river and, in the language of Pattie, "steered for the town." "Marching up to the numerous assemblage of huts in a manner as reckless and undaunted as though we had nothing to apprehend," he writes, . . . "we found it to contain not a single living being except one miserable, blind, deaf and decrepit old man. . . . Our exasperation of despair inclined us to kill even him."

Leaving the old man to finish his acorn mush, they fired the town and swam back to their camp. Then, as "a pleasant scheme to soothe [our] dejection, and prevent lying down to the sleep of despair," they began building dug-out canoes in which to float down to the Spanish settlements that they believed existed at the mouth of the river. The kind of tree used is not mentioned, but it could have been nothing but cottonwood. Eight canoes, united in pairs by platforms, gave a flotilla of four units capable of carrying the whole outfit, including their accumulated catch of furs.

The part of the narrative covering this canoe voyage down

through the delta of the Colorado has few of the glaring discrepancies such as crop out through that relating to the long
up-river traverse. Whether the descriptions are from Pattie's
own observations or interpolations of the Reverend Flint, they
are accurate as to both natural features, flora and fauna.

"The river below its junction with the Helay [he writes] is from
2 to 300 yards wide, with high banks that have dilapidated by falling
in. Its course is west, and its timber is chiefly cotton-wood, which
in the bottoms is lofty and thick set. The bottoms are from six to
ten miles wide. The soil is black and mixed with sand, though the
bottoms are subject to inundations in the flush waters of June. This
inundation is occasioned by the melting of the snow in the mountains about its headwaters. . . . There are but few wild animals that
belong to the country farther up, but some deer, panthers, foxes and
wild-cats. Of birds there are great numbers and many varieties,
most of which I have never before seen. We killed some wild geese
and pelicans, and likewise an animal not unlike the African leopard,
which came into our camp, while we were at work on the canoe. It
was the first we had ever seen."

The leopard-like animal was, of course, a jaguar. It is
rarely if ever seen in the delta region to-day. Most of the
other animals and birds mentioned I saw in the course of my
boat trip down to the Gulf last autumn.

Although Pattie assures us how greatly it would have pained
them to have to kill Indians by whom they had never been disturbed, enough little disturbances seem to have cropped up to
relieve life and the narrative of the dull drab monotony that
would have been theirs without an occasional vivifying splash
of redskin blood across the pages of the both. Two lurking savages, shot down out of a tree so that "they made the earth
sound when they struck it," proved to have been members of
the horse-thief band. They were left suspended from a tree by
the very hempen riatas through which they had been identified.
Some treacherous Indians of a tribe called "Pipi" were also
given a salutary lesson when they discharged arrows at the
boats from the bank.

HAVISAPAI FALLS IN CATARACT CANYON.

CLOUDS AFTER A STORM, SEEN FROM BRIGHT ANGEL POINT.

"As soon as our crafts touched shore [writes Pattie] we sprang upon the bank, took fair aim, and showed them the difference between their weapons and ours, by levelling six of them. The remainder fell flat, and began to dodge and skulk on all fours, as though the heavens had been loaded with thunder and mill stones, which were about to rain on them from the clouds."

With the Cocopahs, of whom Pattie erroneously writes as averaging but five feet and a half against the Yumas' "gigantic stature of from six to seven feet," the party got on very well once the Indians had been duly impressed with the power of firearms. "Apparently frightened to insanity" at first, a surprised camp of Cocopahs "surrendered without making any further effort to escape." A present of meat caused "the ghastliness of terror to pass from the countenances" of the men, and they took measures to stop "the annoying noise" of the women and children who had continued screaming "as if going into convulsions."

The description of the smoking of the Pipe of Peace, with the Indians puffing the smoke toward the sky and uttering mystic incantations, follows so closely that rite as practised by the Sioux that one is inclined to suspect that Flint found the inspiration of it in the Lewis and Clark journals, already published for some years. Neither am I entirely in agreement with Pattie's interpretation of certain cabalistic signs made by the smokers at this juncture.

"They then struck themselves on the breast [he says], and afterwards on the forehead. We understood this to be a sort of religious appeal to the Supreme Being, and it showed more like reverence to him, than any thing we had yet seen among the Indians; though I have yet seen none but what admit that there is a master of life, whom they call by a name to that import, or that of Great Spirit."

That the Mississippi Valley and other Indians (with whom Pattie had heretofore been familiar, and of whom Flint had doubtless read extensively) were given to a worship of a Supreme Being is a long established fact. Beyond Alarcón's and even our fire-place was three feet under water, and our blankets were all afloat."

The description is that of a fully-developed "bore," such as only occurs at the spring and autumnal equinoxes and, in considerably less strength, at the full and new moons of the months immediately following and preceding them. At the end of December I have drifted all night in a scow near the mouth of the Hardy (probably some miles nearer the sea than Pattie attained to) without being greatly bothered by the comparatively slight tidal movement. It is possible that Flint has here interpolated his own picture of the "bore" drawn from the graphic descriptions of Lieutenant Hardy, whose book was out two years before the Pattie Narrative was published. I am rather inclined to believe, however, that Pattie has given a fairly faithful account of what he saw, but on a date at least a month later, or three months earlier, than the one he sets down. Indeed, it is this unfortunate writing-in of exact dates in a story palpably transcribed from memory that discredits so much of the narrative from first to last.

Unable to go ahead on account of the "bore," and unwilling to work back upstream against the current with no prospect of getting horses to carry them to Santa Fé, the trappers paddled along through the bayous to the head of tide-water, buried their furs and set off on foot for the Spanish settlements the Cocopahs had told them would be found on the sea to the west. Here they pass out of our picture. The descriptions of the alkali flats, salt lakes, deserts and mountains crossed or skirted on the traverse to the Pacific are far-and-away the most accurate in the whole narrative, and connote either better observation on Pattie's part or more reliable topographical data available to his editor. If the story of the long journey up the river could only have been done half as well, that part of the narrative would have been one of the most valuable of the historical documents bearing on the Colorado Basin.

On arrival at San Diego the whole party was thrown into

prison by the Mexican Governor. Here the elder Pattie died, and the younger was only released after long incarceration when it was found he was in possession of some vaccine virus that was desperately needed to combat an outbreak of small-pox. Pattie kept the same exact record of arms scratched as he had of scalps taken in his Indian fights. After every one of the thousands of whites and Indians in the whole string of California missions had been innoculated from that precious phial of cultures, our hero took part in a revolution and then set sail for Mexico to claim damages for the furs lost on the Colorado during his imprisonment. Failing to collect the indemnity demanded, he made his way to New Orleans on borrowed money, and so to the Reverend Timothy Flint and the ink-pot.

Pattie was plainly not able to tell much on his own initiative, and Flint's journalistic flair, coupled with a total failure to realize his responsibility as the mouth-piece of perhaps the most remarkable wanderer in Western history, precluded all possibility of producing a record of much worth to posterity. If Pattie could have come to such an editor as Dr. Thwaites at first rather than at second-hand, there would have been a very different story told. As it is, good old Jim Bridger,—with his delectable Yellowstone yarns of the ten-miles-distant elk fired at through a cliff of telescopic glass, and of ground anointed with the astringent water of Alum Creek so as to shrink the distance to be run in escaping a grizzly,—contributed just about as much to the knowledge of nations as did Pattie, and vastly more to their gaiety.

CHAPTER IV

GENERAL ASHLEY ON THE GREEN

THE first boat voyage down any of the canyons of the Colorado was made by General William Henry Ashley in the spring of 1825. This very notable feat of rough-water navigation was undertaken as a part of an extended western trip made by Ashley in planning the campaign of a new trapping partnership he had formed with Andrew Henry to enter into competition with the old established monopolistic fur companies of the upper Missouri and Yellowstone. The record of it is contained in a letter, bearing the date of December 1st, 1825, written by Ashley, on his return, to General Henry Atkinson. This valuable document, preserved for many years in the archives of the Missouri Historical Society, was given to the world in 1918 by Professor Harrison Clifford Dale in his most ably-edited work on the explorations of Ashley and his brave and energetic lieutenant, Jedediah Smith.[1] Prior to that time the only readily available account of this short but historic voyage was a sketchy and sensational version contained in the Jim Beckwourth narrative, a trapper's record no more dependable and even more egotistical than that of Pattie.[2]

William Henry Ashley was a Virginian by birth, but migrated to Missouri a few years before the return of Lewis and Clark struck the spark of action to the hitherto only half-awakened westering impulse of young America. Dabbling in mining and politics, by the early twenties young Ashley had become suc-

---

[1] "The Ashley-Smith Explorations and the Discovery of a Central Route to the Pacific—1822-29, with the Original Journals edited by Harrison Clifford Dale, Professor of Political Science in the University of Wyoming." Cleveland, 1918.
[2] "Life and Adventures of James P. Beckwourth," by T. D. Bonner. New York, 1856.

cessively a General in the state militia, Lieutenant-Governor and defeated candidate for Governor; also a bankrupt with debts estimated at a hundred thousand dollars. It was doubtless the need of money at a time when the fur trade was entering upon a renewed activity that led the enterprising young Virginian to conclude a partnership with the veteran trader, Andrew Henry, formerly of the powerful Missouri Fur Company. The trader, it would appear, brought to the firm money and experience; the politician, vision and energy; though none could charge the brave and resolute Henry with any lack of the latter. In the end, however, it was probably Ashley's vision and executive ability that had most to do with the notable success of the partnership and a policy that ultimately revolutionized the whole western fur industry.

The system under which Ashley and Henry planned to work was based upon securing furs directly from white trappers in their own employ rather than from the Indians through the medium of trading-posts. This method had been followed with success by the Hudson's Bay Company, but on no such comprehensive plan as that now inaugurated. To replace the trading-post as an accumulating point for furs there was substituted what was called a "General Rendezvous," to which the trappers brought their winter's catch each summer. It was scouting out fresh trapping territory and exploring for points best strategically located for the summer rendezvous that led Ashley and Henry and their "partisans" on a series of journeys destined to cover practically all of the hitherto unknown west.

The following advertisement. appearing in the *Missouri Republican* of March 20th, 1822, indicates the means by which the partners recruited their men:

"To Enterprising Young Men:
The subscriber wishes to engage one hundred young men to ascend the Missouri River to its source, there to be employed for one, two or three years. For particulars enquire of Major Andrew Henry, near the lead mines in the County of Washington, who will

ascend with and command the party; or of the subscriber near St. Louis.   (Signed)   WILLIAM H. ASHLEY."

Of the response and the reason therefor John G. Neihardt writes in epic verse:

"One hundred men they flocked to Ashley's call
That spring of eighteen hundred twenty-two;
For tales of wealth, out-legending Peru,
Came wind-blown from Missouri's distant springs,
And that old sireny of unknown things
Bewitched them, and they could not linger more." [1]

And of the spring-time departure that same gifted writer, no less historian than poet, sings:

"When Major Henry went
Up river at the head of Ashley's band,
Already there were robins in the land.
Home-keeping men were following the ploughs
And through the smoke-thin greenery of boughs
The scattering wild-fire of the fruit bloom ran."

Henry pushed on to the mouth of the Yellowstone to erect a fort to serve as a base for his operations, while Ashley returned to St. Louis to look after the recruiting of another force to come on the following spring. This second hundred, commanded by Ashley in person and cordelling two large keel-boats, started up the Missouri as planned, but encountered such serious trouble with the ever-belligerent Arikaras near the mouth of the Grand that it had to fall back and call on both Henry and the military at Fort Atkinson to help clear the way. After a punitive expedition that resulted in about as much punishment to the attacking whites and their Sioux allies as to the Arikaras, Ashley returned to St. Louis, leaving Henry to continue northward overland with the remains of the second hundred.

Numbering on its roster such names as James Bridger, Will-

[1] "The Song of Three Friends," by John G. Neihardt. New York, 1919.

BALANCE ROCK NEAR MOUTH OF NOKAI CREEK,
SAN JUAN.

LOOKING DOWN 1,200 FEET TO COLORADO,
THROUGH CRACK IN CANYON WALL, NEAR
JUNCTION OF GREEN AND GRAND.

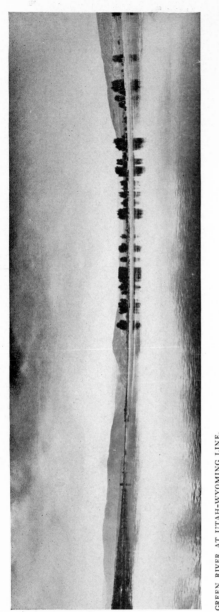

GREEN RIVER AT UTAH-WYOMING LINE.

iam Sublette, Etienne Provot, Hugh Glass, Thomas Fitzpatrick, Seth Grant and Jedediah Smith, this band of frontiersmen marching north under Henry's command is well characterized by Professor Dale as "the most significant group of continental explorers ever brought together." The wanderings of these men during the next ten or fifteen years, he points out, covered "the entire west from the Missouri to the Pacific and from Canada to Chihuahua."

It was the increasing hostility of the Indians on the old route along the Missouri, together with the difficulty of operating in competition with the established fur companies on the upper tributaries of that river, that conspired to turn Ashley's attention to opening up a new field of effort in the untrapped region beyond the middle Rockies. The historic traverse of 1824-25, which carried him to the Colorado Basin at the head of the Green, was undertaken with the dual purpose of establishing touch with men Henry had already thrown into this region and of conducting further explorations on his own account. The record of it, in the form of the letter already mentioned, was evidently dictated shortly after his return to St. Louis in response to a request from General Atkinson for certain information. It is written, according to Professor Dale, "in two different hands, neither of them Ashley's," and covers thirty-six pages of letter paper. Although extremely comprehensive (considering the country described in so comparatively few words) it is also direct and explicit, and, in refreshing contrast to the lurid narratives of Pattie and Beckwourth, puts on the soft-pedal rather than the loud in touching on difficulties and hardships. In short, the record is a succinct, businesslike, modest and thoroughly convincing memorandum of important exploration. Taken quite alone, the document is sufficient to prove that Ashley was possessed of every essential natural prerequisite of a successful explorer, and lacked only scientific training to put his observations on an equality with those of Frémont and Lewis and Clark.

Starting from Fort Atkinson on the 3rd of November, 1824, Ashley overtook his party of twenty-five a couple of days later. Following a route which took him up the North Fork of the Platte, he crossed the Continental Divide on April 1st, 1825, by a route which Dale identifies with Bridger Pass, "paralleling the line of the Union Pacific, but to the south of it." A day or two later the expedition was seriously crippled by the loss of seventeen horses and mules, driven off by a marauding party of Crows. The packs of the stolen animals had to be carried, temporarily, on the backs of the men, and the impossibility of making any considerable progress under such a handicap doubtless had a considerable influence in inducing Ashley to undertake a part of his explorations by river.

Between delays from bad weather and a bootless pursuit of the thieving Indians, it was not until the 18th of April that the party came down to the banks of the river we now call the Green. He describes it as

" . . . about one hundred yards wide, of a bold current, and generally so deep that it presents but few places suitable for fording. Its margin and islands are wooded with large long-leafed cottonwood, box-elder, willows, etc., and judging from the quantity of wood cut upon its banks, and other appearances, it once must have contained a great number of beaver, the major part of which (as I have been informed) were trapped by men in the service of the North West Company some four or five years ago."

There is a military conciseness and exactitude in Ashley's note as to the disposition of his party at the Green. He writes:

" . . . I determined to relieve my men and horses of their heavy burdens, to accomplish which, I concluded to make four divisions of my party, send three of them by land in different directions, and, with the fourth party, descend the river myself with the principal part of my merchandise. Accordingly, some of the men commenced making a frame about the size and shape of a common mackinaw boat, while others were sent to procure buffalo skins for a covering. On the 21st of April, all things being ready for our departure, I despatched six men northwardly to the source of the river; seven others set out for a mountain bearing S.S.W. and N.N.E., distant about thirty miles; and six others were sent in a southern direction. . . . The partizans were also informed that I would descend the river to some eligible point about one hundred miles below, there deposit my merchandise, and make such marks as would designate it as a place of General Rendevous for the men in my service in that country, and they were all directed to assemble there on or before the 10th July following."

As Professor Dale points out, the craft constructed could hardly have been of the size of the Missouri River mackinaw boat, which averaged from forty to fifty feet in length, with a twelve-foot beam. The common name for a skin-covered craft was "bull-boat," and Dale gives the normal dimensions of this type as thirty feet length and twelve feet beam, with a twenty-inch draft. I can hardly conceive it as probable that for a stream so comparatively swift and shallow as the upper Green experienced river men would have risked a craft of even of the latter dimensions. Ashley himself had had no experience of water swifter than that of the lower Missouri, which, from the Yellowstone to the Mississippi, has an average fall of less than a foot to the mile. Others of the party, however, had been in the mountains before, and so must have learned the unwisdom of carrying their eggs in too large and unwieldy a basket. I am confirmed in my belief that this first boat was considerably under the dimensions mentioned by the fact that the initial day's run proved it "too heavily burthened," necessitating a two-days' halt while a running-mate was built to relieve it. In rough, swift, shallow water two small boats are twice as safe as one of double capacity, and four times as handy.

This first camp on the Green could have been but a few miles below the present site of Fontenelle, Wyoming. The initial run carried them past the mouth of the Big Sandy, from whose shallow stream so many forty-niners watered their horses and oxen, and on to a camp not far above the Union Pacific bridge at Green River station. Ashley does not overestimate the dis-

tance in setting it down as forty miles. Here the second boat
was launched the morning of the 24th, and on that day thirty
miles were made through a country somewhat paradoxically
described as becoming "more level and broken." This run
carried the party well below the starting-point of the Powell
and Kolb expeditions, and for the next few days Ashley's descriptions may be checked against those of these later voyageurs.

A "beautiful bold running stream about fifty yards wide,"
emptying to the Green from the west, was Black's Fork, which
Powell describes as "a dirty little stream that seems somewhat
swollen." Powell's entry is under the date of May 25th; that
of Ashley, of the same day of April. The melting snows of
May would easily account for the stream's greater height and
dirtiness on the occasion of the later voyage.

There is something wrong about Ashley's record at this point,
for he writes as though he had taken five days of continuous
river travel to run the comparatively short distance to the
mouth of a creek that can only be Henry's Fork. From a
camp somewhere below Black's Fork he states that they

". . . departed on the succeeding morning (April 26th) and pro-
gressed slowly without observing any remarkable difference in the
appearance of the river or the surrounding country until the 30th
inst., when we arrived at the base of a lofty rugged mountain, the
summit of which was crowned with snow and bearing East and West.
Here also a creek sixty feet wide discharges itself on the West side."

Powell, starting from a camp probably farther up the river
than Ashley's, reached the mouth of Henry's Fork not long
after noon-day dinner. He had marked the spot well as a consequence of making a *cache* of instruments and rations there
the year before, and expresses facetious relief that the Indians
had not borrowed the chronometer wheels for hair ornaments.
As Ashley identifies the place beyond all doubt by stating that
the river enters the mountains for the first time just beyond

(Flaming Gorge), one can only conclude that an error of four or five days was made in transcribing his notes, and that the succeeding dates were moved ahead (probably by his amanuensis) to correspond. If the passage of this short stretch be considered as a one-day run, there is nothing inconsistent in Ashley's statement that "So far, the navigation of this river is without the least obstruction."

Stopping over a day to mark this highly favourable spot as a place of "General Rendevous" in accordance with the understanding with his men, Ashley pushed off into the unknown depths of the canyon below. Doubtless because the head of this gorge marked the limit of even trapper exploration, the yawning, multi-coloured gash where the mountains swallowed up the river had a sinister reputation at this time that extended far beyond the Rockies. What the fanciful Beckwourth called "The Suck" appears to have been regarded as a sort of giant whirlpool, lying in wait, dragon-wise, to wolf down any boat that entered the gorge. These tales must have been somewhat on Ashley's nerves, for his account of the passage, straightforward as it is, suggests rather worse water than is really encountered in this somewhat awesome but comparatively quiet stretch of the Green. The entry of Saturday, May 2nd, covers this run.

"We continued our voyage about half a mile below camp [it reads], when we entered between the walls of this range of mountains, which approach at this point to the water's edge on either side of the river and rise almost perpendicular to an immense height. The channel of the river is here contracted to a width of sixty or seventy yards, and the current (much increased in velocity) as it rolled along in angry submission to the serpentine walls that direct it, seemed constantly to threaten us with danger as we advanced. We, however, succeeded in descending about ten miles without any difficulty or material change in the aspect of things and encamped for the night. About two miles above this camp, we passed the mouth of a creek on the West side some fifteen yards wide, which discharged its waters with great violence."

Powell, who had been assured by old mountaineers that it could not be run, also felt considerable anxiety in heading into what he calls "this mysterious cañon." All that he had to say about it afterwards, however, was: "Entering Flaming Gorge, we quickly run through it on a swift current, and emerge into a little park." Of the same stretch Ellsworth Kolb, after mentioning a quickening of the current, writes: "While there were no rapids, use was made of what swift water we found by practising on the method we would use in making a passage through the bad rapids." Powell speaks of "the foaming crests" of the waves in Horseshoe Canyon, which Ashley would also have run this day, but the imperturbable Kolb merely notes that they encountered only "two splashy little rapids" in going through, "but with no rocks, or any dangerous feature whatever."

Ashley ran about two miles farther than did Kolb in the passage of Flaming Gorge and Horseshoe Canyon, for the latter camped at the "clear, sparkling stream" of Sheep Creek, which is readily identifiable with the one the former mentioned as being that distance above the point where his boats tied up for the night. Ashley's run would have taken him on through Kingfisher Canyon, so named by Powell from the number of those birds seen in that vicinity. Powell's camp, near the foot of a dome-shaped cliff to which he applied the name of Beehive Point, must have been not far removed from the site of Ashley's.

Red Canyon, into which the Ashley party now enters, has the first real rapids encountered on the down-river journey, and though the worst of them are of small moment in comparison with many to be run farther down, the gorge has put a period to the progress of a majority of the less experienced and determined navigators who have attempted to run it. Powell, with his heavily-loaded boats, found the run dangerous almost from the outset. He records letting the boats down with the lines once in the forenoon and once in the afternoon, the latter operation taking so long that camp was made at the com-

pletion of it. The second Powell party fared rather badly in
running this stretch, for one of the boats was capsized on a
rock and another thrown badly out of control by a collision
that tore off one of the rowlocks. Dellenbaugh states that many
"let-downs" were made with lines, and mentions running rapids
with "a current of from six to twelve or fifteen miles per hour."
He also mentions finding the grave of a man named Hook, said
to have been the first mayor of Cheyenne, whose outfit had
been wrecked here in trying to run through shortly after Powell's first passage.

The Kolbs, in the middle of September, had not a little
trouble from shallow water in working down upper Red Canyon. They lined over the rapid where Powell had the upset,
and Ellsworth's boat was considerably banged in running what
he calls "the fifth rapid below Kettle Creek." They also lined
down at least twice on the short run of the following day. The
U. S. Geological Survey party under Topographic Engineer
K. W. Trimble that studied the upper river last summer
stranded one of its boats in a long shallow rapid a mile below
Skull Creek and experienced considerable difficulty in getting
it off.

From this brief summary it will be seen that even the best
equipped and handled expeditions have met with much trouble
and some disaster in navigating that rough, shallow section of
Red Canyon above the one major obstacle now called Ashley
Falls. From the fact that Ashley disposes of this long and
difficult run in a single sentence it is apparent that he was
not endeavouring to cover the voyage in any detail in his letter,
for it is hardly conceivable that his awkward and heavily-
loaded skin boats could have had any less trouble, or made any
better time, than those of these later and better informed navigators. His entry of Sunday, May 3rd, would indicate that
he went right through to, and beyond, Ashley Falls before
camping for the night, a run which Powell and the Kolbs
took from two to three days to complete. It reads:

" . . . after progressing two miles the navigation became difficult and dangerous, the river being remarkably crooked with more
or less rapids every mile caused by rocks which had fallen from the
sides of the mountain, many of which rise above the surface of the
water and required our greatest exertions to avoid them. At twenty
miles from our last camp, the roaring and agitated state of the
water a short distance before us indicated a fall or some other obstruction of considerable magnitude. Our boats were consequently
rowed to shore, along which we cautiously descended to the place
whence the danger was to be apprehended. It proved to be a perpendicular fall of ten or twelve feet produced by large fragments
of rock which had fallen from the mountain and settled in the river
extending entirely across its channel and forming an impregnable
barrier to the passage of loaded water-craft. We were therefore
obliged to unload our boats of their cargoes and pass them empty
over the falls by means of long cords which we had provided for
such purposes. At sunset our boats were reloaded and we descended
a mile lower down and encamped."

Ashley's estimate of the distance from his last camp to Ashley Falls is not far out of the way, and his description of the
way the Falls have been formed by rocks broken from the
mountain tallies very closely with those of Powell and Kolb.
His characterization of the Fall as perpendicular, however, is
both misleading and exaggerated. The drop is not a perpendicular one in any sense, the best evidence of which, perhaps,
will be found in the accompanying photographs and the fact
that both the Kolbs and the recent Geological Survey expedition ran their boats through this narrow chute without difficulty. The Survey party passed here in the medium water of
late July and the Kolbs at the low stage of middle September.
In the higher water of May and June it is not improbable that
they, like Ashley and Powell, would have found lining down
advisable.

Although the fact is not mentioned in his chronicle Ashley,
before leaving the fall to which his name was afterwards given
by Powell, painted his name and the year on a big fragment of
rock above the water, thereby laying the train to much future

LOOKING UP THE GREEN FIFTEEN MILES ABOVE ITS JUNCTION WITH THE GRAND.

speculation and not a little recrimination. William Manly, that stout-hearted teamster-cum-voyageur who tried to reach the Pacific from the Continental Divide by the all-water route in 1849, was one of the first to puzzle over the inscription. It is an interesting fact that he came nearer both to reading and interpreting it aright than did some of the better educated men who came after him. Writing from memory (for his diary was subsequently lost in the wrecking of his boat farther down) he states:

"While I was looking up toward the mountain top and along the rocky wall, I saw a smooth place about fifty feet above, where the great rocks had broken out; there, painted in large black letters, were the words, 'Ashley, 1824.' This was the first real evidence we had of the presence of a white man in this wild place, and from this record it seems that twenty-five years before, some venturesome man had here inscribed his name. I have since heard that there were some persons in St. Louis of this name, and of some circumstances that may link them with this early traveller."[1]

Powell, making a portage trail over the rocks on his first voyage, was the next to come upon the inscription. He read it as: "Ashley, 18-5," adding, "The third figure is obscure—some of the party reading it 1835, some 1855." Dellenbaugh, on the second Powell voyage, read the name correctly and made a drawing of it on a page of his diary, now in the New York Public Library. He writes:

"It was on one of the huge rocks above the river on the left that Ashley wrote his name. This was in black letters, sheltered by a slight projection of the rock which acted as a cornice. Thus it had remained distinct, except one figure of the date, for forty-six years, having been done in 1825."

It was the rather surprising lack of knowledge of Ashley and his travels, not only on the part of Powell but of many latter commentators as well, that was responsible for most of the

[1] "Death Valley in Forty-Nine," by W. L. Manly. San José, 1894.

confusion that arose respecting this historic inscription. Powell's suggesting 1855 as an alternative reading of the date resulted in a (speaking in an editorial sense) wiping of General Ashley completely off the roster of Colorado River voyageurs when the report of the first Powell expedition was reprinted in 1916 as a volume of the Outing Adventure Library. Although Dellenbaugh's drawing of the disputed date, showing it to have been 1825, appeared in his "A Canyon Voyage," published some years previously, the editor of the Outing volume prints this astonishing foot-note at the bottom of the page on which the Powell comment on the inscription appears:

"General Ashley, the fur-trader, made his last journey into the Far West before 1835. The man here mentioned must have been some one else, of the same family name. [Ed.]"

Chittenden, in his "American Fur Trade," and a good many others have insinuated that Powell deliberately misread the date of the inscription in question, possibly in the hope of belittling Ashley's achievement in navigating the upper canyons at so early a date as 1825. There is nothing to support such a charge. The truth appears to be that Powell, surprising as it may seem, knew next to nothing at this time about Ashley and the very considerable prominence he attained as trader, explorer, state Governor and Congressman. This is very evident from the wholly incorrect version he gives of the termination of the Ashley voyage and the subsequent movements of the latter.[1]

The winds and rains of the next four decades must have made considerable inroads upon the historic inscription. The

[1] Mr. Dellenbaugh, to whom I am indebted for much valuable comment on matters relating to the Powell voyages, makes the following very interesting observations regarding the Ashley inscription in a recent letter:
"I never discussed with Powell how he came to misread the date. He read it at the time (the second voyage) as 1835, if I remember correctly, but it did not look like that to me and I drew it exactly as it was. Powell *certainly did not* misread it with any ulterior motive. It looked like 35 to him, that was all, and he evidently did not know then the exact date of

Kolbs, in 1911, reported finding "a trace of the record.   There
were three letters—A-s-h—the first two quite distinct, and underneath were three black dots.   It must have been pretty
good paint," Ellsworth adds, "to leave a trace after eighty-six
years!"   The report of the Geological Survey party of last
summer makes no mention of the name having been seen when
they reconnoitred at Ashley Falls.

Ashley's record of Monday, May 4th, states that they ran
forty miles on that day, with "the navigation and the mountains by which the river is bounded" continuing much the same
as the day before.   Another six miles the following day took
them to a point where the mountains receded from the water
and the river widened out to two hundred and fifty yards.   This
was plainly the beautiful Brown's Hole, later to become famous
as a trappers' rendezvous, but the distance from Ashley's Falls
to the probable site of this camp is greatly overestimated at
forty-six miles.   A day's halt was made here, and then an easy
run of ten miles took them down to a place where several thousand Indians had wintered the previous season.   This splendid
natural camp-ground, two miles above the entrance to Lodore
Canyon, was probably the site of the subsequent summer gath-
erings of the mountain men from all of the middle region of the
Rockies.

Dellenbaugh, who had little but the lurid and erratic Beckwourth narrative upon which to base his statement, gives a
sensational account of the difficulties of the Ashley party in
Red Canyon which is not borne out in a single particular by

Ashley's venture.   Neither did I, but the figures looked a certain way to
me and I drew them as they looked, regardless of what the other men said.
   "I am not sure that the first party saw this inscription—perhaps they did
—I don't remember what was said at the time.   I suppose they saw it, but
it was some distance above the river and there were many huge rocks.
One peculiar thing the Major did was to mix up in his report occurrences
of the two expeditions—some of them at least.   For example, he says:
'We call this Swallow Canyon' (p. 19).   Now I am certain that the first
party did not call this 'Swallow Canyon,' for I was the one who proposed
that name in 1871.   The Major simply forgot that detail, and it does not
matter a bit."

the authentic record by which we have followed the expedition to this point.

"It seemed to have been purely a trapping expedition, and was probably the very first attempt to navigate Green River. They took along few provisions, expecting to find beaver plentiful to the end of the cañon, but after a few miles the beaver were absent, and, having preserved none of the meat, the party began to suffer for food. They were six days without eating, and, the precipitous walls running ever on and on, they became disheartened, or, in the Western phrase, 'demoralized,' and proceeded to cast lots to find which should make food for the others, a proposition which horrified Ashley, and he begged them to hold out longer, assuring them that the walls must soon break and enable them to escape. They had not expected so long a gorge. . . . At last, however, an opening appeared. Here they discovered Provo encamped with an abundance of provisions, so their troubles were quickly over. . . . Provo had plenty of horses, and Ashley and his men joined him going out to Salt Lake, where Provo had come from." [1]

As Ashley's letter makes clear beyond all doubt, he was only well started on his remarkable voyage on reaching Brown's Hole. Immediately below here he passed the Gate of Lodore and entered one of the roughest and most difficult canyons to navigate of the whole Colorado River series. Most unfortunately, only a portion of the run of the first day or two is given with any approach to detail. Professor Dale, who has evidently examined the original manuscript, makes plain the reason for this in the following foot-note:

"From this point, Ashley's narrative seems to be a summary of his journal, rather than a series of extracts quoted verbatim. Be-

[1] "The Romance of the Colorado River," p. 112, on which also appears Dellenbaugh's drawing of the Ashley inscription. Dellenbaugh's conclusion that Ashley left the river at Brown's Hole, and did not enter Lodore, was due to the limited and undependable data available to him at the time his book was written. That he changed his mind on this point in the light of subsequent information is evident from the following extract from a recent letter: "I stated that Ashley left the river in Brown's Park, I believe. I have learned since that he went to the Uinta Valley. . . . Ashley was a splendid character and deserves more mention in history than he has had so far. He was no ordinary trapper-frontiersman."

ginning with the words 'to which place,' the writing continues in a different hand."

The fact that Ashley's entry of May 8th, which practically completes the account of his river voyage, covers a distance that Powell and the Kolbs took weeks rather than days to work down makes it certain that the latter part of the journal relating to the Green trip was most sketchily summarized. This may well have been because Ashley deemed the details of the river work were not essential to completing the information asked by General Atkinson. If this was the case, there can be little doubt that even the earlier parts of the river journal were considerably condensed, a fact which would go a long way toward accounting for the discrepancies in dates and runs to which I have already called attention. Whether or not the complete journal covering this voyage is still in existence I have been unable to learn. Personally I know of nothing I would peruse with greater interest than the plain, straightforward yet comprehensive account Ashley would have written of the desperately difficult task of taking those two flimsy and cranky skin boats down the rock-peppered riffles and rapids of Lodore.[1]

Ashley's entry of May 8th, up to the point where the closer summarization commences, runs as follows:

"We proceeded down the river about two miles, where it again enters between two mountains [the Gate of Lodore] and affording a channel even more contracted than before. As we passed along between these massy walls, which in a great degree excluded us from the rays of heaven and presented a surface as impassable as their body was impregnable, I was forcibly struck with the gloom which spread over the countenances of my men; they seemed to anticipate (and not far distant, too) a dreadful termination of our voyage, and I must confess that I partook in some degree of what

---

[1] Under date of June 11, 1923, Miss Stella Drumm, Librarian of the Missouri Historical Society, writes: "The original Ashley document has not been found; nor have we been successful in our efforts to obtain a likeness of Gen. Ashley."

I suppose to be their feelings, for things around us had truly an awful appearance. We soon came to a dangerous rapid which we passed over with a slight injury to our boats. A mile lower down, the channel became so obstructed by the intervention of large rocks over and between which the water dashed with such violence as to render our passage in safety impracticable. The cargo of our boats was therefore a second time taken out and carried about two hundred yards, to which place, after much labour, our boats were descended by means of cords."

The two rapids to which Ashley refers here are readily identified. The first is a series of riffles in which Powell, on his first voyage, in spite of lining down some of them, got into considerable trouble. The second expedition ran these successfully, as did the Kolbs. The Geological Survey party of last summer had one of its boats holed as the result of colliding with a midstream boulder in what is described as the fifth of the series. Ashley's feat in running this almost continuous succession of bad rapids with no more than "a slight injury" to his awkward "bull-boats" was a really notable achievement.

The second rapid series, where Ashley made a two hundred-yard portage with his cargoes, was that of the historic Disaster Falls. Powell, through the disobedience of one of his crews, lost a boat here, the wreck sowing the seeds of ill-feeling which subsequently culminated in the desertion of the Howlands and Dunn when the voyage was all but completed, and finally led to the death of all three at the hands of the Indians. If Ashley made only one portage here it was at Lower Disaster Falls, a half-mile below the upper rapid. The latter, with great care and some luck, is runable with light boats. The Kolbs got into something of a mess in trying to do this, but Trimble's three boats ran through with only a few bumps from the rocks. The lower fall, because the cliff is deeply under-cut by the river, cannot be run without inviting an almost certain wreck. Ashley's party, like the Kolbs and the recent Survey outfit, probably avoided trouble here by wading in the water and "nosing" the empty boats along the left bank.

Ashley's voyage (though without point in his particular instance) as well as that of Powell is commemorated in the name "Disaster Falls." Powell's entries in this connection not only prove how greatly he was misinformed respecting Ashley, but even suggest a doubt as to whether, at this time at least, he really knew anything at all about his distinguished predecessor except his name.

Under date of June 10th, Powell wrote:

"While the men are building the camp fire, we discover an iron bake oven, several tin plates, a part of a boat, and many other fragments, which denote that this is the place where Ashley was wrecked."

And on June 12th, after the portage around the falls was completed and the question of a name for this savage cataract came up, appears this entry:

"As Ashley and his party were wrecked here, and as we have lost one of our boats at the same place, we adopt the name Disaster Falls for the scene of so much peril and loss.

"Though some of his companions were drowned, Ashley and one other survived the wreck, climbed the cañon wall, and found their way across the Wasatch Mountains to Salt Lake City, living chiefly on berries, as they wandered through an unknown and difficult country. When they arrived at Salt Lake, they were almost destitute of clothing, and nearly starved. The Mormon people gave them food and clothing, and employed them to work on the foundation of the Temple, until they had earned sufficient to enable them to leave the country. Of their subsequent history I have no knowledge. It is possible they returned to the scene of the disaster, as a little creek entering the river below is known as Ashley Creek, and it is reported that he built a cabin and trapped on this river for one or two winters; but this may have been before the disaster."

From this it appears clear that Powell considered the man whose name he had found on a rock in Red Canyon as no more than a common trapper. If, even up to the time he wrote his report, he had heard of General Ashley, famous fur-trader, Governor of and Congressman from Missouri, there is nothing

that he wrote in that document to indicate that he connected
him with the Green River voyageur. While this seems to
show an altogether astonishing ignorance of Western history
on Powell's part, it most certainly blunts the barb in the per-
ennially recrudescent sneer that he deliberately misread the
date of the Red Canyon inscription for the purpose of robbing
General Ashley of the credit of the first voyage through the
upper Colorado canyon series.

The next sentence in the Ashley narrative following that
describing the portage at Disaster Falls reads:

"Thence we descended fifty [50] miles to a beautiful river emptying on each side, to which I gave the name Mary's River."

Here we have two very glaring discrepancies, but both almost certainly the result of a careless copying of the original
journal. The river is plainly the Yampa, which comes in below
the foot of Lodore, and the wholly ambiguous "emptying on
each side" becomes a statement of fact when we substitute
"east" for "each." If we then read "fifteen" for "fifty," we
have a correct approximation of distance, and the sentence becomes intelligible. It would not do to assume, however, that
Ashley ran right through Lodore in a single day. The lengthy
portage inevitable at Hell's Half Mile, of which he makes no
mention, would have taken that long alone. A river that drops
two hundred and seventy feet in twenty-one miles cannot be
taken at a jump.[1] Both Powell and the Kolbs spent nine days
working down that fierce rough-and-tumble of waters. Ashley,
although he would have lost no delays from making observa-

---

[1] The appendix of Kolb's book gives Lodore Canyon a length of twenty
and one-half miles, with a fall of four hundred and twenty-five feet. It
now appears that the latter figure is a good deal too large. The official
figures from the recent Geological Survey party have not yet been published, but in Mr. Wooley's notes, which he has kindly put at my disposal,
there is an entry to the effect that "Lodore Canyon is a little more than
20 miles long and has a total fall of about 270 feet or approximately 13.5
feet per mile." It is the fact that so much of this total drop is concentrated in comparatively short stretches, as at Disaster Falls and Hell's
Half Mile, that makes this canyon so difficult to run.

tions and picture-taking, could hardly have done it in less than half that time.

The remainder of the Ashley river narrative is so obviously a greatly condensed summary that it is hardly worth while to try to follow it in such detail as that relating to the stretches above. His brief description of Echo Park, below the Yampa, tallies closely with that of Powell. What Powell finally decided to call Whirlpool Canyon is recognizable in a gorge

" . . . where the mountains again close to the water's edge and are in appearance more terrific than any we had seen during the whole voyage. They immediately produced bad rapids, which follow in quick succession for twenty miles, below which, as far as I descended, the river is without obstruction. In the course of our passage through the several ranges of mountains we performed sixteen portages, the most of which were attended with the utmost difficulty and labor."

Ashley evidently considered Whirlpool Canyon and Split Mountain Canyon together when he wrote of the succession of twenty miles of bad rapids, although they are really separated by the beautiful little valley called Island Park. His mention of sixteen difficult portages would seem to indicate that this series of gorges bothered him more than did Lodore, which, however, could not have been the case. Although Powell did some lining in both canyons, the Kolbs and the recent Survey party successfully ran all the rapids encountered.

Ashley makes no mention of the time taken to run from the foot of Split Mountain Canyon to the mouth of what he calls the "Tewinty River," which he describes as emptying in from the north with a bold, deep current. This is the stream long known as the Uinta and more recently as the Duchesne, the former branch of that name having been proved to be the main fork. Ashley's estimate of the distance covered on this stretch as seventy miles is approximately correct. Not far below Split Mountain Canyon he must have passed the point at which Father Escalante crossed the river nearly half a century before.

One of the small streams he notes as coming in along both sides now bears the appropriate name of Ashley Creek.

In the concluding entry of that part of the narrative which relates to the river there is nothing to indicate that dangers, or hardships, or lack of food, of anything save the fact that he had explored as far south as he cared to do, caused Ashley to abandon his boat trip. Writing from the mouth of the Uinta, he says:

"I concluded to ascend this river on my route returning, therefore deposited the cargoes of my boats in the ground near it, and continued my descent of the main river to the point marked 5 on the topographical sketch sent you. The whole of that distance the river is bounded by lofty mountains heaped together in the greatest disorder, exhibiting a surface as barren as can be imagined. This part of the country is almost entirely without game. We saw a few mountain sheep and some elk, but they were so wild, and the country so rugged that we found it impossible to reach them."

No trace of the topographical map referred to has ever been found, but fifty miles down stream from the mouth of the Uinta would be not far from the present station of Green River on the Denver and Rio Grande railway. Purchasing some horses from a band of "Eutau" (Ute) Indians encountered soon after abandoning his boats, Ashley returned to the Uinta, "and ascended it to its extreme sources, distant from its mouth about seventy miles;" thence, by a circuitous route, to the Big Horn and Yellowstone, and so to St. Louis by boat down the Missouri.

In the whole history of river boating there is nothing finer than this feat of Ashley's in running some of the worst rapids of the Colorado canyon series in "bull-boats." Save that of Manly—also in a class by itself as a boating exploit—all of the later and more famous Colorado river voyages have been made only after months of careful planning and in expensive craft specially built to withstand the terrific usage of the run. Forced to relieve the burden of his diminished pack-train, Ashley took to the river after but a day or two of preparation, and with nothing but the rifle and the axe to reduce roving buffalo and growing cottonwood to the semblance of a boat. It was a very notable achievement to take craft of that kind through Red Canyon and Lodore. One is divided between thankfulness that the record of it is so unquestionably authentic, and regret that it is so fragmentary and incomplete. It is greatly to be hoped that the original Ashley journal may ultimately turn up to take its honoured place among Colorado River records with those classics of their kind given us by Powell, Dellenbaugh and Kolb.

CHAPTER V

LIEUTENANT HARDY, R. N., AT THE MOUTH [1]

THE voyage of Lieutenant R. W. H. Hardy, R. N., to the head of the Gulf of California in 1826 was no less important an event in the history of Colorado River exploration than the expedition of General Ashley to the Green the year previous. As Ashley gave the first authentic account of the region of the upper Colorado, so Hardy wrote the first dependable description of the remarkable country around its mouth. Of the two men, indeed, the young British naval officer was the far better trained for making and recording scientific

[1] The following notes respecting Lieutenant Hardy were furnished by the Librarian of the Admiralty as the result of a search instituted at the request of Admiral Sir Douglas Brownrigg, R.N.:

"Robert William Hale Hardy: Lieutenant, 20 February, 1815; Commander (retired), 21 October, 1861. The books of the Accountant General's Department show that his half-pay terminated 30 July, 1871, on his death. His will was proved in the Bristol Registry 17 August, 1871, by his executors, the Rev. Charles Hardy (his brother), the Rev. James Wood and Mr. Thomas Skurray. His estate was sworn as under £25,000."

To which Admiral Brownrigg adds: "He was employed nine years on full pay, and the rest of the time, twenty-two years, on half-pay. This looks as if he was of independent means, as he evidently didn't bother to serve very much!"

"Robert William Hale Hardy entered the Navy 8 June, 1806, as Second-Class Boy, on board the *Ganges* 74, Capt. Peter Halkett, lying at Portsmouth, where he shortly afterwards joined the *Royal William*, flag-ship of Admiral Montagu. Between September, 1807, and September, 1813, we find him serving on the East India station, chiefly as midshipman, in the *Monmouth* 64, and *Russel* 74, bearing each the flag of Rear Admiral Wm. O'Brien Drury, *Caroline* 36, Captain Christopher Cole, and *Bucephalus* 32, Captain Barrington Reynolds. While in the *Caroline* he appears to have assisted at the capture of Banda Neira, in August, 1810, as also, in August, 1811, of the island of Java. He afterwards, from January, 1814, until his promotion to the rank of Lieutenant, 20 February, 1815, served in the *Asia* 74, Captain John Wainwright, and *Tonnant* 80, flag-ship of Sir Alexander Cochrane, both on the North America station, where, among other operations, he attended the expedition to New Orleans. He has not since been afloat. Agent: Joseph Woodhead." (Extract from "O'Byrne's Naval Biographical Dictionary," 1849.)

observations. The records of his explorations, moreover, published very shortly after his return to England,[1] are far more accurate and complete than the comparatively fragmentary letter which is all that appears to have survived of the original Ashley journals. That Hardy was considerably in error in locating the mouth of the Gila—or rather in applying the name of Gila on his charts to what was either the main Colorado or an arm of it—detracts no whit from the value of his contribution. From what I have seen of the vagaries on its delta of that most unstable of streams during the last two decades, I am strongly inclined to the belief that Hardy was correct in assuming at the time that the westerly channel, since called the False or Hardy's Colorado, was the main river. That very interesting question I shall touch upon farther along.

Lieutenant Hardy was sent to Mexico in 1825 by the General Pearl and Coral Fishery Association of London for the purpose of investigating certain concessions that concern was contemplating working in the Gulf of California. The cruise to the head of the Gulf was a part of this series of investigations, or rather, he went to the Island of Tiburon to search for reported pearl oyster beds, and subsequently pushed on into the mouth of the Colorado in the hope of replenishing his diminished food supply from the Indians. An incidental hope expressed of "picking up gold dust at the same time" was evidently not very seriously entertained, for Hardy goes on to speak in somewhat facetious vein of the current story of an Italian priest who had obtained two hundred thousand dollars' worth of yellow nuggets from the river.

From the fact that Hardy alludes once or twice in his story to experiences or sights in Patagonia and Maylasia, it seems probable that he had left the Navy after shipping his second stripe

---

[1] "Travels in the Interior of Mexico, in 1825, 1826, 1827 & 1828," by Lieut. R. W. H. Hardy, R. N. (London, 1829). The volume is a very rare one and is found in few American libraries. The copy I have used was placed at my disposal through the courtesy of the Library of Arizoniana of Dr. J. A. Munk, in the Southwest Museum, Los Angeles.

and, in various remote corners of the world, engaged in work similar to that which brought him to Mexico. His early training for and as a naval officer was still much in evidence, however, showing unmistakably both in his language and his way of handling men and meeting emergencies. Beyond all doubt Hardy was the most competent master that ever took a boat into the mouth of the Colorado under sail. It is that fact which makes his story and his observations so valuable.

The craft in which Hardy cruised the Gulf of California was a twenty-five-ton schooner called the *Bruja*. She was broad in beam and evidently staunchly built, both fortunate facts considering what she was called upon to withstand. He describes her as a good sea-boat, but complains that her canvas was in bad shape and that her crew was a lazy and incompetent lot of beach-combers of several different nationalities. All of them knew something of sailoring, however, and appear to have risen to the emergency very creditably when trouble threatened.

Hardy found the natives of Tiburon reminding him strongly of the Patagonian Indian. He describes them as fine physical specimens, and inclined to be friendly once their suspicions were overcome; in short, very much like the Seri of to-day. In spite of the many wild yarns still current to the contrary, there never has been any real evidence that this tribe is addicted to cannibalistic practices of any kind. Hardy quite won them over by curing a number of their ills—including an apparently hopeless obstetrical case—with a few simple remedies from his medicine-chest. He got on rather better with these supposedly blood-thirsty savages (even then the Seri had a sinister reputation) than with the Indians about the mouth of the Colorado.

Hardy apparently had read nothing of the voyages of Ulloa and Alarcón, and although he speaks of certain islands as being indicated upon "Arrowsmith's chart, as well as that by M. Humboldt," he seems to have had the impression that his was the first visit of a white man to this particular part of the Gulf.

Speaking of a point upon the eastern shore to which he had climbed upon landing, he writes:

"I was now gazing at a vast extent of country visited only by the elements and by the animals before alluded to. It is probably in the same state that it was ages ago, and perhaps I am the first person, from creation up to the present time, whose eyes have ever beheld it. Those who love the total absence of sound, and of the 'busy hum of men,' thought I, would here find a solitude so absolutely melancholy, that they would never again quit the society of their fellow creatures."

It was doubtless this thought of being really the first to enter these uncharted waters that led Hardy to take so much care with his soundings and observations, and to see that every point and island, shoal and channel was designated by its good British name. Rocks and sand-spits which *conquistador* and *padre* must have distinguished with the names of half the saints in the calendar now became George and Gore and Montagu islands, while Hardy's chart of the mouth of the Colorado— with its Sea Reach, Lower Hope, and Unwin, Greenhithe and Howard points—somehow awakens old memories of steaming up the Thames. And because Hardy's names were made, along with his careful observations, a matter of record, it is they rather than those of the saints that have stuck; and deservedly so.

All that Hardy had by way of "Sailing Directions" in approaching the head of the Gulf was the admonition from a Jesuit "who was said to have passed close to the mouth of the Colorado," that it was well to bear to the westward. This was hardly explicit enough to be of much use. Running under bare poles before a violent and protracted south-east gale, the *Bruja* was driven in among the shoals in spite of every effort to keep her in deep water. The single sentence with which Hardy sums up the situation is one of the most comprehensive descriptions of the consequences of variable weather at a point where tide meets tide that I have ever read.

"The variable winds of the gulf raise each of them a short sea, and then comes a gale, which swallows up the 'gentle airs,' and roughly superseding their feeble efforts, puts the element beneath into such a state of chaotic wildness, that the vessel will sometimes be lifted up on the top of three conflicting seas at once, which meet under bows, and with their reflux leave a sort of deep vortex into which the vessel tumbles unresistingly, and with such violence, that, to use a sailor's expression, 'everything is made to grin again!'"

Hardy's latitudes and longitudes check fairly well with the positions as established to-day of the various natural features he mentions. This would apply only to rocky points and islands, of course, as bars and spits and all of the lowlands have undergone great changes under a century's accumulation of Colorado silt. He speaks of noting a reddish tinge to the water before coming to Gore and Montagu islands, and of the channels between these two islands and the mainlands to east and west as "the three mouths of the Rio Colorado." This is bringing the estuary rather far down the Gulf, as all riverine characteristics have disappeared some miles above.

It was at six o'clock of July 20th that the *Bruja* came to anchor in the channel between Gore Island and the mainland of Baja California. As there were two fathoms of water under her keel, underlaid with two fathoms more of soft mud, no apprehension was felt, especially as it was believed to be extreme low tide. The sunset, though, did cause a bit of worry, but on quite another score. Hardy, while begging "not to be thought more superstitious than every sailor is allowed to be who is educated on the wild ocean, and reared within the vortex of that innocent creed that seamen always teach," admitted that both he and the whole crew saw in the tumbled sun-flushed clouds the image of a tall ship totally surrounded by Indians. Considerably disturbed by what he calls this "painted warning," arms were cleaned and loaded and a sentinel stationed to guard against a surprise attack by lurking redskins. That there was another and far greater danger than Indians to be feared no one appears to have suspected.

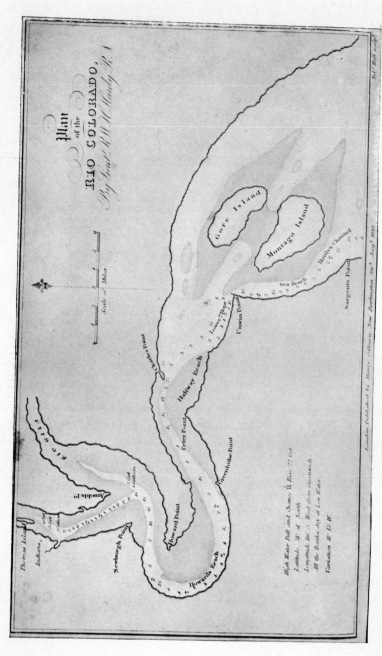

CHART OF LOWER COLORADO BY LIEUT. R. W. HARDY, R. N.

SOME OF THE CHANNELS OF THE DELTA ARE LIKE TROPICAL BAYOUS.

HARDY'S FIRST MEETING WITH THE INDIANS WAS PROBABLY
AT A CAMP VERY CLOSE TO THIS.

DRAGGING UP OUR BOAT TO SAVE IT FROM DESTRUCTION BY THE TIDAL "BORE."
Not far from the point Hardy reached by rowing.

Awakened in the middle of the night "by the dew and the noise of jackals," Hardy got up to find the sentinel and all the crew asleep. Heaving the lead, he found to his astonishment that there was but a foot and half of water. The tide had fallen over ten feet since they had anchored, and was still on the ebb. It was the liquid mud of the bottom, doubtless, that kept the ship from careening. A little later the rush of the returning tide brought the whole ship's company to their feet, arms in hand, to repel what they believed was the expected attack by Indians. As Hardy, in speaking of this tidal disturbance, describes it as no more than "the beating of the ripple against the counter," it is to be inferred that it did not come in the form of a considerable "bore."

Undismayed by a gathering storm the next morning, with "a fog as thick as is sometimes seen in London," they weighed anchor and stood off up-river with a fair wind and a flood tide. Floundering over shoals and nomenclature, heaving sounding names to starboard and larboard as relentlessly as he hove the sounding-lead, Hardy piloted the *Bruja,* through Lower Hope, Half-Way Reach, and Greenhithe Reach, "into Howard's Reach, where the river takes a semicircular sweep to the westward."

Although the Colorado will have cut back and forth in many channels since Hardy's time, his chart indicates that the one he followed this day did not vary greatly from the present course of the river between Gore and Montagu islands and the wretched little bunch of shifting hovels forming the so-called port of La Bomba. The great curving, caving bank to the south and west, undermined by the scouring tides, must have looked just as it does to-day—and been no less treacherous. This is the point where the Mexican power-schooner *Topolobampo* was capsized last fall by the tidal bore, with a loss of close to eighty lives. It is very dangerous even for high-powered craft at any time, and a month either way from the equinoctial tides no sailing craft may venture there without

courting almost certain disaster. Hardy, who seems to have
had not the least idea of what he was getting into, owed his
escape very largely to the sweet little cherubim that sits up
aloft to keep watch o'er the life of poor Jack. Had he come
blithely sailing into the Dragon's Mouth a couple of months
later, encountering the full-moon bore of September at its
height, he would almost certainly have lost his boat, and probably most of her crew.

The *Bruja,* with that nine-knot tide and the wind of a gathering storm on her port beam, would have raced along at a
wonderful speed up the comparatively deep channel of Sea
Reach. Doubling Unwin Point, sheets must have been taken in
smartly as they nosed her close into the wind for the north-
westerly course up lower Hope and Half Way Reach. Then
came the dead beat to windward into Howard's Reach, and, inevitably, trouble. No sailor who has seen the infernal place
could contemplate without a shiver the mad task of beating up
that narrow, tide-swept channel. On one side is a constantly
caving bank half as high as the mast-head; on the other a shoal
alternately bare and covered by the foam-white surges of the
ebbing or flooding tide. With a smart sloop, and a smarter
crew, doubtless the thing could be done every now and then;
but the margin of safety under most favourable conditions
would not be of the kind of which Lloyds would take serious
cognizance.

Hardy, in a somewhat elaborate explanation, blames the
nervousness of the helmsman and the carelessness of his Sailing
Master for the disaster which overtook them, apparently very
soon after they started beating. The "larboard bank of the
river was very high and perpendicular," he writes,

" . . . and in consequence of the narrowness of the channel . . .
it was necessary to stand until our jib-boom nearly touched the
western bank, as otherwise the vessel would not have gathered sufficient way, after once going about, to tack again. Upon one of these
occasions, as the tide, which runs at the rate of nine miles an hour,

swept us along like an arrow, and within ten yards of the bank, the helmsman took fright, and every moment put the helm down to bring the vessel about, without any orders from me. The consequence was that she gathered no way."

On discovering what the trouble was, Hardy directed the Sailing Master to keep his eye on the man at the helm and see that the schooner was kept "clean full" until he himself gave the orders for going about. On the next board, holding on until the jib-boom was within two feet of the towering bank, the *Bruja* "came round like a top," when the order "Down with the helm!" was finally given. This smartly executed manœuvre proved their undoing, however, for Hardy records:

"As soon . . . as we got on the larboard tack, the man at the helm, having now lost his fears, looked round to see the danger from which we had escaped, and thus neglected to pay attention to his duty. Mr. Lindon amused himself with the same contemplation; and the consequence was, that the vessel came up in the wind, lost her way, and in an instant was driven stern-foremost, on to the shore, almost before I was aware of the imprudence, and too late for preventing the consequences of it. . . . The rudder was carried away with a tremendous crash, and I feared that the vessel might have otherwise sustained some serious injury. We now came with our broadside to the bank, and leaping on shore with the end of a jib-sheet, I belayed to the stump of a tree, which had been left there during the high tides, to prevent the vessel from swinging round, which, if she had done, would probably have carried away her bowsprit."

The wreck of the rudder was secured as quickly as possible and, with the ebb tide starting to run out at nine miles an hour, all haste was made to work the schooner into deep water before she was stranded on a shelf of the bank by the rapidly falling water. This very difficult and awkward job was accomplished, in the face of a wind that was driving her against the caving bank, by sending men ashore to shove off with poles until the schooner was worked into a position where sails and current would help to swing her clear. Then they anchored her in "five fathoms of water, though not at a greater distance from the shore than forty yards." Difficulty was experienced even in getting the men on board again, as the rush of the tide kept filling their boat with water.

Plain, blunt sailor that he was, Hardy has done scant justice to the work of himself and his men in extricating their schooner from the extremely precarious position in which she was left on being driven back against the soft and ever-breaking bank. I have worked along the present-day counterpart of that caving crescent of Howard's Reach in tides both nearer to, as well as more remote from, the equinox than those encountered by Hardy, and under the best conditions have found even the operation of making a landing one that demanded all care and alertness. Getting off a schooner disabled and stranded in such a way as was the *Bruja* would hardly be accomplished by the average trading schooner skipper and crew one time out of ten. Nor should Hardy be greatly blamed for getting into such a mix-up in the first place. Beyond question he took an undue risk in entering the river at all without knowing more about the tides and channels. Once in, however, some such sort of a disaster was more or less inevitable sooner or later. That's the kind of a place it is!

Patching up the broken rudder as well as the circumstances permitted, they waited for the slack water that would give them a chance to re-ship it. At the end of a day and a half spent in standing by for the expected quiet at the turn of the tide, Hardy had smoked out another idiosyncrasy of the capricious stream into whose double-fanged mouth he had so lightly ventured.

"But in the Rio Colorado [he exclaims] *there is no such thing as slack water!* Before the ebb has finished running, the flood commences, boiling up fully eighteen inches above the surface, and roaring like the rapids of Canada; we might therefore have waited for the opportunity we sought till the sea should give up her dead, unless we could devise some other plan."

That eighteen-inch boil of the flood tide is a definite measure of the bore as Hardy encountered it, and is just about what one can expect to find now along the same reach at the end of July.

Trying to ship the rudder by sailing with the current the following morning, the *Bruja* was run solidly aground. When the tide fell she was left on a bar two hundred yards from the water's edge. Worse still, when the flood came back it did not approach nearer than a hundred and fifty yards. As it was now four days after the full moon, there was nothing to do but wait for the high tides of the new moon to float her off, "a nice situation," Hardy comments, "especially as we were short of provisions." Realizing that it might not be possible to get her off even at the next high water, he decided not to abandon the schooner as long as there was any chance of ultimately floating her. Fear of being marooned bulked but lightly in comparison with the blow to his sailor's pride, as may be judged from this entry:

"It would have been highly entertaining for some future explorer to have encountered such a monument of our misfortunes as our abandoned vessel would have presented!"

Except for the misnomer, Gila, Hardy's description of what met his eyes in the course of a four-way survey from the deck of his stranded vessel would be perfect to the last word if applied to-day.

"On the western side of the river there are forests of the thorny scrub called Mesquite, an inferior species of the Quebrahacha; and on the banks there was a profusion of stems and large branches of the willow, poplar, and acacia, which had been brought down by the flood, and were now permanently lodged in their present situations. On the eastern bank, where we were aground, there were also wrecks of these trees; but there was no other vegetation but a dwarf sort of reed. From the masthead, nothing on this side was distinguishable, except the waters of the Rio Colorado and the Rio Gila, but an interminable plain; and to the westward rises the Cordilerra, which extends from Cape San Lucas, on the southern extremity of Lower California. To the northward and eastward, there was a long row of lofty trees, which I concluded were growing on the banks of the Rio Gila; that stream falling into the Rio Colorado half a league below us."

From first to last Hardy's descriptions of what he saw of the Colorado River and Delta are just as true to-day as they must have been when he wrote them. From his "Smoky Coast," under its cloud of blown sand, to the caving banks and flooded shoals of Howard's Reach, the mud, the driftwood, the distant lines of trees and the loom of the westerly Cordillera, he missed nothing, and he exaggerated nothing. Not even a certain very vicious brand of horse-fly eluded his observant eye, though, as he admits, he had no luck trying to swat it. It was so active, he writes, that he never knew of one being killed, adding: "They bite so hard that the instant they are driven from the flesh, the blood comes through the puncture made by their sharp and large proboscis."

The descendants of that same fly still prey upon the Colorado voyageur, and, although not numerous (thank heaven!), are just as blood-thirsty to-day as in Hardy's time. I can testify to that fact personally, for I am inclined to think I faced the vampire in less clothes than did my distinguished predecessor. And it is still just as elusive as of old. Working down the Pescadero and Hardy last fall, we—two engineers and myself—made up a pool which paid ten cents for every one of these buzzing grey marauders swatted cold and dead. At the end of four days, with each of us surely averaging all of a thousand diurnal swats apiece, the high man cashed in for only forty cents, and the low man—myself—for ten. The lower Colorado horse-fly is indeed an elusive creature, but it is strange that Lieutenant Hardy, with all the other things he had to worry about, should have noticed it.

No Indians having been sighted since their stranding, Hardy, on July 24th, took a boat, with two of the English sailors, and pushed off up-river on the flood tide for a voyage of exploration. His object, he explains, was to sound out a channel so that he might be familiar with the navigation when the schooner was refloated; also, to see if any cattle were likely to be available for meat. A broad creek which he notes as coming in on the western bank a league above where the *Bruja* was aground could have been nothing else than the tortuous channel by which the great Laguna Salada, beyond the Cocopahs, is replenished and drained. There was a cattle camp at this point when I first boated down the Hardy over fifteen years ago. This was abandoned during the late series of Mexican revolutions, and last summer we found the old building had been undermined by the river and carried away. A few hundred yards inland we found a temporarily deserted Indian wicki-up.

Continuing on up river, Hardy came upon some horses, quietly grazing on the bank, and finally an Indian hut. An old lady, very tipsy on fermented mesquite-beans, called the visitor many bad names, but the attitude of the several men was not especially unfriendly. The old dame he vividly but ungallantly sketches as "shrivelled as a bit of boiled tripe; and her sharp bones protruded, not unlike a sack-full of pans and kettles." Like the *padres* before him, this honest British sailor was as shocked as grieved to find that local sartorial fashions varied materially from those affected by the folks at home. Apropos of the fact that the ladies of this camp had but "a few stripes of the inner bark of the willow or acacia tied scantily round their waists," he observes:

"This was a strange costume, and quite as unseemly as it was new. At first I imagined that that inebriating liquor before mentioned had rendered them unconscious of their nudity, or that perhaps, as they were *fishermen*, out of pure regard for their clothes, they had laid them on one side till their occupation had ceased. But although I examined every part of the hut, I saw nothing which resembled a shirt for the men, or a *chemise* for the women! My astonishment, as the reader may readily suppose, was very great; but equally great were the feelings of compassion which this spectacle awakened!"

As I was compelled to observe when Father Garcés used the same word for the same reason in referring to the Mojaves, compassion lavished upon any white or Indian for an apparent clothes shortage on the lower Colorado in midsummer is distinctly misplaced sympathy.

Although he had provisioned for a three-day trip, the discovery that there were Indians in the neighbourhood made Hardy unwilling to risk spending a night along a stretch of the river where the conditions were so favourable for an ambush. After pondering for a while the advisability of buoying the channel on the chance that it might be of use sometime, he gave up the idea for the reason that any boat venturing there would be carried along so fast by the tide that its velocity would "render nautical manœuvres of no avail." After giving the name of Thomas's Island to an insular bar just above the Indian hut, they returned to the *Bruja,* meeting with considerable difficulties on the way from shallows uncovered by the falling tide. Hardy's head of navigation must have been very close to the site of what was long known as the *Salada* cattle camp, the ruins of some of the buildings of which were still standing when we passed that point last October.

This little half-day jaunt appears to have been the only attempt Hardy was able to make in the way of further exploration. The news of his coming spread rapidly among the Indians, who gathered in the vicinity at such a rate as to make it seem inadvisable to venture far from the stranded schooner. These very primitive savages, while all the time keeping up pretences of friendship, acted more and more suspiciously as their numbers augmented. Hardy entertained small parties of them from time to time on the boat, but always under the noses of his carronades and with small arms laid ready to hand.

No proper precautionary measures were neglected. An attempt to dig emplacements on the bar for a "half-moon battery" having failed because the percolating water caused the sand to crumble, boarding nettings were rigged all the way round the rail and kept up day and night. Another novel safety device was provided through the purchase of a couple of Indian children, on the theory that the expression on their faces might give a hint of brewing trouble if any of the visiting Indians discussed an attack in their presence. "And this plan succeeded so well upon one occasion," Hardy somewhat naïvely concludes, "when the captain and interpreter were on board (and many Indians alongside) conversing probably upon a premeditated attack, that the children began to cry." Upon which he "placed two men with drawn swords and pistols by their sides, over the individuals who had excited the fears of the children, and thereby awakened [my own] suspicions."

Although Hardy appears to have considerably overrated the seriousness of the Indian menace, apprehension on this score did not spoil his appreciation of the continual string of amusing developments incident to his (in many ways) ludicrous situation. His accounts of the funny aspects of the Indian parties on the heeling deck are given with a real humour. His duties as host to guests whom he suspected of desiring to murder him demanded both tact and decision. A chief of especially altitudinous rank, who came aboard wearing a tiny tinkling bell tied to his waist, had to be shorn of this only garment and decoration for fear it might be used to signal an attack from the shore. An uninvited guest at a feast was punished by "a violent blow which laid him prostrate" for deliberately planting his muddy foot in the middle of the table-cloth. An aged hag, described as "not less than a hundred and twenty years old" from the shrivelled condition of her body, had to be placated because the cabin-boy made wry faces at her. This temperamental old dear, evidently a witch of great influence with the assembled *caciques*, was completely won over by Hardy at a crucial moment through the medium "of three or four leaves of tobacco, and a narrow strip of red baize." Promptly re-

linquishing her seat at the Indian war-council, and angrily refusing to pronounce a charm on some of their proffered arrows, she climbed down over the side and went off, singing "in
a loud voice and with long pauses," what must have been a
sort of a Chant of Peace. Hardy, who evidently had a keen ear
for music, reproduces several bars of the weird incantation.

"As for the words [he adds] I knew nothing of them, or of their
import; but they had a marvellous effect upon the captain and interpreter, who hung down their heads, and seemed as if they were
smothering their angry and disappointed feelings. I had now gained
this *witch*, which was perhaps better than winning a battle under
present circumstances! I could not help laughing to myself at the
crest-fallen Indians, whose hopes were blasted at the very moment
when they had apparently every expectation of their speedy frui-
tion!"

This magical, musical warfare was as near to actual conflict
as they ever came, but the increase of the Indians assembling
along the banks to a number which Hardy estimated as not
"fewer than five or six thousand," finally made him decide to
play safe by cutting off communications with them entirely.
Four or five days, mostly devoted to standing watch and
countering the numerous simple and artless pretexts advanced
by the savages to lure the strangers ashore, brought the new-
moon tide and water enough to float the *Bruja* into the main
channel. Favoured by the first interval of slack water they had
ever observed at the turn of the tide, the rudder was shipped
and the schooner went off down the river on the seven-knot
ebb.

But they were still far from clear of the resourceful savages.
The next stratagem of the enemy came pretty near to carrying
them to the inner citadel. Hardy practically admits as much
himself. Scarcely had they started off down the river when two
Indians were observed in the water ahead, supported by a log
of wood.

"As the log went astern [he writes], I put out my hand to lay
hold of one of the swimmers, as the tide was bearing the Indian's
head under water. The hand was held eagerly up; and when I
caught hold of it, I was not a little surprised to find that it belonged
to the slender form of a young lady, of about sixteen or seventeen
years. She no sooner found herself in safety than fear gave way to
maidenly modesty; and she looked about for her bark petticoat;
but, alas! the angry tide had borne it in triumph away! Therefore,
with great gallantry, I took off my jacket, which I presented to her.
This she accepted, and sat down with the utmost coolness on the
deck. I then sent for a sheet for the young lady, as being a more
commodious covering than my jacket. . . . She was rather tall than
short, with enough flesh on her bones to hide the sharpness of their
angles; countenance dark, and not only exceedingly handsome, but
with an expression peculiarly feminine. Her neck and wrists were
adorned with shells curiously strung; her hair, which was dripping
wet, fell in graceful ringlets about her delicate shoulders, and her
figure was straight and extremely well proportioned."

Feasting his lovely visitor on biscuit and *frijoles,* which she
consumed "with as much composure and unconcern as if she
had been amongst friends," the enamoured Hardy speculated
upon a possible reason for so felicitous a sending. Unable to
learn aught from the food-preoccupied minx herself, he finally
came to the conclusion that she meant to propose herself as
governess for the two Indian children he had purchased. Presently the other swimming Indian came upon the scene, making
angry but unintelligible gestures.

"What his purpose might be [writes Hardy], I do not know; but
conceiving that he meant to sell the young lady, I *generously* offered
him *half a yard of red baize for her!* . . . But, however [he concludes gloomily], there was no making a bargain; and when the
party, as I conceived, had been on board a sufficient time, I had
them conveyed on shore in our boat; nor did I ever see them again."

Lest the gallant Lieutenant should be thought parsimonious
in keeping that bid of baize down to half a yard, I might mention that the children he had purchased only cost him a pocket

handkerchief apiece. Doubtless in those far-off days baize
went farther with a lady than it does now, especially with a
lady of the lower Colorado.

In his attempt to get out of the river on the high tides of
the new moon Hardy erred as far on the side of over-careful-
ness as before on that of being over-bold. Fearful of losing
the channel by riding the ebb tide immediately after its turn,
he grounded the *Bruja* again and did not get her off in time to
ride the high water out to the Gulf. Not willing to run the
risk of stranding during the period of receding tides, he anchored in the deep channel of Howard's Reach and waited for
the augmenting tides of the full moon. This was only the sensible thing to do. Firmly grounded on a receding series of
tides, they would have been high and dry again in a day or two,
and in renewed danger from the Indians. Grounding in the
course of a series of increasing tides, they would have had the
higher water of the next day to float free again.

The fortnight that the *Bruja* swung a plaything of the tides
at her precarious anchorage was a period of scarcely less anxiety
than that spent upon the bar above. The Indians were less in
evidence upon the banks, but there was always the danger of
attacks from rafts, or, worse still, of having the schooner battered to pieces by the drift-logs which Hardy realized it would
be so simple for the savages to roll over the banks above and
send charging down on the nine-knot tide. Fortunately, the
Indians appeared to have no definite plan of aggression, and
contented themselves with prowling near and waiting to take advantage of the schooner's getting into trouble on her own account.

More tangible were the assaults of wind and tide in this
ever-treacherous neck of wildly wallowing water. In spite of
a forty-fathom scope of cable to each anchor the *Bruja* was
constantly carried hither and thither, with no small risk at
times of suffering complete extinction under the foundering
banks. Hardy's entry covering the latter part of the "grave-

yard" watch of the morning of August 9th brings back all too poignantly the memories of a night of last November I spent in a large Mexican power-boat at that same ill-starred anchorage.

"At two A. M. [it reads] the fluctuations of the tide commenced, and the vessel was more uneasy at her anchorage than upon any former occasion; so much so, that our superstitious cook insisted that the *old witch* was again at work upon our destinies. The vessel was carried violently to the northward by the ascending tide, where she met an eddy which carried her again astern, till she brought her cable taut abreast; and here encountering the ascending tide, she would sometimes plunge so violently as to take in the water over the bows. After doing this two or three times, I began to fear that she might open at the stern; and therefore had the cable shortened-in, which kept her quiet until the flood set up, when we were again obliged to veer; and at slack water the same violent motions succeeded, which obliged us again to shorten-in cable till the ebb ran strong."

Even so, the *Bruja* made a good deal better weather of it than did the forty-foot launch to which I have alluded. The schooner's anchors seemed to have held fairly well; the light mud-hook of the launch let her back off down stream at all of four miles an hour, and we only kept from going under the caving bank by starting the engine and running against the tide until the wind eased off sufficiently to allow us to return to our former mooring off La Bomba.

Indians continued to collect on the bank in curious groups, and with those who brought fruit and melons some trade was carried on. The *cacique's* daughter and another girl, however, had their petition to be brought aboard summarily denied after Hardy's warily-lifting weather-eye had descried one of them "making a meal of the colonists upon the other's pericranium" while combing the latter's hair in the course of a preliminary primp.

Just before his departure Hardy, dropping for once his altogether delightful bantering note, paid his respects to his at-

tentive Indian friends of a month in an outburst of wild philo-
sophic regret. A lone warrior, standing in Promethean silhou-
ette against the sunset sky behind the western bank, inspired
the thought.

"He wore an eagle's feather fastened to the top of his head; and
as it was blowing hard from the south-east, and the mud pomatum
had been omitted, his long, loose black hair was blown horizontally
over his left shoulder, and he had a tattered covering about his
loins. As he stood on the bank to hail us, he held one end of his
bow in his left hand, resting the other on the ground; and as I
contemplated him I exclaimed, 'What a noble specimen of human
nature is this! But, alas! all that is exquisite and graceful in symmetry is here animated only by the bold and independent spirit of
a superior kind of wild beast—indifferent alike to pity and remorse!' "

The clear-seeing young sailor was right again. The Cocopah never has amounted to much in a spiritual way. And to-
day he is no longer possessed of even that exquisite grace of
symmetry. He is still a beast, though, if not a very wild one.

The tides began to increase on the 10th, but between calms
and a heavy up-river gale it was not practicable to get the *Bruja*
under way until the early morning ebb of the 15th. In spite
of having to beat down through Hardy's Channel against a
troublesome south-east wind, they were clear of the islands
and out into the undiluted brine of the Gulf by noon. Lieutenant Hardy hopes that it will not be necessary for him to
enter at all into the feelings which induced him to fire off their
two heavy guns, "after they had been unshotted," as well as
all of the small arms, and to give a bottle of brandy to be distributed amongst his "almost worn-out crew," who had not
tasted this, "their favourite nectar," since the first day they
had entered the river.

Personally, having been in H. M. S. *Erin*, of the Grand
Fleet, on Armistice Night, I can comprehend perfectly just how
Lieutenant Hardy, R. N., felt and acted, and why. I dare say

that Admiral Beatty's historic signal "to 'splice the main brace' according to immemorial custom" was received by the men of the various units of the Grand Fleet (except by those of the American ships, which had no "splicings") with no less enthusiasm than by the motley crew of the *Bruja*. It's rather fine the way those good old naval traditions are preserved.

Six days after clearing the mouth of the Colorado the *Bruja* anchored in Guaymas Harbor. In one of the bays they found an American brig, the captain of which, according to Hardy, had just died "in consequence of taking a dose of calomel and rhubarb, and shortly afterwards a glass of rum and milk, followed by another of lemonade." This entry has a certain historical value in proving that Yankees occasionally imbibed some fearful and wonderful concoctions almost a century previous to the passage of the Volstead Act.

Of the value of Lieutenant Hardy's record there is no question. The hundred pages of his book devoted to the delta of the Colorado contain more accurate information relative to the physiography, hydrography and ethnology of that region than had been brought out in all of the nearly three centuries that had elapsed since its discovery. Not until Derby and Ives came along twenty-five and thirty years later was any material addition made to Hardy's remarkably accurate observations, and these mostly had to do with parts of the river to which the latter did not penetrate. Up to the point where the *Bruja* was stranded later observations and surveys, except as affected by the constant shiftings of channels, checked very closely with those of the young British officer, notwithstanding his unsatisfactory instruments and the trying conditions under which all of his work was done.

Hardy's error in applying the name of Gila to the easterly channel of the Colorado was undoubtedly due to the faulty maps with which he was provided. These would have shown the Colorado in a single channel, with the Gila as a tributary flowing in from the east somewhere near the mouth of the main river. Not unnaturally, he assumed that the east fork of the first branching he came to was the Gila.

What Hardy really found here, of course, was two channels of the Colorado itself—one the main river, and the other a bayou formed by the tides and the drainage of the June overflow. It has always been assumed (and, it seems to me, on quite insufficient evidence) that the one in which the *Bruja* was stranded, and which we now call the False or Hardy's Colorado, was the back-channel. This conclusion was doubtless arrived at during the considerable period at the end of the nineteenth century when the easterly channel carried the main stream, and the Hardy only the high-water overflow from Volcano Lake. On the theory that this had been the case for a very long time was based the assumption that Hardy was wrong in stating that his schooner was stranded in the main Colorado.

As a matter of fact the Colorado, in building up the alluvial cone of its delta, has probably been swinging back and forth from the eastern to the western sides of that cone at comparatively frequent intervals for many centuries. If anything, indeed, judging from such scourings of channels as remain, it has flowed on the western side of the cone rather more than on the eastern. We found strong evidence in support of this theory last fall while working down across the delta in endeavouring to trace the course of the Colorado after its recent deflection by the Pescadero Dam. When the Colorado broke through to the Bee in 1909, and on to Volcano Lake, it continued to the Gulf by the Hardy, making that its main channel. All attempts to turn it back into its former eastern channel having failed, it has continued to flow by the Hardy ever since. The dam and canal, completed in 1922, throwing it over to the many straggling channels of the Pescadero, cut off the flow into Volcano Lake but not from the lower Hardy. The main Colorado now flows directly over, or at least very close to the point where the *Bruja* was stranded. I am fully convinced that it also did so, quite in accordance with Hardy's belief, at the very time the schooner was aground. The young naval officer's observations were too accurate in all other respects to make it probable he would have been mistaken in his judgment as to which of two channels was a bayou and which a flowing, fresh-water stream. He mentions explicitly the freshness of the water at the point where the schooner was grounded. During the time the Hardy was a back-channel I found, in boating upon it, brackish water far above this point. This would have been the case in Hardy's time had it been anything else than the main channel he states it was. This is not the place to enter into an exhaustive discussion of a point which could be of interest only to a very few. I trust I have said enough, however, to make it clear that while the westerly channel of the great river is appropriately called Hardy's Colorado, the coupling this with the name of False Colorado does an injustice to at least the judgment of a very gallant officer and navigator.

CHAPTER VI

MANLY DOWN THE CANYONS OF THE GREEN

FOR sheer audacity of conception the slap-banging, hell-for-leather run of William Manly and six of his fellow teamsters of a 'forty-niner outfit down the canyons of the Green stands without a rival in the history of Colorado River navigation. Manly was born in Vermont in 1820, and came of good virile old Green Mountain stock. He was taken west with the family at the age of eight, and spent the next ten years in the woods of Michigan, doing his sturdy bit in helping to clear a frontier farm. Dissatisfaction with a life bounded by the narrow circle of the encircling wall of the pines made him an easy victim of the lure of the new lands opening up beyond the Mississippi, and a long spell of chills-and-fever hastened the inevitable capitulation.

With the Grand River flowing but eight miles from the Manly clearing, it was only natural that the young Ulysses should turn to its westerly winding waters to bear him on the first stage of his journey. "Three nice whitewood boards" furnished the material for a boat and a provision chest. These, with their guns, made up the whole outfit of Manly and the neighbour's boy who started with him on his wanderings. Portaging round the rocks at Grand Rapids, they saw nothing in "a small cheap-looking town" and a lot of growing hardwood timber to indicate that the spot was subsequently to become world-famous as the primal fount of antique furniture. Abandoning their boat at Grand Haven, the young pioneers crossed the lake by steamer and fared forth on foot toward the mystic Land of Enchantment beyond the Mississippi.

Beyond all doubt it was that early river voyage through the
126

Michigan woods which was responsible for the writing of one of the most colourful pages in Colorado Basin history. Had it never been taken it is hardly probable that a certain lusty young bull-whacker, standing astride the Continental Divide at South Pass nine years later, would have been sufficiently grounded in the economics of transportation to lead him to hold forth to his mates upon the advantages of water over land carriage—of the river-boat over the prairie-schooner. I have never been able to read without a chuckle Manly's account of the way in which he and a sextette of his bull-whacking companions came to "turn in their whips" and blithely set out to boat from the summit of the Rocky Mountains to the Pacific. He tells of that, and his subsequent wanderings, in the modestly but forcefully written volume containing the story of his varied and interesting life.[1]

"When we came to the first water that flowed toward the Pacific Coast at Pacific Springs, we drivers had quite a little talk about a new scheme. We put a great many 'ifs' together and they amounted to about this: If this stream were large enough; if we had a boat; if we knew the way; if there were no falls or bad places; if we had plenty of provisions; if we were bold enough to set out on such a trip, etc., we might come out at some point or other on the Pacific. And now when we came to the first of the 'ifs,' a stream large enough to float a small boat; we began to think more strongly about the other 'ifs.'

"In the course of our rambles we actually did run across the second 'if' in the shape of a small ferry boat filled up with sand upon a bar, and it did not take very long to dig it out and put it into shape to use, for it was just large enough to hold one wagon at a time."

There were still a number of unsatisfied "ifs," but the announcement of the head of their outfit that, on account of the lateness of the season, he was going to winter in Salt Lake City rendered them of little moment when weighed in the balance against a prolonged contact with the dreaded Mormons.

[1] "Death Valley in Forty-Nine," by W. L. Manly. San José, 1894.

Most of the drivers were from Missouri and had become imbued with a magnified though not wholly unfounded fear of becoming objects of vengeance in retaliation for the outrages inflicted upon the Saints in that state not long before. Manly had little trouble in persuading five of his mates that the unknown terrors of the river were vastly preferable to the swift and certain bullets of the vengeful Danites. At the last moment still another one threw down his whip and announced his decision to "go with the boys."

Manly reveals the Alpha and Omega of their information respecting the unknown river upon which they were about to launch their argosy in stating that: "Both the surgeon and the captain (of their late military escort) said the stream came out on the Pacific Coast, and that we had no obstacles except cataracts, which they had heard were pretty bad." That naïve "no obstacles except cataracts" is a touchstone of the strange blend of innocence and recklessness of which this priceless bevy of bull-whackers was compact. The unexpected cataract is the one danger above all others calculated to give pause to the prospective canyon voyageur. It was doubtless because this particular band had heard more of the deadliness of Danites than of cataracts that they were disposed to regard the latter so lightly.

The prairie-schooners creaked off behind their plodding oxen and the argonauts were left standing behind the pitifully small pile of their worldly goods upon the bank of the Green. Manly, being elected captain, promptly proceeded to get his command in commission and under way. He reports:

"An examination of the old ferry boat showed it to be in pretty good condition, the sand with which it had been filled keeping it perfectly. We found two oars in the sand under the boat, and looked up some poles to assist us in navigation. Our cordage was rather scant but the best we could get and all we could muster. The boat was about twelve feet long and six or seven feet wide, not a very well proportioned craft, but having the ability to carry a pretty good load. We swung it up to the bank and loaded up our goods and then ourselves. It was not a heavy load for the craft, and it looked as if we were taking the most sensible way to get to the Pacific, and almost wondered that everybody was so blind as not to see it as we did."

That optimistic preliminary survey is characteristic of the log of every amateur navigator.

Manly kept a diary covering a considerable part of his wanderings, but subsequently lost it in a fire. Considering that he had no notes from which to work, as well as the fact that his story must have been written after his seventieth year, his descriptions of the river and the surrounding region are remarkably accurate. Although he gives no dates, nor even the names of months, the continuity of topography is so well maintained that it would be possible to follow a considerable part of his voyage quite as closely as I did that of Ashley. As the two trips covered an almost identical stretch of river, however, this would involve rather too much repetition to justify it in a work of this kind. I shall, therefore, sketch in no more than the high-lights of Manly's voyage, identifying only the outstanding topographical features.

From the fact that his ferry-boat, made originally to carry a wagon, was not heavily overloaded with seven men and their outfit I am inclined to believe that Manly underestimated its length considerably in stating it at twelve feet. In any event, however, it would have been a most crudely-built box of an affair, even harder to handle than Ashley's skin-covered bull-boats. Such a craft was bound to come to grief in its first solid collision with a rock, and, considering the bull-whacking technique of Manly's crew, it is a matter of some surprise that it lived to enter the first canyon. Whether a scow of that kind would have been favoured by the low water (the voyage must have been made in the late summer or early autumn, although Manly makes no specific statement bearing on the point) is hard to say. Probably not much, as the increased liability to hit rocks would have been no more than offset by the decreased velocity of the current.

The voyage started auspiciously. They pushed out into the current and commenced to "move down the river with an ease and comfort" that made them much happier, Manly states, than would have been the case had they been going "toward Salt Lake with the prospect of wintering there." A band of Indians, such as could easily have ambushed them had they been on the road, was here reduced to the making of futile gestures from the bank. The river increased in velocity as they proceeded, and so did the number of the "dangerous rocks that were difficult to shun." Navigation appears to have consisted mostly of efforts to fend off from menacing boulders with their poles. This is a difficult and dangerous procedure at best, as the energetic captain soon found at the cost of a wetting. His account of the incident is typical of the breezy zestfulness and buoyant humour with which his whole fine story is told.

"As we were gliding along quite swiftly I set my pole on the bottom and gave the boat a sudden push to avoid a boulder, when the pole stuck in a crevice between two rocks, and instead of losing the pole by the sudden jerk I gave, I was the one who was very suddenly yanked from the boat by the spring of the pole, and landed in the middle of the river. I struck pretty squarely on my back, and so got thoroughly wet, but swam for shore amid the shouts of the boys, who waved their hats and hurrahed for the captain when they saw he was not hurt. I told them that was nothing as we were on our way to California by water any way, and such things must be expected."

Manly estimates their speed at about thirty miles a day at the start, "which beat the pace of the tired oxen considerably." Antelope and elk proved easy to shoot along the bank, a fortunate circumstance in view of the fact that the only provisions secured from the emigrant train consisted of a little flour and bacon. There could have been little thought of danger in those first easy, lazy days, for the shock of the discovery that the whole of the river-road to golden California was not bordered by elk- and antelope-studded meadows and verdant patches of willow and cottonwood caught the skipper fast asleep on the bridge. And yet Manly's description of the approach to the head of Flaming Gorge and the beginning of the Colorado Canyon series, written in a half-jocular vein though it is, is quite as effective as the more studied efforts of Powell and Dellenbaugh, and scarcely less accurate. I quote the spirited passage in full.

"Thus far we had a very pleasant time, each taking his turn in working the boat while the others rested or slept. About the fifth day when we were floating along in very gently running water, I had laid down to take a rest and a little sleep. The mountains here on both sides of the river were not very steep, but ran gradually for a mile or so. While I was sleeping the boat came round a small angle in the stream, and all at once there seemed to be a higher, steeper range of mountains right across the valley. The boys thought the river was coming to a rather sudden end and hastily awoke me, and for the life of me I could not say that they were not right, for there was no way in sight for it to go. I remembered while looking over a map the military men had I found a place named Brown's Hole, and I told the boys I guessed we were elected to go on foot to California after all, for I did not propose to follow the river down any sort of a hole into any mountain. We were floating directly toward a perpendicular cliff, and I could not see any hole anywhere, nor any place where it could go. Just as we were within a stone's throw of the cliff, the river turned sharply to the right and went behind a high point of the mountain that seemed to stand squarely on edge. This was really an immense crack or crevice, certainly 2000 feet deep and perhaps much more, and seemed much wider at the bottom than it did at the top, 2000 feet or more above our heads. Each wall seemed to lean in toward the water as it rose."

Writing almost ten years after Manly, Dellenbaugh, in his "Romance of the Colorado River," describes the startling effect at this same point of coming suddenly upon a wall of mountains apparently blocking the river.

"In the late afternoon we bore down on a ridge, about one thousand feet high, which extended far in both directions athwart our course. It was the edge of the Uinta Mountains. At its very foot the river seemed to stop. It could be seen neither to right nor to left, nor could any opening be detected in the mountain, except high up where Powell pointed out to us a bare patch of brilliant rocks, saying it was the top of Flaming Gorge, the beginning of the canyon series."

Although no voyageurs appear ever to have entered the gateway of the Colorado canyons in more lightsome mood than did those of the Manly party, forerunning warnings of the grim nature of the task ahead seem to have been vouchsafed them from the very outset. Where every one else from Ashley to the Kolbs ran without difficulties through the easy water of Flaming Gorge and Horseshoe and Kingfisher canyons, Manly's clumsy craft had to be helped and humoured at a number of places. An old cottonwood tree with the marks of an axe upon it was the first sign that any one had been through before them. Some mountain sheep were seen, but far out of gun-shot. Their inability to bring down any game at all in this canyon stretch made them "feel the need of some fresh provisions very sorely."

That there was no down-heartedness over the outlook, however, is evident from the skipper's gay description of his flamboyant attempt to perpetuate the memory of his passage upon the canyon wall.

" . . . At one place where the rock hung a little over the river and had a smooth wall, I climbed up above the high water mark which we could clearly see, and with a mixture of gunpowder and grease for paint, and a bit of cloth tied to a stick for brush, I painted in fair sized letters on the rock, Capt. W. L. Manly, U.S.A. We did not know whether we were in the bounds of the United States or not, and we put on all the majesty we could under the circumstances."

The "majesty," I take it, consisted of making the inscription a burlesque military signature. The "CAPT." stood for Manly's skippership of the ferryboat-argosy, and the "U. S. A."

AN INSCRIPTION IN LABYRINTH CANYON LEFT BY THE UNKNOWN
FRENCH NAVIGATOR, DE JULIEN.

ANCIENT INDIAN STRUCTURE ON THE LOWER GREEN.

LOOKING WEST IN THE GRAND CANYON.

for "U. S. of America" rather than for "U. S. Army." One can imagine the guffaws of chesty laughter evoked by this little by-play from that husky crew of bull-whackers.

If Manly has set down the events of his voyage in the proper sequence it is certain that his effort at mural registration was a little idea of his own rather than the result of inspiration born of coming upon a similar inscription left by a previous voyageur. It was not until evening of the day on which he told of having broken out into paint that his party came to a point easily recognizable from his description as Ashley Falls, even before he mentions the name found there.

"Just before night we came to a place where some huge rocks as large as cabins had fallen down from the mountain, completely filling up the river bed, and making it completely impassable for our boat. We unloaded it and while the boys held the stern line, I took off my clothes and pushed the boat out into the torrent that ran round the rocks, letting them pay the line out slowly till it was just right. Then I sang out to—'Let go'—and away it dashed. I grasped the bow line, and at the first chance jumped overboard and got to shore, when I held the boat and brought it in below the obstructions."

Not quite an orthodox piece of "lining down," but perfectly sound practice withal—provided, of course, it was evident the man in the boat had a good chance of bringing it to bank below unaided. The thing could have been done a bit more safely with a man carrying the bow-line down and waiting below the falls, but this very obvious expedient was doubtless impossible on account of the lack of cordage already mentioned by Manly. Considering that Powell portaged two of the boats of his second expedition all the way round the fall, and banged up another badly in lining it down, the work of these drovers in taking their old ferryboat over in safety was a really fine achievement. As I shall point out presently, however, it is not certain that the operation described was at the main fall.

Manly goes on to tell of how, camped below the fall, he discovered the inscription left by Ashley in 1825. Writing from memory he records the date as 1824, still much nearer correct than Powell's two guesses brought him. I have set down the passage relating to this incident in a previous chapter.[1]

If Manly has distributed his days correctly, the final wreck—inevitable sooner or later once he had ventured into the canyons with the craft he had—occurred the next morning. He tells of it without the least suggestion of an attempt to dramatize either the event itself or the state of his mind following what must have seemed at the moment an appalling disaster.

"When we came to look around we found that another big rock blocked the channel 300 yards below the camp at Ashley Falls, and the water rushed around it with a terrible swirl. So we unloaded the boat again and made the attempt to get around it as we did the other rocks. We tried to get across the river but failed. We now, all but one, got on the great rock with our poles, and the one man was to ease the boat down with the rope as far as he could, then let go and we would stop it with our poles and push it out into the stream and let it go over, but the current was so strong that when the boat struck the rock we could not stop it, and the gunwale next to us rose, and the other went down, so that in a second the boat stood edgewise in the water and the bottom tight against the big rock, and the strong current pinned it there so tight that we could no more move it than we could move the rock itself."

That was the end of the old "Pacific-Ocean-or-Bust" ferry-boat. Doubtless (as no further mention is made of attempts to extricate it) it busted very quickly, thereby putting at least the floatable fragments of it in the way of living up to both of the alternatives implied by the name.

In stating that the wreck occurred at a point about three hundred yards below Ashley Falls Manly's memory must have been somewhat at fault. Although there are a few rapids between the falls and the foot of Red Canyon, none is bad enough to seem to fit the description of the place where the

[1] See pp. 92 and 93.

boat was swamped. The likeliest explanation seems to be that the rapid Manly describes lining down successfully was some distance above Ashley Falls, and that the boat was lost at the falls themselves.

Beyond "a few rapid thoughts" as to whether they "would not be safer among the Mormons than out in this wild country, afoot and alone," there is no indication that much time was lost in repining. "Two pine trees, about two feet through, growing on a level place just below," offered canoe material, and they "never let the axes rest, night or day," until two rough dugouts, about fifteen feet in length, were completed. These, lashed together, proving of insufficient capacity, they landed a half mile farther down and set to work upon a second pair. Toiling by daylight and firelight, the task was completed in a very short time. The new double canoe, though its units were of even less beam than those of the first one, was twenty-five or thirty feet long. With Manly, the only expert canoeist in the party, flying his Commodore's flag from the larger craft, the river adventure was resumed with little delay.

Though made from pine instead of cottonwood, these hastily hacked duplex dugouts were identical in type with those built by Captain William Clark on the upper Yellowstone and used to convey his party until it was reunited with that of Captain Lewis on the Missouri. They would have worked better on the swift but comparatively open Yellowstone than in the broken canyons of the Green. They would have stood rather rougher usage than the old ferryboat, but could have been little less clumsy to handle.

The rest of Red Canyon was run without difficulty, and in the easy three- or four-day passage through the beautiful Brown's Hole region smooth water and abundant game made welcome amends for the late hardships. Geese, ducks, otter, deer and elk fell to the rifles of the voyageurs. An enormous bull elk brought down by Manly had horns six feet from tip to tip. Placed on the ground, points downward, "one could walk under the skull between them." To lend still further variety to their feasts, foot-long fish, stupefied by the mud of a rain-swollen creek, came to the surface almost begging to be caught. Unfortunately, according to the narrative, they were very difficult to seize. Mud-stupefied fish are a phenomenon still not infrequently seen during the season of cloudbursts at the mouths of many tributary creeks of the Colorado.

"Cañons deeper and the water more tumultuous" marked the passage of the spectacular Gate of Lodore and the end of the idyllic *dolce far niente* of the peaceful drift through Brown's Hole. Unloading and lining-down was necessary many times a day, and not infrequently even the canoes were taken out and dragged around especially savage riffles. Lower Disaster Falls is readily identified in a passage which also clears up the mystery of the deserted outfit Powell believed to have been the remnants of the supposed wreck of the Ashley party.

"At one place where the river was more than usually obstructed we found a deserted camp, a skiff and some heavy cooking utensils, with a notice posted up on an alder tree saying that they had found the river impracticable, and being satisfied that the river was so full of rocks and boulders that it could not be safely navigated, they had abandoned the undertaking and were about to start over-land to make their way to Salt Lake. I took down the names of the party at the time in my diary, which has since been burned, but have now forgotten them entirely. They were all strangers to me. They had left such heavy articles as could not be carried on foot."

"This notice rather disconcerted us," adds Manly, "but we thought we had better keep on and see for ourselves," thereby confirming an earlier statement anent the predominance of the Missouri element in the party.

Indications of an extremely low stage of water are found in a description of the heavy work of loading and unloading the canoes, "and packing them over the boulders, with only small streams of water curling around between them." They soon learned the wisdom of going barefoot where they were more than half the time in the water which roared and dashed so loud that they could hardly hear each other speak. Far from being dismayed, however, those hard-bitten crews of ex-ox-skinners kept on mastering rough-water technique until they were shortly sitting the thwarts of their plunging dugouts and flicking a paddle with the easy aplomb with which they had lately cracked the curling black-snake from the hurricane bridge of their prairie-schooners. Manly does not state the fact in just those words, but it is plainly readable between the lines: "We kept getting more and more venturesome and skillful, and managed to run some very dangerous rapids in safety."

That sort of a thing could only have one ending. Nowhere is the priceless asset of "an humble and a contrite heart" more devoutly to be desired than in trying to navigate one of those seductive half-and-half blends of white froth and brown boulders called a rapid; nowhere does Pride go more quickly before a fall. In the case of our burgeoning bull-whackers it was a very small fall indeed that started Pride upon the toboggan, to hit bottom—not inappropriately—somewhere near the foot of Hell's Half Mile. Manly writes of the disastrous sequel in considerable detail.

"One afternoon we came to a sudden turn in the river, more than a right angle, and, just below, a fall of two feet or more. This I ran in safety, as did the rest, who followed, and we cheered at our pluck and skill. Just after this the river ran back the other way at a right angle or more, and I quickly saw there was danger below and signalled them to go on shore at once, and lead the canoes over the dangerous rapids. I ran my own canoe near shore and got by the rapid safely, waiting for the others to come also. They did not obey my signals but thought to run the rapid the same as I did. The channel here was straight for 200 yards, without a boulder in it, but the stream was so swift that it caused great rolling waves in the centre, of a kind I have never seen anywhere else. The boys were not skilful enough to navigate this stream, and the suction drew them to the centre where the great waves rolled them over and over, bottom side up and every way."

The account of what followed is a bit confused. For some reason which he does not make plain, the crew of Manly's canoe let go of it and started swimming for the shore. For a while the whole lot of them were struggling in the water. All reached the bank except Alfred Walton who, not being able to swim, went on down through the rapids clinging to his upturned canoe. Retrieving the big canoe, Manly and McMahon threw everything out of it and started in pursuit. Desperate as the situation must have been, Manly refuses to be denied any of the humour of it. "Walton had very black hair," he writes, "and as he clung fast to his canoe his black head looked like a crow on the end of a log."

Overtaking the runaway canoe just before it started into another long rapid, they beached and made it fast before rolling the water out of Walton and laying him up by a fire to dry out and warm up. A few light things, like clothes and blankets, were found in one of the upturned canoes; everything sinkable save two of the guns was lost. Careful stalking on the morrow resulted in the killing of three mountain sheep and the relief of a serious food shortage. This welcome bag prompted the Commodore's loyal crews to opine that they seemed to be having better luck with one gun than with six. "And so," adds Manly, "we had a very merry time after all." Surely of all Colorado canyon voyageurs this one had the most buoyant spirit.

Rapids described as still dangerous in many places, but not so frequent nor so bad as those above, indicated that the dread gorge of Lodore had been put behind and Whirlpool and Split Mountain canyons entered in turn. Finally they were out of the canyons, among barren mountains and hills of "a pale yellow caste." Just where the shot was heard which finally led them to land at an encampment of friendly Indians it is not possible to decide, but it was probably not far from the mouth of the Uinta. When the Indians showed them a collection of knives, guns and blankets, with words and gestures to indicate that these were presents from the Mormons, the astute Manly promptly put his hand to his breast "and said 'Mormonee' with a cheerful countenance. And that act," he explains, "conveyed to them the belief that we were the chosen disciples of the great and only Brigham, and we became friends at once, as all acknowledged." From the leader of an outfit that had preferred to beard the dragon of the Colorado in its den rather than winter among the Saints of Salt Lake that graceful little act showed, to say the least, a notable adaptability to circumstance.

The chief of the band, whose name Manly renders as Walker, appears to have been a most kindly and intelligent Indian, with a topographical sense and knowledge little short of marvellous. On being made to understand that the whites wanted some information as to the further availability of the river as a highway of travel to the big water, he led them down to a smooth sand-bar and proceeded to construct a sort of relief map of the Colorado canyon series. The river and its tributaries were first gouged out in the sand with a crooked stick. Then, with the aid of stones for mountains and fluent gestures to indicate varying height, he began mapping the succession of canyons and valleys from the crossing of the emigrant road down to his camp.

This picture, as far as completed, showed so remarkable a knowledge of the course of the river as it had just been revealed at first-hand to the voyageurs, that they followed Walker with breathless interest as he continued his map downward toward the sea. Canyon followed canyon until a climacteric gorge was represented by a piling of all the readily available stones in a double wall along a sinuous stretch of river.

"Then [writes Manly] he stood with one foot on each side of his river and put his hands on the stones and then raised them as high as he could, making a continued e-e-e-e-e-e-e-e as long as his breath would last, pointed to the canoe and made signs with his hands how

.it would roll and pitch in the rapids and finely [finally] capsize and throw us all out. He then made signs of death to show us that it was a fatal place. I understood perfectly plain from this that below the valley where we now were was a terrible cañon, much higher than any we had passed, and the rapids were not navigable with safety."

When Walker completed the picture by indicating that the deep canyon was surrounded by a tribe of hostile Indians, Manly concluded that he would rather take his chance navigating among Mormons than among the rocks of the river road to California. Four of his companions were of like mind, but the remaining two—McMahon and Field—distrusted the Indians more than they did the river. Since the map they had did not "show any bad places" on the river, they argued that this was the logical way to reach the Coast. Manly writes of wishing them good luck and good-bye "with quivering lips," but a later chapter reveals that repeated warnings from the Indians finally induced them to abandon what probably would have been the first attempt to run the middle and lower canyons of the Colorado series.

Manly's party, travelling on foot with two pack-horses given them by the Indians, reached the nearest emigrant route to fall in with a train on its way to Los Angeles. Trying to reach central California by an ill-defined westerly cut-off, this outfit entered and crossed a sinister sun-scorched gash in the desert mountains which, from their harrowing experiences there, the emigrants gave the name by which it has since been known to the world—Death Valley.

Although the running of the extremely rough rapids of the upper Green in crude hatchet-hacked dugouts is well entitled to be ranked as the one most spectacular feat of Colorado canyon navigation, Manly's breezy but all-too-brief story of it is but a single chapter in his altogether remarkable series of western experiences. Written after he was more than the allotted three score years and ten, his book is still among the

UPSTREAM VIEW OF LOWER END OF BOULDER CANYON.

Johnson went above this point with his steamer, but Ives did not get so far.

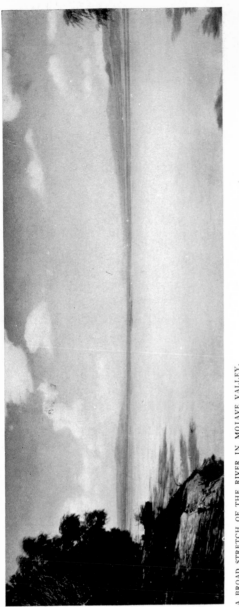

A BROAD STRETCH OF THE RIVER IN MOJAVE VALLEY.
Ives had much trouble from sand bars in passing this stretch.

very best of the records of the stirring days of forty-nine. Knowing all that he went through, and with how high a spirit he trod the path of the pioneer, it is with a real glow of satisfaction that one finds him closing his splendid story with these words:

"I came . . . to this land so pleasant and so fair, wherein, after over forty years of earnest toil, I rest in the midst of family and friends, and can truly say I am content."

I shall hardly need to add that these lines were written in California!

CHAPTER VII

DERBY AND IVES ON THE LOWER RIVER

THE establishment of a military post at the mouth of the Gila for the purpose of protecting the constantly augmenting movement of California-bound gold-seekers was responsible for the first attempt on the part of the Federal Government to explore the Colorado. The provisioning of the fort by pack-train from California having proved extremely difficult and expensive, the alternative of bringing up supplies by the Gulf of California and the lower Colorado was taken under consideration. For the purpose of determining the practicability of such a plan a reconnaissance party was dispatched to the head of the Gulf late in the year 1850. The survey was under the direction of the Bureau of Topographical Engineers of the War Department. Lieutenant George H. Derby, the officer in command of the expedition, as the author of a collection of droll sketches published under the title of "Phoenixana," subsequently attained to a considerable reputation as a humourist. The nature of his report precluded any lapses into lightsomeness in compiling that heavy official document, but a sense of humour must have been a real help to him in interpreting the first paragraph of his orders from the Assistant Adjutant General. Dated October 11, 1850, this reads:

"SIR: The schooner *Invincible* is to be despatched by the chief assistant quartermaster of the division to attempt the entrance of the River Colorado from the Gulf of California, and the ascent of the river as far as the post to be established near the junction of the Gila, with a view to establish that as a route of supply."

If any one in the War Department had gone to the trouble of reading Hardy's book, published twenty years previously and easily obtainable even in the West at that time, they would have been more likely to have dispatched a prairie schooner to ascend the Colorado to the Gila than a hundred and twenty-ton craft officially rated as a "United States Transport." In its failure to take cognizance of information already available this order seems almost in a class with the one which twenty years later, set Lieutenant Wheeler the all-but-impossible task of ascending a stretch of the Grand Canyon already explored by Powell. Derby, fortunately, procured a copy of Hardy's book before sailing from San Diego, and so can have had no illusions respecting the very limited stretch of the Colorado estuary he could expect to navigate with a vessel of nearly five times the tonnage of the little *Bruja*.

Guaymas, evidently, was quite as prolific of bogie yarns about the delta Indians as it is to-day. Derby met a number of old residents who claimed to be thoroughly familiar with conditions at the mouth of the Colorado.

"All of these gentlemen united in saying that the country at the head of the gulf and bordering the river Colorado was inhabited by hostile Indians, from whom we might expect much trouble; and on becoming acquainted with the weakness of our armament, strenuously advised an increase of that and in the number of our crew. I therefore purchased from the captain of a Spanish schooner lying in the harbor two small swivels and eight carbines, with the necessary ammunition, and the captain engaged three additional seamen, increasing the number of our crew to twelve. This force I deemed sufficient for any emergency that might arise."

Arrived at the mouth of the river, however, Derby found the Cocopahs just as ready to fetch and carry as had Alarcón and all who followed him. They supplied him freely with such fresh provisions as they had and proved useful in bearing messages to establish touch with the military party from the fort. Altogether, he gives these aborigines a good character.

"The men are very tall and strongly made as a general thing, and the women are modest, well behaved, and rather good-looking. . . .

We found them very friendly, quiet and inoffensive . . . and though continually on board the vessel, we never missed even the most trifling article. Their arrows were made of reed with a pointed end of hard wood, and their bows of willow, so that if they were disposed to be as hostile as had been falsely represented to us, they would be incapable of doing much damage."

The time of Derby's arrival at the mouth of the river—practically at the winter solstice—could not have been better chosen to find the tides at their least unfavourable stages. Even so, the navigation began to prove very troublesome at points where Hardy's smaller vessel had found fair sailing. Grounding every ebb tide and coming in for a severe bumping at the beginning of every flood, it soon became evident that the head of practicable navigation would fall not far above the Gore and Montagu islands of Hardy. By allowing the schooner to drift up with the flood—using the sails as an aid to control rather than progress—and anchoring during the ebb, she was ultimately worked up to a point about two miles below the mouth of the Hardy. Pushing on from here in a row-boat, the survey of the river was continued until a party under Major Heintzelman was encountered working down from Yuma. As the joint work of the two parties had covered the whole of the river Derby had been sent to study, he did not pursue his own survey farther upstream.

Shortly after returning to the *Invincible* a violent spring tide caused her to part a chain and leave her smaller anchor in the mud. Two nights later the flood-tide wave, running with great velocity,

". . . struck the vessel on her counter as she lay aground with great violence, carrying her around with it with such force as to snap the ring of the large anchor, and we found ourselves drifting rapidly up the stream towards Arnold's Point. Our situation was one of great peril, for this being the highest spring-tide, if we had grounded above, the vessel must have been lost. But the captain with admirable coolness and self-possession seized the helm, and directing her towards the bank, ordered the men to leap from the jib-boom on shore with the kedge anchor, which fortunately brought her up."

This accident was very similar to the one which befell Hardy at almost exactly the same point. Where the young British sailor smashed his rudder, Derby lost his last anchor. If anything, the *Invincible* was left in a more critical situation than was the *Bruja*. Hardy attained comparative safety by pushing off and anchoring in deep water; Derby, with both bowers gone, had to contrive a secure mooring under the caving bank. From the way this was managed, there is no doubt that the skipper of the *Invincible*, Captain Wilcox, was a real Yankee sailor. Derby's description, while neither detailed nor nautical, gives a good idea of how the thing was accomplished.

"We then procured the largest logs we could find, to which, when sunk in the ground, springs were attached from the vessel, and rigged out spars to keep her at a safe distance from the bank."

Precarious as was their position, they hung on here for eleven days, completing their surveying in the vicinity and finally landing the stores brought for the garrison at Yuma. They grounded twice in the two days it took the *Invincible* to drift down to the Gulf on the ebb tides, but got off each time after but little delay. Owing to the lack of any heavy anchors further investigations Derby had planned to make at Tiburon and along the lower California coast had to be given up.

Derby evidently made constant use of Hardy's book and chart, and acknowledges that it, "though very inaccurate in many important points, was nevertheless of much assistance to us in navigating the river." The principal inaccuracy Derby found would have been Hardy's error in applying the name Gila to what was now found to be the main channel of the Colorado. On this point he writes:

". . . We found two branches of the river, the former of which he [Hardy] mistook for the Gila; this is in fact the main channel of the river, the other being merely a slough which divides the river, about a mile from its entrance, into two branches. . . . As there is not water enough in either of these branches to float a whale-boat at low tide, it is evident that the river must have altered entirely since Lieutenant Hardy's visit, or that he never ascended it as he said he did with the Brija [*Bruja*], a schooner of twenty-five tons."

I have already discussed in some detail my reasons for believing that, at the time of Hardy's visit, the main flow of the Colorado came in by the westerly channel, just as he said it did.[1] Neither Derby, nor any one else until the reclamation of the Imperial Valley was inaugurated at the beginning of the present century, saw enough of the spreading delta cone to understand that the main channel of the river had been alternating between easterly and westerly courses at comparatively frequent intervals for many centuries.

In the matter of the navigation of the Colorado between the head of the Gulf and Fort Yuma, Derby concluded that it would be practicable "at any season of the year by a steamboat of eighteen or twenty feet beam, drawing from two and a half to three feet [of] water." He recommended "a small stern-wheel boat, with a powerful engine and a thick bottom," a type he believed best adapted to work against the strong current in a narrow channel "somewhat obstructed by small snags and sawyers."

Commercial navigation of the lower Colorado followed hard upon Derby's demonstration of its feasibility. His reconnaissance was completed in January, 1851, and before the end of that year George A. Johnson landed a cargo of lumber at the mouth of the river and built a flotilla of flatboats in which to freight cargoes to the fort. It is possible that Johnson also built a steamer at the same time, which would account for a stern-wheeler called the *Yuma* which Hobbs says he saw in 1851.[2] The *Uncle Sam*, built in San Francisco and set up at

---

[1] See p. 124.
[2] See "Wild Life in the Far West," by Captain James Hobbs, and "The Romance of the Colorado" (Dellenbaugh).

the mouth of the river in 1852, succumbed to a snag at the end of a few months, and the *General Jesup*, built and run by Captain Johnson, the flatboat freighter, lasted but a little longer before being destroyed by an explosion. Johnson's next steamer, the *Colorado*, had better luck, for its name crops up through the river records of a number of years.

The infiltration of emigrants to and through the valleys to the north and the establishment of new military posts in New Mexico and Utah created a demand for the extension of the river freighting service above Yuma, and that, in turn, calling for further data on the navigability of that part of the Colorado, brought about the Ives expedition of 1857. Lieutenant Joseph C. Ives, chosen to command the first fully equipped exploring party to work directly upon the Colorado, had been chief assistant to Lieutenant Whipple during the latter's survey of the 100th parallel for a railway route in 1854. He seems to have been admirably fitted, both technically and temperamentally, for the difficult work in prospect. He had, moreover, a real gift for description. That, with his sense for the humorous and picturesque, makes the narrative portions of Lieutenant Ives' voluminous report as delightful as informative.

Although the study of the navigability of the river for steamers was the prime object of the expedition, the opportunity for greatly ramified lines of scientific research led to the provision for the collection of data on the geology, ethnology, zoology and botany of the region traversed, together with the making of extended astronomical, barometric and meteorological observations. Distinguished members of the expedition included Dr. J. S. Newberry, in charge of natural history study, F. W. Egloffstein, topographer, who had been with Frémont, and H. B. Mollhausen, artist, described by Ives as "a gentleman belonging to the household of Baron Von Humboldt, and a member of the exploring party of Prince Paul of Württemberg."

The steamer used by the Ives expedition was a steel stern-wheeler, the sections of which were built in Philadelphia, shipped to San Francisco by Panama, and trans-shipped from there to the head of the Gulf for setting up. Ives states that he was forced to resort to this expedient through inability to charter a steamer on the Colorado at a figure commensurate with his appropriation. This is hardly convincing in view, on the one hand, of the abnormal cost of the rushed construction in Philadelphia together with that of the several trans-shipments—including those to and from the railway at Panama—and, on the other, of the fact that the better of the two stern-wheelers already on the river was used for ferrying Lieutenant Beale's party that same winter, and later found time to precede Ives up the river, ultimately to reach a much higher point than he attained with his specially-built *Explorer*. There is an interesting bit of history here which, now that all the parties figuring in it have long since died, will probably never be written. The truth may well have been that some keen theorist in the War Department—or possibly Ives himself—had conceived and designed the steel steamer and so went to considerable lengths in railroading it through to a trial. Certainly the cost of building, shipping and setting up the *Explorer* under the conditions imposed could not have been much less than the charter rate of an ocean greyhound at the height of the U-boat campaign.

Lieutenant Ives, with the machinery and sectional parts of the *Explorer*, arrived off the mouth of the Colorado in the schooner *Monterey* on the twenty-ninth of November, 1857. Drifting in with a three-mile tide the following morning, he remarks a condition that has baffled every navigator approaching this point from either direction: that "the reflection of the rays of the sun, the apparent vibration of the atmosphere, the mirage, and the constant shifting of the outlines of the bars, due to the rapidly rising tide, made it impossible to form an accurate idea of the configuration of the shores."

Ives states that "the usual anchorage for vessels coming from the mouth of the river" was a point on the west bank, not far above Gore and Montagu islands, called Robinson's Landing. Robinson was reported to have established himself here some years previously to search for a treasure said to have been lost in the Hardy when the ship of a certain Count Rousset de Boulbon, filibusterer, went aground as that fugitive was endeavouring to escape up the Colorado after an unsuccessful attempt at revolution in Mexico. As the point subject to the least inundation in the lower delta region, Ives selected the Landing for his shipyard. Although under water at the full-moon tides, there was a four-weeks interval when the slushy silt crusted over in which, with luck and hard work, he hoped to complete the setting up of his little steamer. The problem of finishing this task inside of the time-limit and under the conditions imposed, was perhaps the most difficult that confronted Ives at any stage of his operations.

Unable to moor the schooner against the high, soft, constantly caving bank long enough to discharge the heavy parts, the novel expedient was adopted of warping the vessel into a natural slip formed by a drainage gully. As there was water enough for this difficult and extremely risky operation only at the height of the highest tides, the *Monterey*, to the considerable consternation of her skipper, had to remain there, perched far above the river, until the new-moon rise of a fortnight later floated her back again to the channel.

Waiting for the climacteric stage that would float her up to the natural dry-dock, the *Monterey*, like all of her predecessors, was led a very lively dance as a plaything of the warring waves of the ebbing and flooding tides. The fortunate grounding of the schooner, relieving the strain on her cables, was all that saved her from destruction on one occasion. Narrowly escaping swamping his boat in returning from the shore to the vessel, it appeared for a few minutes that Ives had stepped from the frying-pan into the fire.

"As the tide fell the swiftness of the flow increased, and soon the mighty volume was surging by with formidable violence. The schooner had come to anchor over a shoal, and owing to the rapid fall was aground before its full force was developed; a fortunate occurrence as no anchors could have held much longer. She had no sooner settled down in the sand than a bank commenced forming on the lee side, and in an incredibly short time a mound was raised to a height of several feet, with one or two sluice-ways, through which the water rushed from underneath the keel like a mill-race."

The phenomenon of the formation of the bar under the lee of the stranded ship was the same sort of thing that one experiences when his boat grounds at almost any part of the Colorado. It is a strikingly graphic illustration of the great quantity of sand and silt being carried downward by the rushing waters.

The same night Ives had his first experience of the tidal bore, which appears to have been rather a stronger wave than one would expect so long after the autumnal equinox.

"About nine o'clock, while the tide was still running out rapidly, we heard, from the direction of the Gulf, a deep, booming sound, like the noise of a distant waterfall. Every moment it became louder and nearer, and in half an hour a great wave, several feet in height, could be distinctly seen, flashing and sparkling in the moonlight, extending from one bank to the other, and advancing swiftly upon us. While it was only a few hundred yards distant, the ebb tide continued to flow by at the rate of three miles an hour. A point of land and an exposed bar close under our lee broke the wave into several long swells, and as these met the ebb the broad sheet around us boiled up and foamed like the surface of a cauldron, and then, with scarcely a moment of slack water, the whole went whirling by in the opposite direction. In a few moments the low rollers had passed the island and united again in a single bank of water, which swept up the narrow channel with the thunder of a cataract. At a turn not far distant it disappeared from view, but for a long time, in the stillness of the night, the roaring of the huge mass could be heard reverberating among the windings of the river, till at last it became faint and lost in the distance."

This is quite the most graphic word-picture of the Colorado tidal bore I have ever read. This particular wave, however, must have fallen short by a considerable margin of having the size or the force of the fully developed bores of September and March. The best measure of this is Ives' statement that the ebb tide continued to flow at a rate of three miles an hour. Last October the two engineers who accompanied me on my boat voyage to the mouth of the Colorado made careful tests of the speed of the ebb and flow of the tides at La Bomba, which is some miles farther up river than the long-obliterated site of Robinson's Landing. Among other things, we found that a chip thrown into the ebb after the bore had come into sight down-river travelled so fast that it required a good swinging trot to hold it even running along the bank. That, with other trial runs timed by a watch over measured distances, worked out to about eight miles an hour. So swift an outward flow, of course, required a proportionately large and powerful return bore to overcome it.

The tide that floated the *Monterey* up to her perch in the gully receded to leave the flat a sea of mud. Into this the machinery and sectional parts of the *Explorer* were unloaded, and preparations made for their assemblage. As elevated ways of the usual type would have left the hull too high to be floated off by even the highest of tides that could be expected, it was necessary to lay these in a deep trench in the ground. The work of digging a sufficiently large excavation in the wet, sticky clay proved quite as laborious as dragging in the water-soaked logs of driftwood for the ways. This required several days. Meanwhile the uncrating of the sections of the hull revealed that the steel had been badly bent in the rough handling of transport. Pounding these back into shape proved an especially trying labour. Then there were certain structural defects to be corrected, the most serious of which was a weakness of the hull amidships that had become evident even in the hurried preliminary trial upon the Delaware. The expedient of stiffening the hull by bolting to it on the outside four big scantlings, running longitudinally, was probably the only way out of the difficulty under the circumstances; at the same time nothing could have been devised more effectually calculated to hamper a boat in working up through shallow water.

In addition to driving the work of assembling the hull of his steamer, Ives found time to erect a provisional observatory and begin his astronomical studies. Bothered occasionally by clouds and winds, there were many evenings on which the conditions for observation were ideal.

"The misty wreaths will sometimes suddenly and altogether disappear, unveiling an illuminated sky, upon which the pale constellations of the Milky Way are clustered in a distinct silver band. The dome of the heavens, reflected from the smooth river, is prolonged far below the horizon, and presents a nearly unbroken sphere of radiant sapphire blue, from whose surface myriads of burnished quivering points emit vivid streams of light, while the steadier rays of the planets seem almost to rival those of the moon in splendour."

The young explorer's photographic apparatus was quite probably the first to be used upon the Colorado. As far as results were concerned, however, it might just as well have been left behind. His only mention of his picture-taking experiments reveals clearly the primitive state of the nascent photographic art in the middle fifties.

"I have taken advantage of the mild and quiet interval to experiment, and having constructed out of an india-rubber tarpaulin a tent that entirely excluded the light, have made repeated efforts to obtain a view of the camp and the river. The attempt has not met with a distinguished success. The chemicals seem to have deteriorated, and apart from this the light is so glaring, and the agitation of the atmosphere near the surface of the ground so great, that it is doubtful whether, under the circumstances, a clear and perfect picture could be secured."

The first of the many fine full-page plates in the explorer's report is marked "J. J. YOUNG, from a Photograph by

LIEUT. IVES." The sprightly action of the busy workers in this picture, however, furnishes conclusive evidence that the figures, at least, were not the result of the exposure of a slow-acting wet-plate of early-day photography. Doubtless the impressionistic print teased out from this pioneer negative gave the lithographer no more than a rough adumbration of composition; and a seaward-looking landscape of the Colorado delta is about as strong on composition as the doldrum latitudes of the middle of the Pacific.

The *Monterey*, much to the relief of her skipper, was floated back to deep water on the new-moon tide. One of the two stern-wheelers that came down from Yuma to load the freight brought by the schooner for the post was the powerfully-engined *Colorado* which, under her able and experienced commander and owner, Captain Johnson, would seem to have been the ideal craft for the purposes of the Ives expedition. The latter refers in a friendly passage to the "persevering and energetic proprietors" of the two steamers, who had overcome successfully the many obstacles in the way of establishing navigation of the river. There is nothing either in this, or in any subsequent entry in Ives' journal, to throw any light on the jealousy and rivalry known to have existed between him and the bold and enterprising Johnson.

A severe northwester that forced the *Monterey* to trip anchor and beat a precipitate retreat for open water also carried away the observatory and photographic tents. Protected from the gale in their pit, the shipbuilders worked steadily on. The highly difficult and dangerous operation of lowering the heavy boiler to place was accomplished without accident, and the correction of a troublesome defect in connection with the slots for the connecting rods left the steamer practically assembled. On Christmas Day the boiler was filled and steam got up, regarding which eagerly awaited mechanical trial Ives records:

"The engine ran beautifully—a great triumph for Mr. Carroll after the trouble he has had with it. The boat is well modelled, and presents a gay appearance now that she has been painted. The word *Explorer*, printed in large capitals upon the wheel-house, designates her title and object."

After a couple of days divided between finishing touches and the collection of firewood, the *Explorer* was launched by moonlight at the high tide of December thirtieth. Backing into the stream under her own engine, she was headed round and berthed for the night in the gully lately occupied by the *Monterey*. The next morning she underwent a final inspection, when Ives gives the following description of his argosy:

"She is fifty-four feet long from the extremity of the bow to the outer rim of the stern-wheel. Amidships, the hull is left open, like a skiff, the boiler occupying a third of the vacant space. At the bow is a little deck, upon which stands the armament—a four-pound howitzer. In front of the wheel another deck, large enough to accommodate the pilot and a few of the surveying party, forms the roof of a cabin eight feet by seven. Nearly every newly-launched craft [he adds] is supposed by those interested to excell its predecessors; but I imagine few boats have ever been surveyed by their builders with as much admiration and complacency."

The almost paternal affection expressed in that last sentence somehow strengthens one's belief that the design of the *Explorer* was Ives' brain-child, and helps to account for the length to which he went to give the concrete expression of it a practical trial.

When camp was broken it looked for a while as though the *Explorer* would have to make two runs to Yuma to handle all of the freight. By loading the steamer "down to the extreme limit prudence would justify," however, it was found that all that was left could be towed along in two skiffs. Great care was taken in the final stowage of both human and inanimate freight, for with a bare six inches of freeboard a small list to port or starboard was likely to have serious consequences. Indeed, in pushing off in the night in an overloaded, untried vessel Ives took a tenfold greater chance of complete disaster than in facing the more spectacular but less tangible dangers of the rapids of the canyons above. In the latter the worst that could happen was to run on a rock and stick there; in the surges and eddies of the deep channel under the caving bank of the lower river the least untoward happening would have swamped the open shell of the *Explorer* in the wink of an eye. Once capsized in this stretch, vessel and cargo would have become the core of a new silt-and-sand island the moment it found lodgment at the bottom of the tide-scoured channel, and one out of ten men saved would have been a high rate of rescue.

The air was quiet when the *Explorer* cast off her moorings at midnight, but the first bit of a breeze that sprang up from the north to ruffle the surface of a tide that raced in the opposite direction brought home to Ives the desperate chance he had taken.

"As the wind freshened, waves began to rise and the water to dash into the boat. The prospect was somewhat alarming, for even throwing overboard the cargo would not have saved the open boat from swamping had the breeze continued long enough to have raised a sea, and though near the land, the strongest swimmer would have stood little chance in such a current with nothing to cling to but a steep bank of slippery clay. We shipped so much water that we were on the point of commencing to lighten the boat, and I think if the wind had held fifteen minutes longer the Colorado expedition would have come to a disastrous issue; but the breeze died away as suddenly as it had sprung up; the water again became smooth, and in a couple of hours all danger from winds and waves was over; the low banks on the opposite side came in sight, and the broad and hazardous sheet of water narrowed into a moderately sized and shallow stream."

The remainder of the run to Yuma was marked by the usual succession of petty troubles and annoyances incident to navigating the shifting channel of a shallow mud-banked river. The shipping of Robinson as pilot gave them a man with some acquaintance with the lower Colorado, but certainly not of a river experience comparable to that of Captain Johnson. The nine or ten miles a day averaged for the run from the head of tide-water to Yuma indicates a progress so slow as hardly to be entirely accounted for by the low river and the defects of the *Explorer*. Indeed, the little steel stern-wheeler seems to have acquitted herself fairly well at this stage; it was not until they reached the rocky rapids that the timbers bolted to her bottom became an all but prohibitive handicap.

The scientific and technical members of the party joined the *Explorer* at Yuma, where a two-day halt was made to remedy several fresh deficiencies—nature not specified—which had developed in the voyage from the mouth of the river. Word had recently come to the fort to the effect that the Mormons, at that time at the height of their troubles with the Federal Government in Utah, were stirring up the Indians of the Colorado River valleys. A few days previous to the arrival of the *Explorer* the commander of the post had sent "Lieutenant White, with a detachment of men, up the river, with Captain Johnson, to make a reconnaissance and endeavour to ascertain the truth of these reports." There is nothing in this brief entry to reveal the very natural chagrin Ives must have felt on learning that Johnson, with his larger steamer and more experienced crew, was thus skimming the cream of the river exploration ahead of the government expedition.

The day before the departure from Yuma for the beginning of their real work Ives records:

"The river continues to fall. The Indians say they have never seen it so low. We shall be able to test the experiment of navigation at as unfavourable a stage of the water as will probably ever be experienced."

Since one often has to go on foot with a skiff in threading the interminable sand bars off the mouth of the Gila, it was more or less inevitable that the *Explorer* should find herself solidly aground while still but a short distance above the Fort.

IN CATARACT CANYON.

THE CANYON FILLED WITH CLOUDS.

All the men had to tumble overboard to lighten the vessel sufficiently to work her over the bar, and the four hours and a half required to flounder back to the channel made it necessary to camp in sight of their starting point. Ives humorously remarks that "the delay would have been less annoying if it had occurred a little higher up. We were in plain sight of the fort, and knew that this sudden check to our progress was affording an evening of great entertainment to those in and out of the garrison."

Ives' descriptions of the river as the *Explorer* worked up through the rocky reaches of the Chocolate Mountains are remarkably faithful and, despite his sense of the picturesque and spectacular, singularly unexaggerated. The same can hardly be said of the wood-cuts and engravings made from the sketches of Mollhausen and Egloffstein, which, although plainly executed with rare technique, have a tendency to distort the mountains, cliffs, headlands and other natural features out of all semblance to reality. This fault—rather an unfortunate one, it would seem, in sketches intended to illustrate a record of scientific exploration—became more and more pronounced as these two extremely facile German artists succumbed by degrees to the spell of the grotesque and the fantastic inspired by the great upper canyons. The engravings of "Black Canyon" and "Big Canyon at the Mouth of Diamond River," would be less out of place as illustrations for Dante's *Inferno,* or Poe's "ghoul-haunted woodland of Wier," than as plates in "Senate Document, 36th Congress, 1st Session," as the Ives report is officially designated.

Navigation was beset by increasing difficulties as they proceeded, and progress was proportionately retarded. Snags proved an inconvenience rather than a danger, for the steel of the hull was rigid enough to prevent a puncture from such a cause. Captain Robinson is credited with great skill in avoiding trouble, and much resourcefulness in extricating them from that which they did get into. It must have been a steady ding-dong grind from morning till night, for Ives writes:

"The labor attending the crossing of a bar, carrying out the anchors and lines, heaving upon the windlass, handling the boat-poles, and lightening the boat of the cargo by carrying it ashore in the skiffs is by no means small; and to enable the men to undergo it with less fatigue, they are divided into two gangs or watches, which alternately work and rest for a day."

The Indians, far from being unfriendly, seemed to consider the fire-spouting monster that was always getting stuck on the bars as something sent for their especial entertainment. They soon learned to pick the corners where trouble lurked with unerring judgment, and would gather at such places in great numbers, waiting for the steamer to come along and go aground. It was not long before the congregation of a flock of these stormy petrels came to be taken as the definite assurance of the approach to a bad bar, and the Philadelphia engineer, who thought the Colorado "the queerest river" he had ever navigated, would slow down and begin to run cautiously even before the tell-tale riffle appeared.

Like Hardy, Ives seems to have run afoul of the inevitable Indian witch. This one was a Chemehuevis, a tribe that had expressed particular contempt for a mode of locomotion which, in spite of all the noise it made, did not get ahead as fast as they could pole one of their reed rafts. They were a good-hearted lot, however, and compassion soon took the place of ridicule when they saw how hard the pale-faces and their little puffer were taking their repeated failures to surmount a certain troublesome bar. The old hag was one of several who ran down to the bank to tell the Captain how the thing should be done.

"But as we approached the place she indicated his [the Captain's] knowledge of the river showed him it would not do, and he sheered off without making the trial. The benevolence of the old hag was at once converted into rage, and with clenched fists and flaming eyes she followed along the bank, screaming at the captain, as long as he was in hearing, a volley of maledictions."

Under date of January thirty-first, apropos of the difficulties they had encountered in working up through the shoals to the head of the Great Colorado Valley (probably to about the present site of Parker), Ives writes:

". . . the navigation is more difficult than any yet experienced. One bar would scarcely be passed before another would be encountered, and we were three days in accomplishing a distance of nine miles. A boat drawing six inches less water, and without any timbers attached to the bottom, could have probably made the same distance in three hours."

One would be inclined to have more sympathy for Ives in his difficulties if, immediately following the one quoted above, the following passage did not appear:

"The ascent of the river, under the circumstances, promises to be a tedious business; and as our provisions are half consumed, Lieutenant Tipton took advantage of an opportunity afforded a few days ago by our meeting Captain Johnson, with Lieutenant White and party, returning to the fort, and went back with them in order to bring up the pack-train."

It was on January ninth that Ives had made an entry to the effect that Captain Johnson had been sent up the river "a few days ago." As he now states that it was "a few days ago" that Johnson had passed him, going down the river, it would appear that both parties had been travelling upon the Colorado about the same length of time—something like three weeks. But where Ives, averaging much less than ten miles a day, had made under a hundred and fifty miles of the easier part of the river, Johnson, with a boat more than twice as large, had pushed right through to above the head of Black Canyon, and back again. As it was customary at that time to include what we now call Boulder Canyon as a part of Black Canyon, it seems probable that Johnson went all the way to the mouth of the Virgin before turning back. In that case he covered in *both directions* more than twice the length of river Ives had worked up in equivalent time. The navigability of the lower Colorado had been established, but not by the extremely expensive official expedition.

Considering how heavily Ives had backed his own horse—the freak steel steamer, which had cost so much more in time, money and trouble than Johnson's well-tried river boat could have been chartered for—his discomfiture and disappointment must have been very great. Dellenbaugh writes that he has been told that Ives failed to reply to Johnson's salute when they passed, but, as the transfer of Lieutenant Tipton was made on this occasion, it does not seem probable that an officer and gentleman of the stamp the young explorer had proved himself to be would have given quite such drastic expression to his feelings. It would be very interesting to know the truth of the whole affair, both as regards the building of the *Explorer* and its sequel.

However great may have been Ives' disappointment in having the laurels of exploration thus plucked from his brow, his journal continues a keen and spirited recital of a fine adventure. His description of what we now call Bill Williams' Canyon is a striking bit of word-painting, though I am inclined to think he used rather too much paint. I mean to say that the sombre gorge has never struck me as affording quite the wild welter of colours that Ives has laid upon his canvas.

"The regular slopes gradually gave place to rough and confused masses of rock, and the scenery at every instant became wilder and more romantic. New and surprising effects of colouring added to the beauty of the vista. In the foreground, light and delicate tints predominated, and broad surfaces of lilac, pearl color, pink and white contrasted strongly with the sombre masses piled up behind. In their very midst a single pile of vivid blood-red rose in isolated prominence. A few miles higher a narrow gateway opened into the heart of the mountains. On one side of the entrance was a dark red column, on the other a leaning tower of the same colour overhung the pass, the ponderous rock seeming ready to fall as we passed beneath. Rich hues of blue, green and purple, relieved here and there by veins of pink and white, were blended in a brilliant confusion upon the sides of the cañon, producing a weird-like and unearthly effect, which the fantastic shapes and outlines of the enclosing walls did not diminish. For six miles we followed the windings of the river through this fairy-like pass, where every turn varied and heightened the interest of the pageant, and then the lines of cliff stopped, and we issued suddenly from the cañon into a comparatively open valley."

Neither does "fairy-like pass" quite render the atmosphere of that sun-baked gash of riven granite. The description is magnificent—but not Bill Williams.

Bill Williams' Fork, which was a fine thirty-foot stream when Ives was at its mouth in 1853 with the Whipple party, was now but a bare trickle. The Indians assured Ives that the Colorado was as low, proportionately, as its tributary. While this could not have been literally true, the main river must have been extremely low to form such a rapid as Ives encountered just after sighting the peaks of The Needles.

"As we approached the mouth of the cañon through the Mojave mountains, a roaring noise ahead gave notice that we were coming to a rapid, and soon we reached the foot of a pebbly island, along either side of which the water was rushing, enveloped in a sheet of foam."

When I pulled down Mojave Canyon in a skiff last October the Colorado, flowing perhaps 3,500 second-feet, was not far above its low stage for the year. At that time there was only a slight acceleration of current at the point where Ives found the water tumbling over the rocks in a way to beat it into "a sheet of foam." This would indicate a stage of water probably lower than has been recorded since the time accurate measurement of the river was instituted.

The description of the passage of the gorge through the Mojave Mountains is as fine as anything of the kind ever inspired by the incomparably mightier chasms of the Grand Canyon series. Indeed, as transpires in the course of a further reading of his report, Ives, having exhausted the stuff in his heavy artillery lockers upon the rather insignificant gorges of Mojave and Bill Williams, found himself without adequate ammunition when he came up against the real thing at Black Canyon and the still more stupendous Grand. But this Doré-esque vision of Mojave Canyon, like a Whistler nocturne, is worth while for itself alone, however little it suggests the original inspiration.

"A low purple gateway and a splendid corridor, with massive red walls, formed the entrance to the cañon. At the head of this avenue frowning mountains, piled one above the other, seemed to block the way. An abrupt turn at the base of the apparent barrier revealed a cavern-like approach to the profound chasm beyond. A scene of such imposing grandeur as that which now presented itself I have never before witnessed. On either side majestic cliffs, hundreds of feet in height, rose perpendicularly from the water. As the river wound through the narrow enclosure every turn developed some sublime effect or startling novelty in the view. Brilliant tints of purple, green, brown, red and white illuminated the stupendous surfaces and re-lieved their sombre monotony. Far above, clear and distinct upon the narrow strip of sky, turrets, spires, jagged statue-like peaks and gro-tesque pinnacles overlooked the deep abyss.

"The waning day found us still threading the windings of this wonderful defile, and the approach of twilight enhanced the wild romance of the scenery. The bright colors faded and blended into a uniform dark grey. The rocks assumed dim and exaggerated shapes, and seemed to flit like giant spectres in pursuit and retreat along the shadowy vista. A solemn stillness reigned in the darkening avenue, broken only by the splash of the paddles or the cry of a solitary heron, startled by our approach from his perch on the brink of some overhanging cliff."

The expedition, coming out to the beautiful Mojave Valley before the heat had withered the freshness of the vegetation, found in the lush verdure of the river bottoms a welcome relief from "the monotonous sterility of the country below." The Indians were disposed to be friendly if somewhat superior, and became even friendlier after Ives had established touch with two old acquaintances who had served the Whipple expedition. One of these, Ireteba, signed on with him again, rendering most useful service. Although Ives writes of his relations with the Mojaves in rather a humorous vein (speaking, for instance, of one of his formal addresses as unique in that it contained no reference to the "Great Father at Washington"), there is no doubt that he had a real talent for getting on with primitive peoples; more, possibly, than he had for river navigation.

There was little navigational trouble in traversing Mojave Valley, but renewed difficulties began as soon as they came again to the mountains. A rapid in a canyon entered "through a gate, one side of which looked like the head of a bull" (the present-day Bull's Head Rock, reckoned a possible dam-site), gave the *Explorer* some hard knocks, and after traversing Pyramid Canyon shallow riffles were encountered in "quick succession." One, of which he speaks as "a surging and foaming torrent," they managed to work up under steam, with the aid of a line ahead. Another, less violent of flow but more difficult because obstructed by boulders, nearly brought disaster.

"The river was divided into two channels, in neither of which was there more than two feet of water. The shoal extended for some distance and the bottom was covered with rocks. A long line had to be taken ahead in order to reach a place where there was good holding ground. The boat was lightened and, after several hours of hard labour, had been brought to the crest of the rapid, when the line broke and the *Explorer* drifted down, bumping upon the rocks, and was in imminent danger of having her hull stove. The day's work was undone in an instant, and we were very glad it was no worse. When she finally brought up it was upon some rocks, where she was wedged so fast that it occupied half of the next day to extricate her. The remainder of the day was spent in a second and more successful attempt, and at dark we had the satisfaction of seeing our steamer safely anchored above."

Ives' description of the norther which detained them for the next day or two, during which time they "ate, drank, breathed and saw little but sand," will be appreciated by every one who has boated upon that stretch of the Colorado. The reinforcing timbers bothered them even more here than upon the lower river. Besides increasing the draught they became wedged in the rocks, making the boat very difficult to extricate. Bars where a smooth bottom would have allowed them to pass in hours kept holding them up for as many days. "It is probable that there is not one season in ten," laments Ives, "when even the *Explorer* would encounter one-fourth of the difficulty that she has during the present unprecedentedly low stage of water."

From a camp near the head of Cottonwood Valley, under date of March first, Ives makes an entry which reveals inferentially, more than one interesting fact.

"We have now entered a region that has never, as far as any records show, been visited by whites, and are approaching a locality where it is supposed that the famous 'Big Cañon' of the Colorado commences."

This single sentence shows: first, that Ives either did not know about, or was not impressed with the truth of, Pattie's claim to having traversed this region in the twenties; second, that he fully intended to ignore Johnson's assertion that the latter had pushed his steamer through beyond the head of Black Canyon; and third, that there was no definite information at this time as to where the foot of the present Grand Canyon really was. Indeed, it is not certain that Ives' subsequent explorations of this year entirely cleared up the latter point.

The last twenty miles to the mouth of Black Canyon took five days to accomplish, "a dozen or more rapids of all descriptions" being encountered on the way. The young explorer's discouragement over the outlook is reflected in an entry stating that "the lines have become almost worn out by hard service; the skiff is badly battered and scarcely able to float, and all the oars are broken." As far as navigational investigation was concerned Ives seems to have realized that his bolt was sped. Any lingering hopes he may have entertained of pushing on to the Virgin went glimmering at the mouth of Black Canyon. The long-dreaded blow, when it did fall, came with dramatic suddenness. After surmounting the crest of a rapid a hundred yards below the rocky gateway,

". . . the current became slack, the soundings were unusually favorable, and we were shooting swiftly past the entrance, eagerly gazing into the mysterious depths beyond, when the *Explorer*, with a stunning crash, brought up suddenly and instantaneously against a sunken rock. For a second the impression was that the cañon had fallen in. The concussion was so violent that the men near the bow were thrown overboard; the doctor, Mr. Mollhausen and myself, having been seated in front of the upper deck, were precipitated head foremost into the bottom of the boat; the fireman, who was pitching a log into the fire, went half-way with it; the boiler was thrown out of place; the steam-pipe doubled up; the wheel-house torn away; and it was expected that the boat would fill and sink instantly by all but Mr. Carroll, who was looking for an explosion from the injured steam-pipes."

Three days sufficed to repair the injuries to the *Explorer*, but left her withal in such a state that Ives did not care to risk taking her battered hulk into the canyon without a reconnaissance to determine something of what would be encountered in the dark depths above. Ives, Captain Robinson and the mate made up the party that pushed off in the skiff on the morning of March twelfth. One of the sculls was snapped at the end of a quarter of a mile, but a favouring up-canyon wind gave them a substantial lift when a blanket sail was spread. Eight miles up from the mouth Ives christened as Roaring Rapid a slight riffle that occurs at this point, thereby (as the sinister name has been perpetuated upon the maps) contributing not a little to the gaiety of latter-day voyageurs, and especially that of the hard-bitten river-rats drifting down after surviving the savage cataracts of the upper canyon series.

the *Explorer* to fulfil the high hopes he had built upon her had something to do with it; possibly the increasing hardships of pack-train travel over an arid plateau clipped the wings of his Muse; possibly he was simply overwhelmed; at any rate, the word-painter who had responded so brilliantly to the inspiration of the lesser failed to kindle to that of the greater. The mouth of Diamond Creek is dismissed with:

"The cañon was similar in character to others that have been mentioned, but on a larger scale, and thus far unrivalled in grandeur. Mr. Mollhausen has taken a sketch, which gives a better idea of it than any description."

The accompanying steel engraving looks like a picture of the place where

"Alph, the sacred river, ran,
Through caverns measureless to man,
Down to a sunless sea."

With the shrouded figures of Dante and Virgil mooning on a pinnacle above the gloomy depths it would get away unchallenged with some such title as "Source of the River Styx." A wood-cut of a "Precipice Leading to Cataract Cañon" looks as though it had found its inspiration in a statistical graph showing the growth of wheat elevators in North Dakota under the Nonpartisan League. One should be fortified either with blinders or a sense of humour before attacking these altogether amazing pictures of Mollhausen and Egloffstein.

There is a hundred times the kick of Ives' dread Roaring Rapid of Black Canyon in the slap-banging riffle where the Colorado cascades over the half-mile bar of boulders spewed forth from the mouth of Diamond Creek, but the only comment evoked from the explorer was: "The channel was studded with rocks, and the torrent rushed through like a mill-race."

Somewhere beyond Cataract Creek Canyon Ives must have reached the point where the simple Garcés, greatly moved by the stupendous panorama unrolled before him, "halted at the sight of the most profound caxones which ever onward continue." The *padre's* pack-train was in quite as serious straits for water as was that of the young topographer, but the inspiration of the wonderful chasm lifted his spirit above the petty worries of the day. With Ives, strangely, the feeling aroused was almost akin to revulsion. After stating that "an excellent view was had of the Big Cañon," and referring to "a sketch made on the spot by Mr. Egloffstein" as doing "better justice than any description can do to the marvellous scene," he writes:

"The region last explored is, of course, altogether valueless. It can be approached only from the south, and after entering it there is nothing to do but leave. Ours has been the first, and will doubtless be the last, party of whites to visit this profitless locality. It seems intended by nature that the Colorado river, along the greater portion of its lone and majestic way, shall be forever unvisited and undisturbed."

This statement is as far wrong in stating that those of the Ives party were the first whites to visit the Grand Canyon as in voicing the belief that they would be the last. Ives was quite at the worst when he flung the mantle of Jeremiah over his energetic young shoulders. His prophecy as to the unnavigability of Black Canyon was confuted before he made it; that to the effect that the canyon region would be forever unvisited and undisturbed is still in active process of confutation. Respecting the extent of this cumulative confutation the National Park Service and the Reclamation Service are publishing pertinent figures every year.

After crossing the Little Colorado to the Moqui towns, Ives made a vain attempt to reach the Colorado again in the region of Marble Canyon. Failing through lack of proper guidance, he turned back and pressed on to Fort Defiance, where his party disbanded. Returning to Yuma by stage from Santa Fé, he disposed of the *Explorer* to the "transportation company at

the fort," continued to San Francisco, and took steamer for
New York. The date of his report is 1861, which makes it
very probable that it did not appear until after the first gun
was fired at Sumter. In that event it may well have been that
he never held in his hand the finely printed volume which contains the record of his explorations. Throwing in his lot with
the Confederacy, he was killed in action during the Civil War.

Save for the fiasco of the *Explorer* (for which Ives may not
have been responsible), the Colorado expedition of 1857-1858
was a notable success. The comprehensive scientific observations were a distinct contribution to the knowledge of a hitherto
superficially explored region, while Ives' delightfully-told story
of the day-to-day doings of his party set a mark for descriptive
writing that has rarely been equalled in a Government report.
Powell shot somewhere near it in the report of his first Colorado
River expedition, but with all of his brilliant flair for description the distinguished Grand Canyon voyageur wielded a pen
far less facile than that of the gallant young southern explorer.
Ives' untimely death was a real loss to both science and
literature.

CHAPTER VIII

THE RAFT VOYAGE OF JAMES WHITE

WHAT has always been the most bitterly-mooted question in Colorado River history centred about a voyage by raft claimed to have been made by a certain James White in 1867. For fifty years opinion was divided as to whether this adventurous prospector accomplished a remarkable feat of navigation or a scarcely less remarkable feat of fabrication. It is but recently that demonstration has been made that he fell as far short of the navigational achievement as he did of fabricational intent. As there still remains much that is neither definitely proven nor disproven on both sides of the controversy, however, I am including an account and discussion of an admittedly apocryphal voyage in a record otherwise made up of travels and explorations that have—subject to the inevitable misstatements in, and misinterpretations of, original versions—become accepted history.

White's story may be likened to a bridge of doubtful strength, of which two abutments of established facts are united by a span of unestablished claims. The facts are: that James White was prospecting on the upper San Juan River in the summer of 1867—and that James White reached Callville, floating on a raft, September eighth of the same year. The claims are that White built a raft somewhere on the upper Colorado, near the mouth of the San Juan, and drifted on it down Glen, Marble and Grand canyons to the little Mormon settlement below the mouth of the Virgin. Practically all of those having intimate first-hand knowledge of the middle Colorado canyon series,

171

while freely admitting the strength of the abutting facts, hold that they are not sufficient to support the flimsy structure of the spanning claims; that the claims, in short, will not bear inspection any more than the rapids of the Grand Canyon will bear a man on a raft—and deliver both intact at the other end, that is. That the overwhelming weight of the real evidence is unfavourable to the acceptance of the White story a brief review of the facts will make plain.

White was in his thirtieth year at the time he drifted down to Callville on his raft. Born in New York and reared in Wisconsin, he had gone West when he was twenty-three and divided the next seven years of his life between serving an enlistment in the regular army and working in various capacities. He was described by those who met him at the time (as by those who have known him since) as a plain, manly, straightforward, unimaginative sort of a chap—quite the last type of man, in fact, to tell the blood-and-thunder version of his adventure subsequently attributed to him. Indeed, it appears that White never did detail the several wild and highly sensational accounts that were published describing his voyage, but that these lurid screeds were the result of the expansion and fictionization of his simple unvarnished recital of the facts as he believed them to be. The process was somewhat similar to that by which the narrative of James Pattie's remarkable wanderings was inflated with sensational absurdities in the editing until it became all but worthless as a historical document. The plain, blunt prospector-voyageur, however, appears far clearer of suspicion of having been an accessory-before-the-fact than was the highly egotistical trapper. There is little to indicate that White sponsored any of these more sensational accounts even at the time they were written; since then he has flatly repudiated much of the worst of them.

If White's claims were based on nothing more tangible than these blood-and-thunder thrillers (very brief extracts from one of which will be quoted later to show their character) they

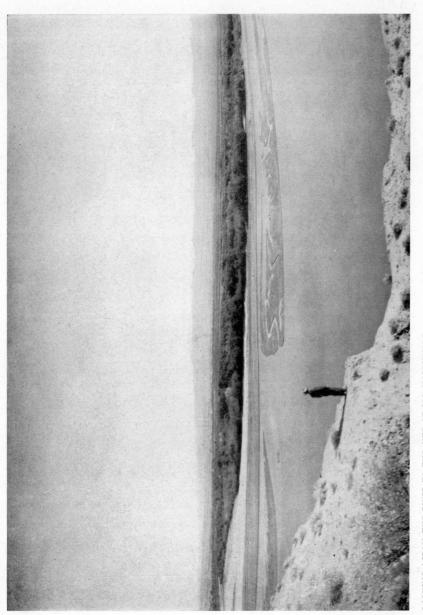

LOOKING ACROSS THE RIVER TO THE SITE OF OLD HARDYVILLE.

It was here that James White told the story of his raft voyage to Dr. Parry.

IN THE GRAND CANYON.

would not be worth the considerable amount of good white paper that has been blackened in the discussion of them. Indeed, much of the severest personal criticism of the man is directly traceable to the absurd exaggerations contained in versions of his story for which he was in no wise responsible. Fortunately, however, he had one highly intelligent, serious-minded chronicler, who realized his responsibility to the extent of setting down as faithfully as he could both the story of the rescued prospector and his own deductions therefrom. This was Dr. C. C. Parry, an eminent engineer and scientist who was attached to the Union Pacific survey party working along the thirty-second and thirty-fifth parallels in 1867. His report, made in duplicate to General William J. Palmer, head of the Survey, and to J. D. Perry, president of the eastern division of the Union Pacific, and subsequently published in the Transactions of the St. Louis Academy of Science, is the most impressive documentary evidence adducable in support of White's claims. If it falls far short of proving that the latter made a raft voyage through the Grand Canyon, it at least convinces one that Dr. Parry honestly believed that such a voyage was made by the man; moreover, it paves the way for one to believe (as any fair-minded person ultimately must if he goes far enough into the facts) that White himself honestly thought —as he still does—that he made such a voyage.

Before setting down the salient passages from Dr. Parry's carefully compiled report I shall quote in full a letter written by White very shortly after his arrival at Callville. In revealing both his lack of education and direct simplicity of thought and expression, as well as the modesty of his original claims, it is perhaps the one most illuminative document bearing on the subject. With a photograph of the original, it was first published in the April, 1907, number of *Outing*. The parenthetical completions and elucidations of misspelled words were doubtless added by the editor to preserve a sense that was otherwise liable to become obscure in places.

"Navigation of the Big Cañon.
"A terrible voyage.
"Callville, September 26—1867.

"Dear Brother it has ben some time since i have heard from you. i got no ans. from the last letter that i roat to you for i left soon after i rote. i Went prospected With Captin Baker and Gorge Strole in the San Won montin. Wee fond very god prospects but noth[ing] that wold pay. then wee stort Down the San Won river. We travle[ed] down about 200 miles, then Wee crossed over on Colorado, and Camp[ed]. Wee lad over one day. Wee found out that Wee cold not travel down the river and our horse Wass sore fite, and Wee had may up our mines to turne back When Wee was attacked by 15 or 20 Utes Indi[an]s. They kill[ed] Baker, and Gorge Strole and myself took fore ropes off our hourse and a ax, ten pounds of flour and our gunns. Wee had 15 millse to Work to [the] Colorado. Wee got to the river Jest at night. Wee bilt a raft that night. Wee had good Sailing for three days and the fore day Gorge Strole Was Wash[ed] of from the raft and down and that left me alone. i thought that it wold be my turne next. i then pouled off my boos and pands. i then tide a rope to my Wase i Went over folls from 10 to 15 feet hie. my raft wold tip over three and fore time a day. the thurd day we loss our flour and fore seven days i had noth[ing] to eat to [except] raw-hide knife cover. The 8 days I got some musquit beens. the 13 days [I met] a party of frendey indes. thay Wold not give me noth[ing] eat so i give [them] my pistols for hine pards of a dog. i ead one of [them] for super and the other [for] breakfast. the 16 days i arriv[ed] at Callville Whare i Was tak[en] Care of by James Ferry. i Was ten days Wih out pants or boos or hat. i Was soon [sun] bornt so i cold hadly Wolk. the ingins tok 7 heed [of] horse from us. i wish i can rite you halfe i under Went. i see the hardes time that eny man ever did in the World but thank god that I got thrught saft. am Well a gin and i hope the few lines Will fine you all Well i send my best respeck to all. Josh anser this When you get it. Dreck your letter to Callville Arizona.

"Josh ass Tom to ancy that letter that i rote him sevel yeas agoe.
"JAMES WHITE."

This letter was written less than three weeks after he reached Callville and probably two or three months before he talked with the members of the Union Pacific survey party at Hardyville, farther down the river. The outstanding impressions in his mind appear to have had to do with the hardships he had undergone (and perhaps the loss of his pack-horses, to which he recurs), rather than with the contemplation of the performance of a remarkable feat of navigation. That this aspect of his adventure was already being brought home to him, however, is clearly evidenced by the flamboyant yellow-journal headings added to the otherwise simple brotherly letter. These are plainly in the same hand-writing as the letter, but the correct spelling of the comparatively long words (where White had been repeatedly floundering over those of three and four letters) proves that the orthography, if not the inspiration of the queer idea, came from another person. People were beginning to assure the still dazed prospector that his voyage was a real head-liner, and of the almost child-like simplicity of his character what better evidence could be asked than his naïve action in scribbling those imitation newspaper headings on the letter to his brother?

No one knew enough about the Grand Canyon at that time to understand that what White claimed to have done (or rather, what it was assumed from his story that he must have done) was all but a sheer impossibility. Dr. Parry had read the Ives report, but nothing that either that explorer, or his geologist, Dr. Newberry, wrote of their glimpses of the Grand Canyon gave a hint of the nature of the river at any point save at the mouth of Diamond Creek. And from Ives' descriptions, both of which I have quoted,[1] one would be justified in believing that the Diamond Creek rapid was far less formidable than the really all but negligible little riffle in Black Canyon to which he had applied the name of Roaring Rapids, and with which every one in the vicinity of Hardyville and Callville was familiar.

This being so, no one—not even the distinguished scientist of the railroad survey—had any background of facts against

[1] See pp. 166 and 168.

which to test the validity of White's assertions. Not unnaturally, therefore, Dr. Parry, taking it for granted at the outset
that White had really come through the big Colorado canyon,
took advantage of the opportunity to gain all the information
possible concerning the hitherto blank space of *terra incognita*
assumed to have been traversed by the voyageur. The latter,
as may be judged from the letter to his brother, can have volunteered very little on his own initiative, so that Dr. Parry, as
he makes plain in his report, was forced to draw out his man
by questions. As White did not know the names of more than
two or three of the main natural features of the country through
which he had come, the questioner had to supply these,
where he could, from his own knowledge. In a sense, therefore, the narrator probably learned almost as much as he im-
parted. Undoubtedly it was the Union Pacific engineers, with
their avid interest and anxiously consulted maps, who first
thoroughly impressed White with the really astonishing nature
of his supposed achievement.

There is some difference of opinion as to just which of the
Union Pacific party besides Parry was present at the interview
with White. The point is not one of great importance, however, as the only other story that claims this meeting as its
inspiration is a sensationally fictionized yarn by Major A. R.
Calhoun which is among those I had in mind in alluding to
certain versions of White's adventure that had done more to
discredit than to strengthen his claims.

The introductory paragraphs of Dr. Parry's report tell how,
in spite of the fact that the exploration of the rest of the West
was almost complete, the Grand Canyon had remained practically a myth.

". . . its actual length, the character of its stream, the nature of
its banks, and the depth of its vertical walls were subjects for speculation, and afforded a fine field for exaggerated description, in which
natural bridges, cavernous tunnels, and fearful cataracts formed a
prominent feature.

"Now, at last [he continues], we have a perfectly authentic account from an individual who actually traversed its formidable depths, and who, fortunately for science, still lives to detail his trustworthy observations of this most remarkable voyage."

He then goes on to tell how, meeting White at Hardyville, he drew from him the connected statement appended "in answer to direct questions noted down at the time." The first part of the narrative that follows is devoted to tracing in some detail what Parry believed were the movements of the prospecting party up to the time it was attacked by Indians near a river he assumed was the Grand. Because the narrative from that point on constitutes the only sane and temperate early account of White's voyage I am setting it down in full.

"They camped at the bottom of this ravine on the night of the twenty-third of August, and on the morning of the twenty-fourth started to ascend the right bank to the table-land. In making this ascent they were attacked by Indians, and Captain Baker, being in advance, was killed at the first fire. The two remaining men, James White and Henry Stroll, after ascertaining the fate of their comrade, fought their way back into the cañon, and, getting beyond the reach of the Indians, hastily unpacked their animals, securing their arms and a small supply of provisions, and proceeded on foot down to the banks of the Grand river. Here they constructed a raft of dry cottonwood, composed of three sticks ten feet in length and eight inches in diameter, securely tied together by lariat ropes, and, having stored away their arms and provisions, they embarked at midnight on their adventurous voyage.

"The following morning, being the twenty-fifth of August, they made a landing, repaired their raft by some additional pieces of dry cedar, and continued on their course. The river here was about 200 yards wide, flowing regularly at the rate of two and a half or three miles per hour. According to their estimate, they reached the mouth of Green river and entered the main Colorado thirty miles from the point of starting. Below the junction the stream narrows and is confined between perpendicular walls, gradually increasing in elevation. At an estimated distance of forty miles from the mouth of Green river they passed the mouth of the San Juan, both streams being here hemmed in by perpendicular walls. From this point the cañon was continued, with only occasional breaks formed by small side cañons equally inaccessible with the main chasm. Still they experienced no difficulty in continuing their voyage and were elated with the prospects of soon reaching the settlements on the Colorado below the Grand Cañon.

"On the twenty-eighth, being the fourth day of their journey, they encountered the first severe rapids, in passing one of which Henry Stroll was washed off and sank in a whirlpool below. The small stock of provisions was also lost, and when White emerged from the foaming rapids he found himself alone, without food, and with gloomy prospects before him of continuing his adventurous journey. His course now led through the sullen depths of the Great Cañon, which was a succession of fearful rapids, blocked up with masses of rock, over which his frail raft thumped and whirled, so that he had to adopt the precaution of tying himself fast to the rocking timbers. In passing one of these rapids his raft parted and he was forced to hold onto the fragments by main strength until he effected a landing below in a shallow eddy where he succeeded, standing waist-deep in water, in making necessary repairs, and started again. One can hardly imagine the gloomy feelings of this lone traveller, with no human voice to cheer his solitude, hungry, yet hopeful and resolute, closed in on every side by the beetling cliffs that shut out sunlight for the greater part of the long summer day, drenched to the skin, sweeping down the resistless current, shooting over foaming rapids, and whirling below in tumultuous whirlpools, ignorant of what fearful cataracts might yet be on his unswerving track, down which he must plunge to almost certain destruction; still, day after day, buoyed up with the hope of finally emerging from his prison walls and feasting his eyes on open country with shaded groves, green fields, and human habitations.

"The mouth of the Colorado Chiquito was passed on the fourth day in the evening, the general appearance of which was particularly noted, as he was here entangled in an eddy for two hours, until rescued, as he says, 'by the direct intervention of Providence.' The general course of the river was noted as very crooked, with numerous sharp turns, the river on every side being shut in by precipitous walls of 'white sand rock.' These walls present a smooth, perpendicular, and occasionally overhanging surface, extending upwards to a variable height and showing a distinct line of high-water mark thirty or forty feet above the then water level.

"His estimate of the average height of the cañon was 3,000 feet, the upper edge of which flared out about half way from the bottom, thus presenting a rugged crest. The last two days in the cañon dark-coloured igneous rocks took the place of the white 'sandstone,' which finally showed distinct breaks on either side, till he reached a more open country, containing small patches of bottom land and inhabited by bands of Indians. Here he succeeded in procuring a scanty supply of mesquite bread, barely sufficient to sustain life until he reached Callville on the eighth of September, just fourteen days from the time of starting, during seven of which he had no food of any description.

"When finally rescued this man presented a pitiable object, ema-ciated and haggard from abstinence, his bare feet literally flayed by constant exposure to drenching water, aggravated by occasional scorchings of a vertical sun; his mental faculties, though still sound, liable to wander and verging close on the brink of insanity. Being, however, of a naturally strong constitution, he soon recovered his usual health and is now a stout, hearty, thick-set man. His narrative throughout bears all the evidence of entire reliability and is sustained by collateral evidence, so that there is not the least reason to doubt that he actually accomplished the journey in the manner and in the time mentioned by him."

This ends the narrative proper, but under the heading of "Conclusions," Dr. Parry adds that

"The following may be summed up as some of the new facts to be derived from this remarkable voyage as additions to our present geo-graphical knowledge of the hydrography of the Colorado river:

"First. The actual location of the mouth of the San Juan, forty miles below Green river junction, and its entrance continuous with that of the Colorado.

"Second. From the mouth of the San Juan to the Colorado Chiquito, three days' travel in the swiftest portion of the current, allowing four miles per hour for fifteen hours, or sixty miles per day, would give an estimated distance of 180 miles, including the most inaccessible portion of the Great Cañon.

"Third. From Colorado Chiquito to Callville ten days' travel was expended. As this portion of the route was more open and probably comprised long stretches of still water, it would not be safe to allow a distance of more than thirty miles per day, or 300 miles for this interval. Thus the whole distance travelled would amount to 550 miles, or something over 500 miles from Grand river junction to head of steamboat navigation at Callville.

"Fourth. The absence of any distinct cataract or perpendicular falls would seem to warrant the conclusion that in time of high water, by proper appliances in the way of boats, good, resolute oarsmen, and provisions secured in waterproof bags the same passage might be safely made and the actual course of the river, with its peculiar geological features, properly determined.

"Fifth. The construction of bridges by a single span would be rendered difficult of execution on account of the usual flaring shape of the upper summits; possibly, however, points might be found where the high mesas come near together.

"Sixth. The estimated average elevation of the cañon at 3,000 feet is less than that given on the authority of Ives and Newberry, but may be nearer the actual truth as the result of more continuous observation.

"Seventh. The width of the river at its narrowest points was estimated at a hundred feet and the line of high-water mark thirty to forty feet above the average stage in August.

"Eighth. The long-continued uniformity of the geological formation termed 'white sandstone' [probably Cretaceous], is remarkable, but under this term may have been comprised some of the lower stratified formations. The contrast on reaching the dark igneous rocks was so marked that it could not fail to be noticed.

"Ninth. Any prospect for useful navigation up and down the cañon during the season of high water, or transportation of lumber from the upper pine regions of Green or Grand rivers, could not be regarded as feasible, considering the long distance and the inaccessible character of the river margins for the greater part of its course.

"Tenth. No other satisfactory method of exploration, except along the course of the river, could be adopted to determine its actual course and peculiar natural features, and James White, as the pioneer of this enterprise, will probably retain the honour of being the only man who has traversed through its whole course the Great Cañon of the Colorado and lived to recount his observations on this perilous voyage."

This statement of Dr. Parry is the one contemporary account of White's adventure that is of any real value in forming a conclusion as to what part of the Colorado was traversed by the prospector's raft. If, in the minds of those having most intimate knowledge of the river section in question, this document constitutes an all but absolute proof that the raft did *not* pass through any portions of the middle canyon series, it is the fault of neither Dr. Parry nor of White. Each appears to have told the truth to the very best of his ability—the scientist as to what he heard, the voyageur as to what he believed he saw.

The other early versions of the White voyage are so palpably fictionized as to be quite worthless as evidence of anything but the facile imaginations of their authors. A few excerpts from one of them will make plain why they all may be dismissed without serious consideration—save for the feeling of nausea that is the inevitable aftermath of dipping into their lurid pages. The most widely read of these thrillers was a story written by Major A. R. Calhoun and published in a book called "Wonderful Adventures," brought out by Evans of Philadelphia, and subsequently, with but slight changes, included in Bell's "New Tracks in North America." Calhoun claimed specifically to have been present at the Parry interview with White and to have thus obtained his material at first hand. As Dr. Bell states that the story was prepared by Calhoun from Parry's notes, it would appear that the journalistic Major gave his imagination a sort of preliminary canter by way of warming up for the real race. Now watch him lengthen out as he eases into the running. The hardships of the prospecting trip had greatly discouraged White and Stroll.

". . . But Baker, who was a brave, sanguine fellow, spoke of placers up the river, about which he had heard, and promised his companions that all their hopes should be realized and that they should return to their homes to enjoy their gains and to laugh at the trials of the trip. So glowingly did he picture the future that his companions even speculated as to how they should spend their princely fortunes when they returned to the 'States.' Baker sang songs of home and hope, and the others lent their voices to the chorus till far in the night, when, unguarded, they sank to sleep to dream of coming opulence and to rise refreshed for the morrow's journey."

To one who knows his Drury Lane melodrama, or even his Wild West movies, the wail of chills-and-fever music from the violins means that some one of the higher-ups of the cast is about to be exposed to serious physical or moral dangers. Following similar methods Calhoun, with those "songs of home and hope," was creating atmosphere for the Indian attack. And, so, climbing back to the mesa the next morning,

". . . the war whoop of a band of savages rang out, sounding as if every rock had a demon's voice. Simultaneously with the first whoop a shower of arrows and bullets was poured into the little party. With the first fire Baker fell against a rock; but, rallying for a moment, he unslung his rifle and fired at the Indians, who began to show themselves in large numbers, and then, with blood flowing from his mouth, he fell to the ground. White, firing at the Indians as he advanced, and followed by Stroll, hurried to the aid of his wounded leader. Baker with an effort turned to his comrades and in a voice still strong said: 'Back, boys; back; save yourselves; I am dying.' To the credit of White and Stroll be it said that they faced the savages and fought till the last tremor of the powerful frame told that the gallant Baker was dead."

Constructing a raft in the depths of the gloomy gorge, they waited, of course, for the witching hour when all of the more deeply mysterious movement of melodrama is set in motion at the click of the relentless inner wheels. But first the fluttering blue-green light, also turned on at the walking of the Ghost.

"They did not consider that even the sun looked down into that chasm for but one short hour out of the twenty-four, leaving it for the rest of the day to the angry waters and blackening shadows, and that the faint moonlight reaching the bottom of the cañon would hardly serve to reveal the horror of their situation. Midnight came, according to their calculation of the dark, dreary hours, and then, seizing the poles, they untied the rope that held the raft, which, tossed about by the current, rushed through the yawning cañon on the adventurous voyage to an unknown landing. Through the long night they clung to the raft as it dashed against half-concealed rocks or whirled about like a plaything in some eddy, whose white foam was perceptible even in the intense darkness.

"They prayed for daylight, which came at last. . . ."

This hastening the Phantom of False Morning by the use of prayer might have suggested to the author the employment of the same expedient when the deep roar of a waterfall was heard ahead. Perhaps, in his case as in that of his hero,

". . . there was no time to think. The logs strained as if they would break their fastenings. The waves dashed around the men, and the raft was buried in the seething waters. White clung to the logs with the grip of death. His comrade stood up for an instant with the pole in his hands as if to guide the raft from the rocks against which it was plunging; but he scarcely straightened himself before the raft seemed to leap down a chasm, and amid horrible sounds White heard a shriek that thrilled him. Turning his head, he saw through the mist and spray the form of his comrade tossed for an instant on the water, then sinking out of sight in the whirlpool."

When the belated prayer-cue did come to the hero the raft must have been back on an even keel, for he seems to have been able to let go his "grip-of-death" for the appropriate gestures. It was only when the roar of the rapid had died down that he dared to look up.

"Then it was to find himself alone [as he must have suspected, however, even before he looked up], the provisions lost, and the shadows of the black cañon warning him of the approaching night. A feeling of despair seized him, and, clasping his hands, he prayed for the death he was fleeing from."

Then a landing "near some flat rocks" and—"Hero's Soliloquy."

"He blamed himself for not having fought the Indians till he had fallen by the side of Baker. He might have escaped through the San Juan valley and the mountains beyond to the settlements. Had he done so he would have returned to his home and rested satisfied with his experience as a prospector. But when he thought of home it called up the strongest inducements for life and he resolved 'to die hard and like a man.' " [Just why renewed inducements to life should prompt a man to resolve to die hard not stated.]

It was while describing how the raft was caught in and ejected from the maw of a giant whirlpool below the mouth of the Colorado Chiquito that White, according to the author, "showed the only sign of emotion exhibited during his long narrative. Red calcium for this one, and "The Maiden's Prayer" on the strings and wood-winds!

"White now felt that all further exertions were useless, and, dropping his paddle, he clasped his hands and fell upon the raft. He heard the gurgling waters around him, and every moment he felt that he must be plunged into the boiling vortex. He waited, he thinks, for some minutes, when, feeling a strange, swimming sensation, he looked up to find that he was circling round the whirlpool, sometimes close to the vortex and again thrown back by some invisible cause to the outer edge, only to whirl again to the centre.

"Thus borne by the circling waters, he looked up, up, up through the mighty chasm that seemed bending over him as if about to fall in. He saw in the blue belt of sky that hung above him like an ethereal river the red-tinged clouds floating, and he knew the sun was setting in the upper world. Still around the whirlpool the raft swung like a circular pendulum, measuring the long moments before expected death. He felt a dizzy sensation and thinks he must have fainted; he knows he must have been unconscious for a time, for, when again he looked up the walls, whose ragged summits towered 3,000 feet above him, the red clouds had changed to black, and the heavy shadows of night had crept down the cañon.

"Then, for the first time, he remembered that there was a Strength greater than that of man, a Power that 'holds the ocean in the hollow of His Hand.' 'I fell on my knees,' he said, 'and as the raft swept round in the current I asked God to aid me. I spoke as if from my very soul and said, "O God, if there is a way out of this fearful place guide me to it." '

"Here White's voice became husky as he narrated the circumstances, and his somewhat heavy features quivered as he related that he presently felt a different movement in the raft, and, turning to look at the whirlpool, saw it was some distance behind, and that he was floating down the smoothest current he had yet seen in the cañon."

The rapids were quieted for good by that appeal, although, unfortunately, only temporarily; two years later Powell, as have all others who came after him, found the very worst of all the falls below the Little Colorado.

With no more thrills to be had from the river, the author now gives the Demon of Starvation his cue. Pea-green spotlight for this, with the tolling of a deep-toned bell—regular Monte-Cristo-in-the-Dungeon effect. Air, "Sailor, Beware!"

"One, two, three, four days had passed since he tasted food, and still the current bore him through the towering walls of the cañon. Hunger maddened him. His thoughts were of food, food, food; and his sleeping moments were filled with Tantalus-like dreams. Once he raised his arm to open some vein and draw nutriment from his blood, but its shrivelled, blistered condition frightened him. For hours as he floated down he sat looking at the water, yet lacking the courage to make the contemplated plunge that would rid him of all earthly pain."

And then the Indians, among whom was a "fiend that pulled him up the bank and tore from his blistered shoulders the shreds that had once been a shirt." A few days more of agony brought Callville and—thank heaven!—Curtain.

This sort of a screed may have a place somewhere in the universe, but wherever that place is it most certainly is not among evidence collected to establish the actuality of any averred happening in air, earth or water. And yet this utterly silly mess of drivel was actually included in a document published a few years ago in an attempt to prove that James White was the first man to traverse the Grand Canyon.[1] Not that the general run of matter that finds its way into Senate docu-

---

[1] Senate Document No. 42, 65th Congress, 1st Session: "An article giving the credit of first traversing the Grand Canyon of the Colorado to James White, a Colorado gold prospector, who it is claimed made the voyage two years previous to the expedition under the direction of Maj. J. W. Powell in 1869," by Thomas F. Dawson.

ments is much more edifying than this particular effusion. Not at all; rather to the contrary, if anything. But what struck me as being rather absurd was that any one could believe that this kind of stuff, far from bolstering up White's always precarious story, would not do it irreparable harm—as anything but scenario material, I mean.

Another lengthy version of the White voyage was published in the January 8, 1869, number of the *Rocky Mountain Herald* of Denver. The writer is unknown, but as he strove to outsoar even Calhoun in wild flights of fancy it will not profit to record the harrowing details here. There is a brief story of the voyage in A. B. Richardson's "Beyond the Mississippi," 1869 Edition. This is not only one of the most delightful, but also one of the most reliable, volumes of Western travel. As its keen and witty author did not encounter White personally, however, his story was merely a summarization of what had already been published. That Richardson, while forbearing himself, was fully alive to the fictional possibilities latent in the spectacular adventure, is evidenced by his closing passage.

"What a romance his adventures would make! Let Charles Reade or Victor Hugo take James White for a hero, and give us a new novel to hold children from play and old men from the chimney corner. But let the novelist for once pity and spare us, and not transform poor White into a walking cyclopedia of all knowledge, recorded and unrecorded, natural and supernatural, like Faria in 'The Count of Monte Cristo,' or Gilliat in 'The Toilers of the Sea,' or Robert Penfold in 'Foul Play.'"

For a year or two, because there was no one with sufficient first-hand knowledge adequately to weigh White's descriptions, Parry's perfectly sincere conclusion that the man had actually traversed the Grand Canyon went unquestioned. The first news of the completion of Powell's voyage was considered rather as confirming than condemning the prospector's story. Much was made in the press of the desertion of three of Powell's party at a dangerous fall that has since come to be known as Separation Rapid. Ignorant of or ignoring the fact that this rapid occurred in the part of the canyon where White had claimed there was smooth going, those interested identified it with the terrible fall where Stroll was lost. That the deserting trio of Powell's boatmen had preferred to face death in the desert rather than risk their lives in running so savage a cataract only served to magnify the wonder of White's lone-handed achievement.

Then came the belated publication of Powell's report, giving facts and figures to prove that there were some hundreds of falls and riffles in the stretch White claimed he had traversed, many of them quite as terrible as the much-talked-about Separation Rapid. This seemed to discredit the story of the raft-voyage so thoroughly as to bring a strong revulsion of feeling toward the man responsible for it. From being a hero, White was hailed as a mischievous liar, and some even went so far as to charge that he had murdered his prospecting companions and invented the story of the canyon voyage to account for it. When later voyageurs brought cumulative testimony as to the almost diametric variance of the canyons White described from the actual Grand Canyon series the feeling that the man had practised a deliberate deception seemed confirmed. The following passage from Dellenbaugh's "Romance of the Colorado River" is probably an accurate epitomization of the best informed opinion of White and his claims three and a half decades after he landed from his raft at Old Callville:

"We have seen various actors passing before us in this drama, but I doubt if any of them have been more picturesque than this champion prevaricator. But he had related a splendid yarn. What it was intended to obscure would probably be quite as interesting as what he told. Just where he entered the river is of course impossible to decide, but that he never came through the Grand Canyon is as certain as anything can be. His story reveals an absolute ignorance of the river and its walls throughout its whole course he pretended to have traversed."

Mr. Dellenbaugh, according to a footnote, formed his opinion of White and his claims from what he believed to be Parry's personal account of the interview with the raft-voyageur, as published in William A. Bell's "New Tracks in North America." As I have already mentioned, however, the story in Bell's book was really written by the fanciful-minded Major Calhoun, and was, in fact, practically identical with the lurid yarn from "Wonderful Adventures," some of the most *recherché* tid-bits from which I have quoted. Considering this, one must admit that the distinguished Colorado River historian expressed himself with admirable restraint. I am inclined to believe, however, that a reading of Dr. Parry's own statement would have resulted in a somewhat less drastic personal criticism of White, though it would certainly not have altered by a hair this essentially fair-minded writer's views respecting the authenticity of the raft voyage through the Grand Canyon.

Meanwhile James White, with a contempt of notoriety beyond all praise, went quietly and unobtrusively ahead earning a living. After working awhile in the West, he revisited his old home in Wisconsin and finally settled down in Trinidad, Colorado. There, working industriously in various ways but mostly as an expressman, he has continued to live to this day, a thoroughly respected member of the community. His fellow townsmen, impressed with his transparent simplicity and honesty, accepted the story of the raft voyage as a matter of course, not because any of them really knew anything at all about the Grand Canyon, but because it was inconceivable to them that a man of White's type and character either could or would invent such an adventure. As for White himself, he was content to consider the voyage as a more or less closed incident of his adventurous past. He told the story with reluctance, and, unless under repeated questionings, very little more than the plain, blunt recital that had so impressed Dr.

CLOUD SHADOWS FROM HOPI POINT.

PLATE IX

Parry. So far as I have ever heard, neither earlier nor later did he ever lift his hand, or even his voice, to capitalize his amazing adventure. This is perhaps the one surest touchstone of the fine, simple character of the man.

It was doubtless some hint of the reputation for honesty and straightforwardness that White had won among his fellow-townsmen that led Robert Brewster Stanton to deem it worth while to visit him in Trinidad in 1907. Stanton, who had voyaged through the Colorado canyons in 1889-90, had subsequently commenced the collection of material for a monumental work on the exploration of the river from the standpoint of an engineer, and in connection with this was going to great trouble in collecting material bearing on the White adventure. Realizing the impossibility of fitting the latter's descriptions to the Grand Canyon as he himself had seen it, Stanton sought a personal interview with the one-time prospector in the hope of finding some more charitable clue to the discrepancies than that advanced by those who called the man an out-and-out liar, if nothing worse. The engineer-historian was accompanied to Trinidad by a stenographer.

White was a hale and vigorous man of seventy at the time, quite clear in his mind and quite untroubled with the tendency to lapses of memory increasingly in evidence in later years. He assured Stanton that he had never looked at a map of the Colorado in all the forty years that had elapsed since his adventure, nor read any account of it save the one in General Palmer's report—Dr. Parry's. With his mind quite unconfused by outside impressions, he told his visitor a story almost identical with that related to the Union Pacific engineers in Hardyville. With an almost Nirvanic placidity and detachment he had allowed the results of two score years of exploration of the region which he claimed to have been the first to traverse to pass him by. Not a whit was he moved when Stanton tried to describe the scores of big rapids that thundered where he had found but one. His invariable answer was, as his visitor put it: " 'Where I went,' or 'Where I was in the canyon,' this and that were thus and so."

The engineer's intimate and intricate questionings, with the answers thereto, were taken down verbatim by the stenographer in shorthand. Assuring the rugged old chap and his family that, while he was no more convinced than before that the raft voyage through the Grand Canyon had actually been made he would miss no opportunity to express himself in praise of White's honesty and good intentions, Stanton took his leave. Carefully worked over and collated with his other material on the subject, the record of this interview was incorporated in the chapters—more than two hundred pages in all—devoted to the White adventure in the manuscript of the engineer's Colorado River book. Beyond all doubt it constitutes the fairest, completest and most intelligent study and discussion of the question that has ever been, or ever will be written.

Stanton's exhaustive two-volume work had not (nor has it to this day, I regret to say) found a publisher when, in 1917, the Dawson document already alluded to was published by the Government Printing Office. Of the facts leading up to the publication of this ably written paper I have never learned. It conveys to me the impression, however, of having been done in a really fine spirit of disinterest by Mr. Dawson—rather a *rara avis* to be hatched so near to the roosts of Capitol Hill. Although the very considerable correspondence carried on indicates that the material was in process of assembling for some months previous, the title page of the document bears the announcement that it was presented to the Senate by Mr. Shafroth May 25, 1917. Just how this august body, which by that time must have heard that the country was trying to participate in the European war, justified itself for taking the time to reopen this already fully discredited tale of far-away and long-ago it would be interesting to know.

That Dawson really believed that White had traversed the

Grand Canyon is perhaps the best evidence that he had little personal knowledge of the middle Colorado canyon series and less of the limitations of rough-water navigation. This is fully borne out by the character of the testimony he introduced under the impression that it was corroborative evidence. In all of the sixty-seven pages of the document there is included nothing (save a later statement from White which I shall touch upon presently) to throw new light on the subject with which it deals, while it does include things—like the blood-and-thunder Calhoun story—calculated to weaken still further an already precarious case. Dawson also goes to considerable trouble to suggest that a belief that White had traversed the canyons had the effect of reassuring Powell that the journey could be made with boats. The chapter under the query "Did Powell Know?" need not have been written had Dawson gone to the obvious source for his facts. Frederick Dellenbaugh could have told him that Powell *did* know of White's claims before he pushed off on his first voyage—and gave them no more credence than has any one else who has been through the canyons. Powell's own knowledge of geology was too sound, as Julius F. Stone has pointed out to me in a recent letter, to fail to tell him that a river as heavily silted as the lower Colorado was not likely to come from a canyon presenting abrupt and insuperable natural obstacles. From which it follows that the pioneer explorer did not, as Dawson would infer, need any adventitious influence to screw his courage to the sticking point of braving the canyon voyage.

White's reconstructed version of his voyage was written in 1916, doubtless at Dawson's request. The spelling and diction are in such great contrast to those of the original letter to his brother from Callville that it is evident this later account was rewritten by a second person from notes or verbal statements from White. Its principal interest lies in the fact that, in the decade that had elapsed since his interview with Stanton, he had finally turned to the maps and written descriptions of the middle Colorado, to be fully convinced that there were really eighteen miles of extremely rough rapids in Cataract Canyon, just below the mouth of the Grand, where he had told of drifting in quiet water. This led him to believe that the Union Pacific engineers had made a faulty interpretation of his original story in bringing in the Grand at all, so he now (doubtless still in all sincerity) concluded that the start was made upon the main Colorado. So this later version reads:

"We travelled all day until about 5 o'clock, when we struck the head of the Grand Canyon of the Colorado river. There we picked up some logs and built us a raft. We had 200 feet of rope when we first built the raft, which was about 6 feet wide and 8 feet long, just big enough to hold us up. The logs were securely tied together with the ropes. We got on our raft at night, working it with a pole. We travelled all night, and the next day, at 10 o'clock, we passed the mouth of the San Juan river. We had smooth floating for three days. The third day, about 5 o'clock, we went over a rapid, and George was washed off, but I caught hold of him and got him on the raft again."

Even yet White was not able to get the successive gorges of the Colorado straightened out in his mind, for what he calls the head of Grand Canyon is located, by his reference to the mouth of the San Juan, as somewhere on the middle reaches of Glen Canyon, and more than a hundred and fifty miles above the head of the Grand Canyon proper. A raft of the kind White describes would have no trouble drifting down the next hundred miles through Glen Canyon to the head of Marble Canyon, but not (for reasons I shall explain more fully in a moment) at an average progress better than from a third to a sixth of that indicated. Even with the elimination of the Grand River and Cataract Canyon, White's reconstructed account of his raft voyage is no easier to accept than the original version.

Although of negative value in forwarding White's claims with any one having a real knowledge of the Colorado canyons, the Dawson pamphlet did a distinct if indirect service in drawing from Robert Brewster Stanton a statement that brought the half-century-old controversy as near clarification as there is any reason to hope it ever will be. The particularly gratifying feature of this statement is that it is not only destructive—in proving to the satisfaction of any reasonable person the absurdity of White's story as applied to the Grand Canyon—but also—in pointing to a stretch of the river to which it might conceivably be applicable—constructive.

The Stanton article, which is appropriately entitled "The Alleged Journey, and the Real Journey of James White, on the Colorado River, in 1867," was published in the September, 1919, number of *The Trail* of Denver. It was contributed in response to a request by the editor of that publication for a reply by Mr. Stanton to the Dawson pamphlet and some further statements by the same author that had appeared in an earlier number of *Trail*. While this paper runs to about twenty-five magazine pages, its author explains that it is only a brief synopsis of "two hundred pages, or more" which he has devoted to the subject in his book. He then goes on to state that, in addition to the record of the White interview, he had spent years in collecting every bit of original material concerning the raft voyage of which he could get any track. This even included the sheet of paper upon which Dr. Parry wrote his original notes when interviewing White at Hardyville in 1868.

In the interview with Stanton in 1907 White had, it appears, stuck doggedly to his original story as to having encountered but one big rapid, and also to his claim that certain of his observations were made by moonlight. The practical impossibility (especially where the effect of being on a half-submerged raft is to accentuate the roughness of the water) of noting but one major rapid where there were scores is obvious; equally so was White's claim to have observed various things by moonlight on specific dates which Stanton, on referring to the calendar of 1867, found had fallen in the *dark* of the moon.

By similar discrepancies Stanton went on to prove not only
that White had not described correctly one single feature of
the Grand Canyon, but that formations and colours that he
stated he had noted did not exist in the greater gorge at all.
White's insistence that he had seen the Little Colorado coming
in on his right hand, between banks that were "not very high"
(whereas it comes in on the left hand between walls as high
as those of the Grand Canyon itself), was perhaps the one
point where it should have seemed easiest to convince him of
his error; but even in the face of the map—which appeared to
convey little to him—he stolidly refused to retract. It was
doubtless the rugged old chap's cocksureness in the matter of
the river he had seen coming in on his right hand between low
banks, together with the impression he had made upon Stanton
of trying to describe things he had really seen, that brought
the clear-thinking engineer to his final conclusion. Here it is,
as set down at the end of twenty-five pages of unassailable exposition and deduction:

"Every one of the above statements by White, describing the
nature and height of the cañon walls which he saw, the nature of the
river, the kind of rapids he passed over and the number of big
rapids he ran, *are his own,* the facts indelibly stamped on his mind
and clearly retained in his memory by reason of their being actual,
personal experiences, and each and every one of them is distinctly
and absolutely true, even to the unknown river he did see coming in
on his right—the Virgin, which Parry so erroneously named; that is,
they are true when applied to that portion of the river from about
Pierce's Ferry [below foot of Grand Cañon] to Callville.

"On the other hand, not a single one of them is even approximately
true; in fact, every one of them is absolutely false, if applied to that
portion of the Colorado above the Grand Wash Cliffs.

"That White has believed, and still believes, from what he has been
told and the continual reading of Dr. Parry's story, *and nothing else,*
that he traversed all the cañons of the Colorado river is nothing more
than the hallucination of a simple mind, devoid of any logical reasoning power. Even if this eye-witness of the whole exploit has this
hallucination, it has not prevented him from testifying truthfully and

consistently on all vital questions, and never altering this testimony in fifty years.

"Therefore, I conclude from his own testimony supported and proved true, that James White never passed through a single mile of the cañons of the Colorado river above the Grand Wash Cliffs; but that he did float on a raft or rafts, on that river, in the year 1867, from a point near the Grand Wash to Callville, Nevada, a distance of about sixty miles—where he stopped and was taken off his raft."

Although the only part of this sixty miles of river I have covered in a boat is that from the head of Boulder Canyon to the ruins of old Callville, I know enough of the stretch between the Grand Wash and the mouth of the Virgin fully to agree with Stanton in identifying it with the portion of the Colorado most nearly fitting White's description both as to rapids and character and colour of the walls. He *could* have drifted down here in the sort of rafts he describes, and he could easily have encountered all the trouble he recounts in doing it. In reconciling White's assertion that he was fourteen days on the river with the comparatively short length of this stretch, Stanton might have pointed out (what he must often have noticed) that an inexperienced man working in rough water always overestimates both time and distance. A man might easily spend six or eight days working a make-shift raft down this particular sixty miles, and—especially in the condition White would have been in after a flight from Indians across the desert—think he had taken twice that long. Not one man in a thousand—not not one in a hundred thousand of White's type—can carry an exact record of river travel in his head. I cannot, for instance, name offhand the camps at which we stopped in the course of a twelve-day trip up Glen Canyon last summer; nor yet, without long thinking, all of the six or seven camps coming down. Still less could White have kept a mental record of a voyage which was started in panic, and continued to be more or less of a panic all the way. Had one not had so much assurance of the man's honesty, the circumstance of his having tried to give a definite and specific accounting for each day would—as in

the case of the James Pattie narrative—incline one strongly
to the belief that there had been fabricative forces in operation.

The one bit of new light I am personally able to shed on a
controversy that has had to receive most of its illumination
from those who have actually boated through the Grand Canyon is from the rafting angle—principally as to the speed of
raft travel. On a number of rivers, but principally the Alsek
of Alaska, the Tigris and the Parana, I have resorted to one
form or another of raft, usually—as in White's case—because
nothing better was available. So far as I am able to learn,
no one who has commented at any length on the White voyage
has had much if any experience of that most cranky and precarious type of craft to which the prospector entrusted his
fate. This has not mattered greatly in the cases of such men
as Dellenbaugh and Stanton, who knew enough of the canyons
to be sure of their ground in any event. But if any one writing
on the other side of the question—Mr. Dawson, for instance—
could have had a first-hand knowledge of the difficulty of doing
anything, or getting anywhere, with a raft in really rough
water, he could not have subscribed to the White story without
very serious misgivings.

A raft built of two or three tiers of logs, well handled, will
survive waves and bumps that would swamp a big batteau. To
work at its best, it ought to have a towing-launch to put it
into the head of a rapid at the right place, and be provided
with sweeps to help in avoiding rocks and keeping out of eddies. The worst enemies of raft-travel are "sweepers"—overhanging trees along the bank that brush passengers off into
the water—and submerged rocks. The Grand Canyon is comparatively free from "sweepers," but is one of the worst of all
places for savage rock-peppered rapids. Once hung up on a
midstream boulder, a raft—on account of its weight—may
well stay there until it breaks up or is carried off by next season's rise. Whether a crew of Canadian lumberjacks could
take a raft of their own design and construction through the

Grand Canyon is a question that arouses interesting speculation. With the most favourable water—perhaps the high-
middle stage of late July—the feat could possibly be accomplished, but it well might take many weeks to cover the distance White claimed to have run in fourteen days.

In endeavouring to compute White's rate of drift down the
stretch which we now know as Glen Canyon, Dr. Parry and
others have assumed that the raft, by keeping "in the swiftest
portion of the current," would have made four miles an hour,
or sixty miles for a fifteen-hour day. To one who has tried
to get anywhere in make-shift rafts this displays a brand of
optimism almost comparable to that of Colonel Sellers in arriving at the total demand for his Elixir of Life by multiplying
the population of the universe by the number of bottles of the
panacea each inhabitant ought to consume. If two inexperienced men, without the use of sweeps, could keep such a raft
as White's in "the swiftest portion of the current" one hour
out of each fifteen-hour day they would be doing well. The
other fourteen hours would be about equally divided in getting
off bars and rocks and floating back up-stream in eddies. In
the Grand Canyon itself the delays from strandings and for
repairs and reconnoitring would be greatly increased. If such
a raft as White describes survived the Grand Canyon passage
at all it could hardly take less than a week for every one of
the six or eight days the prospector claimed he spent on that
part of his voyage.

There is one more point, from the rafting angle, that fits
White's story to the Grand Wash-Callville stretch, while utterly
disqualifying it for the Grand Canyon. He told of tying himself to his raft in order to keep from being washed off. Riding
a loosely-bound bunch of logs in really rough water I can
think of no more certain preliminary to inevitable suicide than
such an action. Over most of the comparatively quiet reaches
below the Grand Wash this might not have got him into trouble
—with luck, that is; but that, thus bound, he could have sur-

vived one major rapid of the Grand Canyon is hardly possible. Anything but a solidly-built raft of considerable dimensions and two or three tiers of logs in thickness will dive and submerge deeply at a bad fall, even if it does not break up. In the Columbia I have seen single logs disappear for over a minute. On a make-shift raft like White's, by letting go and getting completely away from the floundering logs when they were drawn under, a man *might* come up himself with enough wind to last him until he struck the next eddy. But tied to the logs, the only question would be as to whether drowning would precede or follow a rap on the head from his wallowing if not dissolving raft.

With the evidence so complete and overwhelming against the possibility of White's ever having traversed the Grand Canyon on a raft, it only remains to consider whether or not it would have been possible for his prospecting trip to have carried him to the vicinity of the foot of the Grand Canyon rather than to the head of Glen, as he contends it did. That point is interestingly touched upon in a letter from Frederick Dellenbaugh now lying on my desk. As it constitutes the considered and final views of the man who has long been looked to as the first living authority on matters pertaining to the Grand Canyon, I am quoting almost in full the passages relating to the White story. These were written in reply to a letter of mine asking Mr. Dellenbaugh if anything in the Dawson pamphlet had caused him to alter his views of White and his voyage as expressed in "The Romance of the Colorado."

"As for the White story: I have not changed my mind about White, except that, after Stanton's discussion of the matter, I said that I was willing to concede that he was not exactly a liar—only a very ignorant fellow who did not know where he did go, and was led by others who knew no more than he did to believe it was the Grand Canyon he ran through. HIS DESCRIPTION IS NOT AT ALL THE GRAND CANYON. How could any fool go through that sublime gorge and not see anything of it? And find only ONE bad rapid!!!

"My original supposition was that White and the others had a quarrel and that some one was killed. White was only too glad after taking to the river, which he probably did BELOW THE GRAND CANYON, to admit that he had come all the way through the gorge of mystery. Nobody knew anything about it, so he was safe. However, that was only a surmise on my part and may do him an injustice. But I still think that he did NOT go through the Grand Canyon, but that he started in just below its end and went down to Callville on his raft.

"White was doubtless on the San Juan somewhere but he travelled overland for a time. He did not know the San Juan from any other stream. The overland journey was not difficult at that time. Pattie, Carson and many trappers were making it all the time from 1825 on. In 1867 it certainly was not at all difficult.

"The 'Senate' document you refer to has fooled many people. They think it was issued by the government to substantiate White's claim, whereas it was a paper written by a man who had just heard of White's claim and, believing it, wrote this story which was then introduced by one of the senators. There was no real investigation.

"Major Powell *did* know of White's claim in 1869 when he started down Green river. He scouted it. When we went down [Powell's second voyage] we talked about it often and the Major considered it a very flimsy story.

"I do not think it would detract at all from Powell's achievement if White did go through, but there is no sense on that account of allowing a false story to gain ground. I will be glad to concede that White did go through if some evidence can be presented to prove it. Up to the present I have seen no such evidence."

In a later letter Mr. Dellenbaugh mentions a rumour to the effect that a movement has been started to erect a monument to White, and states that he believes it would be a very foolish thing under the circumstances. Beyond all question the distinguished historian and artist is right. If White deserves a monument for anything it would be for the really fine way in which he has always turned his back on a notoriety that was thrust upon him in spite of himself. As a moral achievement that outranks the physical one of navigating the Grand Canyon; there will not, moreover, be any one to question it. Unfortunately, there is more brass than gold in bronze; also in the train of events leading up to the erection thereof. White's real achievement will be more fitly commemorated in the storied urn than by the animated bust.

Robert Brewster Stanton, his great work on the Colorado still unpublished, died last February. That leaves, besides Dellenbaugh, Julius F. Stone, Ellsworth Kolb and Emery Kolb as the most notable, almost the only, survivors of Grand Canyon voyages. With all three of these veterans I have discussed at length the White voyage and the various questions arising therefrom. Each one has expressed views so closely coinciding with those of Stanton and Dellenbaugh that to quote any part of them would be only repetition of what has already been set down.

In the face of all this I submit that if the claim is ever again seriously advanced that James White traversed the Grand Canyon on a raft, it should only be by a man who has tied three drift-logs together and ridden them himself down the rapids of the great gorge. There are still cottonwood trunks to be found on the bars above the San Juan, and Soap Creek Rapids and the old "Sockdologer" are tumbling over themselves just as hard as when Powell first lined or ran them in 1869. Moreover, I know of a man who would volunteer to go along on a jaunt of that kind as Mate, if only a Skipper could be found. His name is Ike Emerson, and he built a raft for me with which we ran Hell-gate on the Columbia three years ago. The last thing he said on parting was: "If you ever hear of a river stunt that no man ain't never pulled afore, lemme know. I'm gettin' old now, but when I whiffs out I want it to be with my river-boots on an' all hell poppin'." [1]

I can conscientiously recommend Ike Emerson to play the Mate of George Stroll to any one who cares to essay the Skipper of James White.

[1] See "Down the Columbia," Chapter X.

CHAPTER IX

ADAMS ON THE BLUE AND THE GRAND

THE exploits of Samuel Adams upon the Colorado and the Grand are recorded in a document of the House of Representatives,[1] and, because he writes so much the way a Congressman talks, one is a bit doubtful as to whether his claims and assertions should be taken at their face value or discounted on the ninety-and-nine per cent basis by which the usual run of Congressional chaff must be winnowed in searching for its possible grain of wheat. The fact that the author of the contents of this document is mentioned in a House Resolution as "Hon. Samuel Adams," as well as his way of speaking disparagingly and contemptuously of the work of others while expatiating fulsomely on that of himself, might suggest that he was, or had been, a professional politician. The fact that he came before Congress praying for Government compensation for services rendered in connection with what were palpably his own personal ventures and adventures also smacks strongly of the way of the political patriot. The charge, however, is not of the sort I would care to go on record as making without direct evidence. Moreover, if Samuel Adams had the nerve to conceive and seriously attempt to carry out the voyage he describes down the Blue and the Grand, one can forgive him much. That run alone, if the account is even approximately authentic, comes pretty near to qualifying Adams for premier honours in rough-water navigation.

The first paper in the pamphlet in question is in form of a

---

[1] "Communication from Captain Samuel Adams Relative to the Exploration of the Colorado River and Its Tributaries." House Miscel. Document No. 37, 42nd Congress, 1st Session.

letter to Secretary of War Stanton. It bears the date of March
29th, 1867, and contains a somewhat heterogeneous assortment
of data and assertions concerning certain trips Adams had made
up and down the lower Colorado during the previous three
years. It appears that he and a Captain Thomas Trueworthy
had brought a small stern-wheeler down from San Francisco
to the Colorado for what Adams characterizes as "the individual and difficult enterprise of demonstrating that it was
capable of being ascended with steamers for over 620 miles
from the mouth." As we have already seen how that very
thing had been demonstrated by Captain George Johnson,
pushing ahead of Ives with the *Colorado* in 1858, one fails to
understand how anything was achieved worth running to Congress to tell about.

Adams describes the company running six or eight little
steamers on the river as a powerful monopoly practising a
wicked imposition upon both the Government and the mining
communities, and in language suggestive of that of a Kansas
Congressman attacking an international shipping combine, he
goes on to tell of the means that were taken to defeat the ends
of his own purely philanthropic mission.

"In proportion as the steamer ascended the river, in that proportion were means the most revolting in their character adopted to
prevent the success of the enterprise, by frequent efforts to injure her
boiler, fire her cabins, destroy her machinery, and by cutting down
the timber for miles along the most destitute localities that sufficient
wood might not be obtained for steam purposes. . . . The bullet and
the knife were brought into requisition to prevent the consummation
of an enterprise so important to the development of the country."

All told, there must be a page or more filled with these dark
allusions to the machinations of the monopolistic octopus,
while even greater space is given to a highly roseate survey—
couched in language that may well have been the model for
subsequent California boosting literature—of the mineral and
agricultural resources of the Colorado valleys. But it was as

a national highway of commerce that the rolling bosom of the River of Red fired (rather than quenched) the sparks of the adventurer's vision. By a priceless coincidence, it was my fortune first to read these stirring lines while engaged in trying to drag a twenty-foot skiff over the occasionally moistened bars between Boulder Canyon and The Needles.

"A singular fatality has from the first been connected with this history of the Colorado river. . . . The letters written respecting it, and the continued effort made by a formidable coalition of corporations [for selfish purposes] to crush out the individual enterprise of proving its national importance, have all been of that revolting character as to do her the most flagrant injustice. The Colorado must be, emphatically, to the Pacific coast what the Mississippi is to the Atlantic. The building timber and ties for the construction of the railroad crossing the continent [now completed] have been carried upon one of her tributaries; and one of her grand purposes will not be completed until the material for the construction of the southern line is borne upon her surface."

This latter consummation would have involved the rafting or barging of the material through the not entirely negligible gorge which we now call the Grand Canyon. One of the most amusing things about these grandiose plans of Adams, as he developed them, is the way in which, in spite of the definite if fragmentary data available to him concerning parts of it in the Ives and Newberry reports, he persists in rating the great central chasm as little more than a myth. He gives the name of "Big Cañon" to what we now call Boulder Canyon, and seems to believe he was truthfully informed when it was "represented as being the largest on the river." After making light of the difficulties Ives and others claimed to have encountered in ascending the lower river, he states:

"From the eminence at the head of the cañon [Boulder] I could see an open valley, sixty miles in length, extending to the northeast. From that point for 350 miles the country has been considered a *terra incognita*.

"From my observations, and from information received from the Indians, and from the maps and correspondence in the Historical Society of Salt Lake City, to which I had free access, through the kindness of George A. Smith, secretary of the same, I am satisfied that there are none of those dangerous obstructions which have been represented by those who may have viewed them at a distance, and whose imaginary cañons and rapids below had almost disappeared at the approach of the steamer."

From his eminence at the head of Boulder Canyon Adams looked easterly up that stretch of the Colorado down which James White was to come drifting in his raft a few months later. He saw where the uplift of the great Colorado plateau bulked monstrously against the sky-line, and he could not have failed to observe that there was no alternative course for the river save through the heart of that lofty mass of rock. "I should have ascended the river farther," he explains, "but my means were exhausted, the exploration of the last two years and a half being attended with great pecuniary embarrassment to Captain Trueworthy as well as myself." But although Adams could not find the means to carry him over the two or three days of land travel that would have taken him to a point where at least a revealing glimpse of the character of his *terra incognita* and its sundering river could have been obtained, he did discover means to hasten to Washington and assure Congress that the unexplored canyon above had "none of those dangerous obstructions which have been represented by those who may have viewed them from a distance." And the House, as pleased about the tidings as was the Senate over the belated news of the White voyage winged by the Dawson pamphlet fifty years later, promptly passed the following "Concurrent Resolutions":

"*Resolved by the House of Representatives* [*the council concurring*], That the thanks of this legislature are due and hereby tendered to Hon. Samuel Adams and Captain Thomas Trueworthy for their untiring energy and indomitable enterprise as displayed by them in opening up the navigation of the Colorado river, the great natural thoroughfare of Arizona and Utah Territories."

There are two or three delicious little things hidden away in these solemn lines calculated to give the spirits of the old Colorado river-rats cheerily to chuckle, but the real guffaw lurks in the climax—that "great natural thoroughfare of Arizona and Utah Territories"! The thought of this ponderous "legislature" putting itself seriously on record as declaring the then even untraversed middle canyon series of the Colorado a "thoroughfare" is almost as inspiring as that of the debate this same august body is said to have held as to whether or not a destroyer was made to chase and catch torpedoes. And I had only half-believed the latter story until I found the former a matter of official record—"spread upon the records of this house," as the order ran.

Robert Brewster Stanton has written that the early accounts of the James White voyage through the Grand Canyon "caused one Army officer, in a report to the War Department, to recommend the building of a huge steamboat to go up the river to explore it, before Major Powell's time!" Is it not probable that Adams' even more positive statement as to the absence of serious obstructions in the middle canyons may have helped inspire this bold idea?

Neither earlier nor later was there anything in Samuel Adams' self-styled explorations of the lower river to warrant more than the passing mention of his name in Colorado Basin history. The only reason I have touched upon his account of them here is because the character of the personal record may serve as a measuring-stick by which a line may be had upon what was, in certain respects, the most remarkable of all Colorado River voyages. The man's report of his activities on the lower Colorado prove him to have been egotistical, prone to make sensational statements, and inclined to arrive at conclusions upon hearsay and insufficient first-hand knowledge. At the same time he showed himself to have been a reasonably faithful recorder of the plain details of his own observations. With these simple facts ready to hand as touch-stones, one is set for a fairly critical reading of Adams' story of his spectacular run down the Blue and the Grand. But subject even to the discounting of these tests, that voyage seems to stand as a really fine and courageous adventure.

The account of Adams' attempt to run the rapids of the upper Grand is attached to a petition to the House of Representatives, "praying compensation for services rendered and expenses incurred in the exploration of the Colorado River of the West, its tributaries, and the country adjacent thereto." It bears the date of December 13, 1869, and makes the specific claim that the investigations on both the upper and lower river were made "at the wish and order" of Secretary of War E. M. Stanton. Because certain anticipated appropriations did not become available, the petitioner states, he had received no aid from the Government, for which reason he prays that the amount claimed in an attached bill be paid him in full for his "time, labour and expense incurred in the explorations contained in the report he has the honour to respectfully submit for your consideration." The amount of the bill is not stated in the printed document, nor have I been able to learn what action was taken on it.

The accompanying report is addressed to the Hon. William W. Belknap, Secretary of War, and is dated November 1st, 1869. As the voyage which it covers was made during the summer months of the same year, it must have been in progress at the same time the first Powell expedition was fighting its way down the middle canyons of the main Colorado. The ambitious character of Adams' plans were made plain in the opening sentence.

"I herewith transmit to you my report respecting the exploring expedition in which I have recently been engaged, the object of this being to descend the Blue river to the Grand, and from thence to the mouth of the Colorado river of the west to the head of the Gulf of California."

Adams, in starting at an altitude not far from twice that of Green River, Wyoming, Powell's point of embarkation, set himself an even more difficult task than that to which the resolute major had committed himself. How inadequate a conception he had formed of the stern work ahead is evidenced by the superficiality of his rushed preparations and the character of his primitive outfit as revealed in an early paragraph of his report.

"About four months after I went to Breckenridge, which is about eight miles from the main divide or summit of the Rocky Mountains, organized an expedition of eleven men, with four boats constructed upon the ground, the largest of which was twenty-two feet in length. The limited time I had to construct these, the quality of the lumber, the capacity of the mill for sawing, and the rapid falling of the water in the river, prevented my building the boats in every respect as I could have desired."

The boats were evidently of rough, newly-sawed lumber, and no mention is made of any decking-over or of water-tight compartments. While one cannot but admire Adams' nerve in coolly tackling the canyons of the Grand in this way, the utter impossibility of the survival of open boats of this character in the sort of water to be encountered almost from the first push-off was about on all-fours with his absurd and unwarrented denial of the existence of important obstructions to navigation in the Grand Canyon. The slap-bang kind of a voyage that was a real joyous adventure in the case of Manly and his crew of bull-whackers became out-and-out fool-hardiness in the case of a man like Adams who, claiming to be something of an expert in rough-water navigation, should have known better than to attempt what he did in the way that he did. Withal, the man must have had real stuff in him to embark upon the adventure, and great courage and determination to push it, as he did, to just about the last gasp.

Two of Adams' boats were put into the Blue very near to Breckenridge; the two others were sent by team to a point twelve miles below. As most of the outfit was dispatched to the rendezvous with the land party, Adams and three of his men must have made their initial run with empty boats. The river was about forty yards wide and of an average depth of two feet. The current is described as rapid, which is easy to believe when it is stated that the descent was from seventy to one hundred and twenty feet per mile. In forming a picture of the conditions imposed by a fall of a hundred and twenty feet to the mile, such as Adams refers to, it may help to point out that the average fall in such canyons as Lodore, Cataract and the Grand Canyon itself, where Powell and most of those who came after him met with repeated disasters, runs in the vicinity of ten to fifteen feet to the mile. Adams does not state what instruments were employed in estimating descent and distance. It may be taken for granted, however, that the figures he gives throughout are very rough approximations, and that his estimates of fall are somewhat exaggerated. Even so, the outfit was in almost prohibitively violent water from the beginning.

The real start with the complete flotilla was made on July 13th. On the same day, the Powell party, the savage cataracts of Lodore far astern, was threading the comparatively quiet depths of Gray Canyon, not far above the junction of the Green and the Grand. Adams records that the mouths of the Swan, Snake and Ten Mile were passed on this first day's run, the combined flows from these considerable streams augmenting that of the Blue very materially. There were no navigational troubles to speak of until the next day, which important French anniversary the torrential Blue seems to have celebrated by doing to the Adams outfit about what the Revolutionists did to the Bastille. The victim's account of what occurred is a good deal more restrained and unsensational than one would have expected after reading his report from the lower river. Follows the complete entry for the day:

"Left camp; ran down the river with the four boats, all performing admirably. The stream being so rapid, it became necessary for the boats, to prevent coming into collision, to run at a distance of several hundred yards apart, and even with this precaution several accidents occurred, and a number of our party were thrown into the stream. This afternoon our largest boat, manned by Messrs. Twible and O'Connor, was leading; my boat, with maps, instruments, papers, &c., in charge of Mr. Day and myself, followed, the other two boats being at proper distances apart. The first boat failing to give us warning in time of the dangerous cañon we were approaching, we could not check the headway of my boat, and on turning the bend in the river, our real danger burst upon us, as we saw, for the first time, the white, foaming water dashing for one mile ahead of us. I called upon Mr. Day to assist me in holding our boat straight in the current. Hardly had he complied before our boat came crashing against a rock; this threw him out into the current, where he was washed upon a rock or boulder below. The boat then swung, and was driven rapidly upon a succession of rocks; the end was knocked out and she filled with water. All my papers, instruments, and maps were lost [together with letters from the late Hon. Thaddeus Stevens, Hon. E. M. Stanton, and General B. F. Butler, who had expressed much interest in the success of the expedition and the development of the resources of the great West]. I succeeded in catching one end of the bow-line as I sank below the surface; this was carried under a rock, and I succeeded in holding the boat quartering across the stream. I remained here two hours [Mr. Adams had doubtless come to the surface and secured a solid footing at some time during this interval, though he fails to mention that rather important circumstance.—L. R. F.], when a rope was tied to my person and I was enabled to get to the opposite shore. Looking up this deluge of water, upon each side of which the walls of the cañon rose one thousand feet, I saw my first boat sixty yards above, completely swamped, and my third boat one hundred yards above this, in the same condition. The roar of the water made it impossible for us to make ourselves understood. The fourth boat being warned in time, did not enter the cañon. I found the fall of water for one mile was two hundred feet."

One might point out after reading the account of this lively interval that a man of Powell's stamp, facing a river of ten per cent of the fall Adams records here, would probably have spent a good deal more time reconnoitring from the banks than in actual boating operations. Adams' cocksureness evidently would not permit him to approach the work in that way, as a consequence of which his haste in trying to run this rocky gorge brought him nearly a week of repentance upon the banks. The entries for the six days following the Fall of the Bastille celebration have to do with repairing boats, sorting and repacking provisions, and a trip "back to the summits of the mountains for additional instruments, papers, and medicine." Although Adams mentions by name the men who supplied these prime *desiderata,* he does not satisfy one's very natural curiosity as to just what kind of "instruments" were so readily to be had in a primitive mountain village. This would be only less interesting to know than an elucidation of the method by which the resourceful leader ascertained the fall of the "water for one mile was two hundred feet"—immediately *after* his original instruments were lost in the river.

The brief entry for July 21st is in itself sufficient commentary upon Adams' all-too-evident failure to learn the lesson of the initial disaster.

"Loaded our boats and started down the river; after running one-quarter of a mile our fourth boat struck a rock and was broken in two in the centre; lost portion of our provisions; was compelled to leave the boat a complete wreck."

However difficult the navigation, for the leader of a party to have held the confidence of his men in the face of this succession of disasters within the distance of a few miles would be too much to expect. The defection which Adams records under date of July 22nd was inevitable under the circumstances.

"Our party was much worn out with the excessive labour we had undergone, and much reluctance to go on was shown by a portion of the men; the argument used by myself, that the heavy falls we had passed in coming through Rocky Cañon was the strongest evidence of fewer below, and that soon we would come to less falls in descending the river below, had no effect upon their excited imaginations, and five of my men left, leaving my diminished party to the dangers from the Indians and the falls; this reduced our party to six persons. . . . This day we put boats down by line two and a half miles."

The next day the reduced party reached the Grand proper, but not before the Blue had exacted further toll, possibly by way of a parting protest against being used as a section of Adams' "great national thoroughfare." The following is a condensation of the entry for July 23rd:

"In consequence of the reduction of our force and sickness, I was compelled to take charge of my boat alone; this was swamped twice by running under a fallen tree, and by being dashed against the rocks below the upper end of Cave Cañon. . . . The river here was fifty feet in breadth; the depth twenty-two feet. . . . My boat was so much injured by the late accidents that I was compelled to abandon it one mile from the mouth. . . . At each accident to our boats we lost tools and provisions; the water penetrating our flour, we were compelled to change it into other sacks—ten times in the last eight days. Such was the rocky character of the river, that the lower edges of my boat were so much worn that I was compelled to cut these down twice since starting. . . . This afternoon at two o'clock, seven miles from Grand river, water running three and a half miles per hour; this was the only place for sixty miles where we found half a mile of smooth water; the fall of water up to this time averaging seventy-five feet to the mile. This smooth surface continued until we entered the Grand river in the Middle Park. . . . The Grand river was here one hundred and forty yards in width . . . and the fall of water, from the place of starting to the junction of the Blue and Grand rivers, was over four thousand feet."

As the exact point from which Adams started is somewhat indefinite, it is difficult to check his figures for the fall of the Blue. This stream enters the Grand at the great Kremling Reservoir site, below which the larger river has been very accurately surveyed. From here on to the end of Adams' adventurous voyage his figures and estimates, wherever the descriptions can be identified, may be checked by the plan and profile of the Grand as shown in Water Supply Paper 396 of the Geological Survey. This publication gives the elevation above sea level of the Grand at a point near the mouth of the Blue as 7,311 feet. Adding to this the 4,000 feet Adams estimated as his descent in reaching that point, it would appear that (provided the latter figure is even approximately correct) the place from which he pushed off below the Continental Divide had an elevation of something like 11,000 feet.

There is an unexplained hiatus of a week in Adams' journal at this point, which does not resume until July 30th, when an easy four-mile run was made in the two remaining boats to near the head of what he calls the Grand Canyon of the Grand River, now on the map as Gore Canyon. Optimism seems to have been completely restored by the long rest, and for the first time the voyageur responds to the appeal of the wild natural beauty of the region to which he had penetrated.

"At our sudden approach in the boats the wild geese and deer started in affright down each side of the river directly for the entrance to the cañon, where we killed a number of each. This afternoon I ascended the height at the entrance to this cañon, looking to the northeast from a point eight hundred feet above the river. A beautiful panorama was extended before me, the clear water of the Grand, like a thread of silver, winding its way through the wide valley, which must soon be the abode of civilization. Struck with the beauty of the scenery, I this evening ascended a point above, the great chain of mountains far in the distance rising higher and still higher toward the snowy range, while Mount Lincoln, towering far above these, bathed in the brilliant moonlight, was superlatively magnificent."

Three days were spent in this pleasant camp. Letters were dispatched, notes written up, provisions re-sorted, blankets dried out and the outfit generally shaken down and tuned up for the grim task of running the canyon below. The upper end of Gore Canyon must be pretty nearly a continuous cascade. The first two miles have a fall of a hundred feet apiece, the third eighty feet, the fourth seventy feet, with the next three or four averaging about twenty feet each. The profile of the gorge looks like something between a graph of the rising cost of living in war-time and one side of a cross section of the Cheops Pyramid. The volume of the Grand here should be not far from that of the Green in Lodore Canyon, but not the steepest of the canyons of the great Colorado series has a fall comparable to that of Gore.

The ten days that elapsed between the emergence of the Adams outfit from the Blue and the resumption of the voyage down the Grand may well have been due to an attempt to get some kind of a line on the difficulties ahead. Adams could have had no illusions by this time as to the utter unworthiness of his boats and the complete inadequacy of his whole equipment for work in rough water. That he was still game to shove off into the head of that sinister tumble of rapids with the remnants of his battered outfit speaks eloquently for the staunch physical courage of the man. He was as determined as ever, if less confident. No attempt was made to repeat the spectacular runs of the first days on the Blue. Chastened by repeated disaster but not beaten, Adams was ready to save his boats and prolong the life of his expedition by every means devisable. He was fighting with his back to the wall now, and a mighty fine fight he made of it. Considering the largeness of language of his outbursts of boosting as presented to the House, the tale he tells here is refreshingly plain and unvarnished. The entry of August 3rd recounts the first round.

"Started into the Grand Cañon of the Grand River with two boats. The entrance to this was fifty feet in breadth; water very swift and deep, the first fall being almost six feet perpendicular a few yards below the entrance; let the empty boat over this fall with a line; loaded our boats and let them down three hundred yards; came to another fall of ten feet perpendicular; packed provisions,

&c., around this sixty yards below; let the empty boat down again by line. I applied my level and found the water to descend, in four hundred yards, forty-five feet. I had never, in any of the deep cañons or rapids of the Colorado River, seen any so great as those of the Blue and Grand Rivers. The walls of this cañon were from nine hundred to one thousand six hundred feet high. After dinner one of our boats, in which were Messrs. Lillis and Lovell, in descending the rapids around an abrupt angle, was struck by the force of the current and dashed against a rock-bound shore. The boat was filled with water and much injured. This accident was a severe one to us, as we lost 100 pounds of bacon, 100 pounds of flour, 1 saw, a bake-oven, 2 canteens of salt, and 35 pounds of coffee, besides other necessary articles that could not be replaced. We were now, with six men, reduced to 150 pounds of damaged flour, 20 pounds of bacon, 12 pounds of coffee, and 8 pounds of salt. Those having charge of the wrecked boat succeeded in hauling her out on land. To these I threw a stone which was attached to a silk fishing line; this was tied to our smallest boat line, and this again to the larger one, and by the latter our boat was swung across the rapid current and prevented from sharing the fate of the other. The width of the river here was one hundred yards, and of great depth."

Camp was pitched by the wrecked boat. "No precautions were taken to guard against Indians," Adams concludes, "as in front of us stood three giant sentinels, a thousand feet in height, guarding the entrance to this gloomy and narrow pass." The most of the following day was spent in making tar and repairing the injured boats. Much difficulty was encountered in lining down the next three hundred yards over a heavy fall, where "sufficient level ground upon which to sleep" led them to make camp again. The next day fresh disaster was in ambush.

"August 5.—Dropped our boats three hundred and fifty yards to the head of the greatest fall we had yet seen. I went down on the left side of the cañon four hundred yards to ascertain if it were possible to take the boat over the rapids, and to get a better view of the falls below. I ascended the steep sides of the cañon eight hundred feet. Looking down I could see the foaming water dashing through the narrow pass, with no apparent method in its motion.

The appearance of the river to the southwest was favorable. Preparing to descend, I saw our party waving their hats. I soon ascertained the cause of all this to originate from the important fact that they had just found, lodged upon the rocks, forty pounds of our lost bacon. This was fortunate for us, as we were reduced to but a few rations of this indispensable article. Finding it impossible to take the boats down on that side, by land or water, we crossed the stream above the rapids and packed our provisions seven hundred yards below, over the roughest and most dangerous portage yet passed. We could make but two trips a day. The boots of my men were completely worn out, and several men were prostrated in consequence of the fatigue occasioned by our constant labour. We then let down our smaller empty boat by line, lifting her over the rocks below. We then started by the same process to let our larger boat down. She swung out into the current, filled with water, was held struggling for an hour in the mad element, when the line parted and our best and largest boat disappeared forever. By this accident we were reduced to one boat; almost everything necessary for the trip had been lost. Here I gave the box in which I had carried my instruments to the waves. We divested ourselves of almost everything of weight, and prepared to try our fortunes in the last boat. The heat was now 110 degrees in the sun, which produced a great contrast to the cold water of the river. Immediately below us, southwest, in a direct course of the river, rose a mountain in the shape of a dome, nine hundred feet high, as if standing upon its broad base to dam up this boiling current of water. I called this 'Dome Mountain.' The fall of water in eight hundred yards was eighty-two feet. I found it impossible to pack provisions up the mountain. We were four days in going three-quarters of a mile."

The meaning of the last two sentences is somewhat obscure. I take it, however, that the attempt to pack provisions "up the mountain" was made in connection with an endeavour to effect a portage along that side. The four days which were spent in going three-quarters of a mile must have included the one following the date of the entry, August 5th, as that was only their third day in this canyon. August 6th must have been mostly devoted to portaging, but Adams' entry is almost exclusively concerned with a discovery which, in his own mind,

seems to vindicate his theory as to the practical non-existence
of a Grand Canyon of the Colorado.

"Made three trips with our boat in taking party and provisions
to the opposite shore. The timber and blocks in the stream I found
to be about as much worn as those I had seen in the Colorado River
three years before. This, to my mind, was an additional evidence
that the cause of this originated from obstructions above, and not
from passing through the exaggerated cañons below, which have been
so brilliantly represented by those who have viewed them at a magnificent distance."

By an extremely interesting coincidence Major Powell begins his entry of August 6th of the same year with: "Cañon
wall still higher and higher as we go down through the strata."
After traversing many hundreds of miles of "exaggerated cañons," the indomitable explorer was writing at the end of his
second day's run into the gloomy depths of the Marble Gorge,
with two hundred and fifty miles of Adams' mythical Grand
Canyon winding below. Adams was quite at his worst in these
silly and rather hysterical attempts to discredit the real explorers of the Colorado River Basin, which makes it the more
surprising that he should have given so simple and so convincing an account of his own dogged fight with the rapids of the
upper Grand. The entry of August 7th is in the form of an
R.I.P. for the foundered Colorado-to-the-Pacific flotilla.

"River very swift. Fall of water one hundred and eighty feet to
the mile. Made to-day four different portages; ran half a mile, and
let the empty boat down by a line through the swift current, as it
was impossible to take her by land. She swung out into the current,
and in a few moments was dashed upon the rocks below, a total
wreck. Our first boat was lost at the mouth of Rocky Cañon; the
second one mile from the mouth of Cave Cañon; the third one mile
from the head of Grand [Gore] Cañon; and the fourth one mile
below this."

This seems definitely to locate the point at which the last
boat was lost as about two miles from the head of Gore Can-

yon. As the Geological Survey profile shows that neither of these miles has a fall of over a hundred feet, Adams' estimate of a drop of "one hundred and eighty feet to the mile" would appear to be considerably exaggerated. It is quite possible, however, that he arrived at this figure by taking the fall of a shorter stretch and figuring it on the mile basis. August 8th, 9th and 10th are covered by a single entry, revealing conditions which make it a matter of no surprise that there was a further desertion of personnel. Indeed, one cannot help marvelling that even a one of the men was willing further to risk his neck for an enterprise which, however spectacular and appealing in its original conception, was now rather less than a forlorn hope. In holding the remnants of the party together the optimism of Adams himself—the confidence that a few more miles would take them over the worst water and to a point from which there would be easy going all the way to the Gulf—doubtless played an important part.

"*August* 8, 9, *and* 10—Found us without a boat, almost destitute of salt, and reduced to fifteens rations of flour, bacon and coffee; our cooking utensils and all our lines and building tools gone, except one axe and a hatchet. Three of our party concluded to leave and return. One of these, Mr. Waddle, had been sick; the other, Mr. G. N. Day, was suffering from excessive exposure. In justice to both, I will say that they had been faithful from the first, and I am convinced that it was only from the force of circumstances that they concluded to return. Our party was now reduced to three. Messrs. Twible and Lillis consented to accompany me. The provisions we had at this time, although much damaged, would have lasted us two weeks. We here constructed a small raft, three feet by six. Upon this we dropped by line our provisions fifty yards below. The perpendicular rocks upon each side made it impossible for us to get our things down in any other manner. We sifted our flour through a piece of mosquito bar, and ascertained that we had thirty pounds, six pounds of coffee, and twelve pounds of bacon. I felt convinced, from the favourable appearance of the country to the southwest, and the nature of the rapids, that we could in a few days make more rapid progress. We then packed our provisions,

&c., down the river three miles, over the most difficult places I had ever travelled. On our way down we found the blankets, shirts, coats, and lead [?] which had been thrown away by the party leaving us three days before."

This three-mile portage took them beyond the heaviest fall of the canyon, and to a point where there seemed a fair chance of navigating a raft. The river, still fairly closely walled in, has a drop of from ten to fifteen feet to the mile for a considerable distance. Adams' estimates of mileage, rough approximations at best, are probably a good deal too high. That, and the fact that he has recorded the events of several days in a single passage, make it somewhat difficult to follow his progress. Their second raft was of cedar, sixteen feet long by five feet wide. Drifting down an estimated distance of thirty miles to what he calls "Rapid Cañon," Adams ascended the mountainside in an endeavour to gain some idea of the character of the river ahead. This struck him as being sufficiently favourable to warrant chancing the canyon with the raft. So while Twible started packing the most indispensable remnants of the dwindling outfit over the mountain, Lillis and Adams shoved off to try their luck with the rapids.

"We pushed her [the raft] out, and in a moment she shot like an arrow down the rapid descent. We both grasped the cross-pieces on the raft to which our provisions were lashed; she sunk four feet under the surface, but rose again in the distance of eighty yards, when, in turning an abrupt angle of the river, she struck and parted. Here we lost a large portion of our provisions. We then took the raft apart, and by swinging three of the logs below formed another, and succeeded in getting our arms and what provisions we had ashore. We ascertained that we now had but eight days' provisions. Here we constructed a third raft, and proceeded twenty miles, the mountains in the southwest becoming less, when we passed through a chain of cañons, the last of which was the most difficult. In this our raft again struck, where we lost all our salt, all our cooking utensils, except one frying pan, and most of our flour and bacon. There was less elasticity to this than the Tulie rafts upon which I passed through the cañons of the Lower Colorado, and in striking with much force against the rocks the material of the cedar raft would part."

Adams could hardly have meant that last sentence as an expression of his serious preference for a tulé raft over one of logs in rough water. The tulé raft, or *balsa,* was used mostly by the Cocopahs of the delta. It was unsuited to voyages of any length, both on account of its lack of strength and because the light reeds of which it was made lost their buoyancy from becoming water-logged after a short submersion.

The entry under the dates of August 12th, 13th, and 14th, after recording the construction and destruction of the fourth and final raft, launches at once into a spirited vindication of what Adams, even at the moment of the complete annihilation of the last of his outfit, declares to have been a highly successful enterprise. Since he was praying for compensation from the Government, doubtless the statement was made to impress Congress with the value of the work performed. That resolution about the "great national thoroughfare of the Colorado" must have gone strongly to the man's head. Follows a condensation of the entry in question:

"Built another raft and descended forty miles further, when again, in turning an angle of the river, she struck a rock, and all our provisions, except five days' rations of flour and bacon, were lost. We were almost worn out by the excessive fatigue and constant exposure in the cold water. . . . We have now descended over six thousand feet. One of the main objects of the expedition had been accomplished, which was to ascertain where was the principal fall of water between the point where we started on the mountains, ten thousand feet above the sea, and the Pacific Coast. I felt satisfied that nothing more could be done by using further arguments to go on; and with the greatest reluctance we concluded to cross the country by land to Delaware Flats, at the base of the Rocky Mountains. I was satisfied that we had gone over the most difficult portion of our route. Three years before I stood at the head of the Black or Big Cañon of the Colorado River, and looking northeast

I could see a valley extending seventy-five miles in length. . . . I now stood at a point above, and looking southwest could see the narrow territory which separated us. I confess that it was with no ordinary feelings that I was compelled to yield to the force of circumstances."

And it is with "no ordinary feelings" that one knowing anything about the course of the Grand and Colorado can read that statement referring to the "narrow territory which separated" Adams' vantage at the head of Black Canyon and the point where he terminated his ill-starred voyage. A credulous Congressman might well have thought that he had boated right chock-a-block against the end of that seventy-five-miles-long valley across which he had swept his northwestering gaze from a point that would have been just about at the site of the great Boulder Canyon dam. As a matter of fact, after setting out to boat from the Rockies to the Pacific, he had covered considerably less than two hundred miles and descended (notwithstanding his claim that it was six thousand) not much over four thousand feet. In doing this he had lost four boats and four rafts, and been deserted by eight men. That is to say, he had lost all of his outfit and most of his men in descending about one-tenth of the "national thoroughfare" he had announced he was setting out to explore and open up. And instead of that negligible bit of slightly obstructed river below him, there were hundred of miles of torrential rapids, boxed in by the most stupendous of all the world's great canyons.

Yet Adams had either the cheek or the ignorance to assure the Secretary of War that this misplanned and mismanaged jaunt of his down the Blue and the Grand furnished

" . . . a strong argument to establish my published statements, over two years before, respecting the country and river, which have from the first been the victim of the wild and extravagant statements of professional letter-writers, who have never seen either, and who act as if they were licensed to give unsubstantial statements to the public, which would at once be ruled out if sought to be intro-

duced in the trial of a petty suit. It is not my purpose here to enter
into the motives, or to dwell upon the character, of that large class
of presumptive men whose vocation it has been to write magnificent
descriptions of that they pretend to know; sooner or later these
will find their level, and a discriminating public will judge them and
their productions."

One chortles to think it was Adams himself who wrote that.
But the funniest thing of all about this, and all the other as-
severations of Adams calculated to wipe the Grand Canyon off
the map, has to do with the date under which it was presented
to Congress. The report to the Secretary of War is dated November 1st, 1869, and the petition to the House praying for
compensation for expenses December 13th, 1869. On August
30th of the same year six gaunt and hungry men, pulling two
terribly battered boats, arrived at the mouth of the Virgin and
told a rather convincing story of a three months' journey
through a very deep, very long, and very much obstructed
series of canyons. That the War Department was somewhat
tardy in learning the news—or at least in realizing its significance—is evidenced by the fact that it sent Wheeler to navigate the Grand Canyon, from the foot upwards, nearly two
years later. But that something of the significance of Powell's
voyage had penetrated to Congress by December 13th is indicated by the fact that no "Concurrent Resolutions tendering
thanks to Hon. Samuel Adams" for his untiring energy and indomitable enterprise displayed in opening up the navigation of
the Grand and the Blue rivers, those great natural thorough-
fares of Colorado, appear to have been spread upon the minutes of the House on this occasion. Neither have I found anything to indicate that the petition brought any response from
the legislature of the ungrateful people whom Adams planned
"to connect more firmly in the bonds of common nationality"
by the "central route of the misrepresented stream of the Colorado."

I shall always regret not having had a chance to consider

Adams' rough-and-tumble, slap-banging run down the Blue and
the Grand as the real dare-devilish stunt that it was, rather
than as an adjunct to his wheedling petition and his audacious
attempts to remould the topography of the Grand Canyon of
the Colorado nearer to his heart's desire.   The Adams that was
a drawer and presenter of petitions, and a maker and repairer
of topography, rather dims the thoroughly wholesome respect
one might have had for the Adams who swooped down and
scooped up the Blue and the Grand in open boats, and who
wanted to batter down the obstructing walls of Gore Canyon
with a tulé raft.

CHAPTER X

THE outstanding figure of the latest half century of Colorado River history is that of Major J. W. Powell, and if the coming years bring any change in its status it will only be to leave it bulking bigger against the sky-line of the future than of the present. We are still too near the great explorer of the Southwest in point of time to consider his achievements in adequate perspective. Historical perspective is only gained in looking down a long vista of years. Thus viewed at the end of the vista of clarifying years it may well appear that Powell, the Scientist and Director of Scientists (through his long work at the head of the Bureau of Ethnology and of the Geological Survey) will loom more impressive than Powell, the Explorer. But that time is not yet. For our very sketchy and superficial present-day review it is with Powell, the Colorado canyon voyageur, that we have to do, one of the most humanly appealing figures in American history.

J. W. Powell was the son of a Methodist minister—a man of "immense mental and moral strength, resolution and fortitude," according to Dellenbaugh, who remarked those qualities in the explorer's father even at an advanced age. That the son had inherited his share of the same good stuff is well evidenced by the fact that he contrived to continue in active service as a volunteer officer of the Union Army even after losing an arm at Shiloh. At the close of the Civil War Powell became connected with the Wesleyan University of Illinois, and his interest in the Colorado canyons was first aroused in the course of vacation studies in Colorado and Wyoming. Out of this interest grew the desire for an intimate exploration of the whole

223

canyon series, and this the man's sound sense and unfailing instinct told him could be properly accomplished only by boating down-stream from the head, not (as the War Department persisted in believing for some years longer) by trying to defy the law of gravity in working up from the foot.

A season's exploration along the upper Green confirming in Powell's mind the practicability of his plan, he returned to Illinois to complete financial arrangements and arrange for the construction of the necessary boats. Funds for the expedition were provided by the State Institutions of Illinois and the Chicago Academy of Science. The only help received from the Government was in the form of a permit to draw rations from the nearest available western army posts. The boats were built in Chicago from designs furnished by Powell, and are thus described at the beginning of his report of the voyage:

"Our boats are four in number. Three are built of oak; stanch and firm; double-ribbed, with double stem and stern posts, and further strengthened by bulkheads, dividing each into three compartments.

"Two of these, the fore and aft, are decked, forming water-tight cabins. It is expected these will buoy the boats should the waves roll over them in rough water. The little vessels are twenty-one feet long, and, taking out the cargoes, can be carried by four men.

"The fourth boat is made of pine, very light, but sixteen feet in length, with a sharp cut-water, and every way built for fast rowing, and divided into compartments as the others."

It seems to me that Powell has never been given sufficient credit for the design and construction of these boats. Considering that he had had no previous experience in rough water, and little if any even in still, the fact that he produced at his first attempt a type of craft fully adequate to the work in hand is a striking example of the man's resource, ingenuity and sound common sense. This is all the more remarkable in the light of the fact that so many later Colorado canyon voyageurs, in attempting to improve upon this original type, have encoun-

tered failure and disaster. The flat-bottomed one-man skiff—
perfected by Galloway and Stone, and used in all of the recent
rough-water work on the Colorado—is a better boat for present-day purposes than the original Powell type. But it would
not have stowed enough freight or passengers to answer the
peculiar needs of that pioneer voyage of 1869, when there was
no chance to replenish either food or outfit in the whole distance from Green River, Wyoming, to the mouth of the Virgin.

As Powell expected to have to winter before completing the
voyage, he provisioned for ten months. Even an assortment of
traps was provided, with a considerable supply of heavy clothing. Scientific instruments included chronometers, sextants,
barometers, thermometers and compasses—everything readily
portable, in fact, for making careful astronomical, meteorological and physiographic records. The photographic apparatus of
that day was doubtless deemed too cumbersome to carry upon
this initial venture. Everything practicable was carried in
duplicate, with the whole outfit so distributed among the four
boats that the loss of one of them would deprive the expedition
of a minimum of indispensable articles.

Powell's report reveals only in incidental mention the origin
of his men, but this is supplied by Dellenbaugh in his "Romance
of the Colorado River." Besides the Major, the party was
made up of the following:

"Sumner, generally known as Jack Sumner, had also been a soldier
in the late war. He was fair-haired and delicate-looking, but with
a strong constitution. Dunn had been a hunter and trapper. Walter
Powell was Major Powell's youngest brother. He had been in the
late war and had there suffered cruelly by capture and imprisonment.
Bradley was an orderly sergeant of regulars, had served in the late
war, and resigned from the army to join this party. O. G. Howland
had been a printer. Seneca Howland was his younger brother.
Goodman was a young Englishman. Hawkins had been a soldier
in the late war, and Andrew Hall was a Scotch boy nineteen years
old."

In this highly varied assortment of individuals it does not appear that there was one thoroughly experienced rough-water boatman. Powell, who must have had a real instinct for judging his fellow beings, simply picked the best men that presented themselves and let it go at that. That considerable dissension should crop out in a party of this kind, bound on such a venture, was inevitable; the really remarkable thing is that Powell should have been able to hold enough of them together to fulfil his plans—another example of the peculiar fitness of the man for the work in hand.

The narrative portion of Powell's report is in the form of a journal, with the incidents of each day entered in sequence. This is not the rough diary kept on the voyage, however, but a considerably polished expansion of it, probably written at least three years subsequently. This is proven by the fact that the author, doubtless writing-in unrecorded occurrences from memory, unwittingly incorporated in his report of the initial voyage incidents which befell in the later one of 1872. These slight anachronisms, as Mr. Dellenbaugh has stated in calling one of them to my attention, are of negligible importance.[1] The narrative itself—with its admirably maintained balance of informative detail, dramatic incident and humorous anecdote—is as much of a classic as a story of scientific adventure, as the voyage which inspired it is a classic of exploration.

Powell's full report, as originally published by the Smithsonian Institute in 1875, occupied a large quarto volume, and even the journal, subsequently republished separately, runs to a very sizable book of over three hundred pages. Obviously, in the restricted space of a single chapter, it is impossible to do even the scantiest justice to an original which itself bears evidence of touching upon only the salient features of the epic voyage. I shall confine myself, therefore, to sketching in occasional high lights of the story, with especial attention to the

[1] See footnote, p. 94.

train of incidents leading up to the dramatic division of the
party at Separation Rapid, with its tragic sequel—the one phase
of the voyage over which there has been, and will continue to
be, serious controversy.

The start was made from Green River, Wyoming, to which
point the boats had been brought over the newly-constructed
Union Pacific, on May 24th.   Powell led the way in the light
scouting skiff, the *Emma Dean*, named in honour of his wife.
The boats, loaded almost to their gunwales, had to be handled
with the greatest care to keep from shipping water, and the
usual number of minor mishaps enlivened the montony of the
easy three-days' run to the head of the first of the great canyons of the Colorado series.   The "flaring, brilliant, red" portal which conducted to the River of Mystery beyond was
christened by the singularly appropriate name of Flaming
Gorge.   Indeed, from first to last, Powell's strikingly fitting
nomenclature has probably never been rivalled in the history
of exploration.   Save for two or three substitutions subsequently made by Powell himself, the names he applied to the
most prominent natural features of the double panorama unrolled in the course of his canyon voyage survive to this
day.

The head of Flaming Gorge was supposed to be the location
of the mythical "Suck," described in the lurid Beckwourth narrative as the terror of the trappers of his time.   The Powell
boats, however, found comparatively smooth going through
the flamboyant portal; likewise in threading the U-shaped
gorge called Horseshoe Canyon which followed.   Kingfisher
Canyon, named from its swarming denizens of the cliffs
and air, was unbroken by fast-running water, and it was not
until the towering sandstone walls of Red Canyon closed
in that anything approaching real rapids were encountered.
That the stern nature of the work ahead did not occupy the
mind of the explorer to the exclusion of the natural beauty of
his surroundings is attested by his description of a vast amphi-

theatre of lofty terraces rising opposite the camp at what he called Beehive Point.

"Each step is built of red sandstone, with a face of naked, red rock, and a glacis clothed with verdure. So the amphitheatre seems banded red and green, and the evening sun is playing with roseate flashes on the rocks, with shimmering green on the cedars' spray, and iridescent gleams on the dancing waves. The landscape revels in sunshine."

A twelve-mile current, with the boats dashing and leaping in the waves like "herds of startled deer bounding through forests beset with fallen timber," gave the first fore-running thrills of rough-water work. Tedious lining-down at several rocky riffles, with a laborious portage of all the cargoes around the sharp pitch at Ashley Falls, revealed something of the reverse of the shield, though perhaps not quite enough. The chastening effect of a bit of real trouble in Red Canyon might well have operated to instill a respect for the power of the river that would have resulted in an avoidance of the disaster lurking below in the depths of Lodore. Of Powell's misreading of the historic Ashley inscription, and of his faulty theory respecting the fate of his distinguished predecessor, I have already written.[1]

Brown's Hole, the famous old rendezvous of the trappers, Powell called by the rather more appropriate name of Brown's Park. Recuperating here from the rough work in Red Canyon, the party, like those of Ashley and Manly before them, revelled in the game that abounds in the beautiful little mountain valley and prepared for the next step into the remoter Unknown beyond the frowning Gate of Lodore. Powell's account of his awakening on one of these idyllic days of sweet-doing-nothing in Brown's Park reveals alike the man's keen responsiveness to the intimate little things of Nature and his whimsical sense of humour. As a transition from the sublime to the ridiculous it is rather a little classic.

[1] See pp. 94 and 133.

DELLENBAUGH'S BUTTE, GREEN RIVER, NEAR MOUTH
OF SAN RAFAEL.

J. W. POWELL, FIRST NAVIGATOR OF THE COLORADO.

PANORAMA OF CATARACT CANYON.

LOW WATER BEND IN THE RIVER AT THE EXTREME EAST END OF HORSESHOE CANYON.

"June 6.—At daybreak, I am awakened by a chorus of birds. It seems as if all the feathered songsters of the regions have come to the old tree. Several species of warblers, woodpeckers, and flickers above, meadow-larks in the grass, and wild geese in the river. I recline on my elbow, and watch a lark near by, and then awaken my bed fellow, to listen to my Jenny Lind. A morning concert for me; none of your 'matinées.'

"Our cook has been an ox-driver, or 'bull-whacker,' on the plains, in one of those long trains now no longer seen, and he hasn't forgotten his old ways. In the midst of the concert, his voice breaks in: 'Roll out! Roll out! bulls in the corral! chain up the gaps! Roll out! Roll out! Roll out!' And this is our breakfast bell."

The reflective note had replaced the whimsical in the concluding passage of the entry of the following day. Forward-cast shadows of events slanted across the explorer's mind on the eve of facing the Innermost Mystery—shadows momentarily darker than the sunset-flung duskiness of the towering Gate of Lodore.

"This evening, as I write, the sun is going down, and the shadows are settling in the cañon. The vermilion gleams and roseate hues, blending with the green and grey tints, are slowly changing to sombre brown above, and black shadows are creeping over them below; and now it is a dark portal to a region of gloom—the gateway through which we are to enter on our voyage of exploration to-morrow. What shall we find?"

According to an old Indian with whom Powell had discussed his voyage the previous year, the prospect was not altogether a cheering one. Describing what happened to one of his tribe whose temerity had prompted him to head his canoe through the flaming gate, the old warrior exclaimed to the accompaniment of fluent gesture:

"Rocks h-e-a-p, h-e-a-p high; the water go h-oo-woogh, h-oo-woogh; water-pony [boat] h-e-a-p buck; water catch 'em; no see 'em squaw any more! no see 'em pappoose any more!"

And so, warned by both word and instinct, Powell headed his little flotilla into the gloomy gorge which, because the water went tumbling down in a way that recalled to one of the men the old school-book jingle, they decided to call the Canyon of Lodore. Scouting ahead in his light skiff according to pre-arranged plan, Powell landed at the head of every doubtful looking place and, leaving a man behind to warn the other boats, went along the bank to reconnoitre the rapid. It was the failure of the crew of one of the boats to heed the halting signal that precipitated immediate disaster and laid the train of ultimate tragedy. The following is a condensation of Powell's account of what happened:

"During the afternoon, we come to a place where it is necessary to make a portage. The little boat is landed, and the others are signalled to come up. . . . I walk along the bank to examine the ground, leaving one of my men with a flag to guide the other boats to the landing place. I soon see one of the boats make shore all right and feel no more concern; but a minute after I hear a shout, and looking around, see one of the boats shooting down the centre of the sag. It is the *No Name*, with Captain Howland, his brother, and Goodman. I feel that its going over is inevitable, and run to save the third boat. A minute more, and she turns the point and heads for the shore. Then I turn down stream again, and scramble along to look for the boat that has gone over. The first fall is not great, only ten or twelve feet, and we often run such; but below, the river tumbles down again for forty or fifty feet, in a channel filled with dangerous rocks that break the waves into whirlpools and beat them into foam. I pass around a great crag just in time to see the boat strike a rock, and, rebounding from the shock, careen and fill the open compartment with water. Two of the men lose their oars; she swings around, and is carried down at a rapid rate, broadside on, for a few yards, and strikes amidships on another rock with great force, is broken quite in two, and the men are thrown into the river; the larger part of the boat floating buoyantly, they soon seize it, and down the river they drift, past the rocks for a few hundred yards to a second rapid, filled with huge boulders, where the boat strikes again, and is dashed to pieces, and the men and fragments are soon carried beyond my sight. Running along, I turn a bend, and see a man's head above the water, washed about in a whirlpool below a great rock.

"It is Frank Goodman, clinging to it with a grip upon which life depends. Coming opposite, I see Howland trying to go to his aid from an island on which he has been washed. Soon, he comes near enough to reach Frank with a pole, which he extends toward him. The latter lets go the rock, grasps the pole, and is pulled ashore. Seneca Howland is washed farther down the island, and is caught by some rocks, and, though somewhat bruised, manages to get ashore in safety."

Gallant and skilful work by Jack Sumner pulling the light *Emma Dean* brought the marooned crew to the bank. The after cabin of the wrecked boat, torn and splintered, was found stranded against a midstream rock a half mile down stream. Powell's first feeling was that even the value of the indispensable barometers in the battered hulk would not justify the risking of life in attempting their recovery, but after a sleepless night he determined the following morning to see what salvage could be effected. Sumner and Dunn, volunteering for the work, piloted the handy *Emma Dean* to the wreck. A ringing cheer announced to the anxious watchers on the bank that the risk had not been run in vain—that at least a part of the valuable cargo of the ill-fated *No Name* still appeared recoverable. Powell, delighted at the joy displayed by his faithful men on finding his precious instruments unharmed, joined heartily in the cheer from the wreck. Presently the boat returned, delivering to the grateful chief all that remained in the broached cabin.

"I find that the only things saved from the wreck [he writes] were the barometers, a package of thermometers, and a three-gallon keg of whisky, which is what the men were shouting about. They had taken it aboard, unknown to me, and now I am glad they did, for they think it will do them good, as they are drenched every day by the melting snow, which runs down the summits of the Rocky Mountains."

Powell's sense of humour appears to have saved the situation at this juncture. Whisky is an almost indispensable adjunct of a hard river trip, but not in the hands of the boatmen. I know where a ten-gallon keg of very ancient Scotch remains cached to this day near the apex of the Big Bend of the Columbia because the leader of a party, himself anything but a teetotaler, distrusted the false courage that mellow old beverage had awakened in his bow-paddler.[1] Powell displayed both restraint and charity in refraining from suggesting (what may very well have been the case) that this particular delegate of John Barleycorn's had a hand on the steering-oar of the unfortunate *No Name* when her crew failed to heed the danger-signal and head in to the bank.

Powell's whole account of the incident which gave the name to Disaster Falls is singularly free from the least hint of bitterness toward the crew whose very culpable carelessness (not to say open insubordination) was responsible for so seriously endangering the success of his expedition. Personally, indeed (whatever may have been said in anger at the time), Powell probably harboured very little resentment toward the men for the wreck itself; the fact remains, however, that smouldering animosities engendered by the incident, kept alive by other clashes of temperament inevitable under the circumstances, were finally fanned into the flame that broke up the party on the eve of the successful completion of the long voyage through the canyons.

Careful lining and portaging carried the three surviving boats through the wild waters of Lodore. An especially violent succession of rock-torn riffles won for itself the name of Hell's Half Mile, one of the few instances Powell, in spite of the provocation, sought nomenclatural inspiration in the infernal regions. I have heard of no subsequent voyageur suggesting a

---

[1] "Down the Columbia"—Chapters VI and VII. I sincerely trust that this allusion will not result in another avalanche of popular interest in the recovery of this buried treasure. My plans are such that I cannot consider heading any sort of a salvage expedition for an indefinite period.—L. R. F.

less sulphurous name for this savage run of falls, however; indeed the expressive title has even been borrowed for several other almost equally annoying little stretches at points lower down the river.   That of Lodore, nevertheless, is the original if not the only Hell's Half Mile.   The Powell party all but lost another boat here, through its breaking away while being lined down.   Fortunately it brought up in an eddy undamaged. What they would have called the place if the fugitive *had* been broken up is an interesting point upon which to speculate. Possibly, since nothing more infernal could have been added to the name, they would have had simply to increase the distance —made an even mile of it, for instance.

To crown the memories of Lodore the camp-fire, scattered by a sudden whirlwind, started a violent conflagration in the dry cedars and willows, driving the whole party into the river. Much clothing and bedding had to be abandoned to the flames, while the cook, stumbling in his flight with the mess-kit, spilled most of the knives, forks, plates and spoons into deep water. Cutting loose the boats, the whole outfit went wallowing off into an unexplored rapid thickly beset with rocks.   Powell, beholding the wild Hegira from the heights beyond sight of the fire, was filled with astonishment at the inexplicable flight.   Luckily no boats were swamped and few indispensable articles lost in the fire.   Powell writes that a few tin cups, basins and a camp-kettle were all that remained of the mess-kit, but adds philosophically: "Yet we do just as well as ever."

Nine days were spent in working through the twenty-one miles of Lodore.   The wild gorge, with its almost unbroken succession of savage rapids, left a deep impression on the mind of the explorer.   Writing from a quiet camp at the mouth of the Yampa, he says:

"This has been a chapter of disasters and toils, notwithstanding which the Cañon of Lodore was not devoid of scenic interest, even beyond the power of pen to tell.   The roar of its waters was heard unceasingly from the hour we entered it until we landed here.   No quiet in all that time. But its walls and cliffs, its peaks and crags, its amphitheatres and alcoves, tell a story of beauty and grandeur that I hear yet—and shall hear."

On the river Powell was content to leave the physical work of handling the boats to his men, but during the long halts he was engaged in almost incessant climbing—most of it in connection with his barometric observations for elevation. The greater part of this was up and down the precarious footings afforded by cracks in the often sheer walls of the canyons. In this sort of effort the lack of an arm imposed a double handicap. It deprived him of a considerable lifting and lowering power, and it impaired his balance. Neither his nerve nor his confidence, strangely, was in the least affected. Indeed, the accounts of his climbings give one an impression of recklessness widely at variance with his extreme carefulness upon the river. More than once he crawled onto ledges or into nooks and niches from which only the nerve and resourcefulness of his companions extricated him without serious consequences. The all-but-tragic sequel to a little clamber up the cliff opposite the Yampa camp is a fair example of the sort of trouble the venturesome explorer got himself into on several occasions. Pulled by Bradley in the light boat, a talus of rocks was reached from which it appeared possible to make an ascent. The entry of June 18th continues:

"Here we find a shelf, along which we can pass, and now are ready for the climb. We start up a gulch; then pass to the left, on a bench, along the wall; then up again, over broken rocks; then we reach more benches, along which we walk, until we find more broken rocks and crevices, by which we climb still up, until we have ascended six or eight hundred feet; then we are met by a sheer precipice.

"Looking about we find a place where it seems possible to climb. I go ahead; Bradley hands the barometer to me and follows. So we proceed, stage by stage, until we are nearly to the summit. Here, by making a spring, I gain a foothold in a little crevice, and grasp an angle in the rock overhead. I find I can get no farther, and cannot step back, for I dare not let go with my hand, and cannot reach foothold below without. I call to Bradley for help. He finds a way by which he can get to the top of the rock over my head, but cannot reach me. Then he looks around for some stick or limb of a tree, but finds none. Then he suggests that he had better help me with the barometer case; but I fear I cannot hold on to it. The moment is critical. Standing on my toes, my muscles begin to tremble. It is sixty or eighty feet to the foot of the precipice. If I lose my hold I shall fall to the bottom, and then perhaps roll over the bench, and tumble still farther down the cliff. At this instant it occurs to Bradley to take off his drawers, which he does, and swings them down to me. I hug close to the rock, let go with my hand, seize the dangling legs, and, with his assistance, I am enabled to gain the top."

Fortunately this was before the Rue de la Paix *motif* had begun to influence the design of male *lingerie*. No such rescue as that could have been effected in any party with which I have ever boated on the Colorado, nor, for that matter, any other stream south of Alaska.

Careful lining took the boats down through the gorges called respectively Whirlpool and Split Mountains canyons. Two days more in easy water from the foot of the latter carried them to the mouth of the Uinta. Here, to allow the making of extensive observations and a visit to the Uinta Indian Agency, camp was established for a week. Frank Goodman, who had accompanied Powell out to the Reservation, decided not to return to the party, saying that he had "seen danger enough." Powell comments:

"It will be remembered that he was one of the crew on the *No Name* when she was wrecked. As our boats are rather heavily loaded, I am content that he should leave, although he has been a faithful man."

Although this passage reveals no trace of resentment, Powell subsequently expressed himself as being far from pleased at Goodman's lack of loyalty to the expedition.[1]

[1] See p. 251.

That part of the Green which Powell had followed to the Uinta had been traversed previously by at least two parties— those of Ashley and Manly. Manly had left the river in the vicinity of the mouth of the Uinta, and Ashley had pushed on to somewhere near Gunnison's Crossing before abandoning his bull-boats. But to the junction of the Green and the Grand Powell probably had no white predecessor. The Macomb expedition of 1859 attained to no nearer than four miles of the junction. De Julien, probably a French-Canadian trapper, whose name, with the date 1836, is carved in the rock of both Glen Canyon and Labyrinth Canyon, would have passed the mouth of the Grand in the event he was making a continuous voyage either up or down the river. As one of his inscriptions has a picture of what appears to be a boat with a sail, there is a possibility that he was sticking to the river and trying to work up-stream. The connection between the two records, however, is too tenuous to base definite conclusions upon.

Desolation Canyon, although by no means as rough as Lodore, was responsible for upsetting the *Emma Dean* and giving Powell, Sumner and Dunn rather a lively time in the water. The most serious result of the accident, however, was the loss of two guns, two rolls of blankets and a barometer. There were spare guns and barometers, but the loss of the bedding prompts Powell to observe that "sometimes hereafter we may sleep cold." The following day Bradley, tossed out of the boat in a swift chute, caught his foot under a thwart and was dragged, head downward, for some distance. Fortunately Captain Powell, who was at the oars, extricated the boat from her difficulties in time to save his mate from drowning.

An overhauling of the outfit during the three-day halt at the Grand revealed the alarming fact that but two months' supplies remained. As provisions sufficient for ten months were loaded at starting, while the party had been on the river less than two months, this meant that the wreck of the *No Name* and various minor mishaps had resulted in the loss or destruction of over half of the original supplies. As it seemed likely that not over half of the distance to the foot of the Grand Canyon had been covered, and that probably the less difficult half, the necessity for an increased rate of progress was readily apparent.

The voyage was resumed on July 21st. The augmented menace of the doubled volume of the river was brought home at almost the first rapid encountered, where the over-venturesome *Emma Dean* was capsized, with the loss of three oars. The other boats were halted, and the rest of the day spent in making a laborious portage. A steady continuation of falls and rapids of great pitch and violence suggested the appropriate name of Cataract Canyon for the great gorge entered below the junction, and there was not enough quiet water found in the course of the week of desperately hard work required to bring the boats safely out at the foot to jeopardize the fitness of the choice. The spectacular towers, pinnacles and spires of the point Powell called Mille Crag Bend marked the end of Cataract Canyon, with its forty-one miles of length broken by some of the worst water on the Colorado.

A nine-mile run down the swift but unbroken current of a terraced gorge which they decided to call Narrow Canyon, brought the *Emma Dean* to the mouth of a good-sized stream entering from the right. Powell records:

"Into this our little boat was turned. One of the men in the boat following, seeing what we have done, shouts to Dunn, asking if it is a trout-stream. Dunn replies, much disgusted, that it is 'a dirty devil,' and by this name the river is to be known hereafter."

This lapse into nomenclatural frivolity—the result of the whimsical humour of the moment—appears to have set somewhat heavily upon Powell's conscience. A fortnight or more later he tried to atone for the act by naming a clear, beautiful stream flowing into the Grand Canyon Bright Angel Creek. This was intended, as he explained, as an offset to the stream they had already named after "the great chief of the 'bad angels!'" Even that did not quite square with the explorer's idea of his responsibility to posterity, however. Some years later he caused the name on the maps of a certain turbid, alkaline, foul-smelling little stream to be changed from "Dirty Devil" to Frémont River. One wonders if the sensitive, high-spirited "Path-finder" ever had to be assured that he was not being paid a left-handed compliment. I believe, however, that Powell had a real admiration for General Frémont.

The next hundred and fifty miles down the quiet-flowing waters of Glen Canyon was a welcome relief from the punishing work among the cataracts in the savage gorge below the Grand. Less spectacular scenically than some of the ampler dimensioned chasms of the upper and lower river, for beauty that allures rather than staggers the tapestried walls of Glen Canyon are without a rival in the whole length of the Colorado. Side streams are frequent, and springs of crystal clearness—each in a sylvan dell of its own—trickle out at the base of the cliffs for mile after mile. These ever cool and inviting little glens—veritable bowers of boskiness—supplied the motif for Powell's name. An especially lovely glen at which he camped below the San Juan is only one of a hundred scattered along this wonderfully appealing stretch of the river.

"On entering it, we find a little grove of box-elder and cotton-wood trees; and, turning to the right, we find ourselves in a vast chamber, carved out of the rock. At the upper end there is a clear, deep pool of water, bordered with verdure. . . . The chamber is more than two hundred feet high, five hundred feet long, and two hundred feet wide. Through the ceiling, and on through the rocks for a thousand feet above, there is a narrow, winding skylight; and this is all carved out by a little stream, which only runs during the showers that fall now and then in this arid country. . . . Here we bring our camp. When 'Old Shady' sings us a song at night, we are pleased to find that this hollow in the rock is filled with sweet sounds. It was doubtless made for an academy of music by its storm born architects; so we name it Music Temple."

Powell ran past the mouth of Aztec Creek with nothing to tell him that an easy six-mile climb in the direction of the towering Navajo Mountain would bring him to the shadow of the striking natural monument we now call the Rainbow Bridge. *El Vado de los Padres* he recognized from the fragmentary portion of Escalante's diary available to him at that time. They camped that night at the historic ford, and on the morrow reached the head of Marble Canyon at the Paria. A place on this day's run, where "the rocks are chiefly variegated shales of beautiful colours—creamy orange above, then bright vermilion, and below, purple and chocolate beds, with green and yellow sands," is readily recognizable as not far above the site of the great Glen Canyon dam.

It was not until a year or two later that the renegade, John D. Lee, fanatical inciter of the Mountain Meadows massacre, established himself and one of his numerous wives and families at the mouth of the Paria. The beautiful little valley was probably uninhabited when the Powell party pitched its hurried over-night camp at the point known for the last fifty years as Lee's Ferry. Some of the second Powell expedition met Lee, and found him, in spite of his sinister reputation, rather an attractive character. His wife Emma, a young English woman of remarkable pulchritude, was spoken of as a person of real charm and character.

The down-stream vista of the Colorado from the mouth of the Paria is singularly empty of threat—to the novice, that is. A gently sloping mesa engulfs the river, but between walls that appear much inferior in height to those of the beautiful Glen Canyon just left behind. It is the rapid downward plunge of the river and the still more rapid up-run of the plateau that make the transition from the open valley of the Paria to the depths of Marble Canyon so astonishing. But that Powell's sound geological sense warned him that they were quit of quiet waters for a while his entry for August 5th attests.

"With some feeling of anxiety we enter a new cañon this morning. We have learned to closely observe the texture of the rock. In softer strata, we have a quiet river; in harder, we find rapids and falls. Below us are the limestones and hard sandstones, which we found in Cataract Cañon. This bodes toil and danger."

This ominous forecast was borne out by the steady succession of fierce rapids into which they plunged but a few miles below the Paria. The canyon walls grew higher and higher, and the falls more frequent and violent. Linings and portages became increasingly necessary, and by one of the earliest of these was passed the long, wild tumble of Soap Creek Rapids, below which the Brown party was to meet disaster twenty years later. The imperative necessity of subjecting the dwindling food supply to the minimum of risk was doubtless responsible for the elaborate care taken to avoid further upsets. Rapids where the danger of drowning would have been faced lightsomely and with jest had the food supply been assured, took on a darker menace with the spectre of starvation stalking every run. The infinite trouble taken to avoid entering a rapid the end of which was not in sight from above is well illustrated by Powell's account of the remarkable expedients resorted to in passing a fall not far below the head of Marble Canyon.

"About ten o'clock we come to a place where the river occupies the entire channel, and the walls are vertical from the water's edge. We see a fall below, and row up against the cliff. There is a little shelf, or rather a horizontal crevice, a few feet over our heads. One man stands on the deck of the boat, another climbs on his shoulders, and then into the crevice. Then we pass him a line, and two or three others, with myself, follow; then we pass along the crevice until it becomes a shelf, as the upper part, or roof, is broken off. On this we walk for a short distance, slowly climbing all the way, until we reach a point where the shelf is broken off, and we can pass no farther. Then we go back to the boat, cross the stream, and get some logs that have lodged in the rocks, bring them to our side, pass them along the crevice and shelf, and bridge over the broken place. Then we go on to a point over the falls, but do not obtain a satisfactory view. Then we climb out to the top of the wall, and walk along to the point below the fall, from which it can be seen. From this point it seems possible to let down our boats, with lines, to the head of the rapids, and then make a portage; so we return, row down by the side of the cliff, as far as we dare, and fasten one of the boats to a rock. Then we let down another boat to the end of its line beyond the first, and the third boat to the end of its line beyond the second, which brings it to the head of the fall, and under an overhanging rock. Then the upper boat, in obedience to a signal, lets go; we pull in the line, and catch the nearest boat as it comes, and then the last. Then we make a portage, and go on."

Although rapids where Powell devised manœuvres no less intricate and laborious than these to minimise the risk of trouble have been successfully run by subsequent voyageurs—notably the Kolbs—this conservative policy was most thoroughly warranted in the case of the pioneer expedition, both because it faced the Unknown and because its food supply was already reduced beyond the danger limit.

The increasing anxieties over navigation and dwindling food supplies, while having the effect of reducing the time and care hitherto given to observations, did not blind Powell to the scenic grandeur of the double panorama unfolded by the running road. He writes of the gleaming colours of the burnished marble walls—"white, gray, pink, and purple, with saffron tints;" and of walking at one place for more than a mile

" . . . on a marble pavement, all polished and fretted with strange devices, and embossed in a thousand fantastic patterns. Through a cleft in the wall the sun shines on this pavement, which gleams in iridescent beauty."

At another point, a bend of the river revealed a wall, "set with a million brilliant gems." On coming nearer they found what might have been a transplanted bit of Glen Canyon— "fountains bursting from the rock, high overhead, and the spray in the sunshine" forming the gems of the bejewelled wall.

Powell called the beautiful bend Vesey's Paradise, after a botanist who had been with him the previous year.

The mouth of the deep, narrow gorge of the Little Colorado, marking alike the end of Marble Canyon and the beginning of the Grand Canyon, was reached on August 10th. A three-day halt was made here for taking latitude and longitude observations, measuring the height of the walls, and overhauling the boats and rations. Only a month's food supply now remained, and this very badly balanced, with coffee and dried apples bulking all out of proportion to flour and bacon. For almost the first time Powell fails to cap the resumé of a dark situation with one of his quaint philosophical witticisms. The gloomy spirit of the deepening gorge ahead must have been brooding near him as he wrote:

"We have an unknown distance yet to run; an unknown river yet to explore. What falls there are, we know not; what rocks beset the channel, we know not; what walls rise over the river, we know not. Ah, well! we may conjecture many things. The men talk as cheerfully as ever; jests are bandied about freely this morning; but to me the cheer is sombre and the jests are ghastly."

The morning after pushing off from the Little Colorado the river re-entered the granite. Rock harder than any yet encountered was ominous in its import of rougher water. The granite towered ever higher as they ran into the sinister gorge until it became a great thousand-foot stratum. Here a heavy roar heralded the approach to a fall which Powell estimated to have a drop of "seventy-five to eighty feet in a third of a mile." This was the savage rapids later called the Sockdologer. Because sheer walls on both sides preclude the possibility of portaging or even letting down with lines, there is no alternative to pushing into the head and taking the chance of coming out right-side-up at the foot. Except at very low water, the channel is not as badly obstructed with rocks as at a number of other rapids above and below; the greatest risk is from the great rolling waves at the foot, estimated by Dellenbaugh to have a height of thirty feet.[1]

Finding that they "must run the rapid, or abandon the river," Powell pushed off in the light *Emma Dean* to show the way through the roaring, foam-white cataract below. His is a good description of the helter-skelter kind of sport that the old Sockdologer is always ready to provide.

" . . . Away we go, first on smooth but swift water, then we strike a glassy wave and ride to its top, down again into the trough, up again on a higher wave, and down and up on waves higher and still higher, until we strike one just as it curls back, and a breaker rolls over our little boat. Still on we speed, shooting past projecting rocks, till the little boat is caught in a whirlpool, and spun around several times. At last we pull out again into the stream, and now the other boats have passed us. The open compartment of the *Emma Dean* is filled with water, and every breaker rolls over us. Hurled back from a rock, now on this side, now on that, we are carried into an eddy, in which we struggle for a few minutes, and are then out again, the breakers still rolling over us."

Swamped and out of control but still uncapsized, the little flagship wallowed through to where the other boats awaited her in an eddy below. "We bail our boat, and on we go again," is Powell's only comment. A few miles more between walls now a full mile in height brought them to a rapid which appeared even more difficult than the one run in the morning. Here they attempted a laborious and intricate combination of lining and portaging which, uncompleted at dark, left them to spend the rainy night huddled in their ponchos upon a narrow strip of wet beach. The next morning a wild, sheer-walled rapid, which had to be run because there was no room to portage, upset one of the larger boats and carried off two of her oars. More of the precious food was spoiled; yet Powell found time to note, and was still in mood that night to write:

[1] This estimate of the height of the waves is probably somewhat excessive, as is also that of Powell of a drop of eighty feet in a third of a mile.

"Clouds are playing in the cañon to-day. Sometimes they roll down in great masses, filling the gorge with gloom; sometimes they hang above, from wall to wall, and cover the cañon with a roof of impending storm. . . . Then, a gust of wind sweeps down a side gulch, and, making a rift in the clouds, reveals the blue heavens, and a stream of sunlight pours in. Then the clouds drift away into the distance, and hang around crags, and peaks, and pinnacles, and towers, and walls, and cover them with a mantle, that lifts from time to time, and sets them all in sharp relief. Then, baby clouds creep out of side cañons, glide around points, and creep back again, into more distant gorges. . . . The clouds are the children of the heavens, and when they play among the rocks, they lift them to the region above."

New oars were sawed out in the course of the hasty halt at the mouth of Bright Angel Creek, but for the dwindling food supply there was no replenishment. With the last of the bacon thrown away, spoiled beyond redemption, and the saleratus lost overboard, rations were reduced to a ten days' supply of musty flour, a few dried apples and a large over-stock of coffee. The barometers were so much damaged that all dependable record of the descent had been lost. Powell's closing entry for August 17th indicates that he was considerably borne down by anxiety and makes understandable his allusion to the possibility of having to abandon the boats and make an effort to reach the Mormon settlements to the north.

"It is especially cold in the rain to-night. The little canvas we have is rotten and useless; the rubber ponchos, with which we started from Green River City, have all been lost; more than half of the party is without hats, and not one of us has an entire suit of clothes, and we have not a blanket apiece. So we gather drift wood and build a fire; but after supper the rain, coming down in torrents, extinguishes it, and we sit up all night, on the rocks, shivering, and are more exhausted by the night's discomfort than by the day's toil."

Powell says nothing of the effect upon the men of a ration that was lacking in quantity, quality and variety, but any one who has had to do hard bodily work on an insufficiency of half-spoiled food will know that the mental depression incident to exertion under such conditions is only less than the physical deterioration. That, with the dangers and hardships of the daily grind, and—most important of all perhaps—the spectre of uncertainty hovering over the ultimate outcome of the voyage, must be considered in coming to a fair appreciation of the harassed state of mind in which both leader and men faced the stark human problem suddenly thrust upon them by an apparently impassable fall.

Two or three days more, marked by several portages and another upset of the little *Emma Dean,* carried the party out of the granite. Renewed hope is reflected in Powell's journal, and a fine run through the easier water of the softer limestone is recorded with "Thirty-five miles to-day. Hurrah." And there is a touch of his old whimsical humour in the account of the "nice, green squashes" foraged from an Indian garden unexpectedly found by the river.

"We carry ten or a dozen of these on board our boats, and hurriedly leave, not willing to be caught in the robbery, yet excusing ourselves by pleading our great want. We run down a short distance, to where we feel certain no Indians can follow; and what a kettle of squash sauce we make! True, we have no salt with which to season it, but it makes a fine addition to our unleavened bread and coffee. Never was fruit so sweet as these stolen squashes."

A footing up of the reckoning that night showed another run of thirty-five miles, and Powell closed the day's log with a line of buoyant optimism: "A few days like this, and we shall be out of prison." But the next morning they re-enter the sinister walls of hard granite, and soaring hope gives way to profound gloom as a landing is made at the head of a fall that appears much worse than any yet encountered. There is no room for a portage around the roaring cataract, and Powell's first impression is that "to run it would be sure destruction." [1] In his eagerness to gain a better view of the lower part of the fall, he worked out so far along a narrow shelf that he was unable to return. Handicapped by the lack of an arm, a line tossed to him by one of the men was of no help, and he was finally extricated from his dangerous position, four hundred feet above the river, only after a half-bridge, half-railing had been contrived out of oars. At the end of an afternoon spent in laborious reconnoitring, Powell figured out a possible course through the rapid and announced to the men that he was going to attempt to run it in the morning.

The situation must have been tense all afternoon, doubtless with a good deal of discussion among the men of their desperate predicament. After supper the elder Howland called the Major aside to protest against continuing farther by river. Powell returned to camp, plotted the course for the last two days, and checked it with a latitude sight, making out that they were not over forty-five miles from the mouth of the Virgin. Awakening Howland, the explorer showed him the result of the plot, and then walked off to turn over the situation in his own mind. He writes:

"All night long I pace up and down a little path, on a few yards of sand beach, along the river. Is it wise to go on? I go to the boats again, to look at our rations. I feel satisfied that we can get over the danger immediately before us; what there may be below I know not. . . . But for years I have been contemplating this trip. To leave the exploration unfinished, to say that there is a part of the cañon which I cannot explore, having already almost accomplished it, is more than I am willing to acknowledge, and I determine to go on."

[1] Due, doubtless, to the rather shattered morale of the party at this juncture, Powell and his men were inclined to exaggerate the difficulties of what has since been known as Separation Rapid. Indeed, he admits as much himself after running it. To the Kolbs it did not appear especially menacing, and that some sort of a portage could be contrived there (at least at lower water) is evidenced by the fact that Wheeler worked his boats *up* at this point two years later.

Awakening the men of whom he is surest, the Major found that, besides his brother, Hawkins, the cook, Sumner, Bradley and Hall were game to stick to the river. At a breakfast as "solemn as a funeral" no word was spoken of the future, but immediately afterward Howland reaffirmed his decision to leave. Dunn voiced a similar inclination. The younger Howland, after vainly trying to persuade these two to remain with the party, decided to throw in his lot with his brother.

The three men leaving were given a gun apiece and offered their share of the rations. Evidently confident of getting game along the way, they refused to take any food. It was decided to abandon the badly battered *Emma Dean,* together with the barometers, fossils, mineral specimens and some ammunition. Each party took one of the duplicate sets of records of the expedition, or rather it was intended that each should have a complete set. It transpired later that, in the confusion of departure, the distribution was unevenly made, each party having portions of records in duplicate. The destruction of the duplicate parts carried by the land party left several gaps in the original record.

Dunn and the Howlands gave a hand to lift the boats over a high rock in portaging the first fall, from the foot of which there was a clear run into the second drop. Here good-byes were said. "It is rather a solemn parting," Powell writes; "each party thinks the other is taking the dangerous course."

Powell led the way in the *Maid of the Cañon,* running through to quiet water in scarcely a minute. The second boat was equally successful. Landing as soon as practicable, guns were fired as a signal to the men above that they had come through in safety. Waiting for a couple of hours on the chance that the others might conclude to follow in the *Emma Dean,* the diminished boating party pushed on down the river. There was a succession of bad rapids all morning, and in the afternoon only the nerve and coolness of the powerful Bradley saved one of the boats that had to be cut loose in lining down a heavy fall. But by night they were out of the granite, and the following noon brought them to the foot of the Grand Canyon. The concluding passage of Powell's entry of August 29th breathes a fervent note of thankfulness, tempered by anxiety for the men left behind.

"Now the danger is over; now the toil has ceased; now the gloom has disappeared; now the firmament is bounded only by the horizon; and what a vast expanse of constellations can be seen!

"The river rolls by us in silent majesty; the quiet of the camp is sweet; our joy is almost ecstasy. We sit till long after midnight, talking of the Grand Cañon, talking of home, but chiefly talking of the three men who left us. Are they wandering in those depths, unable to find a way out? are they searching over the desert lands above for water? or are they nearing the settlements?"

The following day they pulled in to the mouth of the Virgin, where some Mormons—pioneers of a projected town—told how they had been watching for fragments and relics of the supposed wrecked Powell outfit for many weeks. The Major and his brother went out with Bishop Leithead, of the Mormon Church, to St. Thomas, en route to Salt Lake City; Sumner, Bradley, Hawkins and Hall kept on down the river to Fort Mojave. What disposition was made of the historic boats is not stated.

Dunn and the Howlands were never again seen by white men. Powell did not learn of their fate until over a year after the parting near the foot of the Grand Canyon. Faring northward across the Shewits Plateau, the trio, half starved and greatly exhausted, reached an Indian village. They were received kindly, given food and directed to the road to the Mormon settlements. Scarcely were they on their way than an Indian arrived from the vicinity of the Colorado, with a story of a squaw killed by miners. Suspecting their recent visitors of the crime, the Shewits pursued the late voyageurs, lay in wait for them at a certain water-pocket, and filled their bodies with arrows as they prepared to resume the trail after filling their canteens. Jacob Hamblin, the Mormon "Leather-Stocking," gathered the details of the ambush at first-hand.

Most of the controversy that has been raised in connection with Powell's spectacular first voyage has had to do with the circumstances under which Dunn and the Howlands left the party at Separation Rapid. Certain members of the party made statements from time to time calculated to cast some doubt on Powell's version of the unfortunate affair. Jack Sumner, for instance, was credited with the assertion that the three men, far from deserting the expedition in its hour of need, were forced to leave it against their will. Hawkins, the cook, issued a statement in direct contradiction to Sumner's, in that he claims that Powell himself desired to go out to the Mormon settlements, and that only his own (Hawkins') initiative, supported by Hall and Bradley, held the explorer to his original resolve.

It is a significant fact that neither of these statements was given publicity in the quarter of a century and more intervening between the appearance of Powell's report and his death. The Sumner statement was put on paper but has not, I believe, appeared in print. Hawkins, shortly before his death in 1919, wrote a short personal narrative of the voyage of 1869, which was published the following year by William Wallace Bass, the pioneer guide of the Grand Canyon. It is extremely interesting as a human document, but altogether too confused about the natural features of the river to entitle it to serious consideration as a historical contribution. It reveals—what would inevitably have been the case where a number of free mountain men embarked upon so hazardous an enterprise under a man of military training—that there was a great deal of friction and petty dissension, and even some fighting and near-shootings. The bullying ways of the Major's brother, Captain Powell, are credited with being at the bottom of most of the trouble,[1] but the explorer himself is not spared.

It is easy enough to believe Hawkins when he states that the mountain men chafed under the control of the late army officers, that personal feeling ran high at times, and that the men became more and more inclined to throw discipline to the wind in such matters as submitting to the laborious work of portages at rapids they believed were runable. But when he tells how the Major harped for days on the price of a watch ruined in a wetting for which he thought Dunn responsible, and how the explorer finally went to the length of trying to drown the trapper by refusing to throw him a life-line at a critical moment, the ex-cook has concocted something rather more difficult to swallow than even those musty-flour "dough-gods" with which he served the voyageurs in the days following the loss of the salt and saleratus. After that it seems hardly worth while to give serious consideration to Hawkins' account of the way in which he, supported by Hall and Bradley, set the example that kept the Major from leaving the river.

With the passing of Hawkins, the curtain was rung down on the last of the actors who figured in the drama of the first Grand Canyon voyage. For that reason it is not probable that much that is new will ever be brought forward either to authenticate or to discredit Powell's story of his historic journey. That the explorer did not put on record the personal dissensions that were rife in his party was due to two reasons: one, because things of that kind had no place in a government report, and the other, because he was too big a man to let the memory of petty passages due to the irritations of the voyage obscure his appreciation of the fact that it was to the devotion and

---

[1] On this point Mr. Dellenbaugh writes me: "Captain Walter Powell, the Major's brother, escaped from a Confederate prison during the Civil War while suffering from typhoid fever, and wandered in the woods for some days before reaching the Northern lines. It was this experience that made him at times a little queer, and may have been aggravated by the hardships of the Grand Canyon till he was irritable. Ordinarily he was a very mild mannered and agreeable personality."

courage of his men that he owed the triumphant outcome of the expedition. This tribute of Powell to his mates of the pioneer voyage could not have been written by a man with anything rankling in his mind or disturbing his conscience:

"I was a maimed man, my right arm was gone; and these brave men, these good men, never forgot it. In every danger my safety was their first care, and in every waking hour some kind service was rendered me, and they transfigured my misfortune into a boon."

It was not only upon the written page that Powell refrained from setting down aught in malice respecting the men who took him through the canyons. Intimate associates of his earlier and later years have told me that he always spoke of even Dunn and the Howlands with the greatest affection. Frank Goodman, who showed the white feather and deserted early in the voyage, was the only member of the original party of whom he was heard to speak in the least disparagingly.

The name of none of the four men who left the party before the completion of the voyage appears on the Powell monument on the brink of the Grand Canyon, and rightly so. Possibly Powell himself, swayed by his heart rather than his head, would have ruled more leniently could he have been consulted. But in the calm, considered judgment of posterity the men were deserters, and as such did not qualify for commemoration on a monument to honour achievement and fidelity. The appreciation of the greatness of Powell's personal achievement will increase with the years.

CHAPTER XI

WHEELER UP THE GRAND CANYON

PERHAPS the most remarkable feat of navigation ever performed on the Colorado was Lieutenant Wheeler's ascent of the Grand Canyon to the mouth of Diamond Creek in 1871; also—considering its cost and the fact that the expedition covered no stretch of the river not previously traversed—was it one of the most useless. Why the Topographical Engineers of the Army sent Wheeler on this utterly unnecessary scramble into the Grand Canyon provokes speculation no less baffling than that aroused by the action of the same body in providing Ives with his freak sectional stern-wheeler to navigate the lower river. Possibly the same zealous bureaucrat who conceived the *Explorer* also conceived the plan of navigating the Grand Canyon from the mouth upwards, for it is known that the original plan of the War Department contemplated the use of a steamer for the exploration of the great gorge.

To whatever and whomever its inception was due, the mad project must have been materially forwarded by White's story of his raft-voyage, in which he claimed to have drifted in quiet water from far above the mouth of Diamond Creek. That Wheeler attached far greater importance to the prospector's astonishing yarn than to Powell's comparatively accurate observations is proven by the fact that the introduction to his report gives half a page to White and a bare seven lines to the voyage of the explorer-scientist. Powell's second expedition, though it had been under way for some months when Wheeler left Mojave for the Grand Canyon, is not mentioned at all by the army officer, nor do I find it included in his "Chronological

WHERE THE COLORADO EMERGES FROM THE GRAND CANYON.

The Canyon voyage of Powell was completed at this point; that of Wheeler was begun here.

BLACK CANYON, COLORADO RIVER, FROM CAMP 8 OF LIEUT. GEO. M. WHEELER'S EXPEDITION.

Account of Explorations of the Colorado River of the West," although the latter was published as up to the year 1880. Jealousy between rival explorers is no new thing, but Wheeler's palpable disregarding of the work of a man which so far transcended his own is hardly what one would expect from an officer who had the courage and determination to beard in his cavernous den the Lion of the Grand Canyon.

Considered as a feat of navigation rather than as a serious work of exploration, Wheeler's surmountal of the long succession of savage falls and rapids between the Grand Wash and the mouth of Diamond Creek has probably never been equalled among similar efforts in any part of the world. Doubtless, moreover, it is destined to stand as a record in its class. This is not because there are not stretches of unexplored river with rapids as bad as those of the lower Grand Canyon (the Brahmaputra, where it cuts through the Himalayas in descending from Tibet to the plains of India, must have some very rough water), but rather because it hardly seems possible that there will ever occur again the peculiar combination of physiographic ignorance and official stupidity required to force the tackling of such a problem of exploration from what is so obviously the wrong end.

The three boats of the Wheeler expedition were built in San Francisco and shipped to Camp Mojave, on the Colorado, by way of the Gulf of California. They are not described in the report, but from the photographs it is evident that they had flat bottoms and square sterns. The former was a desirable feature for the work in hand, the latter undesirable. A boat designed exclusively for up-stream work should be built with a pointed stern, which minimizes the fluid resistance in towing. A barge belonging to the Quartermaster's Department was added to the flotilla as a carrier of reserve supplies. This was a fortunate provision, although the original expectation that the unwieldy craft could be taken right on up the Grand Canyon was not fulfilled.

among whom was O. D. Gass, of Las Vegas Ranch, Nevada, had ascended to that point in 1864. Wheeler comments:

"I am satisfied that no one has ever ascended the river beyond this point, and Mr. Gass, one of the 4 persons mentioned above, told me in 1869 at Las Vegas Ranch that he considered it impossible to penetrate further. It is for this party to try, however, and if successful to-morrow there will seem to be little doubt of reaching Diamond Creek. Travelled 7½ miles to-day. The narrowest point in the river yet reached is immediately above Tufa Springs—75 feet."

A run of seven and a half miles under the conditions Wheeler began to face at this point indicates remarkably good boat work. It was only made possible by the large crews, averaging nine to a boat; but even such a force must have been handled to good advantage to ascend so considerable a distance. Wheeler's optimistically expressed belief that the surmounting of the immediate obstacles would leave little doubt of their reaching Diamond Creek, makes it certain that he placed little credence in Powell's story, at least the salient details of which must have been available to him. Had he read even a summary of the record of his predecessor through these walls, "the geological horizon of granite" which he mentions reaching this day would have told him that it would be a hard grind all the way. The next morning opened with a bang, and one thing or another kept right on banging all day. Wheeler makes no comment on James White's story of the quiet drifting he had enjoyed through this stretch, but his entry for October 10th proves that a day's education in the way of a Grand Canyon rapid with a boat had left him a chastened man.

"Two boats are lost over the rapid immediately in front of our camp, but secured again without damage. Early to-day a rapid is passed with a direct fall of at least 8 feet. The entire fall of the rapid before mentioned is 35 feet, above which comes smooth water for approximately 1½ miles, flowing along solid granite walls of the cañon on either side. Another rapid met during the day calls for all the strength of the different crews. Much water has been taken by the boats. At last a long rapid of two falls appears, with smooth water at its head, extending for quite a distance. The boats succeed in passing the first one a little after dark. It is not considered safe to try the other, as everything has to be unloaded and the first boat has been very nearly swamped. Therefore a dark and dreary camp is made among the debris of the slopes, where, cuddled Indian fashion, the weary hours of the night are passed. The labour of the past few days has been very wearing upon the men, and one of the strongest Indians was thrown upon the rocks and badly bruised, making two invalids in the party. I have several times during the day despaired of reaching Diamond Creek in time to join the relief party there, as each rapid in turn seems to be more powerful than the last, and the number per mile is evidently on the increase; and, furthermore, it appears unlikely that any party has ascended the river farther than this locality, or that one ever will. Still, the objective point can be reached, it is believed, if the men and boats hold together. Travelled approximately 5 miles and camped on north shore."

In his surprise at the formidable character of the obstructions encountered Wheeler does not seem to realize how well his crews had served him in taking those heavy boats up five miles of that sort of river. Powell, and all who came after him, often spent more than a day working *down* a single rapid. Wheeler's great strength was in his almost unlimited manpower, as there was nothing to prevent his concentrating the whole twenty-seven on the lines of a single boat in case of need. It is a matter of regret, however, that he did not describe the character of the rapids in greater detail, with the methods resorted to in surmounting them. Ives would have written an epic account of such stirring work but—judging from the way in which he exaggerated the difficulties of the comparatively quiet waters of Black Canyon—would possibly have lacked the bulldog qualities to see it through. Wheeler dominated the physical difficulties, but has told the story of his remarkable achievement in the bald, matter-of-fact language of an unimaginative school-boy.

A steady grind of lining and portaging the morning of the 11th brought the party to what proved to be the worst rapid of the trip. Because this savage fall had a bite that was worse than its bark, insufficient precautions were taken in trying to ascend with the first boat, and the penalty exacted imposed an all but prohibitive handicap upon the success of the expedition. Wheeler tells what happened, but without giving a very clear idea of just why.

"This rapid seemed long but not dangerous, however, but the first boat going into it proved differently. The first dash filled the boat with water, the second swamped it, and in this way the lives of two boatmen were endangered. The boat ran back against the rocks almost a perfect wreck, and its contents were washed down below the overhanging rocks. A stout case containing my most valuable private and public papers and data for a great share of the season's report, which for the first time had not been taken out of the boat at a portage, was lost, as well as valuable instruments, the astronomical and meteorological observations, and worse than all, the entire rations of that boat. These losses could not be made good, and these disasters threatened to drive the cañon parties back to the barge station at the crossing, thus pronouncing the trip a partial failure. Night came and the boats dropped back about half a mile to camp. Weary myself and much dispirited, it is still necessary to maintain cheerfulness toward the little party, who see great trouble ahead."

When a search the next morning failed to discover any of the articles or provisions lost in the accident, it was decided to send a "portion of the party" (Wheeler does not state how many men) back to the mouth of the canyon in the damaged boat. This left them rationed about as before, but despondent over the outlook, and with only the leaders still confident that the rapids could yet be passed. "It requires no little courage to continue farther on," writes Wheeler, "since one day later would prevent a return in time to meet the relief party at the river-crossing, and the barge has rations only up to a certain date." The account of the lining of the first boat up what they had named Disaster Rapid gives almost no details of how what must have been a very difficult feat was accomplished.

"Mr. Gilbert and myself propose to reassure the men by taking the first boat across the rapid. Portage of the stores is made to the wash at the head of the rapid, which consumes the greater share of the day, and half an hour before twilight a rope is stretched and the emergency prepared for. The entire force is stationed along the line and the cast-off is made. In five minutes the worst part of the rapid is over, and just as the sun sinks gloomily behind the cañon horizon the worst rapid is triumphantly passed, amid the cheers and exultations of every member of the party."

Just what Wheeler meant by stating that he and Gilbert "proposed to reassure the men by taking the first boat across the rapid," is not quite clear. As he speaks of the entire force being stationed along the tow-line, however, it would seem probable that he and the plucky geologist rode in the boat and fended it off the rocks with poles. That would, of course, have been the post of both the greatest danger and the greatest responsibility. There are a half dozen little things that can happen in the wink of an eye to swamp a boat on the end of a line, while the parting of the line itself leaves the boat almost beyond control. Wheeler's military training would have left him in no doubt of the value of example in restoring the shaken morale of his crews.

The second boat was brought up over Disaster Rapid the next morning, and in spite of the fact that three considerable falls were encountered, nearly six miles were made during the day. The granite had attained a height of from seven to eight hundred feet, confining the river in a narrow channel which at one point was reduced to a width of less than fifty feet. A very difficult and laborious portage was completed after dusk. Wheeler writes:

"It is very severe, since the men are greatly worn. The hope of ultimate success sustains the sinking courage as also the belief that no one will follow speedily in our tracks, thus making the ascending exploration of the river complete and final."

A quarter-mile portage around a bad rapid on the 14th required six hours to finish, and the day's run was a little less than three miles. A slightly greater distance was covered the following day in spite of the handicap of long stretches of perpendicular walls and many rapids. The aneroids indicated the fall of the river steadily increasing. The reaches of comparatively easy water were becoming less frequent, and the labour of towing more arduous, especially in the face of a further reduction of rations. To cap the climax of a depressing day:

"Mr. Gilbert's boat is cast away in pulling through the last rapid, and he and Hecox go so far down the stream that the crew could not reach them, hence they go supperless to bed among the rocks in this wild cañon. Our camp is a little shelving place in the rocks, with scarcely enough room for the little party to sleep among the boulders. Every one is gloomy at the prospect, starvation staring one in the face without the certainty of relief either in advance or retreat."

The entry of October 16th was made as from "Starvation Camp." The lurid name, as the record proves, was not a serious misnomer. The day was a bad one throughout.

"To-day it has often been necessary to climb as high as 100 feet in passing the tow-rope ahead. Two portages of stores were necessary, and one portage of the boats. In passing the third nest of rapids the rope parted and one of the boats was cast away upon one of the roughest rapids in the river. The sight, although exciting, was an extremely sickening one. The boat was caught, however, on the other side, and extricated after much difficulty. Such accidents are disheartening in the face of the presumable dangers yet in advance, the number and extent of which are yet unknown. The boat upon the second trial, however, passed safely. . . . The entire rations of the party scarcely make a re-enforce to my blanket pillow, where they are at night placed as a precaution."

On the 17th a portage was made at a rapid recorded as having a fall of ten feet and a width of thirty-five. This extremely

GRAND CANYON, NEAR PARIA CREEK, FROM PHOTOGRAPH BY
LIEUT. WHEELER'S EXPEDITION.

HERMIT CAMP, GRAND CANYON NATIONAL PARK, ARIZ.

narrow channel (provided the river were not divided) indicates an unusually low stage of water and makes it easier to understand how working room was found for linings and portages at points, such as Powell's Separation Rapid, where the Colorado normally occupies all of the bottom of the canyon even in the months of its most reduced flow. Wheeler, mentioning that he has been standing personal guard over the entire stock of rations for some days, hints of the possibility of having to abandon the boats and strike out for the mouth of Diamond Creek across the mesa.

Three and a half miles were made on both the 17th and the 18th. The run of the latter day, covered in spite of two long portages and the breaking of a line that resulted in an upset of Gilbert's boat, was a fine achievement. Even on reduced rations the men must have been working with great energy and determination. That night, with both boats leaking badly, preparations were made to dispatch messengers to Diamond Creek at daybreak the next morning. "This seems a necessary measure," writes Wheeler, "as the lives of twenty persons are now dependent upon the success of the messengers sent ahead for food."

The overland messengers set out on the morning of the 19th from a point called Look-ahead Camp. Wheeler estimated that there were still seventeen miles of river to be covered by the boats before reaching their goal. What the distance finally proved to be is not stated in the journal, but that it was far short of seventeen miles is attested by the fact that the entry for October 19th was written from the mouth of Diamond Creek. The river party received encouragement early in the day through the finding of "a fish-pole and line with a large salmon attached." A little later there was intercepted a float, on which was found a note stating the messengers had attained their destination. Thus nerved to a final effort, the worn and weary crews won through to the Diamond Creek rendezvous before dark.

After a two-days' rest a portion of the party was sent out overland, while the remainder started in their two battered boats on the return voyage. Wheeler states that Mojave was reached on the evening of the fifth day—probably the fastest run ever made over that particular stretch. This concluding performance was also notable as the only run ever made down any considerable portion of the Grand Canyon in practically open boats.

No mention is made in the journal proper of the use of the photographic outfit during the ascent of the Grand Canyon, but in a note to one of the plates published with his report Wheeler gives an epitome of the activities of that branch of his expedition.

"Mr. O'Sullivan, in the face of all obstacles, made negatives at all available points, some of which were saved, but the principal ones of the collection were ruined during the transportation from Prescott, Ariz., via mouth of the Colorado, San Francisco, &c., to Washington, D. C., thus destroying one of the most unique sets of photographs ever taken."

Viewed from the vantage of the half century that has gone by since it was completed, Wheeler's ascent of the Colorado appears in its proper perspective as a very gallant achievement, carried out, like "The Charge of the Light Brigade," at an unnecessarily high cost because of, and in spite of, the fact that "some one had blundered." If Wheeler had been content to consider it as a record-breaking feat of navigation rather than as an outstanding piece of exploration it would have been more to his credit than a stand calculated to magnify his own work at the expense of that of another man. This, it would appear, he was never willing to do. In a collection of his reports published under as late a date as 1889 he still contends that his wild scramble of two score miles up from the foot of the Grand Canyon completed the exploration of the Colorado River. The fact that Powell had covered this same stretch (together with many hundred miles more of Colorado canyons), two years previous to his own ascent is ignored completely. Yet the handling of the various units of Wheeler's own expeditions of 1871 is characterized as "a masterpiece of successful exploring." It seems rather a pity that a man with the resource and courage required to make that epic ascent of the rapids of the lower Grand Canyon could not have shown a better sporting spirit toward a fellow explorer.

CHAPTER XII

THE SECOND POWELL EXPEDITION

POWELL'S second descent of the Colorado canyons was planned for the purpose of making studies and observations left incomplete on the initial voyage. Constantly faced by the menace of the Unknown, and with the spectre of Starvation stalking ever nearer as the voyage lengthened and the food supply dwindled, it became necessary to accelerate the progress of the pioneer venture to a degree that greatly impaired the thoroughness of the scientific work. The second expedition, planned in the light of what had been learned on the first, was designed to fill in the gaps and deficiencies in the records of the latter.

The success of the first expedition made the matter of securing funds for the second one comparatively easy. Congress made appropriations calculated to cover the study of the river and the region immediately contiguous, and authorized the expedition to draw rations from Western Army posts. The supervision, wisely and fortunately, was placed in the very competent hands of Joseph Henry, Secretary of the Smithsonian Institute, with whom Powell worked in the greatest harmony. The railroads again furnished free transportation for both boats and personnel to the point of embarkation. A failure of the food-supply—the rock upon which the first expedition so nearly came to disaster—was provided against by arranging that fresh rations should be brought in by pack-train to the four most readily accessible points between the mouth of the Uinta and the head of Marble Canyon. Powell spent much of the year 1870 working out these food-supply routes at first-hand.

The fact that Powell took no one of his former party on his second expedition would seem to lend colour to the rumours of the incompatabilities that developed in the course of the discovery voyage. The special knowledge and training gained by the members of the pioneer crews could not but have made the surviving veterans of the voyage of sixty-nine (everything else being equal) more useful, for a while at least, than the best of inexperienced rough-water hands. Whether it was Powell who did not want his former men, or they who did not care to serve again under Powell, or whether (as may well have been the case) there was trouble in getting in touch with each other, I have never been able to learn. In any event, Jack Sumner was the only one of the first party who was listed to go with the second, and he was snowed up in the mountains at the time of departure and so was unable to report.

There was no trouble about getting men, however—and extremely good men, too, as their work proved. The preparations for the expedition were given a good deal of publicity, with the result that Powell was deluged with applicants for places from all parts of the country. Having well in mind the combination of qualities necessary in the man who would stand the physical and mental strain of the canyon voyage, the explorer was sufficiently adept of his fellow beings to pick the best qualified candidates. The recorded fact that his crews were co-operating as harmoniously at the end of their second season on the Colorado as at the beginning of their first is the best testimony as to how well he succeeded.

With some dozens of men urging their qualifications to fill the only remaining place in his party, Powell received a call from a youth recommended by an old army friend. As the youngster advanced across the room, the Major rose to his feet and exclaimed heartily: "Well, Fred, you'll do." And so Frederick Dellenbaugh, not yet eighteen years of age, became a member of the Colorado River expedition of 1871. He started out on the trip as artist to the geologists, and before it was over had become both a trained topographer and a thoroughly seasoned river-rat. The Major's confident offhand appraisal was vindicated; and not for the voyage alone. Frederick Dellenbaugh's achievements as an artist and historian entitle him to a place in Colorado River annals second only to that of the great explorer and scientist who brought the youth to the field that was destined to become that of so much of his life-work.

Among the many debts Western History owes to Frederick Dellenbaugh, none is more considerable than that for his work in rescuing the second Powell expedition from practical oblivion. Although the scientific work of the latter was far more thorough and accurate than that of the first expedition, the explorer—for reasons never fully explained—did not make more than brief mention of it in his reports. While the results of the second expedition were incorporated in these reports, it was not in such a way as to allocate the credit to the specific expedition to which it belonged. This was always a sore point with the members of the 1871-72 party, who, in spite of an unswerving loyalty to their leader, felt that he had been rather less than just to them in this one particular. It was doubtless this feeling that led Dellenbaugh, with the full sanction of Powell, to devote several chapters to a condensed account of the second expedition in his "Romance of the Colorado River," published in 1902. This modest story was subsequently expanded to the wholly delightful volume called "A Canyon Voyage," published in 1908.

Notwithstanding the fact that the second voyage fell far short of the first in spectacular and dramatic incident and atmosphere, Dellenbaugh, with the almost unconscious art of the real artist, has written in "A Canyon Voyage" a story that transcends even Powell's epic tale in brimming human interest. Indeed, I would go farther than that, and say that as a sincere and kindly, yet withal spirited and humorous, chronicle of the doings of a man and his mates this absorbing if unpretentious story has never been surpassed. Its greatest charm is the consequence of a paradox—though written by a man it was told by a boy. The author must have been close to fifty-five when the book was written, yet the spirit of it was captured alive from that young seventeen-year-old who slept his first time out-of-doors the night after the second Powell party pushed off from Green River. This may have been the result of an incomparably clever piece of sheer artistry, aided by frequent references to his original log of the *Emma Dean;* or it may have been due (as I am inclined to suspect was the case) to the fact that the doyen of Colorado River explorers and historians had a no less youthful heart thumping against his chest when he pushed a pen in 1908 than when he pulled an oar in 1871.

Besides Dellenbaugh's very complete and accurate account of the second Powell expedition, E. O. Beaman, the photographer who was with the party for the first season, wrote a very readable story covering the portion of the river traversed in 1871. Beaman had been a pilot on the Great Lakes, and was probably the most experienced oarsman in the party. This fact made him rather less respectful toward rapids than he should have been, and brought him into occasional conflict with his more conservative leaders for running riffles in defiance of orders. He appears to have been too good a sport to let this rankle, however, and it was ill health rather than ill feeling that led him to decide to embark on a photographic expedition of his own to the Moqui towns in preference to continuing a second season on the river with Powell. He wrote a very breezy and spirited account of both his river and land journeys, which was published serially in several numbers of *Appleton's Journal* of 1874. The river story throws many interesting side-lights on the daily doings of the party, but—doubtless because the results of the scientific studies and observations were not available to the writer—was very inaccurate in such matters as the fall of rapids, speed of current, distances and the like.

One of the most notable members of the second party was Professor A. H. Thompson, geographer. He was Powell's brother-in-law, and possessed qualities of leadership rivalling those of the chief himself. Dellenbaugh, who had great admiration and affection for the man, pays him a fine tribute.

"Thompson was from Illinois. He also had been a soldier in the war, and on this expedition was Powell's colleague, as well as the geographer. To his foresight, rare good judgment, ability to think out a plan to the last minute detail, fine nerve and absolute lack of any kind of foolishness, together with a wide knowledge and intelligence, this expedition, and indeed the scientific work carried on by the United States Survey of the Rocky Mountain region and the Geological Survey for three decades in the Far West, largely owe success."

All of the party with the exception of the three youngest— W. C. Powell, the Major's nephew, Richardson and Dellenbaugh—had seen service in the Civil War. This, with the fact that every man was from either the East or the Middle West, would seem to indicate that Powell had made a point of gathering crews that were calculated to be more amenable to control and discipline than those composed of the highly brave and resourceful but all-too-independent mountain men.

The three boats of the second expedition were built in Chicago and, save for a few minor details, followed closely those used by the first party as to type. The decked-over space was considerably increased in the new boats, while that left open was reduced to little more than ample cockpits for the rowers. This gave a good-sized central cabin, decked over flush with the gunwales, and two water-tight compartments at bow and stern. They were rather narrow for their length of twenty-two feet over all, and had, when fully loaded, the very considerable draught of from fourteen to sixteen inches. Eight-foot oars were used for pulling, with one of eighteen feet for steering, the steersman sitting on the after cabin. The experience of the former voyage was responsible for the provision of closed

OWELL'S SECOND EXPEDITION READY TO START, NEAR GREEN
IVER, WYO.

RST CAMP OF POWELL'S SECOND EXPEDITION.

ASHLEY FALLS, GREEN RIVER.

From a photograph taken on the Second

Photo. by E. O. Beaman, 1871.

POWELL'S BOAT WITH THE ARM-CHAIR, IN
WHICH HE RODE THROUGH THE CANYON ON

oarlocks, inflatable life-preservers, water-proof rubber bags for food and clothing, and water-proof boxes for the instruments and records. It was a thoroughly well equipped expedition. Considering the work in hand and the limitations of the time, it would be very difficult to suggest how anything could have been done any better.

Evidently considering that the previous voyage had proved a light pilot-boat unnecessary, Powell's own craft was constructed of the same size, strength and weight as the other units of the flotilla. As a new departure he adopted the convenient but highly precarious expedient of rigging a "bridge" on his flag-ship, this taking the form of an arm-chair strapped to the deck of the midships cabin. This was highly convenient for a post of observation, while at the same time offering the crippled Major a far securer and more comfortable seat than the crown of the cabin deck. At the same time, however, so much weight so far from the keel must have greatly increased the liability of the boat to capsize in rough water, as well as giving her a tendency to roll at all times that could not but have materially cut down the efficiency of the rowers. Dellenbaugh admits that "this had a tendency to make the *Dean* slightly top-heavy," but adds that "only once did serious consequences apparently result from it." The Major himself was, of course, the best judge as to whether or not the game was worth the candle. He was in a better position than any one else to weigh its advantages and disadvantages under all conditions of water, and the fact that he continued to con the canyons from his "arm-chair bridge" to the end is the most conclusive evidence that this novel superstructure was well warranted.

The start from Green River was made on May 22, 1871, two days less than two years after that of the pioneer voyage. Subject to the variation of the season, this would have given both parties practically the same stage of water. Though I have never seen a direct statement on the subject, certain allusions to groundings at various points inclines me to the belief that the later expedition had rather the lower stage of water.

The relief from worries on the score of the food supply and the character of the river ahead made this a happier party than the earlier one from the outset. With no need of hurrying, work on the river was less arduous, the rush of the camp halts less hectic, and the nervous tension decreased all along the line. This made for better personal relations in every way, and the progress of the party in even the worst canyons seemed more like a joyous summer outing than a highly hazardous expedition of exploration. Even an untoward upset in one of the easy upper rapids of Red Canyon which the boats of the first party had run without trouble was rated more as a lark than a disaster. Professor Thompson, misunderstanding one of Powell's signals, headed his boat into the wrong place, with the result that

" . . . the *Nell* was thrown on some rocks projecting from the left wall, in the midst of wild waters, striking hard enough to crush some upper planks of the port side. She immediately rolled over, and Frank slid under. Prof. clutched him and pulled him back, while the men all sprang from the rocks and saved themselves and the boat from being washed away in this demoralized condition. With marvellous celerity Cap. took a turn with a rope around a small tree which he managed to reach, while Steward jumped to a position where he could prevent the boat from pounding. In a minute she was righted and they got her to the little beach where they had tried to land. . . . After about three-quarters of an hour the unfortunate came down, her crew being rather elated over the experience and the distinction of having the first capsize."

No chances were taken at the short, fierce tumble of water at Ashley Falls; all of the loads were portaged, and two of the boats. Here Dellenbaugh turned his pencil to good use by making a drawing of the Ashley inscription, definitely establishing the date as 1825.[1] Equally facile was the young art-

[1] See p. 94.

ist's word-sketch of the highly picturesque camp they made almost in the spray of the falls.

"A brilliant moon hung over the cañon, lighting up the foam of the water in strong contrast to the red fire crackling its accompaniment to the roar of the rapid. A lunar rainbow danced fairylike in the mists rising from the turmoil of the river. The night air was calm and mild. Prof. read aloud from *Hiawatha* and it seemed to fit the time and place admirably."

Except for two or three Bibles, the only books in the party were the works of Longfellow, Whittier, Emerson and Scott— rather an interesting commentary on the character of the men. At the end of nearly all of the less strenuous days it is recorded that either the Major or the Professor read selections from one or another of the poets around the camp-fire. Nor were these the only literary occasions. Now and then, when the current of a quiet stretch permitted, the three boats were lashed side by side and allowed to drift while the Major, from his armchair rostrum, read the stirring lines of Scott or Longfellow. Down through the verdant reaches of beautiful Brown's Park the reading was from *The Lady of the Lake*, which, as Dellenbaugh comments, "seemed to fit the scene well." That picture of Powell drifting down to the jaws of savage Lodore and stiffening the spirit of his men by reading from *The Lady of the Lake* is worth preserving. Dellenbaugh has given us many such pictures, and they make for a sympathetic understanding of the great explorer and his companions such as could be gained from nothing else.

Lodore was entered (as it should be by any outfit with heavily loaded boats) as though there were a cache of dynamite at the head of every rapid, and as a consequence even the wild cataracts of Disaster Falls and the long, wild chute of Hell's Half Mile were passed with no more than minor mishaps. Dellenbaugh gives a clear and detailed description of the approach to the head of Upper Disaster Falls, with its treacher-

ous "sag," which makes it conceivable that the unfortunate
wreck of the *No Name* on the previous voyage might have
been due to carelessness rather than to a direct disobedience
of orders.

Beaman, although redeeming himself with pleasant sallies
of humour now and then, was more inclined to fine frenzies of
writing than was Dellenbaugh. In Red Canyon he writes:

"The walls of rock are closing in, as if to immure us in a monster
tomb, and a certain terror fastens on a man's vitals as the grim
shadows deepen, while yet life itself appears not to fascinate as
does that unknown water-track beckoning us on."

For a description of Brown's Hole the somewhat sentimental
young photographer sought inspiration in *Lalla Rookh*. Of the
scene at the time the Major was entertaining the assembled
flotilla with readings from Scott, Beaman wrote:

"Nature, as it now was pictured before us, enchained the eye
with rarest beauty. . . . Along the banks roses were blooming, as
they might in the valley of Cashmere, and we were enchanted, as
Adam must have been when he awoke in the garden, with none to
dispute his right of enjoyment."

The morning mists of Lodore reminded Beaman of "the veil,
the silver veil, with which the prophet of Khorassan is said to
have covered his features, to hide his dazzling beauty from the
sight of mortals." And yet, as a Turneresque flight with words,
that of the young photographer on this occasion was no mean
effort.

"Soon the brightening and blushing skies denoted the glorious
coming of the sun, and his swift beams began to tinge the peaks of
the loftier mountains with golden colour, that deepened as the day-
god neared the horizon. As the light increased the vapour in the
gulch grew opalescent, and seemed in motion, soft and tenderly agitated as if by the breath of an infant; then its western edge slowly
lifted, and, gradually disclosing the surface of the dark, clear waters,

drifted lightly away until lost in the distant gloom of the eastern hills.

"A mist, nearly as penetrating as rain, then became apparent and palpable for a brief space, when it broke into billowy masses, and slowly wreathed and curled its way up the cañon-walls, lingering in the glens and grottoes far up the mountains, as if reluctant to leave a scene of such witching charm. Now the tops of the mountains began to flame up with volcanic luridness, and in an instant the great radiator rose clearly from its fiery bath, flooding everything with sudden brilliancy and distinctness, and transforming the river at our feet into a stream of molten silver."

All budding writers attack Nature after this fashion, and the result never fails to cause the more sensitive of them a sharp twinge of remorse when, after many years, it flies up to smite them one day like a stepped-on stick. *I know!* Dellenbaugh, as a consequence of the fact that he wrote after arriving at the age of discretion, rode his literary Pegasus with a curb-bit; hence it is he that shall guide us the rest of the way down the Colorado.

Careful handling took the boats through Whirlpool Canyon without trouble. From Island Park the Major, with a lightened boat, pushed on ahead to the mouth of the Uinta to get in touch with the first supply train. The two remaining boats proceeded more slowly, continuing the regular routine work under the direction of Professor Thompson. Of this work, due to the cumbersome and primitive apparatus of that time, by far the most trying was the photographic. The taking of a picture required the presence of a moveable laboratory and dark-room and involved three distinct processes which to-day might be performed thousands of miles apart. The clear glass plate had first to be floated with colodin, then soaked in the silver bath, then exposed wet in the camera, and finally developed, washed and dried on the spot. All of this work had to be done in a portable dark-room, set up for one picture perhaps on the bank of the river, and for the next on the brink of a cliff three thousand feet above. Of the labours connected with the transportation of the formidable picture-taking and making annex Dellenbaugh writes:

"This was the terror of the party. The camera in its strong box was a heavy load to carry up the rocks, but it was nothing to the chemical and plate-holder box, which in turn was a feather-weight compared to the imitation hand-organ which served for a dark-room. This dark-room was the special sorrow of the expedition, as it had to be dragged up the heights from 500 to 3000 feet."

To have carried without breaking great quantities of glass on an expedition of this character would have been a remarkable achievement in itself; to have turned them into a really creditable lot of negatives was a near-miracle. Except where running water and other movement was blurred as a consequence of the slowness of the plates, these negatives of Beaman's are just about as good as any that have ever been made of the upper Colorado canyons. All of the surviving originals are now in the hands of the Geological Survey at Washington, and prints from them are reproduced here through the courtesy of the Director.

On the arrival of the expedition at the Uinta, Thompson went out to the Indian Agency, where he learned that Powell had gone on to Salt Lake. On the Major's return it transpired that it would be necessary for him still further to absent himself in order to put the second supply train on the right road to the Dirty Devil River. Thompson was accordingly directed to continue on down river with the boats to Gunnison Crossing, where Powell would endeavour to join them by the 3rd of September. After stowing away a load of fresh provisions from the Agency and reinforcing the badly worn keels of the boats with iron bands, the party pushed off from the mouth of the Uinta on August 5th.

The absence of the familiar figure of Powell from his "arm-chair bridge" on the *Emma Dean* left more than a corporeal vacancy in the late flagship. Dellenbaugh, writing in a vein of reminiscence, throws a mellow but wonderfully revealing side-light on the intimate human side of the explorer.

"I missed the Major when we were on the water, probably more than any one else in the party, for as we were facing each other the whole time and were not separated enough to interfere with conversation we had frequent talks. He sometimes described incidents which happened on the first voyage, or told me something about the men of that famous and unrivalled journey. Besides this he was very apt to sing, especially where the river was not turbulent and the outlook was tranquil, some favorite song, and these songs greatly interested me. While he had no fine voice he sang from his heart, and the songs were those he had learned at home singing with his brothers and sisters. . . . At times he imitated a certain pathetic yet comical old woman he had heard singing at some camp-meeting. 'The dear blessed Bible, the Fam-i-ly Bible,' etc. He told me one day that his fondness for singing, especially amid extremely unpromising or gloomy circumstances, had on more than one occasion led the men of the first expedition to suspect his sanity. When he was singing, I could see that frequently he was not thinking about the song at all, but of something quite foreign to it, and the singing was a mere accompaniment."

An especial favourite of the Major was the old-fashioned hymn called *The Home of the Soul*, which begins:

"I will sing you a song of that beautiful land,
    The far away home of the soul,
Where no storms ever beat on the glittering strand,
    While the years of eternity roll."

Other numbers in the Chief's catholic repertoire were *The Laugh of a Child* and the *Non Più Andrai* aria from *Figaro*.

There was never a river party but employed close harmony alike as a stimulus to its action and a balm to its repose. This one of Powell's was no exception. Jack Hillers was the only accomplished vocalist, with a repertoire that "contained an exhaustless number, both sad and gay." Some of these, like *What Are the Wild Waves Saying?* and *Come where my Love Lies Dreaming*, have long been smothered in lavender, but I can testify that *Swanee River, Annie Laurie* and *Seeing Nellie Home* were bayed to the moon of Glen Canyon as late as September, 1922.

It was the versatile Hillers, too, who furnished the party with its slogans. Although not an Irishman himself, Jack was possessed of what Dellenbaugh describes as "a fine emerald brogue." The refrain of one of his Hibernian melodies ran: "And if the rocks, they don't shtop us, we will cross to Killiloo, whacky-whay!" This seemed to fit the present situation so well that "it became a regular accompaniment to the roaring of the rapids." And Jack it was who contributed the rallying cry to action, borrowed from the leader of an Irish fire-brigade of ancient New York called the Thirteen Eagles. "Tirtaan Aigles, dis wai!" bellowed through a trumpet, was the fire-chief's call for boots and helmets. Likewise, when the roar and smoke of an imminent rapid smote upon ear and eye, "Tirtaan Aigles, dis wai!" came to echo down the Colorado canyons as the call to oars and life-jackets.

Dellenbaugh's little tales of the human side of camp-life and river-work ring wondrous true, and to one who has done much of that sort of thing they are a sure touchstone of the high spirit and sustained morale of the party.

Professor Thompson maintained the high literary tradition set by Powell. The swarming "paddle-tails" tobogganing down the bank amused the gunners of the party until they found that a pig of lead was a feather for buoyancy compared with a dead beaver; then they were content to pull in and lash the boats together for the floating Lyceum. Dellenbaugh gives us definite assurance on this very interesting point.

"The stream being so tranquil, reading poetry was more to our taste than hunting the beaver, and Prof. read aloud from Emerson as we slowly advanced upon the enemy."

The shallow riffles of the long Canyon of Desolation proved very troublesome on account of the low water, but with plenty of time to spare the party took it easy and saved the boats by careful lining and portaging. Beaman, running one of the rapids contrary to orders, came in for a sharp reprimand that "checked for the time being his tendency to insubordination and recklessness." The little incident failed to ruffle the equanimity of the party, however, for that night the Prof. read Miles Standish by the camp-fire, and a fierce sand storm elicited no complaints.

They reached Gunnison Crossing—formerly the ford of the "Old Spanish Trail" from Santa Fé to Los Angeles and now the site of the Denver and Rio Grande Railway bridge—August 25th, and the Major rode down to the river four days later. Failing after repeated efforts to find a practicable trail to the mouth of the Dirty Devil, Powell had packed in such flour, sugar and jerked-beef as could be obtained in a little Mormon village, in the hope that it would hold the party until the next supply point was reached at the Crossing of the Fathers. Fred Hamblin, who came back with the Major, although he had been fearlessly exposing himself to the attacks of hostile Indians for years, appeared distinctly uncomfortable on the brisk little boat-ride down to the camp. Happy enough on the hurricane deck of a bucking broncho, the Mormon pioneer found the antics of the "water-pony" little to his liking.

After a couple of days spent in writing up the records to send out with Hamblin, the river trip was resumed with a short run late in the afternoon of September 1st. Finding one of the saws was missing, Beaman and Dellenbaugh were dispatched up the bank on foot to retrieve the indispensable tool. The twilight witchery of colour and shadow inspired the young artist to one of his rare attempts at word-painting. The facile sketch is all the finer for its evident restraint.

"The day was ending. Long shadows stole across the strange topography while the lights on the variegated buttes became kaleidoscopic. As for us, we appeared ridiculously inadequate. We ought

to have been at least twenty feet high to fit the hour and the scene.
Gradually the lights faded, the shadows faded, then both began to
merge till a soft grey-blue dropped over all, blending into the sky
everywhere except west where the burnish of sunset remained. . . .
Silence and the night were one as in the countless years that had
carved the dim buttes from the rocks of the world primeval when man
was not. Beautiful is the wilderness at all times, at all times lovely,
but under the spell of the twilight it seems to enfold one in a tender
embrace, pushing back the sordid, the commonplace, and obliterating
those magnified nothings that form the weary burden of civilized
man."

A fortnight of easy running carried the expedition down
through the swift but unbroken waters of Labyrinth and Stillwater canyons and into camp at the junction of the Green and
the Grand. The weird beauties of Bonito Bend and Trin Al-
cove were photographed, and the youthful Dellenbaugh was
honoured by having his name applied to a butte of striking
formation near the mouth of the San Rafael. What stirred the
lad most, however, was the discovery of the stone-slabbed walls
of a cliff-dwelling. It was his first sight of primitive ruins,
and he confessed that they interested him as greatly as did the
Colosseum on a later visit to Rome.

A checking over of the provisions at the Grand resulted in
the party being put on rations. Coffee, three strips of bacon
and a fist-sized hunk of bread to the meal was the allowance
upon which the rough-and-tumble through Cataract Canyon
would have to be made. Taking a notch in their already well-
drawn-in belts, the "Tirtaan Aigles" prepared for the bitter
grind ahead. No unnecessary chances were taken of losing
more of the precious grub. Of the eight rapids encountered on
the first day all were lined but one. A boat broke away while
being let down on the second day, but by great good fortune
was recaptured, right-side-up, in an eddy at the foot of the
rapid. This befell as a consequence of the bow being allowed
to swing too far outward, probably while the stern was fast
against a rock. It is the one thing above all others to be

avoided in lining down, yet it happens to the best and most careful of boat-crews at times.

Punishing work and unremitting care won through to the foot of Cataract Canyon. The increasing coldness of the water made the letting down operations uncomfortable as well as laborious, but with boats of such considerable draught Powell was well advised not to take chances in running any rapids through which he could not figure a clear channel. His problem was a vastly different one from those of the expeditions of later years, with their lighter craft and better chances of obtaining succour in case of disaster. Constantly tinkering at the battered boats, the tired and hungry but indomitable "Aigles" kept plugging along at a safe and steady four or five miles a day, finally to be rewarded by the welcome sight of Mille Crag Bend and quieter water. The last day of September carried them down through Narrow Canyon and in to the mouth of the Dirty Devil, where the ashes of an old fire and a rusty pocket-knife marked the site of the camp of the first expedition.

As it was now a case of neck-or-nothing to reach the Crossing of the Fathers before the food gave out, provision had to be made to complete later in Glen Canyon the work that could not be performed on the present run for lack of time. Accordingly the *Cañonita* was left at the mouth of the Dirty Devil, in order to be available for the use of the crew Powell decided to send in the following season prior to the resumption of river work at the head of Marble Canyon. Packing the reduced outfit into the cabins of the two remaining boats, the party pushed on down between the tapestried walls of Glen Canyon.

Although oars were plied vigorously in the comparatively quiet waters now entered, the relaxation from the grind of portaging and lining the cataracts permitted a resumption of the pleasant literary and social sessions that had marked the passage of the valley stretches above. Dellenbaugh, relieved of his oars, sat on the middle cabin at Powell's feet and divided his time between sketching and listening to the explorer's stories and reminiscences. Powell, with the season's river work all but completed, was in high spirits. Often, half in reverie, he would recite selections from his favourite poets. The closing lines of one of Longfellow's poems seemed especially to appeal to him, and he would repeat several times with much feeling:

> "A boy's will is the wind's will,
> And the thoughts of youth are long, long thoughts."

"Flow gently, sweet Afton!" was often on his lips, doubtless suggested by the "green braes" and "murmuring streams" of Glen Canyon. Or again, it was simply some nonsensical story, like that of the farmer's boy he had known in his youth, who, in spite of the fact that the yokel had no decent hat and clothes and no shoes at all, kept importuning his father for a "buzzum pin," and nothing but a "buzzum pin" would he have.

A good indication of the unusually low stage of water is found in the fact that the boats grounded repeatedly in passing through the broad stratum of sandstone shale now called the Water Pocket Fold. The crews were obliged to walk in the water for considerable distances to ease the boats over the ledges, and the *Nell* finally received a knock that set her badly aleak. Running from twenty to twenty-five miles a day, they passed the San Juan and camped at the beautiful glen Powell had named the Music Temple on the previous voyage. The atmosphere of the lovely dell was somewhat chilled by the discovery of the names of Seneca Howland, O. G. Howland and William Dunn, carved on the rocks by the three men who were murdered by the Shewits after leaving the first party at Separation Rapid. Dellenbaugh wrote that the finding of the names made the Music Temple seem like a sort of mausoleum, and to Powell the memories conjured up by the dramatic parting and its tragic sequel must have been especially poignant.

At a point just below where they ran a "pretty rapid with a clear chute" the party stopped "to look admiringly up at Navajo Mountain," which towered on their left to an altitude of over ten thousand feet. Just as on the first voyage Powell was tempted to ascend the dominating peak of the Glen Canyon region, but again the shortage of food made it necessary to press on. The following day, literally at the end of their provisions, they pulled in to the bench above the Crossing of the Fathers to find a large pile of rations awaiting them on the bank. Powell went out with the pack-train to make preliminary arrangements for the winter's work, and the remainder of the party ran on forty miles farther to the mouth of the Paria. One of the striking natural features passed on the final day of the run was the lone pillar of sandstone to which Powell had applied the name of Sentinel Rock. Although this slender three-hundred-foot-high monolith has impressed almost all who have seen as tottering to an imminent fall, I find that Beaman's photograph of 1871 varies by scarcely the line of a fracture from my own of 1922. Dame Nature is her own Beauty Doctor, but one knows ladies with genuine Parisian enamel complexions who are taking on wrinkles more rapidly.

Old "Leather-stocking" Jacob Hamblin, returning from a parley with the Navajos, came down to the ford at the Paria shortly after the arrival of the boat-party, and a few days later the belated pack-train arrived with a fresh supply of rations. A later messenger brought the news of the burning of Chicago. Making the boats and outfit all snug for the winter, the party fared across the plateau to a camp in the vicinity of Kanab, which was to be the base for their survey work. When the Major came back from Salt Lake he was accompanied by his wife and Mrs. Thompson; also a new Powell baby. Steward, Bishop and Beaman, all of whom were considerably run down from the river work, severed their connection with the expedition here. Assistants for the land work were readily found among the Mormons, and it was hoped that among these sturdy frontiersmen fresh hands for the river could be recruited when the time came.

The winter passed quickly and pleasantly. There was no trouble from the Indians, and the thrifty little Mormon communities provided a fare of fresh meat and vegetables that was a welcome change from the rough and inadequate rations of the river trip. In addition to the survey work a practicable route was found by which a pack-train could reach the bottom of the Grand Canyon at the mouth of the Kanab, thus assuring the food supply for the boating party of the summer. Fennemore, a photographer brought from Salt Lake to replace Beaman, joined the party in March. A copy of *The Count of Monte Cristo* in the newcomer's baggage was pounced upon with delight by the youthful Dellenbaugh.

Finding a way to the mouth of the Dirty Devil, where the *Cañonita* had been left, proved scarcely less baffling than on the previous attempts from the north. At the end of a month of devious wanderings, a party of seven under Professor Thompson found its way down into upper Glen Canyon by following by what was called Trachyte Creek, from the mouth of which the long-sought objective was reached by keeping close to the right bank of the Colorado. This was on June 22nd, and the river was fifteen feet higher than when the party camped there coming down. The flood at its height had surged about the *Cañonita* but a heavy load of sand had prevented her drifting away. Three days of painting and caulking put her shipshape again, and the start for the Paria was made on June 26th. The crew consisted of Hillers, Fennemore, Dellenbaugh and a Mormon called Johnson, probably a progenitor of the family of that name now living at Lee's Ferry. Thompson returned with the pack-train to Kanab.

Drifting along at a comfortable average of little over ten miles a day, the Paria was reached on July 13th. Camp was made again at the Music Temple below the San Juan, where Dellenbaugh records that he cut Jack's (Hillers') name and his own under those of the Howlands and Dunn. It did not prove convenient to stop at this beautiful and historic glen on either our up-stream or down-stream voyage of last summer; nor have I talked with any recent voyageurs who have made a halt there. The names must still be easily found and read, however. The hard sandstone of Glen Canyon has preserved the Julien inscriptions since 1836, and Indian pictographs for perhaps ten times as long.

It transpired that there had been several visitors to the Paria since the Powell expedition arrived the previous November. The first had been a party of prospectors, who had rifled the stores and outfitted for a little raft-voyage through the Grand Canyon. Doubtless the dauntless argonauts were inspired by the story of the James White voyage to seek the gold at the end of the rainbow arching above the great whirlpool at the mouth of the Little Colorado. First and last, prospectors have probably been the victims of nearly all of the unrecorded disasters of Colorado canyon navigation. This particular little band of optimists fared better than many of its successors. The raft went to pieces in the first bad rapid, which chanced to be that same savage run of riffles below Soap Creek where the Brown party met disaster and death in 1889. Everything was lost, of course, including the oars stolen from the Powell caches; but the men themselves managed to climb out to the mesa by bridging some otherwise unscalable places with driftwood ladders.

The next arrivals at the Paria had been the Mormon renegade John D. Lee, with two of his numerous families. The Mountain Meadows Massacre fugitive had come to stay, or at least that was his very evident hope and intention. He had built a fort-like log-cabin and was diverting the water of the Paria to irrigate the rich land at the river's mouth. The outlaw appeared a bit startled at the sudden appearance of Powell's men, and one of the wives hurriedly darted into the cabin, where she was afterwards observed peering suspiciously out at the intruders. "She was a fine shot as I afterwards learned," Dellenbaugh adds significantly.

Once reassured that the strangers were not the officers whom he had been dodging for the previous decade and a half, Lee was very pleasant and hospitable. He invited them to take their meals at his house until the main party came, and allowed them to take what they could use from the garden, the latter a highly appreciated privilege that seems to have been pretty well maintained by Lee's successors to this day. Lee gave them his own versions of the Mountain Meadows affair, claiming that he had tried to prevent it. Failing in this, he retired to his house and wept, thereby gaining from the scornful Pai Utes the nickname of *Naguts*, or Cry-baby. That the story would not go in court was subsequently proven when this dangerous but engaging fanatic paid the penalty of his undeniable guilt by being shot in Mountain Meadows in 1877.

Johnson's little voyage down Glen Canyon had given him his fill of river work, and he departed with Lee on July 14th. Andy, the cook, and Clem Powell came down with a wagonload of provisions a few days later. Waiting for the Major and Thompson, the men of the river-party worked about the garden and irrigating ditches and won what appears to have been a more or less standing invitation to the table of the aimiable Mrs. Lee XVIII. This was the handsome and spirited Sister Emma, of whom all who met her for many years spoke with the greatest kindness and admiration. Lee came back in time to preach the Sunday sermon and incidentally furnish not a little amusement for the irrepressible Andy. Knowing the renegade's jumpiness in the matter of lurking officers of the law, the mischievous cook quietly slipped in behind him and punctuated the exhortation by cocking his rifle with a sharp click every now and then. "Lee would wheel like a flash to see what was up," wrote Dellenbaugh.

Knowing Lee's sinister record, one would think that the

facetious Andy would have preferred to play safe with some comparatively innocuous amusement like pounding dynamite caps; yet this cruelest of murderers appears to have taken the pleasant little by-play quite in good part. He had the whole party over to dinner and supper on the Mormon holiday of July 27th, and continued to be "genial, courteous and generous" during all the remainder of their stay at the Paria.

By the time the Major arrived, early in August, Fennemore, who had been ailing for some days, decided against venturing on the river trip. As no other recruits had become available, this left only the original party, now greatly reduced. "Only the 'Tirtaan Aigles' remained," wrote Dellenbaugh, "and there were but seven of these now." As it was impossible adequately to man three boats with this number, it was decided to leave the *Nellie Powell*, already considerably damaged. Mrs. Thompson, Powell's sister, given a couple of rides when the repaired boats were being tried out, became so enthuiastic over the exhilarating sport that she made a strong plea for inclusion in one of the crews. After a farewell dinner with the hospitable Lee at which the first watermelons of the season were served, the party pushed off on August 17th.

It was a hard, lean, cool-headed bunch of river-rats that guided the boats into the head of the final great gorge. In spite of the time lost in climbing out over the constantly heightening walls for observations and photographs, something like ten miles a day was averaged all the way through Marble Canyon. A careful portage avoided trouble at Soap Creek Rapid where the ten rafting miners had come to grief, and the boating party found some solace for its rifled caches in picturing the fly-like climb that had been necessary to take the marauding would-be navigators back to the outer world. Improved lining technique seems to have made comparatively easy work at places where the first party met considerable difficulties. Only once did they appear near disaster, and the impending menace seemed a very real one.

"At one place as we were being hurled along at a tremendous speed we suddenly perceived immediately ahead of us and in such a position that we could not avoid dashing into it, a fearful commotion of the waters, indicating many large rocks near the surface. The Major stood on the middle deck, his life-preserver in place, and holding by his left hand to the arm of the well secured chair to prevent being thrown off by the lurching of the boat, peered into the approaching maelstrom. It looked to him like the end for us and he exclaimed calmly, 'By God, boys, we're gone!' With terrific impetus we sped into the seething, boiling turmoil, expecting to feel a crash and to have the *Dean* crumble beneath us, but instead of that unfortunate result she shot through smoothly without a scratch, the rocks being deeper than appeared by the commotion on the surface."

A fine run of eighteen miles on the 22nd carried them to the mouth of the Little Colorado. There had been a descent of four hundred and eighty feet in the sixty-five miles of Marble Canyon, and of the sixty-three rapids passed, four had been portaged and six lined.

After four days at the Little Colorado for observations and photographs, the boats were cast off and headed into the main gorge of the Grand Canyon. Straining his back severely in helping work the boats down a heavy fall on the second day, Hillers toppled over into the swift water and had a narrow escape from being carried away. The injury—one of a sort all too frequent in lifting and tugging at a heavy boat from an insecure footing—left the plucky photographer considerably crippled temporarily and of little use to the party for several days. During Hillers' disablement his boat work was taken over by Andy, the cheerful and versatile cook.

No cook is ever taken on a rough-water river trip for his culinary accomplishments alone. He need not necessarily be an accomplished river-rat, but if he is not at least a willing water-dog he cannot count on holding his job beyond the next recruiting point. Indeed, a hard river trip offers about the only sort of conditions under which a camp-cook can be kept on an equality with ordinary mortals. Anywhere else he is allowed to develop into a temperamental tyrant who might be the offspring of the union of a Bolshevik statesman and an Italian prima donna born in Kansas.

The ominous up-run of the granite heralded the imminence of the dreaded Sockdologer. Dellenbaugh was no less impressed by the savage tumble of rollers than was Powell. He writes:

" . . . We could look down on one of the most fearful places I ever saw or ever hope to see under like circumstances,—a place that might have been the Gate to Hell that Steward had mentioned. We were near the beginning of a tremendous fall. The narrow river dropped suddenly and smoothly away, and then, beaten to a foam, plunged and boomed for a third of a mile through a descent of from eighty to one hundred feet, the enormous waves leaping twenty or thirty feet into the air and sending spray twice as high. On each side were the steep, ragged granitic walls, with the tumultuous waters lashing and pounding against them in a way that precluded all idea of a portage or let-down. It needed no second glance to tell us that there was only one way of getting below. If the rocks did not stop us we could 'cross to Killiloo. . . .' "

Powell decided to run the *Emma Dean* through first, leaving the crew of the *Cañonita* to watch the performance and learn what they could from the result. The Major and Jones donned their life-preservers, but Hillers and Dellenbaugh, to avoid being hampered in rowing, merely laid their jackets ready to hand in case of an upset. Hatches were battened down and a camp-kettle left in each standing-room for bailing. Pulling up-stream in order to have room in which to manœuvre, they turned the bow out and swung down upon the enemy.

"Nearer and nearer came the angry tumult; the Major shouted 'Back water!' there was a sudden dropping away of all support; then the mighty waves smote us. The boat rose to them well, but we were flying at twenty-five miles an hour and at every leap the breakers rolled over us. 'Bail!' shouted the Major,—'Bail for your lives!' and we dropped the oars to bail, though bailing was almost useless.

. . . The boat rolled and pitched like a ship in a tornado, and as she flew along Jack and I, who faced backwards, could look up under the canopies of foam pouring over gigantic black boulders, first on one side, then on the other. Why we did not land on top of one of these and turn over I don't know, unless it might be that the very fury of the current causes a recoil. However that may be, we struck nothing but the waves, the boats riding finely and certainly leaping at times almost half their length out of the water, to bury themselves quite as far at the next lunge."

Bailing out in an eddy at the foot, they waited for the arrival of the *Cañonita* before pushing back into the stream. Rain and darkness ambushed them half way through a difficult portage and they pitched a cheerless camp among the granite boulders. All the following forenoon was spent in working the boats down the next three hundred yards, the lines having to be carried along a ledge a hundred and fifty feet above the river. Here it was found that the battered boats were in sore need of repairs, and before these were completed another night had fallen. To make a bad situation worse, the river began suddenly to rise, pounding the boats at their mooring and threatening to cover the rocks upon which the outfit had been piled. A narrow ledge, fifteen feet above, was the only refuge, and to this everything but the boats was laboriously hoisted. The latter were lifted out and made as snug as possible on the rocks below.

A dark and lowering morning succeeded to a rainy night. The boats were launched with all haste and loading was about to commence when a jet of water, two fingers wide, was discovered pouring into the middle cabin of the *Dean*. Preferring to run the risk of swamping on the river to that of being held over for another day in so dreary and dangerous a hole, the Major ordered them to ram a sack of flour against the leak and push off. The loss of an oar and one or two other mishaps threatened more trouble and delay, but they finally got out into the current and ran down to a beach where repairs could be completed under less difficult conditions.

The week that followed was just one darn thing after another. All the care in the world will not prevent occasional mishaps in so rough and continuous a series of rapids as that through the heart of the Grand Canyon. One day Jones, knocked out of the boat by the back-kick of an oar, was dragged for some distance hanging by his knees to the gunwale and his head in the water. Another day the *Dean's* abnormally high centre of gravity, due to the presence of the Major on his "arm-chair bridge," brought her to grief at a rapid in which the other boat appears to have had little trouble. Failing to find a landing place at the head of an ugly fall, Powell ordered the boat to head back into midstream to make the best of a run. The explorer and Jones were wearing their life-jackets; those of Dellenbaugh and Hillers were on the thwarts beside them.

"The plunge was exceedingly sharp and deep, and then we found ourselves tossing like a chip in a frightful chaos of breakers which almost buried us, though the boats rose to them as well as any craft could. I bailed with a camp-kettle rapidly and Jack did the same, but the boat remained full to the gunwales as we were swept on. We had passed the worst of it when, just as the *Dean* mounted a giant wave at an angle perhaps of forty or fifty degrees, the crest broke in a deluge against the port bow with a loud slap. In an instant we were upside down going over to starboard. I threw up my hand instictively to grasp something, and luckily caught hold of a spare oar. . . . The *Cañonita* was nowhere to be seen. . . . I was about preparing to climb up on the bottom of the boat when I perceived Jones clinging to the ring in the stern, and in another second the Major and Jack shot up alongside as if from a gun. The whole party had been kept together in a kind of whirlpool, and the Major and Jack had been pulled down head first till, as is the nature of these suctions on the Colorado, it suddenly changed to an upward force and threw them out into the air."

The boat was righted and brought to bank without drifting into further bad water. When the Major landed a little farther down to make a geological examination of the walls, his irre-

pressible crew suggested that it was in continuation of the geological examination of the bottom inaugurated in the rapid
above. As a matter of fact he must have had a very close
squeeze. I have never heard any one complain that *two* arms
were any too many, even in a comparatively mild rapid. Powell's nerve in facing the sort of water encountered in the Grand
Canyon is beyond all praise.

Before night the Major, Dellenbaugh and Jones were all
floundering in deep water again, this time as the result of a
combination of miscalculation and hard luck in trying to make
a hurried landing at the head of a rapid. Hillers saved the
boat by sticking to his oars. Dellenbaugh scrambled back
to help a few moments later, and the two of them contrived a
precarious landing at the very brink of the fall.

The mouth of the Kanab was reached on September 6th.
The packers with the supply train had been waiting for several
days. Finding one of Andy's discarded shirts stranded on the
bar one morning, they took it as heralding the destruction of the
whole expedition, and were not a little relieved to have their
fears proved groundless. There had been a fall of eight hundred and ninety feet in the seventy miles from the Little Colorado. One hundred and thirty-one rapids had been run, six
lined and seven portaged.

It had been the plan all along that the present expedition,
like the first, should continue on to the foot of the Grand Canyon. It was consequently somewhat of a thunder-clap when
the Major, the second morning after the arrival at the Kanab,
suddenly announced: "Well, boys, our voyage is done." He
and Thompson had been discussing the question for a day or
two, and the decision appears to have been arrived at on the
ground that the comparatively small amount of work to be
done below did not warrant taking the risk of running the lower
canyon at the difficult stage of water prevailing. A warning
from Jacob Hamblin that the Shewits were preparing to ambush
the party may also have influenced the decision. In any event,

Powell was the most competent judge as to whether or not the danger and expense of completing the voyage were worth incurring.

Dellenbaugh's regret at leaving the *Emma Dean* and the *Cañonita* will touch a responsive chord in the heart of every man who has run the river road.

"We unpacked the good old boats rather reluctantly. They had come to possess a personality as such inanimate objects will, having been our faithful companions and our reliance for many a hundred difficult miles, and it seemed like desertion to abandon them so carelessly to destruction. We ought to have had a funeral pyre. . . . I tried to persuade the Major to pack the *Dean* out in sections and send her east to keep as a souvenir of the voyage, but he would not listen to it, though years later he admitted that he regretted not taking my suggestion."

Returning to the Kanab with his own party three years later Dellenbaugh was prepared to carry out his original plans for saving the historic boats. It was too late, however. He learned that one of them had been sawed in two, shortened, and used in an attempt to tow up the canyon. It had been abandoned at the end of a short distance, and, with its mate, was destroyed by the next flood. All that remained at the Kanab camp was the hatch from a middle cabin and the Major's old "arm-chair bridge." The latter was taken out to Salt Lake and presented to Bishop, who resided there at that time. The young artist himself fell heir to the silken flag of the *Emma Dean,* and that jaunty little banner was shaken out to the Grand Canyon breezes again when the bow oarsman of the pilot boat of the second expedition, full of years and honours, returned for the unveiling of the Powell Monument nearly fifty years later.

In a tribute to his fellow voyageurs at the end of "A Canyon Voyage" the author writes: "Never was there a more faithful, resolute band of explorers than ours." To which one well might add: "And their chronicle is worthy of the men who inspired it." But there is more to Dellenbaugh's fine story than

electric power have made coal a comparatively unimportant commodity in the southern Pacific region. Indeed, the discussion which followed its subsequent presentation to the American Institute of Civil Engineers was almost entirely sympathetic. This was only the engineering view, of course; hardheaded Wall Street was never seriously impressed even by Stanton's extremely effective advocacy.

Brown incorporated his projected line under the name of the Denver, Colorado Canyon and Pacific Railway, becoming its first president. He appears to have been a bold, confident man, quick to conceive and act, and very affectionately regarded by his friends—probably the best type of the Western promoter. But promotion and canyon navigation are widely divergent activities, and what makes for success in one will not necessarily do the same for the other. Brown's very confidence seems to have been the main factor in his undoing. Nor would the fact that he picked assistants of great resource and courage in Stanton and Hislop justify the belief that he was possessed of much talent for judging men. An altogether too sizable proportion of the party left the survey in the lurch at its most critical stage to allow one to credit the run of the personnel with a very high order of the right sort of stuff properly to qualify them for the character of venture for which they were chosen.

On March 26th, 1889, Brown drove the first stake at Grand Junction, immediately after which he went East to complete preparations for the boat trip down the canyons of the main Colorado. The survey down the Grand River to its junction with the Green was made by F. C. Kendrick as chief engineer. This voyage was made in a second-hand skiff purchased from a ferryman. Being quite unfitted for work in rough water, it had to be portaged for twelve miles in passing one of the canyons.[1] Towing up the Green to meet the main party at the crossing

---

[1] Mr. Dellenbaugh is in error in stating that "this was the first party on record to navigate, for any considerable distance, the canyons of the Grand River." Samuel Adams had run a greater distance, and in rougher water, in 1869. See Chapter IX.

of the Rio Grande Railway, the Kendrick survey ran out of provisions and only the opportune discovery of a cattle-camp saved them from serious privations. The inadequacy of the arrangements for this preliminary trip was prophetic.

There were several accounts written of the unfortunate Brown expedition, most of them agreeing except upon minor details. Stanton wrote both technical and popular papers, Ethan Allen Reynolds, a guest of Brown on the trip, wrote a magazine article, and Dellenbaugh has written a critical discussion in his "Romance of the Colorado." The last makes a special point of refuting the charges that Powell and Thompson, from whom Brown had sought advice in Washington, had not sufficiently impressed their caller with the seriousness of his undertaking. Professor Thompson is quoted in an emphatic declaration that he not only advised Brown to provide life-preservers, but that "he was warned over and over again to neglect no precautions." Powell's report alone should, to the ordinary man, have been a sufficient antidote for overconfidence. But Brown, in his bold optimism, passed these warnings by, and paid the price.

Stanton, who had not been consulted in the matter of preliminary arrangements, confessed that he was dismayed at the first sight of the boats. Pretty enough to look at and probably adequate for smooth-water work, they were faulty in design and construction and, indeed, deficient in every important particular as a craft for Colorado canyon navigation. Reynolds gives the nearest to a detailed description of the fleet of the expedition as it was assembled at Green River, Utah.

"Our outfit consisted of six boats, five of them cedar, clinker-built, fifteen feet long, forty inches wide, and half decked, with brass airtight compartments in each end. The sixth was an open dory made of pine, ribbed with oak, and very strong. . . . Five water-tight compartments of zinc cased with pine, originally intended to fit in the middle of each of the five cedar boats, were loaded with duplicate lots of provisions, and lashed together end to end, making what we called a flotilla, about twelve feet long, which we intended to tow after us." [1]

The inclusion of the open dory in the outfit, and the attempt to raft provisions down the cataracts on the astonishing "flotilla," need no comment. With the five specially-built boats the trouble was more on the score of poor design and construction than of poor material. Cedar has been used successfully in some of the later canyon boats. But a length of fifteen feet, a beam of but little over three, and a weight of a hundred and fifty pounds, for a boat that was to carry three or four men and a heavy load in rough water gave a fair line on both Brown's buoyant confidence and lack of common sense. Putting such craft in the hands of a party the majority of whom were both inexperienced and unwilling to stand the gaff of disaster was like greasing the ways for—just what happened.

The party which left Green River on May 25th consisted of sixteen men. Rather an illuminative side-light on its character is thrown by one account which lists two of its members as "guests of Brown," and two others as "coloured servants." As far as I can learn, this is the only Colorado canyon expedition in which either the "guest" or the "servant" figured on the rolls. The negroes, at least, as appeared when the showdown came, displayed the stuff of real river roustabouts. Respecting the guests, the record is not quite so clear.

The expedition reached the junction of the Grand and the Green on the 29th of May, and the following day the survey which had been brought down the former river by the Kendrick party was taken up. The "flotilla" had to be cut loose at the very head of Cataract Canyon to prevent the towing boat from following it over the first rapid. "This was regarded at the time as a great misfortune," Reynolds writes, "since it carried nearly one thousand two hundred pounds of food. As it turned out, however, it was the most fortunate thing that could have happened to us."

[1] "Down the Colorado Cañons," *Cosmopolitan*, November, 1889.

The "fortunate thing" alluded to was the finding of a fragment of the float, with a few of the provisions, a little farther down, but the reasoning by which the regaining of a portion could be reckoned as better than a retaining of the whole is a bit hard to follow.

Up to June 2nd Reynolds writes that all of the trip had been "a perfect picnic," but from that time on disaster was incessant. Of one of the first upsets he says:

"We had such good luck in shooting around points of rock, that the next morning Brown, Hughes, and myself determined to try it again with the first boat. Brown sat in the prow with the oars; I sat in the middle, on the load, and Hughes sat in the stern with the steering paddle. We started in comparatively smooth water, and made the first point all right, but just as we attempted to run in shore, a huge 'fountain' burst up by the side of the boat, and pitched us into the middle of the worst rapid we had yet encountered. Brown, who was very powerful, struggled to keep the boat head on, and for a few seconds we succeeded in riding two or three enormous waves successfully, then, in spite of all efforts, the boat turned sidewise, was thrown in the air, and came down bottom up. As she went over Brown and Hughes managed to catch hold of the ends, but I could not get a hold and was pitched clear of the boat. I thought that the expedition, so far as I was concerned, was ended, but a lucky wave washed me against the side of the boat, and, when we finally got ashore, we found ourselves on the opposite side of the river from the balance of the party, and two miles below where we had been thrown in."

Reynolds' description of his boat being "thrown in the air" is, as Mark Twain characterized the report of his own death, "somewhat exaggerated." The way of a wave with a boat is not quite so much like the way of a bull with the mangled corpse of a *matador* as the line would imply. On rare occasions a sharp up-tossing of a boat may pitch a man into the water, but to suggest that a wave may pitch a boat out of the water is to disregard the native fluidity of the tossing medium, to say nothing of the truth.

Both Reynolds and Stanton lay considerably more stress on the force of the so-called "fountain" than any one who had preceded or has followed them on the Colorado. The sudden up-boiling tumble of water is encountered under certain conditions on all rough rivers and is probably no worse on the Colorado than on any other stream having equal fall or sand content. One form of it occurs in deep water at the foot of rapids as a sort of compensating action to the down-suck of whirlpools. A commoner form is caused by the caving of submerged sand-bars. Both of these may be very troublesome in throwing a boat out of control in a bad place, but neither is quite the thing of terror pictured by Reynolds.

"Where the river is broad, deep, and swift, the bottom seems to be covered with pit-holes in the sandstone, and to have great heaps of constantly changing quicksand mounds. This causes numberless cross-currents underneath the surface, and at times these seem to combine, resulting in an enormous up-shooting wave, which breaks through the surface of the water with a swish and roar that is appalling, and tosses everything which it may strike. The noise these 'fountains' make is something between the boom of a cannon and the swish of an enormous sky-rocket, and they can be heard for a mile."

At Rapid Number 10 the boat called *Black Betty* was smashed to kindling wood on a ragged boulder, and nearly all of the cooking utensils and a large batch of supplies were lost. At this early stage Stanton records that all of the boats "were badly damaged, two of them entirely gone." They had still the worst part of the canyon to pass. Reynolds, borrowing the name that Powell had applied to a torrential stretch near the foot of Lodore, calls the obstructing cataracts "Hell's Half Mile." The name is appropriate enough, though the second use of it on the same river indicates either a lack of knowledge or imagination. Just the same, several of the worst pitches in Cataract Canyon, with quite as much fall and three or four times the volume of Lodore, are every bit as infernal as the original Hell's Half Mile.

The finding of the skeleton of a man, complete save for a missing lower jaw, did nothing to cheer the party at this juncture. Wherever possible they kept to the bank, confining navigation to lining the boats down one side of the river, avoiding even the crossings. Tempted by a short stretch of easier water, two of the boats essayed another run. The first went through in safety, but the other, with Hughes steering and Reynolds at the oars, furnished the regular daily disaster.

"Just as we passed a jutting pinnacle of rock, we were unaccountably swept into a small but vicious whirlpool which was behind it. Around and around we spun, and, although I rowed with all my might, we drew steadily nearer the vortex. Finally my end of the boat began to sink, and Hughes's end to rise in the air. Finding we were going down, I let go of the oars, and hung on to the seat of the boat. I saw Hughes twirled around once or twice, and then the boat seemed to end straight up, and I went down clean under the water together with half of the boat. I suppose that I was under but half a minute, though I found myself getting short of breath. The sensation was very queer, but there was a pleasant relief from the roar of the water. Suddenly, the vortex being choked, it released its grip, and the boat shot into the air. As I came up Hughes called for me to hold on. I called back asking him if I was not holding on, and shook the water from my eyes just in time to see a huge wave roll over Hughes and give him a beautiful ducking. The boat did not capsize, and although we had lost an oar, we managed to paddle into the current, and soon reached shore, where we bailed out. The others then tried it, and came through all right, except Number Five, which had a hole knocked in her in the attempt."

A day or two later boat Number 1, after dragging Hughes over the rocks and spraining his ankle, broke away and went off down river. Brown, after a vain pursuit of four miles, came back to report that there was still much bad water ahead. The finding of a section of the runaway "flotilla," with its flour, beans and cornmeal still intact, eased the food shortage momentarily, but another two days of disaster reduced the party to starvation rations. There is a considerable divergence between the respective versions of Reynolds and Stanton regarding the breaking up of the highly demoralized party which took place at this juncture. The former merely passes it over lightly with:

"After two more days of loss, as we had only three boats, it was decided to divide the provisions we had left, throw away every unnecessary article, and that five of the surveyors should start on foot to carry along the line, while the rest of the party should attempt to reach the placer mines, which we knew were below, to get provisions if possible."

Stanton, in one of his engineering reports,[1] gives a far more revealing and convincing account of what happened:

"On the 16th of June, by the upsetting of the boats all of our provisions were lost except a sack and a half of flour, a little coffee, sugar, and condensed milk. This looked very desperate for a party of sixteen hungry men in such a country as the heart of Cataract Cañon. The next morning, President Brown, with a picked boat's crew, started for the placer mines, some 35 or 40 miles down the river, to procure supplies. The scarcity of provisions and the separating of the party alarmed the men, and the greater number decided to desert the work and to follow Mr. Brown, leaving, as they did, their instruments standing upon the line. Knowing that, if we abandoned the survey then, we could not return to that point and complete it, and believing that the work could be completed to Dandy Crossing with the food on hand, which was divided equally among all the men, the writer determined not to leave if a sufficient number of men would remain to assist him. The first assistant, Mr. John Hislop, together with C. W. Potter, one of the flagmen, and the two negro servants, Henry C. Richards and G. W. Gibson, the cook, volunteered to remain and continue the survey. These men deserve special mention and praise for the faithful and uncomplaining manner in which they pushed on the work till the evening of the 20th. It requires more than ordinary nerve to do the work of an engineer-

[1] Transactions of American Society of Civil Engineers—No. 523 (Vol. XXVI, April, 1892).

ERT BREWSTER STANTON.

LOOKING DOWN FROM THE RIM OF MARBLE CANYON TO THE MOUTH OF SOAP CREEK.

It was in a rapid just below here that Brown was drowned.

ing party over such a country with only about one-tenth of the amount of solid food that a healthy man requires."

In another account[1] Stanton tells how the survey was carried on at the rate of four miles a day on a ration of "one small piece of bread, a little coffee and milk for our morning and evening meal, and three lumps of sugar and as much river water as we wished at noon." For those who stood by him the engineer had unstinted praise.

"The men worked on without a murmur, carrying the survey over the rocks and cliffs on the side of the cañon, and handling the boat through the rapids of the river. At night, when they lay down on the sand to sleep, after a meal that was nine-tenths water and hope, and one-tenth bread and coffee, it was without a complaint. Those who could stand the privations best divided their scanty store with those who suffered most. At the end of the sixth day we were met by a boat, towed up the river, with provisions. Our sufferings were over, except from the effects of eating too much at the first meal."

The steady stream of wreckage that had been floating down past Dandy Crossing for a fortnight had given the miners warning that the Brown party was in trouble among the cataracts, so no time was lost in going to Stanton's relief when the President himself came through. There seems to be a considerable difference of opinion as to just what became of Reynolds at this juncture. Dellenbaugh, who got all his facts at first hand from Stanton, states explicitly: "At Dandy Crossing three of the party left the river—J. N. Hughes, E. A. Reynolds, and T. P. Rigney." Hughes and Reynolds were the men down on the list as Brown's guests, and as such were the ones who could have most readily detached themselves from the party without laying themselves open to the charge of lack of loyalty. Yet Reynolds, for some reason, strove in his magazine article to convey the impression that he had continued in person with the expedition through to its tragic finale in Marble

[1] "Down the Colorado Cañons," *Scribner's Magazine*, November, 1890.

Canyon. Of the voyage down Glen Canyon he writes: "For the next hundred and fifty miles we had no difficulty whatever, while we enjoyed the scenery to its utmost." [1] He gives circumstantial accounts of the two upsets, before concluding, still very much in the first person, with:

"So we climbed up wearily the steep sides of the side cañon, and, guided by compass, started for where we supposed Kanab should be. After some miles of search we found a cattle camp, and bronchos to carry us to the nearest railway. Thence we reached home after two months of wandering."

It seems hardly conceivable that a man should have used so many "we's" had he not actually been with the party to the last, as he describes; but Stanton puts the question beyond doubt when he accounts as follows for the eight men who are known to have made up the party that finally entered Marble Canyon:

" . . . It was decided that Mr. Brown and myself, together with six others, Hislop, McDonald, Hausbrough, Richards, Gibson and Photographer Nims, should go on and make an examination of the lower cañons, take notes and photographs, but without an instrumental survey."

The point at which Reynolds left the Colorado is of small importance historically save as it affects his story of the Marble Canyon disasters. Since it is certain he did not enter any part of that gorge he is disqualified as a first-hand witness of what happened there, leaving that of Stanton as the only dependable account extant.

By an interesting coincidence the party had found Jack Sumner of the first Powell expedition at Dandy Crossing. Sumner had proved one of the handiest and most dependable men of the pioneer voyage; the only one, indeed, whom Powell appears

---

[1] Ellsworth Kolb in the Appendix to "Through the Grand Canyon" says: "Hughes, Terry and Rigney left at Glen Canyon, Reynolds left at Lee's Ferry, and Harry McDonald joined the party."

to have made an effort to include in his second expedition. How this veteran was impressed with the Brown party, and what advice he gave them, does not appear in any of the published accounts, though it is doubtless covered in Stanton's records. Certainly an effort would have been made to get Sumner to join the party, and it would be interesting to know his reasons for declining to do so. Only one man was obtained in Glen Canyon. This was Harry McDonald, described as a "frontiersman and an experienced boatman."

Brown having secured fresh supplies from Kanab, the start from Lee's Ferry was made with three boats on July 9th. Ten miles were traversed the first day, an extremely creditable run considering that portages were made at Badger and Soap creeks. The rapids below the latter are the ones in which the rafting prospectors had come to grief after rifling the caches of the second Powell expedition at the Paria. It is always dangerous to run, but not difficult to line or portage. The Brown party had passed the worst of the rapid and made camp at a point where they considered it safe to run with the boats again.

Marble Canyon differs from all of the other great gorges of the Colorado in that the river, instead of entering a mountain as at Lodore, by cutting down through a rapidly rising plateau, seems to be burrowing into the very bowels of the earth. None has entered it but to confess to the depressing effect of seeming literally to be leaving the surface of the earth and descending to some subterranean inferno. Brown, with his original expedition reduced by half in both men and boats, was, as might be expected, especially susceptible to the brooding spell of the gloomy gorge. Of that, and of what followed, Stanton writes:

"President Brown seemed lonely and troubled, and asked me to sit by his bed and talk. We sat there late, smoking and talking of our homes and our journey on the morrow. When I awoke in the morning, Mr. Brown was up, and, as soon as he saw me, he said,

'Stanton, I dreamed of the rapids last night, the first time since we started.' After breakfast we were again on the river in very swift water. Mr. Brown's boat, with himself and McDonald, was ahead; my boat, getting out from the shore with some difficulty, was a little distance behind. In two minutes we were at the next rapid. Just as we dashed into it, I saw McDonald running up the bank waving both arms. We had, for a few moments, all we could do to manage our own boat. It was but a moment. We were through the rapid and turning out into the eddy I heard McDonald shout, 'Mr. Brown is in there.' I looked to the right, but saw nothing. As our boat turned around the whirlpool on the left, the notebook which Mr. Brown always carried shot up on the water, and we picked it up as we passed."

From McDonald it was learned that the leading boat, after passing safely the worst of the rapid, had been upset by an "up-shooting wave"—doubtless the same sort of boil Reynolds had called a "fountain." Brown was thrown into the whirlpool, McDonald into the current. To McDonald's encouraging "Come on!" Brown answered with a cheery "All right!" Mc-Donald was carried under three times before the heavy current threw him against the bank. Brown was still swimming round and round in the whirlpool as his companion ran up the bank for help, but less than a half minute later Stanton found only a floating note-book. A day's vigil at the treacherous bend revealed nothing more.

It was Stanton's heart rather than his head that caused him still to go on after this staggering disaster, although one has to read between the lines to discover it. In one of his engineering reports he writes: "Being very desirous to complete the work, the writer concluded to push on, even then not fully appreciating the utter worthlessness of the boats and the other means provided for making such a journey." As there really could have been nothing left to learn of the utter worthlessness of the whole outfit after the Cataract Canyon experiences, one will do better to seek the mainspring of Stanton's courageous but reckless resolution in his parting tribute to his late chief.

"In that whirlpool poor Brown battled for his life till, exhausted in the fight, he sank, a hero and a martyr to what some day will be a successful cause."

It was loyalty to the memory of a friend and what amounted almost to a consecration to that friend's cause that impelled Stanton forward in the face of inevitable disaster. He had snatched the banner from the hand of a fallen leader and his indomitable spirit would not brook a retreat. Indeed, as a standard bearer of the Colorado Canyons railway project Stanton never did back up, either earlier or later. Even the culminating disaster of the present expedition acted as no more than a temporary check.

Starting the morning after Brown was drowned, the voyage and survey were continued without serious trouble for three days. Twenty-four bad rapids were successfully run or portaged, the marble walls rearing steadily higher and higher as the river cut deeper into the earth. After a Sunday rest work was resumed on Monday at the head of two rough rapids. The first of these and a part of the second were portaged, and at a point where it appeared that the river run could be resumed Stanton and the photographer remained to complete their work while the boats ran down to await them at a sand-bar half a mile below. Stanton writes:

"The first boat got through with difficulty, as the current beat hard against the left cliff. My boat was the next to start. I pushed it out from the shore myself with a cheerful word to the men, Hausbrough and Richards. It was the last they ever heard. The current drove them against the cliff, under an overhanging shelf. In trying to push away from the cliff the boat was upset. Hausbrough was never seen to rise. Richards, a powerful man, swam some distance down stream. The first boat started out to the rescue, but he sank before it reached him.

"Two more faithful and good men gone! Astonished and crushed by their loss, our force too small to portage our boats, and our boats unfit for such work, I decided to abandon the trip, with then and

there a determination, as soon as a new outfit could be secured, to
return and complete our journey to the Gulf."

The last night in the gorge was marked by a terrific storm.
Baulked of its prey, the Dragon of the Canyon roared its protest in such an outburst of thunder and lightning as Stanton
had never experienced in all his years among the Rocky Mountains. In such a theatre, and following so soon upon the heels
of the river tragedies, the besom of the onslaught might well
have impressed the cowering fugitives as a direct visitation of
the Wrath of the Gods. Stanton, however, evidently of a
deeply religious nature, read into it a higher meaning.

"Thunder with echo, echo with thunder, crossed and recrossed
from wall to wall of the cañon, and, rising higher and higher, died
away among the sides gorges and caverns thousands of feet above
my head. For hours the tempest raged. Tucked away as a little
worm in the cleft of the rock, the grandeur of the storm spoke to me
as to the Psalmist of old; and out of the stillness came a voice
mightier than the tempest, and said, 'Be still, and know that I am
God.'"

Fully determined to go on with the survey just as soon as a
new outfit could be provided, Stanton cached the remaining supplies in a marble cave to await his return. The ascent of the
walls was made at a point near the beautiful bend Powell had
called Vesey's Paradise. A climb of twenty-five hundred feet
gained the plateau, where the rain-pools from the late storm
favoured their progress toward the Mormon settlement. A
team from a cattle-ranch took them on to Kanab, where Bishop
Mariger did everything possible to help them reach the railway
in comfort.

At the time that Stanton succeeded Brown as the dominant
figure in the Colorado Canyons railway project he was in his
early forties. Although born in Mississippi, he came of good
old New England stock—Stanton and Brewster. Following his
graduation from Miami University in 1871 he went into the

engineering department of the Atlantic and Pacific Railway, subsequently taking part in many Western surveys and having to his credit very notable construction work in Colorado. Both by training and temperament he was admirably fitted for the severe task to which he now turned his unflagging energies.

After returning to Denver and reviving the spirits of his discouraged directors, Stanton gave his attention to the creation of an adequate outfit for the canyons. This took over four months, but when he again turned his face toward the river at the end of November it was at the head of an expedition which, both in equipment and personnel, had none of the glaring deficiencies of its ill-starred predecessor. That Stanton had learned his lesson is plain from his description of the new outfit.

"It consisted of three boats twenty-two feet long, four and one-half feet beam, and twenty-two inches deep. These were built of oak, from plans of my own, with ribs one and one-half by three-quarters of an inch, placed four inches apart, and planked with one-half inch oak, all riveted together with copper rivets. Each boat had ten separate air-tight compartments running all round the sides. The best cork life-preservers were provided for all the men, and they were required to wear them whenever they were upon the water. All stores and provisions were packed in water-tight rubber bags made expressly for the purpose."

The party consisted of twelve men, four of whom had been with the previous expedition. These latter were Stanton, Hislop, McDonald and Nims. The eight new men must also have been hand-picked, for they showed good stuff from first to last. The outfit was hauled by wagon from the railroad to Crescent Creek, a point in Glen Canyon just above Dandy Crossing. Christmas dinner was eaten at Lee's Ferry, and three days later the push-off into Marble Canyon was made. The rapid where Brown had been drowned was found much less menacing at this low winter stage and it was passed without trouble. A day or two later, however, serious misfortune overtook them when Nims, the photographer, climbing too boldly in an attempt to get an effective composition, fell twenty feet and broke his leg.

Setting the fracture as well as possible under the difficult circumstances, the injured man was taken to a boat and carried down river a couple of miles to a side canyon by which it was hoped a way could be found to the plateau. Starting early in the morning, Stanton reached the top at noon. While his two companions returned to guide the party that was to attempt to carry Nims out of the canyon, the engineer set out on foot to cover the thirty-five miles to Lee's Ferry. Arriving there after midnight with blistered feet, he snatched a few hours' sleep before starting back for the rim with a wagon. The return journey was slower on account of having to circle the head of the side canyons with the wagon, and darkness found them still many miles from their destination. Stanton writes with much feeling of an incident of their night-halt on the wind-swept plateau.

"It was late and we camped for the night on the open prairie—the old Mormon, his little son and I. A snow storm was driving from over the mountains. Our supper was cooked by a sedge-bush fire—the bacon, the coffee and the bread; but before it was eaten my friend knelt on the ground, and turning his face up to heaven, while the snow-flakes fell upon his white beard, offered up a fervent prayer for blessings upon ourselves and upon those at home, for care for the wounded man, and strength for ourselves and the horses till we could reach him and take him to a place of safety. I would that all my Christian friends had the spirit of kindness and charity that it has been my good fortune to find among the Mormons in northern Arizona and southern Utah."

The sentiment is one that will be heartily echoed by every wayfarer who has traversed the trails of that part of the Southwest the so-called Mormon has reclaimed from the desert.

It was noon of the next day before the rescue party reached the rim above the point where the accident had occurred. The injured photographer had been waiting since mid-afternoon of the day before. Wrapped tightly in blankets and tied firmly to a stretcher improvised from a piece of canvas and two oars, he had been borne and hoisted up the steep ascent by eight of his companions. The distance was four miles, with a climb of seventeen hundred feet. "In two places," writes Stanton, "the stretcher had to be hung by ropes from above, while the men slid it along a sloping cliff too steep to stand upon, and in two places it was lifted up with ropes over perpendicular cliffs ten and fifteen feet high." The final half-mile was up a forty-nine degree slope over a slide of loose rock. It is a remarkable fact that the plucky Nims made the ascent in comparative comfort and that none of the carrying party was injured.

The Mormon into whose kindly hands the injured man was delivered was W. M. Johnson, who had been for a while with the second Powell expedition. The little son whom Stanton mentions in describing the camp in the snow was probably one of the two Johnson boys who now operate the ferry at the mouth of the Paria—fine manly fellows both.

The loss of Nims was an especially hard blow to Stanton from the fact that he was preparing to make the novel experiment of surveying the canyons by photography. His ingenious conception contemplated making a practically continuous panorama of both walls by taking hundreds of overlapping photographs, all exposed in duplicate or triplicate to minimize chances of loss of the record. It was his idea that these twin panoramas, supplemented by copious geological notes and records of altitudes, would answer all the practical purposes of a preliminary survey with comparatively cumbersome instruments. The newly-perfected roll-film made the problem of photographic supplies a comparatively simple one, and Nims, a professional photographer who had shown his mettle on the previous expedition, had entered into the plan with great enthusiasm.

Stanton's first feeling was that the loss of Nims would make further photography impossible and thus practically nullify the engineering work of the expedition even in the event of its success from a navigational standpoint. Then, with characteristic confidence and determination, he decided to handle the cameras himself. Every good engineer has, or should have, the patience, carefulness, common sense and eye for distance essential to the making of successful if not highly artistic photographs. Stanton speedily mastering the simple technique of the cameras, went to the work with enthusiasm—and stuck to it. That he succeeded in exposing something like sixteen hundred negatives with only ten per cent of failures seems less remarkable to-day than it did in 1890, when the comparative simplicity of the roll-film was hardly appreciated. It was a notable achievement under any conditions, however, and very revealing as to Stanton's ready resourcefulness.

Continuing on down the canyon to the place called Point Retreat from the fact that the previous expedition had there left the river, the supplies cached in a marble cave were all found in good condition. Stanton measured the speed of the boats in some of the rapids above this point, and found that on several occasions they ran as fast as twenty miles an hour. This figure from an engineer is as valuable as interesting. The tendency of the average river voyageur is greatly to overestimate both the speed and the fall of rapids. Ten miles below Point Retreat the body of Peter Hausbrough, easily recognized from the clothing, was discovered. Of the burial service at the foot of an overhanging cliff Stanton writes:

"We stood around the grave while one short prayer was offered, and we left him with a shaft of pure marble for his headstone, seven hundred feet high, with his name cut upon the base; and in honour of his memory we named a magnificent point opposite—Point Hausbrough."

The mouth of the Little Colorado was reached January 20th. The sinister Upper Granite Gorge was entered eighteen miles below. Here, warned by Powell's experiences, the party proceeded very slowly and cautiously. On January 29th they came to the head of the great Sockdologer, which Powell has estimated to have the greatest fall of any rapid on the river— eighty feet in a third of a mile. Where both of the former ex- peditions had been forced to cast loose and run this whole violent tumble of surging water, the extremely low midwinter stage of the river suggested to Stanton that his boats might be successfully let down by line. The sequel proved this to be one of the not infrequent instances where the most cautious course proves also the most costly.

The upper end of the rapid was passed in safety by all three boats, but in endeavouring to continue the *Marie* was caught by a cross-current, turned half way over, filled with water and jammed between two submerged boulders. Working with lines tied to their waists to keep from being carried away, re- lays of men succeeded in bringing to bank all but two sacks of provisions. The boat herself, however, defied all attempts at dislodgment, and she was still held fast when darkness forced the abandonment of salvage efforts and the making of camp "literally upon the sharp edges of the broken granite." A timely overnight rise of two feet forced the rocky jaws to re- lax their hold by the following morning, but the shattered wreck that was dragged ashore bore little semblance to a boat. One side of it was smashed and half of the other gone entirely. Only the keel was unbroken. Stanton describes one of the most remarkable pieces of repair work ever made upon the Colorado.

"We pulled her upon the rocks and at once set to work. We cut four feet out of her centre, drew the ends together, and with five days' hard work we had a new boat. In those five days we were not a moment without the awful roar of that mighty torrent in our ears, with hardly wood enough to cook our meals (the last two days cooking done with the shavings from the broken boat), and the ever-returning question which boat would go next?"

The lower part of the rapid was run and the remainder of the First Gránite Gorge passed without further trouble. At a fall not far below Bright Angel Creek, characterized as "one of the most powerful and unmanageable rapids" encountered on the river, there was tried an experiment that invited, as it brought, certain disaster. The first attempt at a let-down, essayed with a two hundred and fifty-foot line "strung out ahead," resulted in the swamping of a boat in the eddy below but, luckily, did her no injury. This method of lining (because almost no control over the direction of the boat is retained) is extremely risky in anything but a clear, unbroken chute of water, yet nothing in comparison to the sheer toss-up next resorted to as an alternative. Stanton describes the latter as "Major Powell's plan . . . of shooting the boat through and catching it below." Powell's report reveals no mention of the employment of such an expedient; indeed, it is one that no experienced rough-water boatman would use in a broken rapid except as a very desperate last resort.[1]

The rebuilt *Marie* was led down for the slaughter. Stanton describes the result in a single comprehensive sentence.

"She rode gracefully the high waves at the head of the rapid, but in the middle she turned, partially filled with water, shot to one side, struck against the cliff, sank in the worst part of the rapid, and came up in pieces about the size of tooth-picks—our five days' labour and our boat gone together!"

No further experiments were tried. The next morning the remaining boat, the *Lillie*, was taken out of the water and portaged round the rapid on the rocks.

A day or two later Harry McDonald left the party and

[1] The Little Dalles on the Columbia is one of the few points occurring to me where one might be justified in taking the chance of turning loose an empty boat. There are violent whirlpools here, but little white water. The whirlpools are too much for a small, heavily-loaded boat to hope to win through, but an empty skiff *might* float high enough to elude them. I considered trying this with the light lake skiff I used in that part of the Columbia, but finally portaged.

started out by a side canyon to tramp to Kanab. McDonald
was the experienced riverman who had joined the first party
at Dandy Crossing following the shake-up of personnel after
the Cataract Canyon disasters. He was pulling with Brown
at the upset which resulted in the former's drowning below
Soap Creek. From the fact that Stanton refers to him as "our
first boatman" it would appear that he had been directing the
navigational end of the second expedition. This brings up the
very interesting question as to whether McDonald may have
left the party as a consequence of unpleasantness over the loss
of the *Marie*. If he was responsible for that highly ill-advised
attempt to save the labour of a portage he may well have come
in for sharp censure for its failure. On the other hand, if he
had advised against it and been overruled he would have been
more than human not to voice some sort of a protest. If Mc-
Donald was really the experienced boatman he is said to have
been, it is inconceivable that he should have countenanced a
plan so certain to result in disaster. Stanton's story gives no
clue to the trouble, if there was any.[1] Turning "a keen, untroubled face home to the instant need of things," he merely
records:

"The rest of the party seemed to take on a more determined feeling that the exploration should go on to a final success. Special

[1] In a subsequent reading of Mr. Stanton's report and the discussion
thereof by his colleagues in the paper of the Transactions of the American
Society of Civil Engineers already alluded to, I find a statement that
throws a little further light on the departure of McDonald. Replying to
a suggestion that he might have done better to have employed skilled boatmen from the Northwest, Mr. Stanton writes:
"I am fully aware of the value of 'skilled labor' in any undertaking,
under ordinary circumstances. Yet in selecting my men for the second
expedition, although strongly advised to secure the lumbermen Mr. Sears
refers to, I rejected all such labor with but one exception, an experienced
boatman in such waters, and he deserted the expedition in the Grand
Cañon when we most needed him."
This would indicate that McDonald left on his own initiative, though
whether from trouble over the loss of the *Marie* or because he was tired
of the hard grind it is not clear.
In a continuation of this statement Mr. Stanton gives his reasons for
picking the character and type of men he did for the second expedition:

praise is due to Mr. John Hislop [1] and Mr. Reginald Travers, for the determined and manly spirit with which they stepped into new and trying duties, and the perserverance with which they carried them through."

"It has been my experience many times during the past twenty years that for such work, whether on land or water, where prolonged hardships and privations, and especially scanty food, and perhaps starvation, are to be faced day after day, the man who has an object to gain, with of course the qualities of body and mind to quickly acquire 'experience,' is far more efficient, and a better man to tie to in a wilderness, than the laborer, however skilled he may be, who is simply hired for so much a day."

In confirmation of this undeniably sound contention, Stanton cites the case of Reginald Travers, whose only preparation for the work of the expedition had been that of a New York stock-broker and "an amateur oarsman on Flushing Bay." But Travers had the right stuff. Inside of a week he was just about the best riverman in the party.

Since writing the above I have received the following note from Mrs. Anna Stanton Burchard:

Mr. Stanton's diary, containing the daily "log" of the expedition, gives some pages to McDonald's departure, which he strongly condemns as a desertion. He quotes the reason given by McDonald for his desertion,—the extra work thrown upon him by the shirking of two others, whose "utter worthlessness" Stanton admits, for which Stanton says he gave him extra wages; and, on the other side, Stanton says: "McDonald has been for years a hunter and trapper and prospector, going and working by fits and starts as he saw fit, and this regular work, day after day, week after week, for several months, is too much for him, and he is dissatisfied and makes—and—an excuse.

"2nd. The rich quartz veins we have passed are tempting him back, for he says he will only go out far enough to get a horse and outfit and come in to prospect."

Under date of February 10, 1890, Stanton takes McDonald's signature to a receipt in full on a page of the diary and adds a note strongly condemning his conduct.

A diary entry of February 7, 1890, three days before the paying off, gives a vivid contrast in character: "McDonald spoke up in an angry manner and said . . . that we could never get to Peach Springs, and would have to go out soon any way, and, for his part, *he* would just as [soon] leave—start out now, from here.

"I simply answered, it was the privilege of any one to leave when they thought best, and the conversation ended.

"I was much surprised to see Mac show the white feather so soon and only sorry because of its effect upon the other men.

"Hislop says he has come to stay,—the same as he did last year. And, with him, I 'shall fight it out if it takes all summer.'"

The loss of the *Marie* is not mentioned in the diary as having anything to do with McDonald's leaving.

[1] John Hislop was subsequently Chief Engineer of the White Pass and Yukon Railway in Alaska. I distinctly recall spending an evening with him in Skagway, when he and three or four other railway men made up a grub-stake for myself and another youthful runaway from Stanford to the newly discovered Porcupine Creek diggings. My only recollection of him is of a sizable, bearded Scotchman, with a quiet, steady eye. At that time

Stanton, naturally, was more concerned in his reports with engineering than with scenery. Few of the natural beauties were lost on him, however, and he pauses occasionally to sketch some striking scene with a few quick, telling strokes. This, as the aftermath of a rainstorm that assailed them in the vicinity of the Kanab Wash, is rather a gem of its kind:

"As the clouds rose we were treated to scenes rare and beautiful in the extreme. Over the brink of the upper walls came—first one and then another—hundreds of little streams, shooting far out into the air, and dropping hundreds and hundreds of feet over the cliffs, breaking into sparkling spray before they struck the bench below. These formed thousands of smaller rivulets as they dropped farther and farther down, till the whole of the bright scarlet walls seemed hung with a tapestry of silver threads, the border fringed with white fleecy clouds which clung to the tops of the walls, and through which the points of the upper cliffs shone as scarlet tassels. As the sun broke through some side gorge, the cañon was spanned from side to side, as the clouds shifted their position, with rainbow after rainbow, vying to outdo in brilliancy of colour the walls of the cañon themselves."

Stanton observed with great interest that, although the walls for many miles below the Kanab were almost vertical to a height of three thousand feet, there was a bench of solid marble, running almost parallel to the grade of the river, wide enough to carry the rails of a four-track line. Rapidly rising water in this sector brought an acceleration of current. A mile and a half-long rapid was run in just four and a half minutes by the watch—almost exactly twenty miles an hour. A little farther down the party was witness of one of the strangest phenomena ever seen by Colorado canyon voyageurs.

I had never heard that he, or any one else for that matter, had voyaged through the Grand Canyon. A recent letter from Anna Stanton Burchard identifies the Alaskan engineer with her father's right-hand man in the Colorado canyons. "After all the dangers he had gone through," she writes, "he was killed by a street car when he was home on a visit." —L. R. F.

"About 2.30 P. M. we heard a deep, loud roar, and saw the breakers ahead in white foam. With a great effort we stopped upon a pile of broken rock that had rolled into the river. When we went ahead to look, much to our surprise, the whole terrible rapid that we had expected to see had disappeared, and there was only a rushing current in its stead. While we stood wondering, there rose right at our feet those same great waves, twelve to fifteen feet in height and from one hundred to one hundred and fifty feet long across the river, rolling down stream like great sea waves, and breaking in white foam with a terrible noise. We watched and wondered, and at last concluded that this was the forefront of a great body of water rolling down this narrow trough from some great cloudburst above. Believing that discretion was the better part of valour, we camped right there on that pile of rocks, fearing that, although our boats would ride the waves in safety, we might be caught in one of these rolls just at the head of a rapid, and, unable to stop, be carried over the rapid with the additional force of the rushing breakers."

At the time Stanton was unable to suggest any adequate explanation to account for the sudden appearance of the waves other than that they were the result of a great cloudburst somewhere above. In a footnote he states that he learned some weeks later of the occurrence at about this time of a cloudburst upon the Little Colorado. Mr. W. W. Bass, the veteran Grand Canyon guide, writes me a very interesting letter bearing on this remarkable phenomenon. I reproduce the essential parts of it without subscribing to the criticism of Stanton's judgment. After summarizing Stanton's account of the incident and his explanation of it, Bass continues:

"Now a cloudburst in February here [the Little Colorado] is a most unusual thing. I never knew of one in 40 years. But if true, how did the rushing torrents get past his outfit without their knowledge and then turn back up the river to engulf them? Now just take a little squint at the map of this particular portion of the Colorado River and you will plainly see that Cataract Creek Canyon intersects the Colorado River just below where he had to camp, but strange to relate, he never mentions seeing it at all. . . . Now here is the secret of that awful bank of up-drifting water he describes:

You will read that he mentions rainy weather—the only storms during the entire journey. The winter during January and February had been a severe one in the San Francisco mountain range and heavy deposits of snow covered the entire upper surfaces on the northern slopes and plateaus. Cataract is a synclinal cañon and receives the entire drainage of this region from the Friscoes to Floyds, a distance of nearly 100 miles. I had constructed a large reservoir in the upper reaches of this drainage and the rain storm Stanton mentions was responsible for the melting of this great body of snow and every tributary of Cataract was a raging torrent for several days. My large reservoir was filled to overflowing but could not withstand the force of the great body of water and it gave way all at once and resulted in flooding the entire Indian reservation 50 miles below. By reference to my diaries I find that the exact date that this body of water joined the Colorado was the same as Stanton gives in his report for the incident he describes. You will readily see that this wall of water 40 or 50 feet high when released at this point from a narrow gorge would naturally rush up stream."

It is just possible that the breaking of the Bass reservoir as described may have been responsible for the remarkable waves seen by the Stanton party. The engineer did not, however, state that the waves were surging *up* the river, as Bass infers. On the contrary, he states explicitly twice that they ran *down* stream. As he was still above the mouth of Cataract Creek Canyon, any disturbance from that direction would have had to come in the form of an *up*-running series of waves. This makes it hard to reconcile the broken reservoir theory with Stanton's account.

My only first-hand experience in the sudden augmentation of the flow of a river was on a greatly reduced scale from that which Stanton encountered, but I give it briefly for what it is worth. I was running down the old Alamo channel through Imperial Valley last summer on a stream of five hundred second-feet, when four hundred additional second-feet were turned into the waste at Sharp's Heading. The forefront of this increased flow, overtaking me between sheer walls four miles above Holtville, carried my boat against a cliff, rolled it over and finally broke it in two amidships. The flood came very much as Stanton described—in a series of swift under-running waves that were hardly perceptible in the deeper water but which broke violently over the shallows. I do not, therefore, find it hard to fall in with the engineering party's theory that the abnormal waves they saw were the result of great cloudbursts in a not-too-remote part of the upper basin.

The coldest weather of the voyage followed the rains, and when rapids were run in the early mornings a thin sheet of ice from the spray formed on boats and rowers alike. The photographic work was considerably complicated by the fact that a fire had to be built to thaw the ice from the cameras before every series of exposures. The mouth of Diamond Creek was reached March 1st. Here all but one of the crew of the lost boat left the river, reducing the party to eight. Records and photographs were sent out from this point and a fresh lot of supplies brought in from Peach Springs, on the railway. In the course of an eleven days' halt men and boats were stiffened for the final battle.

With the Lower Granite Gorge beginning ten miles above Diamond Creek, they were in bad water again from the first push-off. Stanton mentions several rapids where the impossibility of portaging made it necessary to run willy-nilly. The crucial test came on the afternoon of the second day at a rapid which he calls "No. 465." This is readily identifiable as the savage series of falls at which the first Powell party divided. Professor Thompson subsequently called it Catastrophe Rapid, but it has since come to be known by the rather more appropriate name of Separation Rapid. If anything, Stanton's description makes it possible to form a more comprehensive mental picture of this baffling tumble of cataracts than does that of Powell. Two streams, entering almost directly opposite each other, are responsible for bringing down the boulder dams which so effectually obstruct the river.

"These make three drops or falls in the one great rapid, that in all has a fall of perhaps thirty feet. On the right side is a perpendicular cliff, fifty to one hundred feet high, extending two-thirds of the length of the rapid. On the left side is a perpendicular cliff of one thousand feet or more in height, and extending the whole length of the rapid. The current, turned from the right side by the large number of boulders from that creek, dashes, after passing over the first fall, against the left cliff, just at the head of the second fall, and is thrown back with awful force, and, as it meets the current from the right, curls up in angry waves fifteen to twenty feet high, first from one side and then from the other. From this the whole current is thrown against the right wall, as it curves out into the stream, just as at the head of the fall."

Rested, freshly provisioned and sustained by the knowledge that the rapid had already been run successfully, Stanton's party was assailed by none of the doubts and dissensions which operated so potently to split Powell's worn and somewhat demoralized voyageurs at this point. Once assured that a portage was out of the question, the engineers hastened back to their boats and prepared for the plunge without a moment's debate or hesitation. It was a wild ride—for some reason, much rougher than Powell's.

"In a moment we were at the head of the first fall, and over or through a half dozen huge waves, and approaching the second fall. As I looked down into that pit of fury, I wondered if it were possible for our boats to go through it and come out whole, and right side up. I had no time for a second thought. We were in the midst of the breakers. They lashed us first one side and then the other, breaking far above our heads, and half filled our boats. For a second we were blinded with the dashing, muddy waters. In another second we were through and out, and right side up. I turned to look to see if all the men were safe. They were all in their places; but our boat, though right side up, had been turned quartering with the current, and we were being carried with fearful force toward the right cliff. Every instant I expected to be dashed again the cliff ahead, where the whole current of water was piled up in one boiling mass against the solid granite; but just as I thought the last moment had come, our sturdy Scotch helmsman, Hislop, gave the boat a sudden turn, and, assisted by the rebounding wave, we went by the cliff, and I shouted to the men: 'That's good! that's good! We are past!' But the words were hardly out of my mouth when, as we rounded the point into the third fall, our boat, thrown in by a huge wave, crashed into a rock that projected from the shore, and she stopped. We were all thrown forward. The boat filled with water, sank upon the rock, and stuck fast. Wave after wave in quick succession rolled over us. I tried to straighten myself up, when a great wave struck me in the back, and I was washed clean out of the boat into the whirlpool below the rock. For an instant I knew nothing; but as I was drawn down my consciousness returned, and as I was carried by that whirlpool down, down, down, I wondered if I should ever reach the bottom of the river. The time seemed an age. The river seemed bottomless. In a few moments I was caught as by two forces—one around my legs, and another around my neck—and twisting in opposite directions; they sent me whirling away, and I was shot to the surface fifty feet (I am told) down the rapid from where I went in."

The second boat, missing her stranded sister by a scant two feet, ran the drifting Stanton a neck-and-neck race for the foot of the third fall. He states that Edwards, the cook, jerked him into the one boat quite as mercilessly as he had been dashed from the other. When finally dislodged, Stanton's boat showed a ten by eighteen inch hole in her side. Kept from sinking by her water-tight chambers, she was drifted down to a point where she could be dragged out for repairs. An hour's work completed a fairly tight and serviceable patch of copper. Another "roaring, tumbling rapid" that was run late in the afternoon was probably the same which, at different stages of water, has given later voyageurs quite as much trouble as the dreaded falls at Separation Rapid.

The almost unbelievable differences varying stages of water make in rapids is the explanation of the diverse experiences of successive canyon navigators at the same points. The fact that Wheeler was able to effect portages at Separation Rapid and several other difficult points in the Lower Granite Gorge is accounted for by the almost unprecedentedly low water of the late fall of 1871 and the fact that he had almost unlimited man-power for his lines.

Stanton was out of the Grand Canyon on March 17th, and, continuing his survey down the lower river, reached the head of the Gulf of California April 26th. To the great regret of all, the two staunch little boats that had carried them nearly twelve hundred miles without an upset had to be abandoned to the ignominious fate of a final resting place in the mud of the tidal flats of the delta.

Although Stanton's courage and loyalty in completing the canyon survey after the disastrous and tragic finish of the Brown expedition were universally acclaimed, and although the most conservative of his colleagues were almost a unit in agreeing that his work had established the feasibility of a railway down the Colorado from an engineering standpoint, the odds against the economic justification of so costly a piece of construction threw the balance against it in the financial scales. During the last three decades of his active professional career Stanton did notable mining and civil engineering work in various parts of the world, including Sumatra, Cuba, and Canada. Perhaps his outstanding achievement was the solution of a troublesome and costly landslide problem for the Canadian Pacific after all other engineers had failed.

Neither his failure to imbue others with his own faith in the canyon railway project nor his active work in diverse and distant fields ever caused any waning of interest on Stanton's part in the Colorado River. His dream of a great work covering the history of the exploration of the river from the viewpoint of an engineer may well have been contemporaneous with his dream of a canyon railway. He began gathering material for it not long after his surveying voyage, and his compilation and preparation of material occupied the leisure hours of most of the remaining years of his life. His eldest daughter, now Mrs. Lewis S. Burchard of New York, writes me that in order to secure accurate data bearing on the earliest expeditions from Mexico to the lower river "records of Spanish expeditions were translated, checked up and verified even to the astronomical observations;" also that he corresponded with the Vatican in an endeavour to connect the "De Julien" inscriptions of 1836 with some early Catholic missionary. A line on the exhaustiveness with which every subject was handled may be gained from the fact that two hundred pages of manuscript were devoted to documents and discussion bearing on the raft-voyage of James White. Some hint of the fair-mindedness and accuracy which characterized Stanton's work may be gathered from the brief extracts from and comment on some of this matter in my own chapter on White. The completed work was planned to be of two volumes and to bear the title: "The Exploration, Navigation and Survey of the Colorado River of the West, From the Standpoint of an Engineer."

There was a strange fatality attendant upon all of Stanton's Colorado River ventures, from the tragic culmination of the Brown voyage to the defeat of his hopes in the canyon railway project and the failure of an ambitious gold-dredging enterprise he subsequently launched in upper Glen Canyon. But perhaps the bitterest disappointment of all—because it came near the end of a long career—was the failure to interest a publisher in his long-laboured-over book. The most ambitious and comprehensive record of Colorado River history attempted up to this time was still in manuscript form when the author died early in 1922, and it remains so to this day.

The very completeness of the Stanton work on the Colorado has been the rock upon which it has stranded in seeking publication through the regular channels. It is doubtless destined to find its way to the world through the efforts of some historical society or foundation. This consummation could be brought about in no more fitting way than through co-operative action on the part of the several such organizations in the seven states of the Colorado River Basin.

Robert Brewster Stanton will not find his true niche in Colorado River history until after the publication of his book. Until then full appreciation of the man and his work will only be possible to those who knew most intimately both the one and the other. Frederick Dellenbaugh knew the man for many years; knew what he was doing, what he was trying to do. In answer to one of my letters of inquiry Mr. Dellenbaugh writes:

"You can safely say all you wish to about Stanton's ability, his nerve, his honour, his devotion to duty and all that. He was an *absolutely* fine character in *every* respect. I had and have a profound admiration for him."

CHAPTER XIV

GALLOWAY AND STONE AND A NEW CANYON BOAT

THE final decade of the nineteenth century ushered in a new era of Colorado canyon navigation. The navigators of the period previous to this had come in carefully organized and outfitted expeditions, working collectively for a common end, such as scientific exploration in the cases of Powell and Wheeler, and seeking data for railway construction in those of Brown and Stanton. With preliminary exploration practically complete, and no further demand for railway surveys, the canyon navigation was open for individual enterprise. And here, nearly three-quarters of a century after Pattie and Ashley, reappears the strangely anachronistic figure of our old friend the trapper. Nathan Galloway would doubtless have been another Pattie had he lived in 1825, except that it is not probable that he would ever have been tempted to break into print. To the man's utter indifference to publicity is due the very regrettable fact that the exploits of the outstanding lonehand Colorado canyon navigator must remain all but unrecorded.

Galloway was a hunter and trapper—one of the greatest the upper Colorado Basin has ever known. Julius F. Stone, who met him first in the Henry Mountains in the early nineties and hunted with him on and off for many years, writes me that the man had the most intimate and accurate knowledge of everything pertaining to his vocations; that he understood wild animals really better than they understood themselves, in that he knew what they would do under all varying conditions and circumstances. Galloway probably sought the more inaccessible Colorado canyons because their very remoteness meant better trapping and hunting. Reaching these places demanded skilled boating, and bringing to bear upon the problems of this the same keen faculties that made him so successful with gun and trap, he not only became very adept in working in rough water but practically evolved a new type of Colorado canyon boat and revolutionized the whole system of navigating those canyons.

Galloway was not able to afford the comparatively large and expensive boats such as were used by Powell and Stanton, nor (working alone or with a single companion as was his wont) would he have been in a position to man such craft had they been available. He needed something he could handle alone or, at worst, with the aid of a single partner. Realizing at the outset the futility of trying to build a boat strong enough to withstand repeated collisions with rocks and cliffs, he tackled the problem from the other end by trying to build a boat with which rocks and cliffs could be avoided. That is to say, he sacrificed strength to lightness and handiness. Decked over until the open space was little more than a cockpit for a single oarsman, and with water-tight compartments fore and aft to preserve buoyancy when swamped or capsized, Galloway lanched the forerunner of the type of boat in which all of the rough-water work of the Colorado canyons is done at this day.

By pulling up-stream while facing down-stream in the rapids the necessity of the former steersman was done away with. Steering was managed by slanting the bow to port or starboard across the current. Being able to see where he was going, the oarsman picked his own course and no longer had to endure the tension of waiting for orders with his back to the sphere of action. Pulling against the current had the effect of checking headway by so much and thus lessening the force of impact of a possible crash. This method—sometimes called "drifting"—has been used in Canada and Alaska for many years. It is, indeed, the plan of action that a man of good common sense, turned loose alone with a skiff on a swift river, would quickly work out for himself. The method *was* new to the Colorado canyons, however, while the Galloway type of one-man row-boat for working in rough water was a distinct and notable innovation.

While Galloway doubtless did some boating through the upper canyons previous to that date, his first extended river trip was in 1895, when he left Green River, Wyoming, and went right through to Lee's Ferry. Who his companion was on this trip I have been unable to learn. It is not improbable that he made the whole run by himself, for the following year, on September 15th, he *did* start through the upper canyons alone. Shortly after pushing off on this trip a trapper by the name of William Richmond was encountered, a stranger to Galloway and also working down-river by boat. They agreed to join forces and trap the canyons down to Lee's Ferry, pooling their joint catch and dividing it at the end of the voyage. It was their intention right up to reaching the mouth of the Paria that the voyage should be terminated at that point and the return made by way of Kanab. It was entirely the consequence of some bantering remark on Galloway's part—possibly in the form of a dare taken up by the spirited Richmond—that they continued on through Marble and the Grand Canyon. After considerable hardship but no serious disaster, they reached Needles on February 10th, 1897. There is no published record of this fine sporting little jaunt; Julius Stone, who had some verbal account of it from Galloway, gives me the bare facts. As Galloway would have known better than to expect any trapping along the bare, water-swept cliffs between the Paria and the Virgin, the result of this bit of midwinter madness on the part of that game pair of trappers may safely be put on record as the one Grand Canyon voyage really made for the fun of the thing.

Galloway had been trapping down the Green for a number of winters when Julius Stone, in whose company he had hunted on several occasions, suggested another Grand Traverse, this time for the purpose of securing a complete collection of photographs covering the whole Colorado canyon series. The trip was planned for the fall months of 1909, Galloway going to Stone's home in Columbus to help plan the outfit.

Stone, who had been at the head of a large manufacturing company for many years, was the one man needed to perfect and standardize the type of boat evolved from Galloway's practical experience. An outdoor man all of his life, he had spent much time upon one sort or another of water, which included some canoe experience upon Canadian rivers. Combining his own considerable knowledge of boats with that of Galloway, the design was draughted, and blue-prints sent to a well-known builder in Detroit. The principal modifications of Galloway's boat embodied at Stone's suggestion in the new design were a broadening of the stern, so that the blow of a wave would have the effect of checking headway, a canvas shield to keep the cockpit dryer in splashy water, and a detachable skeg to make steering easier in the long quiet stretches of hard pulling. This was to be taken off while working in rapids, where it would have the tendency to impede speedy turning of the boat. Mr. Stone gives me the following description of the four boats built for his trip of 1909:

"The boats were 16 feet, 4 inches long, 48 inches beam, and 16 inches deep. They were built of ⅝ inch Michigan White Pine, with butt joints so as to be more readily kept water-tight by caulking. The bottom of each was flat and had a rake of 10 inches fore and aft from the centre. The empty boat weighed 243 pounds, being built as light as possible and intended for only one man, together with the necessary provisions, camp equipment, etc. The compartment immediately in front of and to the rear of the cockpit was covered with canvas ticking, held down at the ends and sides by such fastenings as are now used in attaching automobile curtains to the frame. There was a supposedly water-tight compartment at the extreme bow and stern of each boat, but this proved by experience to be a delusion."

This is the boat which, with slight modifications affecting size and weight rather than design, was used by the Kolbs in their notable voyage down the whole canyon series in 1911, and by the Geological Survey in Cataract Canyon in 1921. The three boats used on the latter trip, with one addition, were to be reconditioned for the Geological Survey work of the summer and fall of 1923 in the Marble and Grand Canyons. The boat is called by several names, varying according to where and by whom it was last used. Now that it is a proven and established type it is high time that usage settled to one. For this I would suggest Galloway-Stone as a name that is both comprehensive and appropriate.

The Stone party pushed off from Green River, Wyoming, on the 12th of September, 1909. There were four boats. Stone and Galloway each had one to himself, as did Charles C. Sharp of Nelsonville, Ohio. S. S. Deubendorff of Richfield, Utah, carried the photographer, R. C. Coggswell, as a passenger. Of Deubendorff's work and personality Stone writes with the greatest enthusiasm. Although quite without previous boating experience, he was always ready to do more than his full share, quickly developing into a most valuable riverman.

No party previously entering the Colorado canyons ever had so skilful and experienced a guide as Galloway. As a consequence of his knowledge of the river much laborious reconnaissance work was avoided, with its accompanying uncertainty and loss of time. Ashley Falls in Red Canyon were run with no damage save to one of the oar-locks of Stone's boat. Lodore was passed in four days. Split Mountain Canyon called for hard, careful work, but brought no serious trouble. One of the rough, shallow riffles of Desolation Canyon was responsible for the first mishap, of which Stone writes:

"Mr. Sharp's boat was caught between a couple of rocks at the upper end of one of the last rapids of Desolation Canyon and filled with water, hanging there until the rest of us had landed at the foot of the rapid and cut a small tree which we used as a lever in freeing

the boat from the rocks, after which we lightened it of all the articles
it contained, which naturally were water-soaked; but these, including Mr. Sharp, were soon dried out around a roaring camp-fire, and
early the next morning we put a patch on the bottom of his boat,
where it had been somewhat cracked, and went on without further
difficulty."

The junction of the Grand and the Green was reached on
October 15th, at the end of rather less than thirty days' running time from Green River, Wyoming—probably the best record ever made for this stretch.   Before entering Cataract Canyon a halt of a day and a half was made for the rigging up of
canvas fenders around the cockpits.   The builders having failed
to install the iron stakes designed to support this protective
shield, green black-willow stakes were substituted, answering
the purpose fairly well.   The canvas was tacked permanently
to the boat all around the cockpit.   Four rings, sewn to the
fabric and slipped over the ends of the stakes, served to keep
the fender elevated.   Small holes were cut in the canvas to
permit the functioning of the oars.   Capable of being quickly
raised against splashy water or lowered to avoid a head-wind,
Mr. Stone found this simple contrivance added considerably
to the comfort of the work in rough rapids.

Cataract Canyon, because it is so easily approached through
deceptively quiet water from both the Grand and the Green,
has entangled more unskilled navigators—mostly prospectors,
doubtless—than any other of the gorges of the Colorado.   The
inevitably resultant tragedies have earned for this sinister
tumble of almost continuous rapids the gruesome but appropriate name of "The Graveyard."   Few of those passing it
successfully but have reported finding evidences of recent disaster, and in this respect the Stone party was not an exception.

"At the head of Cataract Canyon [writes Mr. Stone in a personal
letter] where our first camp was made we found signs of a party
consisting of two men and a half-grown boy, apparently not more
than three or four days ahead of us.   These evidences continued until

we reached the head of Rapid No. 24, where we found their boat jammed in the rocks and wrecked, beyond all hope of extrication. Nearby we found a coat on a rock, the underside of which was still wet, showing that the disaster must have occurred not more than 24 hours before.

"We hurried along as fast as we could in the hope of overtaking whoever it might be and helping them, but found no evidence of them whatever at any point below, and careful inquiry throughout that region at every point where they might have reached civilization failed to disclose any evidence that they succeeded in doing so."

In the course of the two following years Mr. Stone learned of the finding of wrecked boats and bodies that indicated that at least seven men had lost their lives in Cataract Canyon between 1909 and 1912, none of them identified.

The cataracts furnished considerable excitement but brought no serious trouble to the Stone party. Deubendorff was caught among the rocks in Rapid No. 18 and in the resultant upset lost his watch, notes and a part of his load. A useful lifebelt prevented serious consequences to himself. An experience near the end of the canyon effectually cured Mr. Stone of tempting fate by trying to make snappy action for the camera.

"Wishing a picture of a boat in turbulent water, I purposely went into the largest waves of Rapid No. 23, with the result that the boat failed to rise over the second wave; also the third one. Both of these broke entirely over the boat, the first one carrying away the fender and everything else moveable in the boat except myself. The print shows indistinctly the boat just before it disappeared under the second wave, and you see by the result that our experiment was practically barren of the object sought. In other words, 'the game wasn't worth the candle,' though I had a lively experience for a few seconds in trying to keep right side up, but I quickly got over to the right hand side of the stream where there was a convenient sand bar on which I tipped the boat over, freeing it from water, but it was the last time I voluntarily tried such an experiment."

Sharp, for business reasons, had to leave the party at Dandy Crossing. His boat was cached at that point. Lee's Ferry

was reached October 27th. A fresh supply of provisions was
expected here, and the failure of the pack-train to arrive put
the party on uncomfortably short rations until Galloway's
useful rifle replenished the larder with goat-meat on the second day in Marble Canyon. This great gorge brought the usual
run of hard work, notwithstanding which the mouth of the
Little Colorado was reached in not much over three days from
Lee's Ferry—record time again. Mr. Stone ran a level on the
great Sockdologer, and reported a fall at that point of only
thirty-four feet, nine inches. Whether this covered the exact
third of a mile where Powell estimated a fall of eighty feet it
would be very difficult to say. There is still considerable that
is not entirely clear regarding the location of this famous rapid.
Doubtless the Geological Survey work of this summer will
gain some interesting data on this somewhat controversial
point.

Reaching Bright Angel Creek November 2nd, the party
climbed out the following day to the south rim at El Tovar.
After replenishing supplies and films, the voyage was resumed
on the 5th. On the 8th, in trying to run what Stone calls
"Conquistador Aisle" (Rapid No. 95 from the head of the
Grand Canyon), the plucky Deubendorff provided further
thrills. Mr. Stone sends me the entry from his diary covering
the lively interval.

"At 3:15 P.M. we reach one that looks pretty bad,—it has a
narrow channel with very high waves for a long distance. However,
we decide to try it. Galloway picks out his course along the right
hand side where there are some rocks but no big waves. He goes
first, I next, and Deubendorff last. As I drop into the eddy below
the first rock I see Galloway has been unable to follow the channel
decided upon and his boat strikes a partly submerged boulder 20 ft.
from the place he tried to reach; therefore, I at once decide to go
into the heavy waves which turns out to be the proper thing, as I
go through all right, but on looking around at the first place I can
safely do so, I see Deubendorff's boat on the crest of a big wave
near the upper end of the rapids, then it goes out of sight and re-

appears in the act of turning over almost endwise. It comes down among the waves, bottom up, while now and then I get a glimpse of Deubendorff's head bobbing up a moment and then disappearing again, but out of sight the greater part of the time. I call to Galloway and try to reach the bow line of Deubendorff's boat as it reaches me, but this I am unable to do because of the high canvas sides of my own. Galloway, however, slips his line through the iron handhold at its stern, takes a hitch around his leg and so tows the boat to the right bank before it reaches the next rapid. I gather up the balance of the things that float down, and then we set about righting the boat which is soon done and emptied of water. In the meantime, Deubendorff, who so suddenly decided to run this rapid head-first without a boat (and succeeded) has crawled out about 300 yards below the place where the accident happened and has come down to help us. His head is pretty badly cut and he looks like hell, but his first words are 'I'd like to try that again. I know I can run it.' So do we, because we saw him do it. He doesn't seem to know what fear is; but all is well that ends well and we cross to the left bank, build a fire (wood is a little scarce), Deubendorff puts on dry clothing, I tinker up the cuts in his head, the wet things are spread out to dry, and but for a broken oar there is little evidence of trouble."

Separation Rapid, where the Powell party divided and where Stanton had so much trouble, did not greatly bother the Stone party. Just below there, however, a rapid which both of the previous parties had run (one at higher and one at lower water) impressed Stone as being the most dangerous he encountered on the whole voyage. Later the Kolbs ran the upper part of this rapid on what was probably a somewhat lower stage. This is striking evidence not only of the well known fact that the same rapids vary greatly at different stages of water, but might indicate considerable physical changes in all but the cliffs and bedrock as well.

While reconnoitring this rapid Stone slipped and fell in such a way as to catch his heel in a crevice between two large rocks. He hung down, helpless, with his back to the boulders, until Deubendorff and Galloway succeeded in lifting his pen-

NE OF THE NARROWEST PARTS OF MARBLE CANYON.

At this point Mr. Stone's party found driftwood 107 feet above water.

RUSSELL AND MONETTE NEARING THE NEEDLES.
The "flags of victory" are their undershirts.

**GALLOWAY WITH
A COUPLE OF
TRAPPED BEAVER.**

dant body sufficiently to release the foot. A badly wrenched and swollen ankle was the only result of what might have been a very serious accident.

The whole outfit was taken out of the water in passing this troublesome rapid. An intricate and skilful piece of lining reduced the portage to a minimum, but even as it was a large part of two days was consumed in completing it. This was the last fall of any consequence in the Grand Canyon, the mouth of which was reached on November 15th. Four days later the voyage was completed at Needles.

Of linings and portages Mr. Stone writes:

"We took our boats out at seven different places, usually only in order to get around one or two bad rocks, say 25 or 30 feet. The longest distance we portaged them was about 150 ft. in Lodore Canyon. We also lined them in twenty-one instances, but only in one case for a greater distance than the length of the bow line—30 ft."

The voyage of the Stone party was a record-breaking performance in several respects. It was not only much the fastest trip ever made through the whole Colorado canyon series, but it was far ahead of any other passage in the number of rapids run. The record for time still stands as the best ever made between Green River, Wyoming, and Needles; the Kolb brothers, two years later, made a slightly better record for rapids run. The arrival at Needles also marked the completion of Galloway's second voyage through all of the canyons, and to date he is the only man to attain that distinction. Mr. Stone admits (but does not claim) the honour of being the oldest man ever to make the long canyon voyage. Although he hardly looks that age even to-day, this vigorous sportsman must have been well along in his fifties in 1909, and Galloway was almost as old. Between them these two veterans share one more Colorado navigation record that is not likely to be equalled for many years. Each brought his boat through the whole voyage without an upset, and with but a single light collision with a rock while under control by the oars.

His interest in the Colorado canyons stimulated rather than satiated by his first trip, Mr. Stone laid plans for another voyage down the river in 1912. The untimely death of Deubendorff in 1911 rather took the heart out of the venture for the two surviving veterans of the former trip, and 1913 saw the passing of Galloway himself. Stone dropped the plan of the Colorado trip for good then, but in 1917 could not resist the invitation of Ellsworth Kolb for a fling at the Black Canyon of the Gunnison. Limited in time on account of business, he was able to enjoy the old-time thrill of only a few slap-banging rapids and the tonic of a ducking or two before hastening back to his desk in Columbus. Ellsworth has given me a delightful description of the cool-headed veteran coming up after an upset in a boiling riffle and deliberately adjusting his eye-glasses as if for a reading of the morning paper.

With the news of the preparations for the Geological Survey trip down the Marble and Grand Canyon this summer Mr. Stone turned again a longing eye to the Colorado. Confessing a strong temptation to seek permission to go along in his own boat as a sort of supernumerary for the pure fun of the thing, he adds:

"But while Father Time has dealt very graciously and very kindly with me, I am afraid there are some exactions that he has not withheld, and it may be that the requisite strength and endurance are two of the essentials which I do not possess, though the impulse to horn in is very strong. . . . I shall envy you and Kolb your every moment on the River, but not in that selfish grudging spirit which would deny to others the delights that are beyond our own reach."

And therein lies some hint of the stuff of which the real Colorado canyon navigator is compact. Personally, I should be heartily glad of the assurance that I was going to have an honest-to-goodness hankering for nosing a boat into the head of the Mable Gorge any time after I was within twenty years of three score and ten.

   .   .   .   .   .   .

There were two other highly courageous Colorado canyon voyages completed during the time Nathan Galloway was trapping on that river, one (and possibly both) of which owed its inspiration to the work of that masterly pioneer navigator. It was in 1895 that the Mormon hunter and trapper first demonstrated the possibilities of the light decked-over boat in rough-water navigation by his voyage from Green River, Wyoming, to Lee's Ferry. On August 27th of the following year a man by the name of George F. Flavell pushed off from Green River in a boat believed to have been modelled closely upon that of Galloway. He was accompanied by a single companion whose name has not been preserved. They were equipped for trapping and prospecting. In December of the same year the two men arrived at Yuma, where Flavell (who was also called Clark) is reported as boasting that he ran every rapid on the river. It is very probable, however, that the plucky voyageur made no such absurd and bombastic claim. He wrote one letter to Robert Brewster Stanton telling of his progress down the river, and others of similar character to former assistants of that engineer. These letters were later collected by Stanton, who states that: "In them Flavell tells the number and exact location of all the rapids he did not run, and around which he portaged and let down by lines, and the number of times his boat 'got stove in' against the rocks and had to be repaired and rebuilt." [1] It is a matter of real regret that there is no full and authentic record of this pioneer light-boat voyage through the Grand Canyon.

A prospecting expedition which left Green River, Utah, in September, 1907, had the first, and probably the best steel boats ever used in the Colorado canyons. The men composing

[1] *The Trail*, Denver, September, 1919, p. 13.

without disaster. There is some conflict of evidence as to just how and where their first boat was lost. The lurid magazine story referred to has it that Monette was stranded on a rock in running the Sockdologer, while the packers at the Grand Canyon had a somewhat more circumstantial account of how the boat was carried away by the rising river when the two voyageurs were camping beside the Hance Rapid. It is certain, in any case, that Monette came to the foot of the Bright Angel Trail riding as a passenger on Russell's boat; also that the departure from this point was made in that order.

The one remaining boat broke away as they were lining it down Hermit Creek Rapid—the same place at which Stanton had lost his *Marie* while trying to shoot her through empty eighteen years before. Climbing up the granite, Russell and Monette found a trail which led them to the camp of a prospector by the name of Bouchre. With his help the boat was recovered from a whirlpool five miles below the point at which it had broken loose. After three gaping holes in its sides had been repaired, the still undismayed navigators packed up and pushed off to complete their voyage. When Needles was reached in February, 1908, Russell was flying a "Flag of Victory" in the form of a cotton undershirt tied to an oar. It would be as interesting to know how they contrived to pass Separation Rapid as to know how they contrived to spare an undershirt at the end of a voyage on the Colorado.

As in the case of that of Flavell, one regrets that the story of this highly courageous voyage of Russell and Monette has never been adequately chronicled.

CHAPTER XV

THE KOLB BROTHERS AND THE FIRST MOVING-PICTURES

THE 1911 voyage of the Kolb brothers, latest of the Grand Traverses of the Colorado canyons, was notable in several respects. It was an extremely fine piece of rough-water navigation, it made possible the first moving-pictures ever taken over any extended section of the Colorado canyons, and it was the inspiration of one of the most modest and sincere yet at the same time graphic and wholly delightful books ever written by a river voyageur. This rather impressive lot of achievements was accomplished in the face of the fact that neither brother had ever cranked a moving picture camera before, and that Ellsworth, who wrote the story of the adventure, was just about as much of a stranger to the pen as to the oar he took up for the first time when the little expedition pushed off from Green River on the way to the canyons. The explanation of the thing is comparatively simple once you know the Kolbs—just two uncommonly well balanced heads set on two pairs of unusually capable shoulders. Add to that an apparently bottomless reserve of nerve—or what is less politely but more expressively called guts—and you have the complete formula.

Probably no one ever dreamed of the voyage through the Colorado canyons longer or more persistently than did the Kolbs. They had lived for years on the brink of the Grand Canyon, where their photographic studio had brought them into intimate contact with the surviving veterans of earlier voyages returning to gaze down on the scenes of former adventures as old sailors drift back to look upon the sea. Dellenbaugh told them of Powell; Stanton, Stone, Galloway, Russell and

Monette they met themselves. The whole long run was made in fancy many times before it became possible to tackle it in fact. With commendable patience they waited until they had both the time and the money to do the thing properly—and the Grand Traverse costs about as much in both one and the other as a hunting trip to Africa. Their outfit as finally assembled at Green River was complete in every respect, even to an extra man to help with the movies.

The two boats were built from designs furnished by Julius Stone and conformed in practically every respect to those used on his voyage with Galloway, save that the heavier construction throughout slightly more than doubled the weight. In order to insure complete protection from the water the forward compartment in each boat was lined with carefully soldered tin. Unfortunately the advantage of this highly desirable precaution was completely nullified by the neglect of the builders to make the hatch-covers water-tight. "Loose boards, with crosspieces, fastened with little thumb-screws—there they were, ready to admit the water at the first upset." The oversight was especially annoying on account of the delicate moving-picture camera, but with a falling river there was no time to delay further for repairs which demanded special materials.

The start, to the usual accompaniment of bucolic advice, was made on September 8th, 1911. Emery had already had some rowing experience; Ellsworth managed to master the essentials if not the niceties of the operation in the six easy care-free days that were taken by way of holiday in covering the sixty miles to the head of Flaming Gorge. "Jimmy," the moving-picture assistant, although he had a liquid baritone and was willing enough to sing around camp of a wet sheet and a flowing sea, never did develop any real affinity for their riverine counterparts of a wet seat and a flowing stream. After leading an unhappy and not altogether useful existence through Red Canyon and Lodore, ominous forebodings of coming illness in his family in California led him to apply for an in-

GRANITE LEDGE RAPID, BELOW BRIGHT ANGEL.

SUSPENSION BRIDGE ACROSS THE COLORADO AT GRAND CANYON.

definite leave of absence, to run concurrently with the continuance of the river trip. Same was granted, to the not inconsiderable relief of both parties to the agreement. Later the brothers came upon their recent assistant, the centre of a knot of spellbound auditors on the main street of Vernal, Utah. He was holding forth on the dangers of canyon navigation and, as Ellsworth dryly observes, "evidently keeping them interested."

"Jimmy's" family is a large one, with a surprising number of the ilk taking to photography and then to river travel. It must have been an uncle of the Kolbs' little helper that signed on with Julius Stone as photographer in his canyon voyage of 1909, and it was probably a nephew I had sent to film my run down the Columbia in 1920. Neither Mr. Stone nor myself managed to find in our respective assistants quite so prolific a fount of comic relief as did the genial Ellsworth in the amiable Jimmy.

Confidence mounted with perfected technique, and the successful running of the opening rapids of Red Canyon nerved the brothers to have a try at some real big game by shooting Ashley Falls. Both boats bumped but neither was much hurt. Lodore proved the usual ding-dong grind. No undue liberties were taken with that savage tumble of rapids, and, between carefully conning the course ahead and making many pictures, nine days were required to pass through to the foot of the gloomy gorge. The upper Disaster Fall was run and the lower lined. In the course of the latter operation Emery, busily cranking the picture camera, allowed his not unvociferous brother to be dragged off into the river by a runaway boat, fortunately without serious results. Art will be served. That sort of thing happened several times before the trip was over.

A day or two after passing Disaster Falls both boats stranded in somewhat lesser rapids. The guns were lost and, through the faultiness of the bulkheads, just about everything, including the cameras and some of the film, came in for a soaking. It was recorded that the wetting of movie film did not affect its usefulness in the least—for kindling fires, that is. The outfit was portaged around Triplet Falls and the boats lined down. Hell's Half Mile brought heart- and back-breaking work. First there was a three-quarter mile portage over mud-slippery rocks and sloping walls—nine loads to a boat. This was followed by a hard stretch of rough laborious lining of the empty boats; then the boats themselves had to come out. This latter portage was made imperative by a tree which had lodged on the bank at an unrunable point in a way to prevent even further lining. Ellsworth's description of the problem presented here and of the way it was solved gives some idea of the resourcefulness and dogged determination characterizing the work of the navigator brothers from beginning to end.

"Directly underneath and beyond the roots of the tree were large rounded boulders, covered with slippery mud. Past this barrier the full force of the water raced, to hurl itself and divide its current against another rock. It was useless to try to take a boat around the end of the rock. The boat's sides, three-eights of an inch thick, would be crushed like a cardboard box. If lifted into the V-shaped groove, the weight of the boats would wedge them and crush their sides. Fortunately an upright log was found tightly wedged between these boulders. A strong limb, with one end resting on a rock opposite, was nailed to this log; a triangle of stout sticks, with the point down, was placed opposite this first limb, on the same level, and was fastened to the upright log with still another piece; and another difficulty was overcome.

"With a short rope fastened to the iron bar or hand-hold on the stern, this end was lifted on to the cross-piece, the bow sticking into the water at a sharp angle. The short rope was tied to the stump, so we would not lose what we had gained. The longer rope from the bow was thrown over the roots of the tree above, then we both pulled on the rope, until finally the bow was on a level with the stern. She was pulled forward, the ropes were loosened and the boat rested on the cross-pieces. The motion-picture camera was transferred so as to command a view of the lower end of the barrier, then the boat was carefully tilted, and slid forward, a little at a time, until she finally gained headway, nearly jerking the rope from our hands, and shot into the pool below." [1]

Jimmy left the party below the foot of Lodore, and from there on to the foot of the Bright Angel Trail in the Grand Canyon the brothers had no help either with navigation or pictures. Whirlpool and Split Mountain Canyons provided much good practice and a few thrills but little trouble. Likewise the rough, shallow riffles of Desolation and Gray Canyons. Steady pulling in the long, quiet stretches of the Uinta Valley and Labyrinth and Stillwater Canyons hardened the muscles; familiarity with the river was breeding much respect but no contempt. Physically and mentally the voyageurs came to the stern grind of Cataract Canyon in the proper fettle. Confidence is an indispensable adjunct to rough-water work, but only when used as a reserve rather than as a spur. The admirable balance of the Kolbs is shown by the fact that the brilliant success of their work in the upper canyons had no tendency to make them underrate the grim character of the task still ahead. Ellsworth is engagingly frank about his own feelings in the matter. Looking down into the forbidding depths of Cataract Canyon from the broken plateau above the junction of the Green and the Grand, he writes:

"For the first time it began to dawn on us that we might have tackled a job beyond our power to complete. Most of the parties which had safely completed the trip were composed of several men, adding much to the safety of the expedition, as a whole. Others had boats much lighter than ours, a great help in many respects. Speaking for myself, I was just a little faint-hearted, and not a little overawed as we prepared to return to the boats."

Thus humble and contrite of heart, those two timorous photographers clamber back to the river and forthwith proceed to put up a record that must stand for all time by running every

[1] From "Through the Grand Canyon from Wyoming to Mexico," by E. L. Kolb. The Macmillan Company, New York, 1920.

one of the rapids of Cataract Canyon. When it is explained that this gorge, so aptly called "The Graveyard of the Colorado," is but forty-one miles long, that the foot of many a fall all but spills into the head of the next in line, and that the current in places attains a speed of from twenty to twenty-five miles an hour, to state that all of the rapids were run might well conjure up a picture of a helter-skelter, hell-for-leather unbroken dash of two or three hours' duration. This was hardly the case. The Kolbs spent at least five days between the walls of Cataract Canyon, on four of which they were working practically from daylight to dark. Most of the time was spent in looking over the rapids to find a runable course; most of the remainder in drying out clothes and bailing out boats. The actual runs through the rapids were, of course, a matter of but a few minutes each.

On the first day in Cataract Canyon the *Edith*, Emery's boat, pulled ashore somewhat carelessly while they were looking over the course ahead, drifted out into the current and ran a rapid on her own account. A hard stern-chase by her skipper in the other boat overtook the truant just as she was about to repeat the experiment at a second fall. With insufficient room in which to handle a towing job, Emery had to turn the runaway loose again and pull to the bank to get his wind. Rather under the weather for several days, his violent effort had completely exhausted him. Ellsworth promptly took his place, ran the rapid and caught the fugitive where she was chasing her tail in a big whirlpool. They camped that night with a lone trapper who, without the least idea of what was ahead of him, was laboriously working an open boat through the canyon by leading it along the banks.

A quarter-mile rapid choked with submerged rocks, encountered toward the end of the afternoon of the second day, looked all but impossible for running. Tossing in logs and watching their eccentric actions, it was finally concluded the thing might be done "by shooting up, stern first, on a sloping rock near the shore," and then swinging and making for the only clear channel, the entrance to which was otherwise blocked by a projecting shore. Emery started first.

"He got his position, facing stern downstream, gave the slightest shove forward, and the released boat whizzed down for fifty feet and ran up on the rock. She paused a moment, as the water prepared to return. He gave two quick pulls, shooting back again, slightly to the right, until he struck the narrow channel, then reversed his course and went through stern first exactly as we had planned it."

Ellsworth made a less delicately finessed operation of it, and so came in for rather a bad wetting.

With Emery's indisposition aggravated by rough work and rainy weather, the experiment was tried the following day of allowing him to concentrate upon the photographic work while his brother ran both boats through the rapids. This latter expedient was made possible by the fact that Cataract Canyon, in spite of its great declivity, rarely has sheer walls on both sides of a rapid. This made it possible to clamber back for the second boat after running the first. The plan worked admirably. The second run, in the light of what was learned during the first, was always much easier. With two days' rest in camp, Emery was himself again and ready for the heavy central cataracts where most of the canyon's fall is concentrated in a few miles. Both had good scares and bad wettings in running the big rapid at the mouth of Dark Canyon, in many respects the worst of the series. Emery's boat was slammed down on a rock; Ellsworth's missed the rock but broke a row-lock, finishing with one improvised from a crooked knee. He draws an extremely graphic picture of Emery's run in the *Edith* as it appeared from the foot of the rapid.

"Separated from my brother in this instance, I had an opportunity to see the man and water in conflict, with a perspective much as it would have appeared to a spectator happening on the scene. I was out of the heat of the battle. The excitement and indifference to danger that comes with a hand-to-hand grapple was gone. I heard the roar of the rapid; a roar so often heard that we forgot it was there. I saw the gloom of the great gorge, and the towering, sinister shafts of rock, weakened with cracks, waiting for the moment that would send them crashing to the bottom. I saw the mad, wild water hurled at the curving wall. Jagged rocks, like the bared fangs of some dream-monster, appeared now and then in the leaping, tumbling waves. Then down toward the turmoil—dwarfed to nothingness by the magnitude of the walls—sped the tiny shell-like boat, running smoothly like a racing machine! There was no rowing. The oar-blades were tipped high to avoid loss in the first comber; then the boat was buried in the foam, and staggered through on the other side. It was buffeted here and there, now covered with a ton of water, now topping a ten-foot wave. Like a skilled boxer—quick of eye, and ready to seize any temporary advantage—the oarsman shot in his oars for two quick strokes, to straighten the boat with the current or dodge a threatening boulder; then covered by lifting his oars and ducking his head as a brown flood rolled over him. Time and again the manœuvre was repeated; now here, now there. One would think that the chances were about one to a hundred that he would get through. But by some sort of a system, undoubtedly aided, many times, by good luck, the man and his boat won to land."

That is an admirable description of its kind, especially as suggesting the mental view of one good boatman watching another good boatman. That sort of thing—as long as all goes well—usually looks worse to the man on the side-lines than it feels to the one in the thick of the action.

A rather complicated run through the difficult island rapid near the foot of the canyon finished the cataracts, and a quiet camp was made that night under the fantastic pinnacles of Mille Crag Bend. An easy run down the long, straight stretch of Narrow Canyon the next morning carried them to the mouth of Frémont River—Powell's "Dirty Devil"—and on to the Hite ranch, near the site of the former Dandy Crossing. Here they talked with John Hite, whose home had been a refuge for the survivors of Cataract Canyon disasters for many years, and

with Bert Loper, who told them how he failed to catch up with
Russell and Monette in time to accompany them through the
Grand Canyon.

Glen Canyon was a rest-cure after the cataracts, although
there was bitter disappointment over missing the mouth of
Aztec Creek and so gaining the distinction of being the first to
reach the Rainbow Natural Bridge from the river. The work-
shop of a dredging outfit at Lee's Ferry offered a chance for a
final going-over of the boats before entering the main gorge.
Here they found a letter from an old friend from Kanab who
had recently been in to the Ferry in the hope of a visit with
the voyageurs. He stated that he had twice been troubled with
ominous dreams about them, and advised especially against
their trying to run the savage Soap Creek Rapid, where Brown
had met his death. That well-intentioned warning had much
better never been given, for Ellsworth writes:

"Rust should have known us better. With all the perversity of
human nature that letter made me want to run that rapid if it were
possible. Why not run the rapid and get a moving picture as it
was being done. Then we could show Rust how well we had learned
our lesson!"

A near-upset for Emery and a bad drenching for both in running the twenty-foot drop of Badger Creek Rapid ought to have
brought the adventurous pair to Soap Creek in a properly chastened mood. Here there was a fall of twenty-five feet in a
quarter of a mile, most of it in the first fifty feet. At the brink
of the fall was a submerged boulder with an eight-foot tumble
of water over it; at the foot the usual whirlpool, followed by
the smaller rapid in which Brown was lost. Finally they decided to attempt a run with one boat, "depending," Ellsworth
writes, "on our good luck which had brought us through so
many times, as much as we depended on our handling of the
boat." This was riding the fair and propitious Lady Luck
rather hard. Like confidence, luck (where rapid running is

concerned) had better be kept for a cushion to break a fall rather than as a spur to drive one to it.

The plan was for Ellsworth to run the boat, while his brother trained the camera upon the point below the big rock where, if it occurred, an upset was bound to take place. After completing the film, he was to run to the foot of the rapid and fling a life-preserver to the survivor—if there were any. About the only thing that came off according to this highly conditional schedule was the event least desired—the upset. The big rock was missed, but a second stuck out a foot so trippingly that the surprised boat turned on her side and spilled a still more surprised oarsman into the water. An instant later she swung off the rock and righted herself, giving her indignant skipper a chance to clamber back and, in spite of a cockpit full of water, work her to the shore at the foot of the rapid. Emery did some intermittent cranking during the diversion, but not enough of it at the proper time to give unbroken continuity to the picture.

Ellsworth, who was considerably peeved over the upset, must have been downright mad when he found everything in the boat soaked, including the contents of the supposedly water-tight case containing the photographic supplies. A state of high dudgeon is the most comprehensible explanation of his action in forthwith stalking back to the head of the rapid and pushing off with the *Edith* into the deepening dusk. Emery, reluctantly consenting to the attempt on the chance that it would save a day's portaging, kindled a fire as a guiding beacon at the foot of the rapid.

No real rough-neck of a rapid could be expected to stand for that kind of liberties, and especially one that already had a reputation as a killer. Its greeting to the *Defiance* had been hardly more than a friendly nuzzle compared to the wolfish snap with which it gulped the *Edith*. An unseen side-current caught the brave little craft and carried her straight over the big rock, where an up-curling wave stood her on end, spun her round, and flopped her down bottom-up. Considering the

THE KOLBS' CAMP AT RAPID 23 IN CATARACT CANYON.

Photo. by Julius F. Stone.

THE STONE PARTY AT SUPPER IN DESOLATION CANYON.

Photo. by Fred. Harvey.

RUSSELL RUNNING THE RAPIDS BELOW BRIGHT ANGEL TRAIL.

multiplicity of overlapping incidents on such an occasion, Ellsworth's recollections run in very fair sequence.

"It was all done so quickly, I hardly knew what had occurred, but found myself in the water, whirling this way and that, holding to the right oar with a deathgrip. I wondered if the strings would hold, and felt a great relief when the oar stopped slipping down,— as the blade reached the ring. It was the work of a second to climb the oar, and I found I was under the cockpit. Securing a firm hold on the gunwale, which had helped us so often, I got on the outside of the boat, thinking I might climb on top. About that time one of the largest waves broke over me, knocking me on the side of the head as if with a solid object, nearly tearing me from the boat. After that I kept as close to the boat as possible, paddling with my feet to keep them clear of the rocks. Then the suction of the boat caught them and dragged them under, and for the rest of the rapid I had all I could do to hang to the boat."

Emery was waiting in the *Defiance* at the foot of the rapid, but the castaway was so benumbed with cold that he had to be lifted into the boat by main strength—no mean task in view of the fact that Ellsworth outweighed his brother at the time by about forty pounds. The swamped *Edith* was overtaken only to drag the pursuing boat with its two passengers over the next rapid—the one in which Brown had been upset and drowned. With Emery at the oars and Ellsworth holding to the over-turned boat they struggled in the darkness to make a landing. Once they had all but grounded when the deep-floating fugitive dragged them back into the current again. Two more small rapids were floundered through before they finally reached the shore over a mile below the main fall and on the opposite side from that on which the *Defiance* had been unloaded. After a wet and uncomfortable night on the rocks, most of the next two days were spent in drying out and re-assembling the scattered outfit, developing wet plates, and meditating on the pride which goeth before a fall—especially one with a big rock at the brink of it.

That the prime desideratum of "an humble and a contrite heart" was again in at least temporary ascendency is indicated by Ellsworth's account of coming to a fall "so much like the Soap Creek Rapid in appearance that a portage was deemed advisable." The next day, after nearly losing the *Edith* in trying to line her round an overhanging rock, they took the *Defiance* out of the water and dragged her past the rapids along a sandbank twenty-five or thirty feet above the water. That must have been a punishing task for two men, especially since the water-soaked boats weighed a good deal over their original five hundred pounds apiece.

The remainder of the rapids of Marble Canyon were run carefully and without untoward incident. The cave where Stanton cached his provisions after the culminating disaster of the Brown expedition was readily recognized; also the verdant, water-sparking walls of Vesey's Paradise. The final swift run down to the mouth of the Little Colorado revealed transient but welcome glimpses of points long familiar from hunting and photographic expeditions from the Grand Canyon home. At last they emerged from the Marble Gorge and tied up near a rock on which, a year and a half before, they had sat and talked of the time they would come barging down on that red flood in boats. They found the very grass-patch upon which they had pastured their burro, and chuckled at the recollection of a mad plan they had discussed of building a raft and floating the little beast down with them to Bright Angel. Now they knew it was just as well that the delectable stunt had not gone beyond the discussional stage.

With the beginning of the Grand Canyon as the head of the home stretch, they pushed on into the big gorge without allowing sentimental memories to tempt them to camp at the Colorado Chiquito. The next morning they entered the granite of sinister import. The threatening aspect of the Hance Rapid, with its confused channel and forty-foot fall, made a portage appear advisable. One boat and all of the loads were carried

down before nightfall, and in the flush of the next day's early
morning confidence the other was run through—luckily without trouble. Running the second section with his loaded boat,
Emery was thrown out into the water in much the same way
as his brother had been in his first attempt at Soap Creek.
Back again in the wink of an eye, he rode his half-filled boat
to the bottom no worse for the sudden spill.

The Sockdologer and the other 'tween-cliff, "big-water"
rapids bothered the Kolbs far less than they had Powell and
Stanton. Heavy fall and high waves made it rough going and
wet going; likewise fast going. The twelve miles from the
Hance Rapid to Bright Angel Creek were made in five hours,
most of that time, of course, spent reconnoitring from the
banks. That night their signal fire was lighted from a previously selected point in Bright Angel Canyon known to be
visible from their home on the south rim. The next day, after
making boats and outfits secure, they climbed out on foot.

After a month to rest and check over photographic results
the voyage was resumed on December 19th. Two fresh recruits accompanied the veteran voyageurs down from the now
snow-covered rim to their waiting boats. One, a brother,
Ernest Kolb, was to be given a dash of river life and water
in the short run to the foot of Bass' Trail; the other, Bert
Lauzon, signed on for the duration of the voyage. He proved
a most valuable acquisition in every respect.

The river had fallen a couple of feet since they left it and
there were occasional fringes of ice around the shaded pools.
An easy two-mile run carried the boats through a splashy little
rapid they had promised to shoot for the entertainment of a
bunch of tourists assembled upon the plateau, and the new river
party made a cheery first-night camp by the grave of a prospector whose skeleton had been found near that point five
years before. The next day some heavy rapids were run, including Granite Falls and Hermit. At all of these the helpers
worked the cameras from the shores and stood-by to throw

life-preservers in case of trouble. The following day there were several places where they had to ride through willy-nilly for lack of room to walk round. In light rapids the passengers were allowed to sit upright and enjoy the fun, but in dubious water they were made to sprawl flat to keep the centre of gravity as low as possible and thus minimise the chances of upsets.

Ellsworth, confessing to a plan to give his younger brother a proper baptismal introduction to the Colorado, reluctantly gave up the idea when he found how much colder the water had become. That, at least, is the way he tells it; in any event he would hardly have chosen the "reverse whirl" at the back of a submerged boulder as quite the proper place to bestow this little testimonial of brotherly affection. Doubtless it is true, as he claims, that he was drawn into the sinister hole entirely as a consequence of carelessness. At any rate, the upset was all that could have been desired as far as the brother was concerned, and just a bit more as regards the boat. Ernest, thanks to his two life-preservers, came up about thirty feet below and was hauled ashore to drain and dry out. Ellsworth, like a proper skipper, stuck to his ship, but rather too busy with little personal details to prevent the carrying away of the hatch-cover and the flooding of the compartment containing the motion-picture camera. The film in the latter came in very handy for kindling the warming fire. Ellsworth admits he was considerably bothered over the whole affair, but it is noticeable that his chagrin did not take the form of going back to do it over again, as at Soap Creek. It took two days' work to clean the sand and silt out of the movie camera, and even then a drop of moisture was left in the lens cell which had the effect of fogging all of the next roll of film.

Ernest went out by the Bass Trail, leaving the party of three to push on for a little Christmas Eve celebration of its own. For obvious reasons, brother Emery is the one who writes the most intelligible and collected account of what happened. At

the fourth rapid below the Bass Trail there was a difference of
opinion as to the best way through, so every one took his own
course. Emery picked a channel down the right-hand side,
Ellsworth tried the left, while Lauzon pinned his faith to one
over the rocks along the bank. The sequel proved the recruit
was the best picker. Emery ran into a nest of jagged rocks
almost at once and had to make a precarious landing to prevent a smash-up. He was just trying to figure how the others
might be able to rescue him by letting down a rope from above,
when he saw that the *Defiance* was having troubles of her own.

"She was caught in a reverse whirl in the very middle of the
pounding rapid, bouncing back and forth like a great rubber ball.
Finally she filled with splashing water, sank low, and the water
pouring over the rock caught the edge of the twelve-hundred pound
boat and turned her over as if she were a toy; my brother was holding to the gunwale when she turned. She was still held in the whirl,
jumping as violently as ever, then turned upright again and was
forced out. Ellsworth had disappeared, but came up nearly a hundred feet below, struggling to keep on top but going down with
every breaking wave. When the quieter water was reached, he did
not seem to have strength enough to swim out, but floated, motion-
less, in a standing position, his head kept up by the life-preservers.
The next rapid was not over fifty yards below. If he was to be
saved it must be done instantly."

Without hesitation Emery plumped to take the ninety-nine
chances of disaster for the one chance of success that might let
him reach the foot of the rapid in time to be of help. But the
odds were too great. The bow of the *Edith* cracked like an
egg-shell against a hidden rock a few moments after she cleared
the bank, and she drifted aside, a hopeless wreck, into an eddy.
Ellsworth, fortunately carried against the cliff twenty feet
above the next rapid, had strength enough to hold on until
Emery clambered down and dragged him out. Lauzon running
true to expected form, swam out and tumbled over the side of
the *Defiance* just as she began to pick up speed above the head
of the second rapid. A complete novice in propelling a boat, it

was no finished exhibition of oarsmanship he gave in flailing the derelict into a convenient eddy, but no one took him to task on that account. He came ashore with a grin, facetiously complaining that they were losing a lot of good pictures.

Sitting on a rock half way down Bright Angel Trail a year or two ago, Bert Lauzon gave me his version of that merry little Christmas Eve party. It did not differ greatly from that of Emery, save that he insisted in treating his own part in the affair quite as a joke. A man like that, with the instinct and nerve to act promptly in emergency, is worth a hundred Dismal Jimmies or Gloomy Guses on a rough-water voyage. Human sunshine sheds a very genial glow in depths that may never be plumbed by the direct rays of Old Sol.

The *Edith* was repaired on Christmas Day. The smashed side-ribs were replaced with new ones hewn from mesquite and the gaping hole in her side was closed with boards from the loose bottom. Covered with canvas and tin, this patch proved quite water-tight and left the wrecked boat as seaworthy as ever. Although every fibre of Ellsworth's battered body continued to ache for many days afterward, he was not seriously handicapped in his river work.

Emery came in for a neat and very unexpected upset near the end of the granite. Neither man nor boat was the worse for it, but the chastening effect of the recent submersions was evident in Ellsworth's statement that a portage was made near the end of the second granite section. With the revealing frankness of a riverine Marie Bashkirtseff, he adds:

"If we were a little inclined to be proud of our record above Bright Angel we had forgotten all about it by this time. We were scarcely more than sixty miles from home and had experienced three upsets and a smashed boat, all in one week."

Another portage was made at Lava Falls, where the river had once been dammed by the flow from an active volcano. Hot springs still attested the thinness of the crust of the earth, and the steam from these gave welcome relief to hands and legs numbed in working down the boats in the ice-cold water. A third portage was made not far below, and in the afternoon they passed the wide canyon mouth where the half-starved members of the first Powell expedition had looted an Indian garden of melons. Also short provisions at this juncture, the Kolbs construed this act of lawlessness on the Major's part as justifying their angling for otherwise unapproachable salmon with a stick of dynamite. The results of the cast were so good that they regretted that they had not brought more bait.

Replenishing provisions by a trip out to the railway by way of Diamond Creek and Peach Springs Wash, the river voyage was resumed on January 8th. The temperature of the upper world was found to be hovering around the zero point, and even the greatly depressed river levels were maintaining an uncomfortable and unwonted wintriness. Two hours below Diamond Creek they came to a double rapid which, in spite of all they had been through, made them catch their breaths. A portage all the way round would have involved taking the boats over a three or four hundred-foot cliff, while all of the rapid was certainly not runable. Finally, after taking great precautions, they managed it by running the first fall and portaging the second. The portage proved unexpectedly easy on account of the ice on the rocks, which made it practically a sledding operation for the boats. The *Defiance* did a bit of tobogganing on her own account at one point, bringing up against a rock that punched a hole in the side near the stern. Luckily the puncture was above the water-line and so easily repaired.

Rapids were violent all that day and most of the next. Separation Rapid, with its sheer walls and three heavy falls, was reached at the end of the second day. It looked troublesome but, in the Kolbs' opinion, by no means bad enough to have given pause to the three mountain men of the Powell party who left the expedition there. Ellsworth expresses the belief that the separation, with its tragic sequel, was due to the culmination of previous dissensions rather than to any real fear on the part of Dunn and the Howlands of running the falls.

The following morning the Kolbs ran the first pitch, avoided the second by floating their boats through an ingeniously conceived and constructed little by-pass along the side, and ran the third. The *Edith* came near to stranding on the great sloping rock in the middle of the third section, but after pausing a moment, "came down like a shot and whirled to the side without mishap." With two feet more water Ellsworth thinks that they could have run right through, as had Powell and Stanton.

Lava Escarpment Rapid, the last heavy fall in the Grand Canyon, was approached with some trepidation. The conservative Julius Stone, who considered it the worst on the whole river, had warned the Kolbs especially against it. It looked bad to them, very bad, when they finally reached the head after many false alarms. Forty big rocks, just showing or slightly submerged, were counted in two sections near the head of the half-mile-long tumble of broken water. But while the low stage prevented running—as Powell had done with one of his boats after having the other break away in trying to line,— it gave them room to work below instead of lining from a ledge, eighty feet above the water, as others had had to do. By carefully and laboriously skidding the boats on logs around the worst places, the most dangerous section of the rapid was avoided. The rest was a clean run in water so swift that the oars were snatched from their hands if they tried to do more than keep the boat straight with the current. They camped that night out of sound of the roar of water.

Five mountain sheep created a diversion which prevented their clearing the mouth of the canyon the following day, but on January 13th they passed the Grand Wash and ran on far toward the Virgin. Looking behind to the towering bulk of the Colorado Plateau, they wondered if the river had ever dropped in a precipitous fall over the face of the wall as at Niagara, working back year by year after the way of the great cataract

VIEW FROM BEND OF BRIGHT ANGEL TRAIL.

© Kolb Brothers.

WINTER IN THE GRAND CANYON.

to form the gorges they had been following for a thousand miles. Five days later the *Edith* and *Defiance* were taken out of the water at Needles, to be carefully preserved for possible future use. So far as there is any record, these were the first boats completing the Grand Traverse to be saved from the ignominious fate of falling a final prey to the floods which they had so bravely and successfully defied.

The *Defiance* at the present moment is docked beside the front entrance of the Kolb studio at the Grand Canyon, where some little vigilance is required to keep tourists from registering their names and address on her honourable bow and stern. The *Edith*, after carrying Emery through Cataract Canyon again in the summer of 1921, is carefully housed in the shadow of the old John D. Lee cabin at the mouth of the Paria awaiting the next call to action.

From a photographic standpoint the canyon voyage of the Kolbs proved quite as great a success as it did from the navigational. The illustrations in Ellsworth's book bear graphic testimony to the work of the ordinary cameras. That of the moving-picture machine, in spite of the adverse conditions under which it was operated, was no less striking. The destruction of films in the upsets left big gaps in the complete record, of course, but enough survived to tell the story. These have been shown at the Kolb studio at the Grand Canyon ever since the completion of the historic voyage, usually with a talk by one of the brothers. On a number of recent occasions when both of the veteran navigators were absent, Emery's daughter Edith, for whom his canyon boat was named, has told the stirring story.

Their Grand Traverse of 1911 was not the end of Colorado River navigation for either of the Kolbs. A year or two later Ellsworth, dropping casually off the train at Needles, bought a boat from a Mojave Indian and pushed off that night on the crest of the spring rise. Riding the flood all the way, he reached the head of the Gulf of California at the end of eight days—probably a record for that four hundred miles of sinuous and sandbar-choked river. By way of change from the comparatively placid lower Colorado, he next tried the teeth of the Westwater Canyon of the lower Grand, hitherto considered unrunable. Accompanied by Bert Loper, veteran of the Russell-Monette party, Ellsworth boated down the Grand from the Shoshone Dam to Moab. Westwater presented no insurmountable difficulties to these two seasoned river-rats from the canyons of the big river.

The Black Canyon of the Gunnison, tackled the same season, proved a harder nut to crack. Ellsworth had been assured that the region offered wonderful photographic possibilities; also that the Gunnison disappeared into a natural cave and came back to the surface of the earth far below. For this subterranean passage he had a special outfit made, including a watertight trunk, a padded jacket of kapok, and a football headgear. The journey through the earth turned out a very tame experience after all, for the great natural cavern proved to be only the diversion tunnel of the U. S. Reclamation Service, described in a subsequent chapter. The Black Canyon itself, however, offered some compensation by turning out just as black as it was painted. In one way or another, every foot of it between Cimarron and Grand Junction was traversed, but four boats were worn out in the passage.

In 1921 Ellsworth Kolb handled the boats for the U. S. Geological Survey party working down Cataract Canyon, Emery accompanying the expedition with his motion-picture outfit.

CHAPTER XVI

THE GEOLOGICAL SURVEY COMPLETES POWELL'S WORK

POWELL'S two Colorado River voyages were undertaken in the interest of Science, but after the completion of the second of these in 1872 nearly half a century went by before another important expedition dedicated to that cause navigated the canyon sections of that stream. This was due to the fact that not until well toward the end of this period had conditions arisen creating a demand for scientific data of sufficient value to justify the expense and risk of further boating expeditions through the canyons. When such a demand arose —in connection with comprehensive plans for the utilization of the waters of the river for power and irrigation—canyon navigation was resumed. It is extremely fitting—in a sentimental as well as a practical sense—that the United States Geological Survey, of which Major Powell was one of the first Directors, should be the body to swing the circle back to scientific exploration as it again navigates the Colorado canyons to complete the work of the first great canyon navigator.

Although not until recently carrying on work that involved further extensive navigation of the canyons, the Geological Survey has been active in the Colorado Basin from the time of its creation in 1879. Much of this work was in continuation of that initiated by Powell in the years following his final voyage. Supplementing the earlier reconnaissance topography covering almost the entire basin, more than 50,000 square miles of this region has been surveyed and mapped on standard scales. Systematic stream measurement was begun in 1889 with the establishment of three gauging stations. Stream-flow records have since been collected at more than three hundred points, and seventy-seven regular gauging stations are now being maintained.

The work preliminary to, as well as the early development of Federal irrigation systems were conducted by the Geological Survey from 1888 until March 9, 1907, when the Reclamation Service was separated from the Survey as a co-ordinate bureau in the Department of the Interior. During this period the four projects in the Colorado Basin now operated by the Reclamation Service had been initiated, and construction work was well advanced on three of them. Studies were made of several projects on which construction has not yet been undertaken; investigations and surveys of reservoir sites for the control of the Colorado were also made in this period.

Special surveys, showing plan and profile of streams and with sufficient topography to cover all possible locations for structures needed in a comprehensive scheme of water development, were begun in the Colorado Basin in 1909. By the end of 1923 such surveys will afford continuous maps from Green River, Wyoming, on Green River, and from Grand Junction, Colorado, on the Colorado (formerly the Grand), to the Mexican boundary. These maps will cover an aggregate distance of 1500 miles. Several hundred miles along the principal tributaries have also been similarly surveyed.

Much of this special survey work was done by land parties, but in reaching several extended stretches of the river inaccessible by other means boats had to be resorted to. Principal of these were the canyons of the upper Green, Cataract Canyon, and the continuous gorge formed by Marble and Grand Canyons. The first and second of these sections were surveyed by parties of the seasons of 1921 and 1922; the third section, completing the mapping of the Colorado, is to be covered by a party which plans to go through Marble and Grand Canyons during the late summer and early fall of 1923.

Cataract Canyon was surveyed by an expedition under W. R. Chenoweth during the fall of 1921. E. C. La Rue was Hydraulic Engineer of the party, Sidney Paige, Geologist, and Frank Stoudt, Recorder. Ellsworth Kolb had charge of the boats, and Emery Kolb was attached as photographer. The work was done in co-operation with the Southern California Edison Company, which had already made extensive studies of its own in Glen Canyon. The surveying party used three boats of the Galloway-Stone type. Two of these were somewhat larger and heavier than those of the Kolbs; the third was somewhat lighter than the latter. Emery Kolb used his *Edith* of the previous voyage.

All of the boats were shipped by rail to Green River, Utah, from where Cataract Canyon was reached by an easy voyage down the quiet waters of the Green. The survey was started at the junction of the Green and the former Grand on September 15th, and carried down to the head of the first rapid of Cataract Canyon the same day. The stage of the river was little if any higher than the Kolbs had in 1911, with weather conditions more favourable for work in the rapids. At all of the worst rapids Ellsworth Kolb ran each of the survey party boats through himself. Thus six rapids passed by the outfit in a day meant that the indefatigable head-boatman had run eighteen. Yet I find in his diary an entry exulting: "I get the same kick out of the rapid-running that I formerly did."

No one has gone through Cataract Canyon without finding evidence of previous disasters. These have usually taken the form of fragments of boats, parts of camping outfits, clothing, and occasionally the skeleton of an unlucky voyageur. This survey party found what might be called an epitaph on a tombstone of that "Graveyard of the Colorado." It was chiselled on a rock on the north side of the river above Rapid Number 14, and read:

"CAMP NO. 7. HELL TO PAY.
SUNK AND DOWN."

It was believed to have been cut by a member of the Best party, an ambitious but badly equipped and handled prospecting outfit that met disaster in Cataract Canyon in July, 1891.

Although the survey was repeatedly showing the fall of the successive rapids as being considerably less in feet than had previously been estimated, the Kolbs found the same old kick in the tumbling water and the same old impact in the obstructing rocks. Ellsworth records a somewhat busy interval at Rapid 23.

"I ran three boats and had some trouble with each one. Boat 1 hit a rock, whirled bow first, submarined and an extra oar was washed off and gave me a chase to the head of the next rapid before it was recovered. Run 2, an oarlock separated and I used an extra paddle to recover it. *Static* also hit a rock, but no harm was done and we muddled through."

Through the first forty-four rapids of Cataract Canyon the Kolbs maintained their remarkable record of the previous voyage—everything run, with no linings or portagings of the boats. With the larger and more heavily-loaded boats this meant even finer work than that of the earlier run, and if only a clean score could have been made all the way through the achievement would have been an outstanding one. It was the cataract of sinister repute at Dark Canyon, officially designated as Rapid 45, that spoiled the record. A brief entry in Ellsworth's diary gives a laconic account of what—to him more than to any one else in the party—must have been a particularly annoying brace of accidents.

"About noon we arrive at Dark Canyon. The rapid has not improved with age; in fact it is much worse—has about fifty rocks badly placed on the south side, and has a dangerous turn, filled with great rocks. Still I thought it could be run and save a lot of time. Evidently I was mistaken. One loaded boat, the *L. A.*, was put in, landed in a nest of rocks 50 feet from the south shore. Got a line from shore, but our combined efforts failed to budge it. I cooned the line to shore. The *Edison*, half loaded, did a little better; lodged on a flat rock but was shoved off and landed safely.

"The *Static* was emptied, started better, but went into the turn and capsized. I hung to the boat until it approached the Island Rapid, where I swam out."

The *Static* was recovered from an eddy a hundred feet below. The *Edith* had to endure the ignominy of being lined down the side of a rapid she had run with flying colours on her first voyage. The unlucky *L. A.*, with the water surging over two-thirds of her length, had to remain in midstream all night. The following day, by an ingenious contrivance of lines and pulleys devised by Emery Kolb, the fifteen-hundred-pound load of the stranded boat was landed with but slight damage from the water. Thus lightened, she was soon pried free of the rocks and after a little lining brought safely to bank and reloaded.

Island Rapid, the last of the cataracts, proved much less menacing than on the former Kolb voyage, and was run without trouble. Two days later the survey was completed to the mouth of the Frémont and tied into the line of a previous party. Mr. Chenoweth retained a portion of the party for work on a land survey, the others proceeding by boats down Glen Canyon to Lee's Ferry. This boat party, landing at the mouth of Aztec Creek, proceeded up six miles to the Rainbow Natural Bridge. This was the first occasion on which that remarkable monument had been reached from the Colorado.

The voyage of 1922 for the mapping of the hitherto unsurveyed canyons of the Green was undertaken by the Geological Survey in co-operation with the Utah Light and Power Company. K. W. Trimble, topographical engineer of the Geological Survey, was chief of the party, with Ralf R. Woolley as hydraulic engineer and recorder, and J. B. Reedside as geologist. H. L. Stoner was representative of the Utah Light and Power Company. The veteran, Bert Loper, acted as head-boatman, with Leigh Lint and H. E. Blake as assistants. The three boats were of the Galloway-Stone type, and practically identical with those used by the party surveying Cataract Canyon the previous year.

The start was made from Green River, Wyoming, July 13th. The first sixty miles of the river had been covered by the Reclamation Service survey of 1914, so the work of the present party was not commenced until just above the head of the Colorado canyon series at Flaming Gorge. The water appears to have been at an extremely favourable stage for boating—probably better than Powell had found it early in the spring, or Stone and the Kolbs later in the summer. Loper and his men also handled the boats with much judgment and skill. As a consequence of good water and clever navigation the three boats of this party were taken through the canyons of the Green with just a bit less lining and portaging than those of any of their predecessors, including Stone and the Kolbs.

One of the boats, stranding rather solidly in a shallow rapid of upper Red Canyon, was knocked loose as the consequence of being bumped by a sister going to her assistance. A boat that was slightly holed above the water-line by bumping a rock not far below the Gate of Lodore was about the worst casualty, and an hour's work removed the traces of that crash. Ashley Falls were run without trouble, as was also Upper Disaster Fall. At Lower Disaster Fall a part of the loads was portaged and the lightened boats lined along on the side opposite to the treacherous under-cut cliff. The three sharp pitches at Triplet Falls were all run. Most of the loads were portaged around Hell's Half Mile. The boats were successfully run through all but about forty yards near the lower end, along which they were lined. One boat hung up on a boulder near the upper end of the rapid was the only hitch in an extremely well-managed passage. The forty-three trips over the long portage trail made that rather the most infernal part of Hell's Half Mile to most of the party.

Whirlpool, Split Mountain and Desolation canyons provided the same sharp, lively runs Stone and the Kolbs had enjoyed in those gorges, but no rapids that caused serious trouble. On September 9th the work was tied to a previous survey near the foot of Desolation Canyon, and there was little to do the remainder of the run to Green River, Utah. The work of this

GEOLOGICAL SURVEY PARTY AT MILLECRAG DAM SITE

GEOLOGICAL SURVEY PARTY'S BOATS IN COLORADO CANYON, 1921.

CAMP OF GEOLOGICAL SURVEY PARTY ON LOWER GREEN.

party completed the accurate mapping of the Green-Colorado from Green River, Wyoming to the head of Marble Canyon.

It is interesting to compare the accurate figures for fall of rapids and canyons of these two late surveys with those of the early navigators of the river, especially Powell. The latter, who probably ran few levels on the river, must have made most of his estimates of the fall of rapids more or less offhand. Careful and inclined to conservatism as he was, the fact that the pioneer canyon navigator was constantly liable to the almost invariable human error of overestimating the descent of large volumes of falling water is evidenced by the fact that his figures were usually too high. Where Powell made the same error in estimating the descent over considerable sections the fault must have been largely in his crude and roughly used barometers. The figures for descent given by later navigators (with the exception of Stanton and Stone) have largely been based on those of Powell. I can only cite a few instances to show how hitherto commonly accepted figures have varied from those finally established as accurate.

Where Powell's description would indicate a descent of over fifty feet in the immediate vicinity of Disaster Falls, the diary of Ralf F. Woolley of the late survey speaks of the descent in a three-mile section including at least the lower fall as "a little more than 25 feet per mile." Where the Kolbs speak of a fall of seventy-five feet in the three quarters of a mile which includes Rapids 21, 22 and 23 of Cataract Canyon, E. C. La Rue's notes from the late survey indicate that the actual fall for that particular section is thirty feet. These adjustments of facts and figures have not reduced the menace these rapids hold for the canyon navigator by a hair. Quite to the contrary, indeed, judging by the experience of the Kolbs. In 1911, when that intrepid and resourceful pair *thought* the sinuous tumble of water at Rapid 45 in Cataract Canyon was twenty-five or thirty feet, they ran it without trouble; ten years later, when they *knew* there was only an insignificant fourteen-foot drop there, they messed up just about all the boats they had in floundering through.

Powell's estimate of a drop of four hundred and thirty feet in the forty-one miles of Cataract Canyon is not far from the four hundred and fifteen indicated by the survey. Split Mountain Canyon is one of the few instances where the error was reversed. Powell gave the descent as ninety feet in nine miles, while the survey found a fall of one hundred and thirty-one feet in seven.

Considering the instruments with which, and the conditions under which Powell worked, the discrepancies revealed by these figures are not surprising. As for his overestimating the heights of individual rapids, it is a universal human tendency to be free with a finite measuring stick when applying it to a thing of infinite power and menace; and the Major was nothing if not human. I have heard an engineer of the Cataract Canyon surveying party express the greatest admiration for the practical results of the observations and studies made by Powell in the course of his two Colorado canyon voyages.

At the moment of writing the only section of the Colorado not accurately mapped is that included in the practically unbroken gorge of Marble and Grand Canyons, but by the time these lines appear in print it is hoped that data for the closing of this gap will have become available. A party headed by Colonel Claude Birdseye, Chief of the Topographic Branch of the Geological Survey, and including E. C. La Rue of the Water Resources Branch, is scheduled to push off into the head of Marble Canyon about the first of August of this year. When it emerges from the foot of the Grand Canyon sometime in the fall it should have completed the work envisioned by Major Powell in 1869 when he embarked upon the first Grand Traverse of the Colorado.

Part II

BINDING THE RIVER

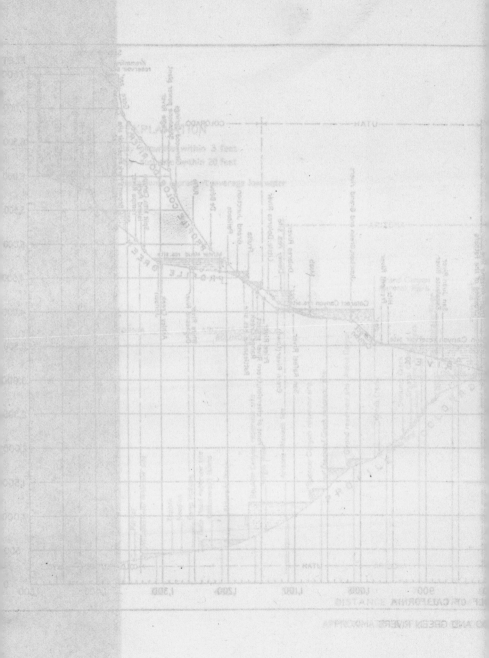

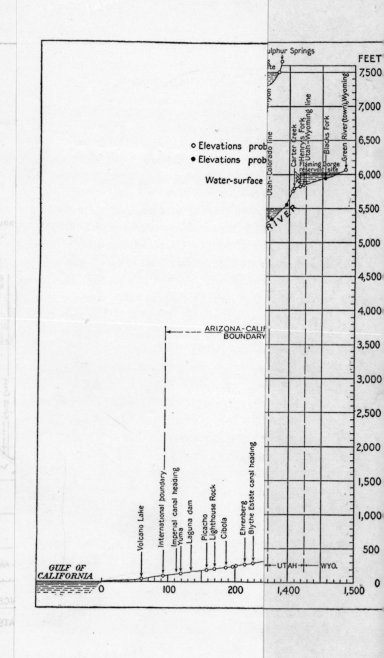

CHAPTER I

THE WILD BULL OF THE COLORADO

SOME rivers are like good old barnyard cows that stand quietly chewing their cuds while milking is going on, without once trying to kick over the pail or even flick their tails in the face of the milker; others, like wild range steers, never yield any dividends until their hides are on the fence, their meat converted into bully-beef and their bones into fertilizer. The Colorado might be likened to a blooded bull standing at about the bovine mean between the barnyard bossy and the Texas high-tail. Roped, dehorned, blind-folded, harnessed and put to work it can be made worth a whole herd of dairy cows or range steers. I have told the story of how the Colorado was found by man; the story of how it was bound by man can not be written for a decade or so yet. Here it can only be indicated how the *toro colorado*—the great red bull— must be thrown and dehorned.

The first service a good bossy-cow river performs for the man who finds it is to give him a water-way by which to get around and explore the country. Later it floats his logs, runs his mills, waters his fields and—if it is a big enough stream— bears his commerce. The Tigris and the Yangtse, the Rhine and the Danube, the Ohio and the Mississippi did all, or nearly all, of these things in turn, and with only an occasional protest in the way of a springtime flood. But the turbid flood of the Colorado was hostile even to the first explorers. The stout-hearted *conquistador* gave the river his best a few score miles above the tidal flats; the trapper who came alive from his first battle with the upper gorges rarely risked renewal of the conflict. For three centuries the hundreds of miles of middle canyons were hardly crossed, let alone navigated.

369

Where the pioneer had been unseated there was little tendency on the part of his softer brother who followed to take a chance at a fall. Mostly these stayed on the ground by building their mills and watering their fields by or from docile tributaries. But those of them who had the temerity to try to work *el toro colorado* himself approached the unbroken brute from the wrong direction. Trying to irrigate the lowlands of a great delta before the river that formed it is controlled above is like grabbing by the tail a bull that can only be handled by the horns. The attempt to reclaim the below-sea-level area of Imperial Valley before a control dam was built somewhere in the Colorado canyons was—and is—one of the most desperate gambles with wealth and human lives in modern history. How dramatic, how wonderfully courageous, has been the fight to hang on to the tail of the great red bull of the Colorado until he can be subdued by the horns will be touched upon in another chapter.

Although the Colorado is often called the American Nile, there are some respects in which it bears more resemblance to the Yangtse than to the great North African river. Like the Yangtse, the Colorado takes its rise among the snows of lofty mountains, cuts through great central gorges, and flows across a great alluvial valley to the sea. The Ichang Gorges of the Yangtse, however, are as insignificant in comparison with the Grand Canyon of the Colorado as are the Rockies to the Himalayan peaks among which the great Chinese river has its birth. The Nile draws most of its waters from tropical rains rather than from the snows of lofty mountains, and it flows through no great central canyon series. It is the fact that the African river, like the Colorado, brings an inexhaustible flow of water to a fertile but naturally desert sub-tropical basin that gives real point to the name American Nile. The lower valleys of both rivers are in nearly the same latitude, have similar climates, similar crops and similar problems. The following table from E. C. La Rue's "Colorado River and Its Utilization" makes a number of interesting comparisons between the Nile and the Colorado:

"Total area of the Nile Basin............square miles   1,112,000
Total area of the Colorado River Basin...   "   244,000
Length of the Nile (source of Kagera to sea)...miles   3,946
Length of the Colorado (source of Green to Gulf)   "   1,700
Total fall in the Nile (source to mouth)........feet   6,600
Total fall in the Colorado (source to mouth).... "   14,000
Irrigable area of Nile Valley in Egypt.........acres   6,663,000
Irrigable area of the Colorado Valley below Virgin "   2,734,000
Area irrigated in Nile Valley in Egypt in 1913.. "   5,351,000
Area irrigated in Colorado Basin below Virgin in
    1913 .... "   367,000
Mean annual run-off of the Nile at Cairo,
    Egypt ....acre-feet 68,000,000
Mean annual run-off of the Colorado at
    Yuma, Ariz. ....·....   "   17,000,000"

The first cultivators of the Colorado Basin were the Yumas and Cocopahs. They doubtless practised methods similar to those followed by the Egyptian *fellaheen* of the time of the Pharaohs—scattering seeds in the mud of the receded overflow and letting Nature take its course. Both *fellaheen* and Colorado Indian do the same thing to-day. Neither took—or takes —any liberties with the rivers themselves. That remained for the audacious and irreverent white man to do—occasionally to his cost, but to his ultimate profit.

The cliff-dwellers and their progenitors were the first to raise crops in the basin of the Colorado River by the artificial conveyance of water to the land. The river benches below many of the long-abandoned cliff-houses show evidences of having been ditched and watered. Considerable irrigation systems may still be traced in the valleys of the Gila and Little Colorado, while the ancient canals of the Salt River Valley would have been equal to serving a quarter of a million acres of land. The Jesuit *padres* were the first white irrigators, water diversions transforming the regions of their missions into veritable gardens. Father Escalante even turned an investiga-tive eye upon the main river. At two or three points in the narrative of his famous *entrada* of 1776 he speculates upon the possibility of diverting water for irrigation, but without opti-mism as regards the Colorado itself.

The Mormons, the real Fathers of American Reclamation, began irrigating from the upper waters of numerous westerly-heading tributaries of the Colorado as fast as their migrations carried them to these fertile valleys from the Great Basin of Salt Lake. Their first works were modest diversions for the watering of convenient river-bottoms; later reservoirs were constructed and higher and more extensive areas brought under ditch. Few indeed even among the Government-financed and engineered reclamation projects have produced communities to rival in prosperity, beauty and richness of life those of these irrigated valleys of the Latter Day Saints.

None of the early explorers appears to have visioned the main Colorado as furnishing water for any extensive scheme of land reclamation. The impossibility of diversions anywhere along the many hundred miles of the middle canyon series was evident to the veriest novice, while the difficulty of devising any plan to control floods and the overflow of the lower valleys was almost equally plain. Ives, working up through Cotton-wood Valley in 1858, noted the richness of the level lands but wrote that any attempts to bring water to them would be likely to result in disaster. As far as all efforts to irrigate this fertile area to date go, the explorer was right.

Powell's report of his pioneer voyage through the Colorado canyons reveals no indication of a belief that the keystone of a comprehensive reclamation project must ultimately rest in those very gorges, but it would seem that something of the true perspective of the great problem was sharpening to focus in the lenses of his imagination even at that early date. Frederick Dellenbaugh writes me an illuminative comment in point:

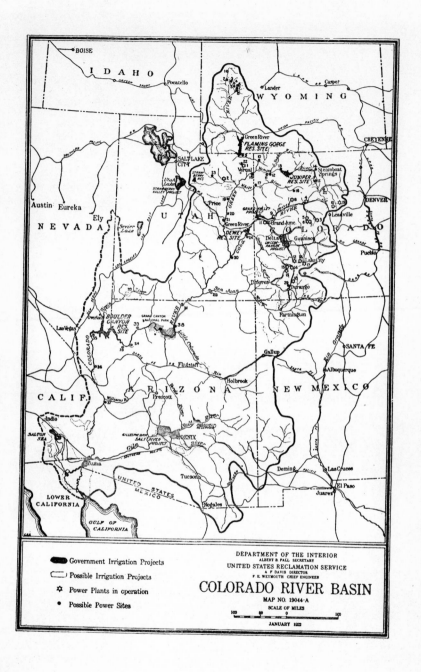

BOISE

I D A H O

Pocatello

WYOMING

Lander   Casper

Green River
FLAMING GORGE
RES. SITE

CHEYENNE

Steamboat
Springs

SALT LAKE
CITY

Vernal

JUNIPER
RES. SITE

DENVER

Utah
Lake
STRAWBERRY
VALLEY PROJECT

Price

Leadville

Austin Eureka

Ely

GRAND VALLEY
PROJECT

U T A H

Green River

Grand Junc.

C O L O R A D O

N E V A D A

DEWEY
RES. SITE

Delta

UNCOM-
PAHGRE
PROJECT

Gunnison

Pueblo

Lake City

Dolores

Durango

Farmington

BOULDER
CANYON
RES. SITE

Las Vegas

Overland

GRAND CANYON
NATIONAL PARK

Gallup

SANTA FE

Albuquerque

Flagstaff

Holbrook

C A L I F.

A R I Z O N A

N E W   M E X I C O

Prescott

Indio

SALTON
SEA

GILLESPIE DAM
SALT RIVER
PROJECT

PHOENIX

Yuma

Tucson

Deming

Las Cruces

El Paso

Nogales

Juarez

LOWER
CALIFORNIA

UNITED STATES
MEXICO

GULF OF
CALIFORNIA

Government Irrigation Projects

Possible Irrigation Projects

✿ Power Plants in operation

• Possible Power Sites

DEPARTMENT OF THE INTERIOR
ALBERT B. FALL SECRETARY
UNITED STATES RECLAMATION SERVICE
A F DAVIS DIRECTOR
F. E. WEYMOUTH CHIEF ENGINEER

COLORADO RIVER BASIN

MAP NO. 19044-A

SCALE OF MILES

100   50   0   100

JANUARY 1922

SKY-LINE CANAL, STRAWBERRY VALLEY PROJECT, UTAH.

"I don't remember whether or not the Major ever had any vision of Reclamation during our Canyon Voyage, but he did very soon after and his "Lands of the Arid Region" was the result. He then took up the problems of reservoir sites and secured the establishment of a survey for the purpose of surveying and reserving such sites. Congress, however, as usual, had no vision in the matter, and penny wise and pound foolish as always, refused to continue the work."

Of his own idea of what to do with the Colorado the eminent historian, doubtless with a chuckle at the recollection of the dream of the seventeen-year-old youngster he was at the time, writes:

"I had an idea of making dams in the Grand Canyon, but not for Power—merely to make it possible to navigate. My plan was to tunnel side cliffs and then blow the cliff off into the river with dynamite! People laughed at me but I enjoyed talking about it anyhow."

Although it is hardly probable that any one realized it at the time, the key to the problem not only of taming the Colorado, but also to that of making a faithful servant of it, was found with the discovery of practicable long-distance electrical transmission toward the end of the nineteenth century. After that hydro-electric development and irrigation went hand in hand, striding ever faster as the economic feasibility of longer and longer power transmission was proven. Reclamation projects of a magnitude and character impossible to finance for irrigation alone became economically justified when the incidental development of power could be saddled with most of the costs. The great majority of the Government's most successful reclamation projects would have never come up even for serious consideration but for the fact that the generation of power at the dams or on the canals made it possible to complete them without charging a prohibitive share of the costs against the land. And that is why it has at last become possible seriously to consider the roping and harnessing of the Great Bull of the Colorado. Because power can be made to pay the bills, flood-control and irrigation projects on a scale impossible to finance by themselves may now be planned and carried out.

The ideal plan for the development of the Colorado below the great middle canyon series would have provided for a number of projects based upon a foundation of complete river control. Like the foundation of any other structure, this one should have been built first. Thus the bull would have been seized and held by the horns, instead of being grabbed, and not held, by the tail. Western initiative and confidence, on the one hand, and Governmental inaction and lack of vision on the other, conspired to bring about work upon the superstructure before anything had been done about a foundation. A little less initiative by the one, and a little more by the other, might have brought the sequence of construction somewhere near the proper order. If the buoyant Western dreamers could have restrained their eagerness to bring about fulfilment a decade or so, or if the Federal Government could have advanced its action toward control of the Colorado a decade or so, both the losses of the past and the very real menace of the present would have been avoided.

Neither the Government nor the men who dreamed the dream of the Imperial Valley can be greatly blamed for what has happened; as for the much more terrible blow that yet may fall, responsibility for it may only be apportioned after the event—which it is devoutly to be hoped may never occur. In 1892, when the plans for the diversion of water from the Colorado to the below-sea-level area south of the Salton Sink first began to take tangible shape, the financial, if not the engineering, obstacles to a canyon control-dam for that river were quite insuperable. The young giant of Electricity, in his swaddling clothes at the time, had not yet pulled on his Seven League Boots of long-distance transmission. Men could dream of creating a rose-blooming desert by bringing to it a stream from the river, but not of paying for it by another less ponderable stream run along a copper wire. And so the dreamers concentrated on their dream of making a few thousands of millions of blades of grass grow where none had grown before, and failed to concentrate upon a couple of rather important realities—the Colorado River floods and the Law of Gravity. In fulfilment of their dream they reared a wonderful super-structure—and forgot the foundation. Jacking up that super-structure and building a foundation under it before Nature lets the Colorado and gravitation loose to destroy the whole thing is going to be a difficult and costly piece of emergency work, especially as it must, or ought to, be a rushed job.

Even when the Federal Government went into reclamation work on its own account in 1902 neither the possibility, nor yet the need, of adequate control of the Colorado appears to have been fully realized. With characteristic conservatism and common sense, however, the Reclamation Service located all but one of its Colorado Basin projects upon fairly manage-able tributaries. Even the Yuma project, which diverted water from the main river at the Laguna Dam, did not contemplate the reclamation of any considerable acreage of new land that was subject to inundation. But in bringing water to lands al-ready in private hands a sizable area liable to flooding was in-cluded in the project, and the effectual protection of this has been one of the most troublesome and costly problems con-fronting the Service at this point.

Of the four irrigation projects undertaken and completed by the Government in the Colorado River Basin, two are in the north and two in the south. A fifth takes its water from the Basin of the Colorado and delivers it to land in the Salt Lake drainage area. The story of the remarkable transforma-tions wrought by this notably successful quintette of projects is succinctly but comprehensively told in the following tables, specially prepared by the Reclamation Service from the latest figures available and placed at my disposal through the cour-tesy of its late Director, Arthur Powell Davis:

Salt River Project, Arizona

Net construction cost of project $10,550,000
Repayment of construction charges to Oct. 31, 1922.. $955,000
Irrigable acreage of completed project.............. 213,000
Cropped acreage under irrigation, 1922............. 192,000
Gross value of irrigated crops, 1922............... $12,898,000
  Per acre cropped $67
Gross crop value for 10-year period, 1912 to 1921...$111,000,000
Estimated increase in farm land values as a result of
  reclamation $30,000,000
Number of irrigated farms....................... 5,000
  Population 33,600
Number of project cities and towns............... 14
  Population .... 42,500[1]
Number of public schools........................ 60
Number of churches............................. 65
Number of banks................................ 20
  Deposits $17,776,000
  Number of depositors........................ 38,000
Roosevelt dam: Storage dam; type, rubble masonry arch, gravity;
  height, 280 feet; crest length, 1,125 feet; volume, 342,325
  cubic yards; area of reservoir, 16,832 acres; capacity of
  reservoir, 1,305,000 acre-feet. Cost of dam and appurtenant
  structures, $4,100,000.
Granite Reef dam: Diversion dam; type, rubble concrete weir;
  height, 38 feet; crest length, 1,000 feet; volume, 40,000 cubic
  yards; cost, $627,000.

Yuma Project, Arizona-California

Net construction cost of project.................... $8,951,500
Repayment of construction charges to Oct. 31, 1922.... $954,000
Irrigable acreage of completed project.............. 110,000
Cropped acreage under irrigation, 1922............. 54,000
Gross value of irrigated crops, 1922 .... $2,682,500
  Per acre cropped $50
Gross crop value for 10-year period, 1912 to 1921......$25,422,000
Estimated increase in farm land values as a result of
  reclamation $10,000,000

[1] Includes population of Phœnix, 29,053 in 1920.

Number of irrigated farms...................... 1,200
    Population 4,800
Number of project cities and towns............... 6
    Population 6,665
Number of public schools....................... 16
Number of churches............................. 12
Number of banks................................ 5
    Deposits $1,927,000
    Number of depositors.......................... 6,000
Laguna dam: Diversion dam; type, Indian weir, concrete and rock fill; maximum height, 10 feet; crest length, 4,780 feet; volume, 442,000 cubic yards; cost, including headworks, $1,948,-000.

Grand Valley Project, Colorado

Net construction cost of project....................$3,899,000
No repayments on construction charge as charge not yet announced.
Irrigable acreage of completed project.............. 55,000
Cropped acreage under irrigation, 1922 11,800
Gross value of irrigated crops, 1922................. $366,000
    Per acre cropped.............................. $31
Gross crop value for 6-year period, 1916 to 1921.......$2,121,000
Estimated increase in farm land values as a result of reclamation $3,000,000
Number of irrigated farms....................... 400
    Population 1,000
Number of project cities and towns................. 6
    Population .... 11,250[1]
Number of public schools....................... 23[2]
Number of churches............................. 28[2]
Number of banks................................ 7[2]
    Deposits ....$3,621,400[2]
    Number of depositors.......................... 11,000[2]
Colorado River diversion dam: type, masonry ogee weir with roller crest 10 to 15 feet high; maximum height, 24 feet; crest length, 546 feet; volume, 25,680 cubic yards; cost, $500,000.

[1] Includes population of Grand Junction, 8,665 in 1920; adjacent to project and whose growth has not been affected particularly by the work of the Reclamation Service.
[2] These items include area adjacent to project.

Uncompahgre Project, Colorado

Net construction cost of project...................... $6,700,000
Repayment of construction charges negligible as public
    notice announcing charge issued only recently.
Irrigable acreage of completed project................ 97,400
Cropped acreage under irrigation, 1921............... 63,600
Gross value of irrigated crops, 1921................. $2,614,300
    Per acre cropped................................ $41
Gross crop value for 10-year period, 1912 to 1921......$22,170,900
Estimated increase in farm land values as a result of
    reclamation $7,000,000
Number of irrigated farms......................... 1,640
Population 6,170
Number of project cities and towns.................. 3
Population 7,450
Number of public schools.......................... 27
Number of churches............................... 27
Number of banks.................................. 8
    Deposits $3,219,800
    Number of depositors........................... 11,000
Gunnison tunnel, bringing water from Gunnison River to Uncom-
    pahgre Valley, 30,645 feet long; capacity, 1,000 second-feet;
    cost, $3,039,000.

Strawberry Valley Project, Utah

(Portion of water supply brought through Strawberry Tunnel from
the Colorado River drainage basin through the divide into
the Great Basin where the project is located.)

Net construction cost of project......................$3,472,500
Repayment of construction charges to Oct. 31, 1922.... $318,000
Irrigable acreage of completed project................ 55,400
Cropped acreage under irrigation, 1921............... 47,200
Gross value of irrigated crops, 1921.................$1,557,100
    Per acre cropped................................ $33
Gross crop value for 6-year period, 1916 to 1921.......$9,192,800
Estimated increase in farm land values as a result of
    reclamation $5,000,000

Number of irrigated farms.......................... 2,740
    Population 6,500
Number of project cities and towns................... 12
    Population 16,000
Number of public schools............................ 22
Number of churches................................. 23
Number of banks................................... 6
    Deposits $1,750,000
    Number of depositors............................. 10,000
Strawberry Dam: Storage dam; type, earth fill, reinforced concrete
    core wall; maximum height, 72 feet; crest length, 48 feet;
    volume, 108,000 cubic yards; cost of dam and appurtenant
    structures, $224,400.

The majority of these projects called for very bold engineering, especially those of Strawberry Valley and Uncompahgre. The irrigation plan of the former provided for the storage of waters in Strawberry Reservoir, in north-central Utah, and their carriage through the four-mile Strawberry Tunnel to the Diamond Fork of the Spanish Fork River and their diversion from that stream to the irrigable area. This project, due possibly to the fact that the lands were largely taken up by Mormons who were trained irrigators, has been highly prosperous and successful in every particular.

The Uncompahgre Project receives its water from the flow of the river of that name, supplemented in the early spring and late summer by a diversion from the Gunnison River. This supplementary supply is furnished through the Gunnison Tunnel, six miles in length and passing twenty-two hundred feet below the summit of Vernal Mesa. Four hundred and seventy miles of canals and laterals are comprised in the distribution system. In spite of its costly engineering features, the considerable area of this project has enabled it to be completed with the comparatively modest charge of seventy dollars an acre against the land.

The Grand Valley Project consists of a strip of land about

forty miles in length and from two to five miles wide extending
along the northern edge of the valley from which it takes
its name. The water is diverted from the Grand River,
now called the Colorado, by a low dam of the weir type. Because the valley is protected by the mountains from severe
storms, the climate of the project is comparatively mild for so
considerable an altitude, as a consequence of which there is
a remarkably long growing season of one hundred and eighty-
two days.

As all three of these Upper Basin projects have an elevation
of close to a mile above sea-level their crops are the usual
staples of the higher latitudes of the temperate zone—wheat,
alfalfa, sugar-beets and deciduous fruits. The two Lower Basin
projects, on the other hand, with their low altitudes and intensely hot summer climates, raise the products of the sub-
tropics and even the tropics.

The Salt River Project was the most costly to complete of
any in the Colorado River Basin, but owing to its considerable
size the charge per acre against the lands will prove less than on
some of the others. With an irrigation season of three hundred
and sixty-five days a year and a growing season of almost equal
length, the farmers in the Salt River Valley were almost too
successful for their own good. Lucrative returns from stock-
fattening and dairying, from alfalfa, garden truck and both
citrus and deciduous fruits, made them ready to play for still
higher stakes with cotton when the price of that temperamental
staple was sent skyward by the war demand. This rocketing
action brought the usual stick-like fall. Being a government
project, the impact was better distributed than in the Palo
Verde and Imperial valleys on the California side of the Colorado. The buoyancy and resiliency of the Salt River Valley
farmer brought an immediate rebound, and now he is back on
the earth with both feet, and scratching his rich, sandy loam
with both hands.

The Yuma Project furnishes the only instance where the

REPLACING A BROKEN OAR IN BAD WATER.

READY FOR A RAPID.

Note the collar on the life-preserver to keep the boatman's head up in case he is knocked unconscious in an upset.

LAGUNA DAM SLUICEWAY, YUMA PROJECT.

Reclamation Service, in the face of many temptations, has made an extensive diversion of water from the lower Colorado. Thanks to sound engineering and conservative management, it is on the highroad to notable success where a privately promoted project attempting the same work could hardly have avoided the difficulties that have weighed so heavily upon Blythe and Imperial. Water is taken into a canal system heading on the California end of the Laguna Dam, ten miles northeast of Yuma. After serving the irrigable lands on the west side of the Colorado, including those of the Yuma Indian Reservation, the canal passes under the river through an inverted siphon to carry water to the Yuma Valley. In this latter section there is served a considerable acreage near the river which was already under cultivation when the project was inaugurated. The providing of drainage and levee-protection for these low-lying lands has called for much difficult and expensive work. Indeed, the variety and the scope of its activities (besides irrigation, levee-work and drainage, there is also operated a railway and a pumping system) have conspired to make the burden of the Yuma Project farmer a heavy one—heavier, perhaps, than could have been borne by those of a project of less wealth of resource.

One of the most interesting phases of the development of the Yuma Project—that of pumping water to the Mesa—has but recently been entered upon. The several thousand acres now under canal on the slightly elevated plain of the Yuma Mesa is rated as approaching nearer to the ideal for citrus culture than any other known lands. The report of the Reclamation Service says:

"The climate is unique among citrus districts of the country since it has the smallest rainfall, lowest relative humidity, and greatest percentage of sunshine, a combination which makes possible the production of fruit of fine quality, high colour, and with an early ripening period. The frost hazard is a negligible factor in this district, and should give the prospective citrus grower no concern."

Although the charges against these Mesa lands for the cost of irrigation works alone will amount to $200 per acre, the unique advantages of the restricted area suitable for successful citrus culture makes the offering probably the most outstanding thing in the bargain line ever made available by the Reclamation Service.

During the time these five Government projects have been in process of completion considerable irrigation development by private capital has been carried on. Most of these projects have been on the smaller tributary streams of the Upper Basin, and where the promoter and the land-shark have not figured in the development, reclamation has been generally successful. The most uniformly consistent irrigation development has been undertaken by the Mormons, mostly on tributaries of the Colorado heading in or flowing through Utah. These Mormon projects have succeeded for the same reasons as have those of the Reclamation Service—because they have been soundly engineered, conservatively managed and run for the benefit of the farmers taking up the land. If the former have shown a higher average of financial returns than the latter it will be because they have had the advantage of a larger proportion of farmers experienced in the use of water.

One would have thought that the object lesson furnished by the Imperial Valley trying to keep its head above water would have provided an effective deterrent against taking further liberties with the lower Colorado until effective flood control had been provided. The lesson was not lost upon the Reclamation Service, which confined its efforts to making the lowlands of its Yuma Project as safe as possible and the beginning of studies looking to the ultimate minimization of the inundation menace by dams in the canyons above. Nor did the United States Indian Service take any chances with lands subject to overflow in the installation of its pumping plant for the irrigation of several thousand acres of the Colorado Indian Reservation. But the private promoter, tempted again by an easy diversion and the profits of subdividing a great area of rich and readily irrigated land, was still ready for a fling. During the very continuance of the Colorado outbreaks of 1905 and 1906 by which the whole Imperial Valley was threatened with submergence, a company was formed to acquire the former Blythe rancho and its water rights. As a colonization scheme the project was a success almost from the outset. Seventy thousand acres of level and extremely fertile land were put under ditch and placed on the market, finding ready buyers. Several towns grew up in the valley, the largest of which was Blythe, with a present population of over two thousand. For the rest, the story of the Palo Verde project just about parallels that of Imperial—a long uphill and only partially successful fight to prevent the river from claiming its own. There are several reasons why the great wild bull of the Colorado should be thrown and tied without further delay, but the one above all others that calls for speedy and vigorous action is to save Imperial and Palo Verde from a goring to the death.

CHAPTER II

TRYING TO HOLD THE BULL BY THE TAIL

THERE have been many brave fights against odds in the history of colonization, but for indomitable courage few to rival that of the settlers of Imperial Valley. Those who would expect success in pitting their efforts against great natural forces should fight free and unhampered, and should make no strategical errors. Those who started the fight for Imperial made just about every mistake there was to be made, and they fought with a sword suspended above their heads from the first. Beaten to their knees time and again, they kept up the fight until every enemy that could be grappled by the throat had been mastered. There remained—and remains—only the Damoclean Sword of the menace of the Colorado hanging by its often all-but-parted hair of emergency levee protection. Against that threat Imperial Valley must have help, and speedy help, or a fight that is otherwise all but won will be irretrievably lost.

Perhaps nowhere in the world—on the Nile, the Tigris, the Indus—has there been an opportunity for desert reclamation so nearly ideal as that offered by the lands of the ancient and modern delta of the Colorado, handled at the proper time and in the proper way. And nowhere in the world is there a place where an attempt at desert reclamation would be fraught with a more certain aftermath of difficulties and disaster than the attempt to bring water and settlers to the Imperial Valley, handled when it was and as it was. The proper way to have handled the Imperial Valley project would have been through the medium of the U. S. Reclamation Service, and as a unit of a comprehensive programme which included complete flood control of the Colorado. The proper time would have been when it was economically feasible, and politically possible, to go ahead with the first great control dam. Whether that reclamation millenium has arrived even to-day has yet to be proven.

The Salton Basin, which roughly corresponds to the Imperial Valley, has been very aptly defined and delimited as the area that would ultimately be submerged if the Colorado discharged inland instead of into the Gulf of California. That delimitation suggests both the ease of the diversion of Colorado River waters to the depression of the Valley and the dangers incident to such a diversion. Fully to understand the situation one must picture the delta of the Colorado as a low, rounded dam cutting off the present head of the Gulf of California from the extensive below-sea-level area corresponding to its ancient head. In comparatively recent geological time that arm of the sea extended some distance to the north and the west of the Imperial Valley of to-day. Possibly it lapped near to the bases of the Chocolate and the San Jacinto mountains, although the most clearly defined of the ancient beaches are some miles from either range.

The silt-laden flood of the Colorado, dropping its mud and sand as it entered the side of this narrow arm, finally built up a solid dam all the way across to the foot of the Cocopah Mountains. This barrier turned the northern end of the Gulf into a great inland sea which, cut off from the ocean and deprived of all but intermittent flows of the Colorado, ultimately dried up. Then the river, flowing now this way, now that, down the sides of its delta cone, filled the bed of the ancient sea with a great depth of silt. When the northerly flow persisted for any length of time a new inland sea was formed, but only to disappear by evaporation a few years after a silting up of the river's channels diverted its red flood again to the Gulf. This process evidently went right on up to the time of the inauguration of the Imperial Valley reclamation project, for McDougal writes:

"The earliest existence of Salton Sea within historic times is that shown in Roque's map, 1762. . . . Collated reports give the presence of flood water in some volume in the sink in 1828, 1840, 1849, 1852, 1859, 1862, 1867 and 1891." [1]

It is a remarkable fact that although the 1891 replenishment of the Salton Sink was actually taking place at the time the plans for irrigating Imperial Valley were under preliminary discussion, none of the promoters of the scheme appears to have read it as a danger signal. Disinterested scientists and engineers read the sign aright, and gave warning. Those of them that were not ignored entirely were just as effectually dismissed as knockers. The fathers of Imperial Valley reclamation are often spoken of as having seen great visions. This is true; but the brightness of those visions so dazzled their eyes that they failed to take note of some rather important realities.

The opportunities for bringing water to the parched desert of the old silt-filled sea-bed were so fair, and so plain for even one who ran to read, that it was inevitable that the first thoughtful man to see the lay of the land could not but be impressed with the possibilities of the situation. Melchior Díaz crossed either to the mud volcanoes near Salton Sea or to those north of Black Butte before he was killed by falling on his own spear; but the *conquistador* was mainly after gold. Father Escalante, and probably Garcés, would not have missed noting the opportunity for making the desert to blossom as the rose if only the *entradas* of either had carried him by the route that revealed the way for the water. Pattie, with a mind for nothing but beaver and fair señoritas, passed the key-route to the south, leaving it for Oliver Meredith Wozencraft, a 'forty-niner, to discover.

Dr. Wozencraft conceived the idea of bringing water from the Colorado to the arid lands of the Salton Sink during a somewhat arduous journey across that forbidding region in the

[1] "The Salton Sea," by D. T. McDougal. The Carnegie Institute, Washington, 1913.

spring of 1849. His plan, which was worked out in collaboration with Ebenezer Hadley, Surveyor of San Diego County, provided for the diversion of a portion of the flow of the Colorado
to the old Alamo channel, and thence to what is now called Imperial Valley, substantially as under the later project. In 1859
Dr. Wozencraft secured the passage of a bill through the California Legislature giving him all state rights to sixteen hundred
square miles of the desert region in question in consideration
of their reclamation. In the fall of the same year a bill was
presented to the House of Representatives designed to secure
the consent of the Federal Government to undertake the work.
The plan was outlined as follows:

"This bill proposes, in consideration of the introduction of a
wholesome supply of fresh water to the Colorado desert, to cede
to Oliver M. Wozencraft and his associates the said desert tract as
described in the bill. This tract embraces (according to Lieutenant
Brigland) about 1,600 square miles in the basin of what is now
and must remain, until an energetic and extensive system of reclamation is inaugurated and brought to successful completion, a valueless and horrible desert. The labour of reclamation must be commenced within two years and be completed within ten years. As
fast as the water shall be introduced, upon a report to that effect
being made to the government by a duly appointed commission,
patents shall be issued for the parts reclaimed, and when all the
conditions are fulfilled, then, and not until then, shall the title rest
in said grantee."

The outbreak of the Civil War deferred immediate action on
the bill and the post-bellum depression resulted in its shelving
for many years. After an interminable succession of post-
ponements and disappointments, just as his bill was finally
about to be brought up for a hearing, Dr. Wozencraft died in
Washington, perhaps the first of the many to be broken in heart
and pocket by Colorado Desert reclamation.

Except for the fact that it is rather a decenter sort of thing
to die in action on the desert than of stagnation in Washington,
it is just as well that events happened as they did. Success in

Washington could only have prepared the way for inevitable failure in the desert. If the promoters of the present Imperial Valley project were twenty years ahead of their times, Dr Wozencraft was fifty. He would have failed for lack of railway transportation and for lack of the Western markets that have helped keep Imperial going financially. But attempted reclamation of this region in the sixties, or seventies, or even the eighties would hardly have stopped at simple failure. It is rather more than probable that a canal to the Alamo would have started the Colorado flowing to the Salton Sink at the first high water, just as it did in 1905; and with anything less than the aid the Southern Pacific gave in closing the latter breach, the river never could have been stopped until the Salton Sink was filled high enough to overtop the dam of the delta and drain down to the Gulf of California. The disaster which Imperial Valley avoided by a hair in 1905 and 1906, and by which it is still threatened, would almost certainly have been visited upon any reclamation project attempted before the time of the railways.

Just how much the inception of the present Imperial Valley project owed to the work and the plan of Dr. Wozencraft I have been unable to learn. Probably very little. It first took definite shape in the mind of C. R. Rockwood, an engineer who was sent to the lower Colorado in 1892 to report upon the feasibility of an irrigation scheme in northern Sonora, doubtless the one now known under the name of the Del Rio Project. It was a typical land-promotion scheme, with some stock in the company sold even before the plan had been reported upon. Finding the Sonora project quite impracticable, Rockwood, on his own responsibility, made a tour of investigation along the old channel of the Alamo to the Salton Sink. The same things that had struck fire to Wozencraft's imagination forty years before kindled in the mind of the young engineer a vision of which he was never to lose sight.

It may be that if Rockwood's vision of a green and blooming

MAIN CANAL OF THE IMPERIAL VALLEY IRRIGATION SYSTEM.

CREST OF THE JUNE FLOOD OF THE COLORADO BEATING AGAINST
THE PESCADERO DAM.

THE BEATEN COLORADO QUIETLY FLOWING INTO THE PESCADERO CUT.

garden could have been more frequently clouded with a cut-in of a red and raging river his splendid effort would have been better balanced. First and last, he made the mistake of over-rating the blooming desert and underrating the raging river. A desert may bloom, as the Imperial Valley is doing to-day, and yet leave much to be desired; but a raging river that is doing a balancing act down the crown of a delta cone was not, and is not, a thing to be taken lightly.

To the land boomers in Denver one project was as good as another. The name of their concern was changed to the Colorado River Irrigation Company and enough stock was sold to make it possible to send Rockwood back for a real survey. This was completed by the spring of 1893, to be followed by several years of vain efforts to raise the money to begin pre-liminary work. Much of the trouble of the next decade was traceable to commitments and promises of this early period of high and low finance. The best thing that happened in this interval was the elimination of the original land boomers and their replacement in a reorganized corporation called the California Development Company by men of energy, ability and—in one or two instances at least—integrity.

The project for the reclamation of the desert of the Salton Sink came in for considerable publicity in the course of this early financial campaign, and one of the consequences was a warning from a high authority. In the Report of the Smith-sonian Institute for 1907 F. H. Newell, subsequently Director of the Reclamation Service, wrote:

"If we go into this depression below sea level and interfere with natural conditions, or—as we say—'develop the country,' we are brought face to face with the great forces of the river and the uncertainty as to whether it will desire to continue in the channel in which we happen to have found it."

Difficulties over the heading on the Colorado and the right-of-way for a canal through Mexico complicated the matter of finance, and then, with the latter all but assured, the outbreak of the Spanish-American War forced another postponement. Financial backing was finally secured in 1900, and that, fortunately, from a man who was a builder as well as a capitalist. George Chaffee, who had already done important reclamation work for two of the provincial governments of Australia, lost no time in getting to work. His contract for canal construction was entered into in April, 1900, and in May of the following year water was flowing upon the desert lands of Imperial Valley. Equal energy was displayed in the extension of the distribution system, and in the brief span of twenty-two months which covered Chaffee's construction activities more than four hundred miles of canals and laterals were built. Considering the financial and other handicaps under which he laboured, this pioneer builder did a fine, honest job. George Chaffee's sound practicality was a useful balance-wheel alike to the visions of Rockwood and the fervid enthusiasms of the sales department. There is little doubt that if a man of his common sense and integrity could have had a controlling hand in directing the destinies of Imperial Valley during a longer period of its earlier development a good many serious difficulties would have been avoided.

The idea of creating a veritable sunken garden in the desert appealed strongly to the popular imagination, and the great amount of publicity given to the Imperial Valley project created a ready demand for the land and appurtenant water-rights. With the company in financial difficulties from the outset, largely due to the promiscuous distribution of water-script at ten cents on the dollar by the original boomsters, it was only natural that sales should have been pushed with the realization of money, and still more money, as the prime objective, and with scant regard for the future welfare of the buyer.

It has been well said that for the farmer of desert land forty acres is enough, eighty an abundance, one hundred and sixty a misfortune, and three hundred and twenty a calamity. Where the newly created Reclamation Service was strictly limiting the holdings of settlers to small tracts, the Imperial Land Company was allowing nothing but the bank-roll of a prospective settler to limit his purchase. Capitalists made money by buying large holdings for speculation, but many an optimistic colonist bought straight calamity by filing upon and buying the water-rights for a full half-section.

Government engineers and experts issued several further warnings during the year or two following the bringing of water to the Valley. One was against the risk attendant upon diverting water from the Colorado without a dam or weir; another had to do with the dangers incident to the provision of insufficient drainage; a third was against the menace of alkali in the soil. The people of the Valley—and especially those engaged in speculative enterprises, who were the hardest hit—felt considerably aggrieved against the Reclamation Service and the Department of Agriculture for the issuance of statements which had the undeniable effect of restricting their prosperity. They are even inclined to this day to attribute the reports in question to an animosity engendered as a consequence of the fact that Imperial was not a Government project. Nothing could have been more absurd. There was trouble at the Heading almost from the outset, and inside of four years this had led up to an actual outbreak of the river into the Valley. Imperial has been anxious for years to abandon Hanlon's Heading for the Government-built Laguna Dam, and a bill now before Congress provides for such a consummation.

On the score of drainage trouble, also, the worst that was warned against has come to pass. With the rising of the water-table consequent upon the lack of provision to carry off the surplus from irrigation thousands of acres of what were once the best lands of the Valley have reverted to worthless desert. These are now in process of re-reclamation by the excavation of a scientific drainage system; but that does not affect the fact that the Government's original warning was entirely justified by the conditions that prompted it.

The report on the soils of the Valley was the only one of these three Governmental warnings that proved to have been unduly pessimistic. According to Circular Number 9, of the Bureau of Soils of the Department of Agriculture, a very considerable area of the Valley was so considerably impregnated with alkali as to be almost if not quite useless for agriculture. This gloomy picture was discredited almost at once by the bountiful yields that were had from a large part of the pre-condemned lands just as fast as they were put under water. There are areas in the Valley that from the first have been worthless on account of alkali; others have become more heavily impregnated through injudicious handling of water and poor drainage. Yet the fact remains that the whole acreage affected by alkali is but a fraction of that indicated by the unfortunate Circular Number 9. Even so, however, the conclusions embodied in that report were no more than ordinary errors of judgment, such as even perfectly competent government experts are liable to. There was no more animosity to the Valley expressed or implied in it than in the thoroughly vindicated opinions of the Reclamation Service.

My first sight of the reclaimed desert was in the winter of 1904 when, as a youngster, I traversed Imperial Valley from end to end in going through to the lower delta on a hunting trip. Water had been working its miracle for over two years and a half and—between heat and a wonderful soil—accomplishing what could not have come to pass in twice the time under ordinary conditions. Settlers were swarming in by every train, land and water-rights were in hot demand, and one breathed enthusiasm and optimism with the very desert dust. Water was short at times but irrigators were reconciled to silt-blocked ditches and canals by the sedulously fostered belief that such of the red flood of the Colorado as did reach their lands was little short of liquid gold in its richness in fertilizer.

All of the wonder-workers were in the field at the time and, going or coming, I had more or less intimate glimpses of the visioning Rockwood, the dynamic Heber, and that smiling, steady-eyed, level-headed engineer C. N. Perry, who appeared to be the only one of the lot to realize that the wild bull of the Colorado was going to be a difficult brute to handle by the tail. Perry, scouring Mexicali with me in an endeavour to charter a deep-dust-navigating mule-team for the plunge into the unknown below the border, told me something of his work in building headings on the Alamo Canal—fine, sound work it proved, too, when the test came.

There was a lot to stir a boy's imagination in the amazing transformation that was taking place there in the desert, as there was in the men who were bringing it about; yet my one outstanding memory of that visit has to do with an uncannily prophetic vision with which none of them had the least to do in conjuring it up. With a single hunting companion I had crossed the International Boundary Line at a point where Calexico and Mexicali were scarcely more than names upon the map and was pushing southward into the then comparative *terra incognita* of the Colorado River delta. It was a day of brassy sunniness, with the dome of the sky gleaming metallically where it was smitten with the blinding glare thrown off from the heat-drenched plains that were destined shortly to become among the richest and most extensive of North American cotton-fields.

Sprawling over the seat of the creaking wagon, I piloted my team of Mexican mules toward the ever-receding heat-wave lakes that lapped in shimmering mirrors to the erosion-sculptured slopes of the distant Cocopahs. The true mirage of reflection and the false mirage of dancing heat milled and melted and merged in the fantastically jumbled landscape ahead. Upended cliffs gave way to inverted mesas, and these to spreading cloudburst moraines and patches of overflow flats peppered thickly with mesquite and palo verde.

It was doubtless the change of my angle of vision that brought a double line of willows into view beyond the silver-grey of the mesquite, but something in the wizardry of the projectoscope of the mirage made the transition as sharp and sudden as the shifting of slides in a stereopticon. One instant I was gazing on a sky-hung projection of tree-blotched alkali, the next at a yellow-red flood—sinuous, ropy, leonine of power as of colour—swirling between two parallel bands of fringing willows.

My map told me that the nearest point on the Rio Colorado was all of fifty miles as flies the south-bound goose; likewise my common sense told me that the great drainage ditch of the Southwest was not suspended from above like a piece of drop scenery. But I knew that rolling River of Red in an instant, all topsy-turvy though it was. I even awakened my drowsing companion when I called it by name right then and there. But the true significance of that apparently impetuous northwest-ward flow across the sky eluded me until an evening, some days later, when the Cocopah guide who was leading us back into the mountains after sheep interpreted the sign as read by the visioning eye of the tribal seer.

"It is the spirit of *El Rio Colorado* seeking its ancient home in the great salt sea to the north," explained the dusky Monanza, where we rested on the crest of the pass and watched the westering sun declining to the silver sliver of the Laguna Salada; "and because our wise men tell us that one day the body shall follow the spirit, we Indians build our homes at the foot of the mountains and leave the white man to dispute the lowlands with the river that built the floor of the valley, and which in its own good time shall come to claim it again."

Monanza the Cocopah spoke less trippingly than I have quoted him, but such was the gist of his explanatory comment. I smiled indulgently at the picturesque conceit and promptly changed the subject to pig-hunting. Faring south down the winding Hardy toward the head of the Gulf, a week's chase of deer and cougar and the temperamental *javelina* wiped the slates of memory clean for the time being of all recollection of the questing spirit of the shifty Colorado.

Something over a year went by and then, one morning, heavily-headed dispatches to the Los Angeles papers recalled to my mind the strange words of the Cocopah guide. The Colorado, it was stated, for reasons not clearly explained, had broken through the lower Mexican heading of the Imperial Valley Canal and was discharging its full volume into the Salton Sink by way of the channels of the Alamo and the so-called New River. The fight was joined, it seemed. The Colorado was preparing to lap again its ancient beaches at the foot of the San Jacinto Mountains. The body of the great river was about to follow its questing spirit.

The break-through of the Colorado at what was called "Intake Number 3" need never have occurred in the first place, nor need there have been any great difficulty in closing it once it did occur. From the outset everything and everybody seems to have played into the hand of the river, and the shifty Colorado took quick advantage of every opening offered by unsound engineering and gross carelessness. The cutting of an emergency intake in the soft earth on the Mexican side of the boundary appears to have been due to two things—primarily, to the fact that the canal below the original Chaffee gate at Hanlon's Heading had become so silted up as to be unable to deliver sufficient water for the fall irrigation of 1904; secondarily, to the fact that the Federal Government was contesting the right of the Valley to divert water from what was still technically a navigable stream. The Mexican heading was a double-bladed sword cutting the Gordian Knot of both difficulties. Heber, after vainly trying to get a bill through Congress recognizing the right of the Valley to water from the Colorado, went to Mexico and closed a contract with President Diaz for the use of water diverted on the Mexican side of the line under the provision that one half of the diversion should be available for future irrigation in Baja California. Then Rockwood made the projected cut, but with few precautionary provisions against possible trouble in the event of an unexpected rise. This was in October, 1904.

By resorting to three successive deepenings of the channel enough water was brought to the Alamo Canal to carry the Valley through November, December and January. High water was not expected to occur until spring, and it was the intention temporarily to close the cut in February. Three unseasonal rises in that month hampered preparations for the work, and when the closure was finally attempted toward the end of March Rockwood was spending most of his time in Los Angeles, locked in a political struggle with Heber for the control of the California Development Company. The endeavour to close the widening breach by dredging a mud dam across it met with two failures. A soundly devised plan of Perry to turn back the rising flood by means of anchored brush mattresses was half completed when Rockwood, who had finally won out in the annual meeting of the company, arrived and ordered work suspended.[1]

Rockwood's plan to divert the river from the break by means of a half-mile jetty had to be abandoned uncompleted, and probably had the effect of hastening the break-through of the whole flood of the Colorado early in August. Another plan of Rockwood, involving the use of a gate and by-pass, was abandoned when that engineer relinquished active control of field work and took over the business management of the company in Los Angeles. Another jetty, this one planned and constructed by F. S. Edinger, a Southern Pacific Railway bridge-builder, was swept away by a flood from the Gila in November.

The waters of the Colorado were finding their way to the Salton Sink by two channels, both winding through the reclaimed areas of the Valley for many miles. All of the flood

1 "The Story of the First Decade of Imperial Valley," by Edgar F. Howe and Wilbur Jay Hall (Imperial, 1910).

VIEW OF ROOSEVELT DAM AND SPILLWAYS, SALT RIVER PROJECT, ARIZONA.

GILLESPIE DIVERSION DAM ON THE GILA.

which could crowd into the bank-full main canal went out through the waste-gates at Sharp's Heading and sought the bottom of the ancient sea by the channel of the Alamo. The overflow drained southwesterly to Volcano Lake, and then north by the channel of the New River. Both the Alamo and the New, having heavy gradients, scoured out great gorges through the silt and clay of the Valley, but without doing great damage save to the lands actually torn down and washed away. Irrigation of the unmenaced areas went on about as usual and there was surprisingly little check to the prosperity and progress of the new desert garden.

During the continuance of this early overflow the people of Imperial Valley greatly underrated the threat of the Colorado. Fortunately another highly interested party not only realized the danger, but had both the initiative and the means to act to avert at least the immediate threat. This was the Southern Pacific, which was deeply concerned both because it had taken over a controlling interest in the California Development Company and because its main line tracks were threatened with submergence by the rising Salton Sea. Rockwood was given unlimited backing when he returned to the field with a more comprehensive plan in December, 1905, and on his final resignation from the company the following spring the railway took the whole task directly upon its own shoulders. H. T. Cory, an engineer of great energy and resource and high technical training, was put on the job, with orders to close the break regardless of cost.

As nothing could be done to check the flood through the crevasse during high water, the Valley was forced to face another severe inundation in the course of the spring rise of 1906. A part of Mexicali was undermined and destroyed, and Calexico seriously threatened, before the "cutting back" action of the New River excavated a gorge sufficiently wide and deep to drain off the overflow. Then followed a considerable period of suspense during it which it was feared that the cutting back, greatly to be desired in relieving the overflow in the Valley, should continue all the way back to the Alamo and so to the Colorado. That was the real menace in 1906, as it is to-day. Perhaps it will be in order to explain why.

It is a fact well understood by hydraulic engineers that every large river flowing over an earth rather than a rock bed and carrying much silt and sand, tends to equalize its descent. This is done by a natural cutting and filling, much in the same way as a railway equalizes its grade across a broken country. The middle and lower Missouri is a good example of such a stream, and I believe I have already cited the fact that the descent of that river from the mouth of the Yellowstone to the Mississippi maintains an invariable eighty-five hundredths of a foot to the mile for the whole distance.

Through the action of this law the lower Colorado, during the time it flowed unchecked to the Gulf of California, had an even fall of something like a foot to the mile from the Chocolate Mountains to tide-water. But as the gradient of the floor of the Imperial Valley from the Mexican boundary to the lowest point in the Salton Sink is three or four times as great as that of the Colorado, the result of the unchecked flow of that river to the depression of the ancient Gulf would be to spread the descent out equally. In other words the cutting back process would continue up the Colorado until some point was reached where boulders or bedrock put a stop to the action. This would, of course, undermine and destroy the present Laguna Dam, above Yuma, and, infinitely more disastrous, excavate so deep a gorge all the way to the Salton Sea that all of the resources of modern engineering could hardly be equal to the task of diverting the Colorado again to the Gulf before the whole of the Imperial Valley had been completely submerged. The threat of a submersion that could not but endure for hundreds of years grows steadily greater with every spring overflow that adds another foot or two to the crown of the delta cone.

When the exhaustion of the floods from the melting snows of the Rockies had reduced the flow of the Colorado to twenty-five thousand second-feet, Cory, after months spent in assembling materials, began his work. That there was no longer any misconception of the magnitude of the task is evident from his account of the preparation. Ample railway trackage had already been provided and the local stone quarry at Pilot Knob developed to its utmost.

"First the channel proper was narrowed by jetties to six hundred feet. Next a brush mattress consisting of fascines sewed by three-eighths inch galvanized iron rope to heavy three-quarter inch cables, eight feet apart, was successfully woven and sunk across this six hundred foot channel, the mattress reaching fifty feet both up and down stream from the centre of the dam to be. This work was completed early in September. Then followed a very substantial pile trestle carrying an extension of the railroad spur already mentioned. Meanwhile teams had thrown up dikes over the sand bars exposed by the receding flood waters, from either edge of the water to the banks proper, which were over half a mile apart. Brush was piled under the trestle and sunk by rock obtained in the quarry by Pilot Knob, loaded with steam-shovels, hauled hither by train loads and dumped from above by car loads. Similarly dirt was brought from the 'clay pit' and unloaded along the earthen dikes at each side of the crevasse proper. At the same time levees were started running from the concrete headgate to the Rockwood gate and from the south end of the earthen dike across the break down along the river several miles."

This impressive offensive was a vastly different affair from Rockwood's first futile attempts to hold back the Colorado by throwing up a mud levee with a dredge; but even in this plan there was a faulty link. Weakness in the headgate developed almost as soon as it felt the force of the flood, and on October 11th two-thirds of the structure suddenly lifted up and carried away. Cory had learned something, however, which was that "putting rock in the breach faster than the rushing current could carry it away was more than a forlorn hope. . . ." By drawing to his utmost upon every quarry between Los Angeles and Nogales, three weeks more of feverish effort closed the crevasse and turned the Colorado back on its former course to the Gulf of California. This was on November 4th. No time was lost in strengthening the defensive works, but on December 7th another savage flash flood from the Gila came down, broke through the unfinished levees a half mile south of the closure, and at the end of thirty-six hours the whole river was again flowing.

Even the Southern Pacific was staggered by this latest defeat and, unwilling to stand the expense of further effort unsupported, turned to the Federal Government for financial aid. President Roosevelt, acting with characteristic promptitude, avoided the delay of asking Congress for an appropriation by requesting E. H. Harriman to make the closure at Government expense. The effort, which occupied the first six weeks of 1907, was considered by the great financier and railroad man as the crowning achievement of his career. By practically closing the Los Angeles and Tucson divisions of the Southern Pacific, and by running many special trains with piling and timbers from as far as New Orleans, the breach was finally filled on February 14, 1907. This time the defences held.

A saving feature of this period of flood was the fact that, although the Alamo Canal was filled to overflowing with the diversion from the Colorado for a large part of two years, there was no breakdown of the service to the uninundated lands of Imperial Valley. This was due almost entirely to the sound design and construction of the wooden structures erected by Perry at Sharp's Heading. The destruction of the waste-gate to the old Alamo at this point would have cut off the supply of irrigation water completely and reduced the Valley to its former desert state within a few weeks. But this gate, though called upon to handle a discharge many times greater than that for which it was originally designed, came through the ordeal unscathed. Water was supplied with fair regularity to an increasing acreage of cultivation and the demand for new lands was unabated. Remarkable as it may seem, the Valley continued to progress even with the knife held close against its jugular vein, just as it has during the succeeding years when the point of the still threatening blade was somewhat farther removed.

But although the Colorado was confined again to its former channel along the base of the Sonora Mesa to the head of the Gulf of California and the immediate menace to the Imperial Valley removed, the great inland sea remained. And in that important respect this flood differed from all other floods of modern times. The Hoang-ho and the Mississippi had inundated great areas, but never for more than a few weeks at a time. By old channels or by new the flood waters had always drained on seaward when the seasonal rises were over. But the Salton Sink, lying from two to three hundred feet below sea-level, had no outlet, no drainage. Once there, nothing but the slow process of evaporation acted to reduce it, and that, as it turned out, was barely sufficient to offset the waste from normal Imperial Valley irrigation.

The lesson of this tremendous preliminary skirmish was plain for all to read. Hitherto none but engineers had realized the character and imminence of the impending catastrophe. Now the blade of the Damoclean sword hanging above the Valley was unsheathed for all to see. If a part of two seasons' overflow of the Colorado was sufficient to create an inland sea of 285,000 acres, a man could figure on the back of an envelope how long it would take to create a sea reaching beyond the Mexican boundary and putting every town, every home, every acre of the American section of the Imperial Valley permanently under water. But Imperial was not settled with the kind of men who gave ground before a threat. Had it been, other difficulties fought and overcome as they developed would have caused the Valley to revert to desert years ago.

With a controlled Colorado bringing life to their valley, and with an uncontrolled Colorado threatening it with certain death, the basic elements of the problem were simple enough. Control of the river was the thing. Cost what they might, said the increasingly numerous and prosperous people of Imperial, levees high enough and strong enough to keep the Colorado on its direct course to the Gulf of California must be constructed. Forthwith, carrying the war into the enemy's country, men and materials were sent into Mexico to do all that could be done by money and science to guard against another rush of the destroyer to the north. Great and impressive progress was made in the defensive campaign, and for a while opinion in the Valley was sanguine of its success.

Even in those early days, however, there were far-seeing engineers who pointed out that the protective effort was being made in the wrong sector. A river was like a man, they said. You could hamper a man, and perhaps trip him up, by tackling him about the knees; but if you were going to throw him down and keep him there you would have to grip him by the throat. The throat of the Colorado was up in the encanyoned middle river. Build a flood-control dam there and your inundation problem on the lower river was solved for all time.

This contention was as sound in theory a decade and a half ago as it is to-day; it was the practical aspects of it that seemed to present insurmountable difficulties. The raising of fifty million dollars for a flood-control dam appeared a sheer impossibility. Electricity at that time was just getting beyond its first tentative toddles in long-distance transmission, so that it never occurred to any one that power might ultimately be made to pay the whole bill. Since there was no doubt that the Federal Government would not, and that the Valley could not, assume the full cost of such a dam, there was nothing left to do but keep piling dirt on the protecting levees. This was all right while the levees held, but the cumulative effect of it was simply to elevate and render more terrible the threat of the hair-hung Damoclean Sword of the final inevitable breach.

Stopped in its direct frontal onslaught of 1905 and 1906, the Colorado adopted siege tactics in preparation for a flank attack. Building up its bottom with silt for three years, it picked a vulnerable sector of the defence a few miles south of its original breach and poured its flood into one of its old high-water back-channels called the Bee. Fended off from the Alamo and the New River drainage basins by rushed levee work, it continued on into the broad shallow expanse of Volcano Lake. Here, after depositing its silt, it drained—by the countless spreading channels of the Hardy and Pescadero—to the tide-waters of the Gulf.

While the Colorado had failed in its attempt to reach the Salton Sink at a single bound, this break-through of 1909 to Volcano Lake was distinctly in the class of a major advance, a clean-cut strategical victory. It rendered necessary the lengthening by many miles of the levee system and so weakened defensive effort by dissipating it over an extended front. A few more feet of silt to raise the take-off for the next spring, and the way to the Imperial Valley and the Salton Sink would again be open.

Realizing the seriousness of the situation Congress, for the first and last time where the threat to Imperial Valley was concerned, acted with promptness and decision. A million dollars were appropriated and the best engineering talent available was sent to close the crevasse and turn the river back to its former channel. There is some difference of opinion as to the soundness of the practice followed in building the Ockerson Levee, and as to whether or not it could have been made to answer its purpose had more money been available for its construction. At any rate it failed at the first test of strength with the river. The summer floods of 1911 breached it at many points, among which was another broad opening of the cut to the channel of the Bee. Considerable stretches of the embankment remained intact, but the failure at vital points was so complete that nothing further was done to restore it.

Nor has another attempt been made to put the river back into
what was by far the most direct course to the Gulf of California, and the one, therefore, in which its flow would be the
swiftest and the minimum of silt deposited. Between the
growth of vegetation and the accumulation of silt in overflow
seasons, this channel may now be considered as closed for a
very long period of years. So completely has it been filled and
overgrown that, in boating through to the head of the Gulf last
summer, the engineers who accompanied me were quite baffled
in their endeavours to locate the point where the old and the
new channels came together.

Following the near-knockout of the destruction of the Ockerson Levee, Imperial Valley, like a fighter sparring for wind,
settled down to strictly defensive tactics. An elaborate system
of levees was built from Hanlon's Heading all the way across
to Volcano Lake and on to the rising ground near the foot of
the Cocopahs, and these were raised foot by foot as every year's
deposit of silt built up the crown of the delta. The Colorado
was playing the same game with Imperial as has the Hoang-ho
for so many centuries with China. The other name for the
Hoang-ho is "China's Sorrow," and trying to back up the Colorado with levees was only preparing a greater sorrow for Imperial Valley.

For the Valley, gaining all the while in wealth and population in spite of the handicap under which its people laboured,
it now became a question simply of holding on until permanent
relief could be obtained. All hopes of vanquishing the Colorado on the delta were given up. The Valley began, as it were,
watching and praying by its sodden levees in flood season and
working and praying for a control-dam in the upper canyons
the rest of the time. As the hopes of finally clearing the way
for a dam brightened with the passing of the years, the threat
from the failure of wide sections of levees increased. At length
there came a rise which was only prevented from overtopping

the Volcano Lake Levee for many miles by the wooden barrow-way along the top.

Beaten to its knees again on the defence, the Valley turned to the last resort of a failing defensive—an offensive. Since the river had proved that it could raise the silt-bed of Volcano Lake faster than dirt could be piled on top of the levees, there was nothing left to do but to try to keep the river out of that great settling basin. The Valley, in short, was left no alternative but to try to do what the Government had signally failed to accomplish in 1911.

The plan prepared by Chief Engineer Ray Carberry of the Imperial Irrigation District contemplated the diversion of the Colorado, not to its original channel east of the breached Ockerson Levee, but to the network of drainage channels of the Pescadero, a tributary of the Hardy. During the winter of 1922 a channel was excavated through the divide between the Bee and the Pescadero at the most favourable point, work on a diversion dam being pushed at the same time. No elaborate engineering went into the construction of the barrage. Cory had learned that the only way to beat the Colorado was to dump blocks of rock into it faster than they could be carried away. That was the bludgeoning method employed here, and by a fortunate chance there was available for Superintendent of Construction a young engineer with the chest of a prize-fighter and the jaw of a bulldog, called Frank Higley.

Higley was licked half a dozen times, according to reliable reports, but because he was so engrossed countering the rough-stuff of the river with some rather hefty little jolts of his own, never seems to have known about it. All through the spring rise he fought a rough-and-tumble with the roaring wild bull of the Colorado. Time and again rock-trains were nearly lost, and once a pile-driver with its crew. The bulldog strain in the young engineer kept him plugging away at what just about every one else felt was a losing fight, and one morning in June, coming up a bit groggy for what he expected to be the final round at the crest of the rise, he was rewarded by finding a tamed and beaten antagonist slinking off down the Pescadero Cut with its tail between its legs.

Four months later, trying to boat through to the Gulf after visiting the dam-sites of the upper canyons, I picked up Frank Higley at Andrade and took him on down into the delta on a hunt for the maverick Colorado. Ray Priest, Chief Engineer of the Yuma Project, was also added to my crew. He and Higley occasionally discussed some technical point of the Pescadero diversion job in the course of the week we fought mud and mosquitoes down the track of the lost and wandering river, but about all I ever got out of the boss of that notably successful piece of engineering was to the effect that he had bet ten dollars with his Chief, Carberry, that he would make the dam stick, and that he had come pretty near to losing the money.

Greatly to the credit of Ray Carberry and the engineering staff of the Imperial Irrigation District as is the turning of the Colorado into the Pescadero Cut and away from Volcano Lake, even those who so brilliantly planned and carried out the work do not consider it as other than a stop-gap calculated to reduce the threat to Imperial Valley until a control dam can be built in the canyons. The dam across the Bee may go out in the spring floods of this year, or, by constant strengthening and levee work, it may be possible to keep it intact for five or ten years. That is largely on the lap of the Gods of the Thunder who slap down the sudden cloudbursts onto the Gila drainage basin. Just where the Colorado decides to put down its next silt barrage will also have something to do with it. Not far below the four-miles-long Pescadero Cut we found where the flow of the late diversion had left behind it a stratum of mud half way up to the tops of the mesquite. No levee gang can compete for long with a river capable of building up the crown of a delta cone ten feet and more a year.

With the ever imminent threat of destruction by the Colo-

rado, with the handicaps imposed by the fact that the project
was originally financed on a shoestring and has been hard put
for money ever since, with the ever formidable difficulties in-
separable from desert reclamation, and finally with the visitation of troubles that have descended upon farmers generally
in the post-war adjustment period, it would not have been
surprising if Imperial Valley had faltered in its fight for existence, or even abandoned the struggle entirely. That this has
not happened has been largely due to two causes. The first
of these is the fact that the project—with abundant water, a
great area of rich land and a remarkable growing climate—
was so basically sound that it had the strength to struggle
ahead under a load that would have crushed to earth an ordinary farming community. The second is the fact that the very
nature of the fight for life the Valley was making drew to it
a population of fighters. The process was selective. Those
who could stand the gaff remained on the fighting line; those
who could not retired to the softer life of the established communities. The resident-owner of a farmstead in Imperial Valley to-day is the exemplar of as indomitable a courage as was
ever shown in that most inspiring chapter of American history
so well called the Winning of the West.

Unlike the farmers under the projects of the United States
Reclamation Service, who have been carried by the Government during bad years, those of Imperial have had to finance
themselves from the outset. With lands liable to complete and
permanent submersion not unnaturally rated as practically
prohibitive risks by the bankers, this has become increasingly
difficult with the passage of the years. Then there has been
the cost of levee work and other flood protective measures, and,
more recently, the assessments for the comprehensive drainage system which should have been constructed years ago. At
the same time there have had to be combated the evils of a pernicious system of tenant farming, fastened upon the Valley as
a consequence of a disproportionate number of absentee own-

ers. And, finally, in the face of the after-the-war slump that hit farmers so hard all over the country, there has had to be devised and perfected an adequate co-operative system of handling the Valley's unprecedentedly large production of melons, lettuce and other perishable crops, involving intricate and difficult problems of shipping and marketing.

And yet under the burden of these all-but-prohibitive handicaps the Valley has never ceased to go ahead, even in times of deepest depression. There have been years of restricted prosperity but none of restricted progress. The early boom towns grew into modern cities, and an extension of irrigation did not prevent the intensification of cultivation. A half million acres have been brought under canal on the American side of the line, and over half that area on the Mexican. The annual value of crops produced in the lands north of the international boundary now averages over $60,000,000 a year; that from those south of the line perhaps thirty percent of that figure.

In every sense but a political one the irrigated area below the Mexican line is an integral part of Imperial Valley, and should be considered and treated as such. It has been developed by American money and brains, and it has drawn its supplies and equipment from the American side just as it has marketed all of its products there. Having been held from the first in comparatively large tracts, this southern area has been better financed, better farmed and better managed as a whole than that on the American side. It has, therefore, probably averaged better returns to the acre. This is notably true in the case of cotton which, profitable only in spots during the last three or four years north of the line, has continued to yield good returns on the large scientifically farmed ranches below the border. Not in Egypt nor even the famed Delta region of Mississippi will one see finer cotton fields than those through which he rides for miles in driving from Calexico to the head of the Gulf.

The integrity of the American and Mexican sections of the

Imperial Valley should be borne very fully in mind in any final adjustment of Colorado River problems. The same dog-in-the-manger lot of politicians who have so far succeeded in preventing the ratification of the Santa Fé Pact by Arizona would, if they could have their way, deprive the Americans opening up the Mexican end of Imperial Valley of water for further development—possibly even of that which they have heretofore used. International law would doubtless intervene to prevent so gross an injustice, but the exercise of just a little common sense and common decency, to say nothing of a spirit of fair play, should make legal arbitrament unnecessary. Not that a professional politician could be expected to exercise any of these amenities; but when it comes to a final show-down on Colorado Basin affairs there is not much doubt that there will be rallied enough plain, honest, every-day citizens to do a few important things in spite of the politicians.

The fact that the annual value of crops produced in the Imperial Valley will amount to over $100,000,000 if another decade is passed without an inundation would seem to be sufficient argument on the practical side as to why the Government should expend half that sum on a control-dam to insure the continuance and increase of that production. The saving of Imperial Valley alone, to say nothing of the similarly endangered Palo Verde Project, would warrant double that expenditure as insurance. There are a number of other practical reasons for the step, all of which I shall touch upon in my next chapter.

But there is still another reason—classifiable, I fear, rather as sentimental than practical—that I should like to advance in support of Imperial Valley's claim to a helping hand from the Government at this time. Although it has eventuated chronologically half a century and more after the advent of the original pioneers, nothing in American history has more strikingly typified the fighting spirit of all American pioneers than the struggle of the people of Imperial Valley to save their homes from the Colorado. The fights of the first pioneers have become matters of history. They have been celebrated in song, in story and in bronze. *This* fight has been in our own time; it has been put up by our own contemporaries. Some even of us outsiders have been at times in the thick of it; all of us have read of it in our morning papers. What more peculiarly fitting tribute could America pay to the memory of her whole army of pioneers than by erecting a great control dam on the Colorado for the benefit of the brave band that will have fought to a victorious finish the last, though by no means the least, of America's pioneering battles?

CHAPTER III

TRYING TO SEIZE THE BULL BY THE HORNS

BECAUSE a series of great dams in the middle canyon section of the Colorado River would serve three distinct if somewhat interlocking purposes, the adjustment of problems leading up to such development is peculiarly complicated and difficult. A dam intended to provide only for flood control might vary in type and location from one intended to store and divert water solely for irrigation. Similarly, development of the river for power alone would call for a different disposition of dams than for flood control or irrigation. The joint solution called for, obviously, would be a compromise between the ideal solution of each.

Although it was realized from the outset that any dam erected in the Colorado canyons would have to be of a size and cost incomparably greater than those of any similar structures hitherto constructed, the technical aspects of the problem never awakened serious doubts in the minds of engineers. The need of such a dam was recognized from the time it became evident that the endeavour to control the lower Colorado by levees was no more than an emergency expedient. In the early years of the present century the apparent hopelessness of making a control-dam yield other than indirect returns prevented the serious consideration of so costly a project. Then came the extension of practicable long-distance electrical transmission and the great increase of the southwestern power market, and the financial part of the problem was solved almost over night. A dam large enough to furnish adequate flood-control and at the same time enormously increase the volume of water available for irrigation, could be made to pay for itself out of the sale

411

of power. That left nothing but political obstacles blocking the otherwise open road to fulfilment. The differences between the seven states of the Colorado River drainage basin remained to be ironed out and an appropriation secured from Congress to defray the cost of the work. The former was in order to be adjusted first. Congress could not be expected to appropriate money for a project that was liable to be tied up indefinitely by inter-state disputes.

Besides the usual run of petty jealousies fostered by the state politician and booster, there were important and honest differences between what have been called the Upper and Lower Basins of the Colorado. The four states of the Upper Basin were apprehensive that a great expansion of irrigation below the dividing middle canyons would, in accordance with American law, establish water-rights covering so considerable a part of the flow of the river that development in Utah, Colorado, Wyoming and New Mexico would be permanently restricted. The states of the Lower Basin, on the other hand, feared that irrigation might become so widespread in the upper states that there would not be enough water left in the river to serve the ultimate needs of Arizona, Nevada and California. The fact that the whole low-water flow of the Colorado had been turned into the canals of the Yuma and Imperial Projects was as much of a danger signal for one group of states as for the other.

There were two ways open for clearing up the points at issue —one by litigation and the other by arbitration. As water-right cases between certain of the upper states had already been in the courts for ten or twelve years, the futility of litigation except as a last resort was evident. The plan of arbitration adopted reflected the sound common sense of those who devised it. A Colorado River Commission was formed, consisting of one Commissioner from each of the seven states of the Basin, with Herbert Hoover, Secretary of the Department of Commerce, as Chairman. This body was authorized to meet and frame a compact under which a comprehensive plan of de-

ARTHUR POWELL DAVIS, DIRECTOR U. S. RECLAMATION SERVICE.
An outstanding figure in Colorado River development.

AT PEACH SPRINGS, ON WAY TO DIAMOND CREEK DAM SITE.

Left, Arthur P. Davis; middle, the Author;
right, W. S. Norviel.

velopment for the Colorado could be undertaken. This was finally accomplished in the now historic gathering of November, 1922, in Santa Fé, New Mexico.

The signing of the Santa Fé Compact was an epoch-marking event in more respects than one. Outstandingly important as the first tangible step toward the settlement of the vexing problems of the Colorado Basin, it also has the distinction of being the first successful instance of arbitration between more than two states of the American Union. That an agreement was arrived at in so comparatively short a time is attributable to three things: first, that the conflict of interests between the several states was more fancied than real, due to the fact that the properly conserved waters of the Colorado are sufficient for the needs of all of them; second, that commissioners representing the several states were men of open and flexible minds; and third, that Herbert Hoover was Chairman of the Commission. Possibly the latter was the most important consideration of the three. There is only one Hoover, and it needed a man with his genius for conciliation, his clear-sightedness, his sincerity of purpose to develop the strategy of the situation. In any event, the fact that the Pact was framed and signed with so little friction and in so conciliatory a spirit bodes well for the future relations of the states of the Colorado Basin once they are lifted out of the wallow of cheap politics.

The distribution of the irrigable land in the seven states of the Colorado Basin is shown in the table on page 414.

The crux of the problem of the Colorado River Commission was that of assuring each state a water supply sufficient not only for its land already irrigated but for that potentially irrigable as well. When it was shown that the average annual flow of the Colorado—in excess of 15,000,000 acre-feet—was more than equal to this service if adequately conserved in reservoirs, the problem became one of devising a plan under which this water should be fairly divided among the states entitled to its use. The real touch of genius in the Compact was contained in the provision that the waters of the river—subject to certain limitations—should be equally divided between the Upper and the Lower Basins, leaving the states of each basin to work out the ultimate distributions among themselves.

Table of Colorado River Acreage

	Acreage irrigated 1920.	New acreage.	Total acreage.
Lower basin:			
Arizona	507,000	640,000	1,147,000
California	450,000	490,000	940,000
Nevada	5,000	35,000	40,000
Total	962,000	1,165,000	2,127,000
Upper basin:			
Colorado	740,000	1,018,000	1,758,000
New Mexico	34,000	483,000	517,000
Utah	359,000	456,000	815,000
Wyoming	367,000	543,000	910,000
Total	1,500,000	2,500,000	4,000,000

Secretary Hoover gave the following reasons for dividing the Colorado River and its tributaries into two basins, as provided in Article II of the Compact:

"(a) The commission, upon analysis, found that the causes of present friction and of major future disputes lay between the lower basin States and the upper basin States, and that very little likelihood of friction lay between the States within each basin; that the delays to development at the present time are wholly interbasinal disputes; and that major development is not likely to be impeded by disputes between States within each basin. And in any event the Compact provides machinery for such settlements.

"(b) The drainage area falls into two basins naturally, from a geographical, hydrographical, and an economic point of view. They are separated by over 500 miles of barren canyon which serves as the neck of the funnel, into which the drainage area comprised in the upper basin pours its waters, and these waters again spread over the lands of the lower basin.

"(c) The climate of the two basins is different; that of the upper basin being, generally speaking, temperate, while that of the lower basin ranges from semitropical to tropical. The growing seasons, the crops, and the quantity of water consumed per acre are therefore different.

"(d) The economic conditions in the two basins are entirely different. The upper basin will be slower of development than the lower basin. The upper basin will secure its waters more by diversion than by storage, whereas the development of the lower basin is practically altogether a storage problem.

"(e) The major friction at the present moment is over the water rights which might be established by the erection of adequate storage in the lower basin, as prejudicing the situation in the upper basin, and regardless of legal rights in either case. The States are now divided into two groups in opposition to each other legislatively, with little hope of the cohesion that is necessary before Federal aid can ever be secured.

"The use of the group method of division was therefore adopted both from necessity, as being the only practical one, and from advisability, being dictated by the conditions existing in the entire basin."

Next to the equal division of the water of the Colorado between the states of the Upper and the Lower Basins, perhaps the most important point established by the Santa Fé pact is that so lucidly and explicitly set forth in this statement of Secretary Hoover—that the problems of these two great areas, separated by hundreds of miles of desert, are radically divergent and that those of each should be treated as a unity. This would seem to indicate that it was in the mind of the Commission that each division should work out its peculiar problems independently of the other. If this first great flood-control, irrigation and power project can be construed as primarily a problem of the Lower Basin, certainly one of the most potentially troublesome sources of friction has been removed at the outset.

With each basin free to act independently in determining

what projects are best suited to its own peculiar needs, and free to present its claims to the Federal Government for assistance, the chances for future interbasinal disputes are reduced to a minimum. Even with a ratified Compact, an attempt to locate the great initial project at some compromise location where it would be calculated to serve equally the states of each basin would inevitably result in an interminable series of disputes that could hardly fail to culminate in a complete deadlock. With both basins at liberty to concentrate on their own problems, subject only to the limitations imposed on each as regards the total amount of water used (and, of course, ability to secure financial help from the Federal Government), no insuperable difficulties ought ever to arise.

It is Secretary Hoover's idea that the development of the Lower Basin should be under the direction of a conservation board created by and acting on behalf of California, Nevada and Arizona. Once the pact is ratified, such a board would take up the question of deciding the character and location of the dam or dams best calculated to facilitate the three prime *desiderata*—flood-control, irrigation and power development—for the mutual benefit of the states of the lower division. This board would act subject to another wise provision laid down by the pact, namely, that agriculture shall take precedence over power. As Secretary Hoover has said: "It has been the feeling not only of the Commission, but practically unanimously through the West, that it is far more to the interest of America that we should develop homes out under the blue sky than that we should stifle our agriculture for the benefit of our industry."

The principle thus established may be interpreted to mean that flood-control shall be given first consideration in any comprehensive plan of development on the Colorado, that irrigation shall be reckoned as second in importance, and power as third. On the other hand it is established that, in paying for this development, the order shall be reversed. That is to say, the sale of power shall bear the bulk of the burden, with irriga-

tion and flood-control to be assessed for a share of the costs
only in the event power proves unable to carry the whole load.
By establishing this order of priority at the outset a potentially
dangerous source of friction is avoided, for there are many
deeply interested parties who contend that, as power is to pay
most if not all of the cost of all construction, the exigencies
of power development should be given consideration before all
others.   There is undeniably much to be said for this contention, but as the specific ruling of the Commission definitely re-
moves it from the controversial stage, that phase of the question will not arise in the event of the ratification of the Compact.

The possibilities of a Colorado harnessed and put to work
make a serious demand upon the imagination.   More than
four million horse-power of electric energy delivered to the
railroads, mines and factories within a five-hundred-mile radius
of the point of generation; four million acres of new land
brought under cultivation; homes and work for from three to
six million people—that is a way of putting it by and large.
But that glittering side of the shield has already come in for a
disproportionate amount of attention.   Ultimate possibilities
are all very well to carry in the back of the head, but of far
greater relative importance at the present juncture are the
practical aspects of getting under way at the earliest possible
moment with a single project that will lift the menace from
the Imperial and Palo Verde Valleys and at the same time furnish power for the already depleted markets of the southwestern states.   It is estimated that a dam adequate for these purposes will be twice the height of any in existence at the present
time, and of ten times greater storage capacity.   It will require
from five to ten years to build, and at least two years for the
entire flow of the river to fill the reservoir created by it.

Three further steps will have to be taken before the way
to the actual construction of such a dam is open.   In the first
place, the Compact as signed at Santa Fé must be ratified by

the legislatures of the several states of the Colorado Basin and by Congress. Failing such ratification there is no way to final adjustment save through the courts, and, judging by the rate at which litigation of this character has moved in the past, El Centro and Brawley might well be a hundred feet below the level of Salton Sea before a decision is reached.

The ratification of the States and of the Federal Government once secured, the next step will be for the boards of conservation acting for the respective basins to come to decisions as to where the first great dam of each shall be built and of what size and type it shall be; all of this, of course, under the advice of the best engineers available and in the light of the comprehensive studies that have been and will be made of the intricate problems involved. As a third and final step leading up to construction, an appropriation to cover the cost of the work will have to be secured from Congress. This, of course, is the order of action only in the event that the whole of the development is carried out by the Government. In the event certain projects, or series of projects, are turned over to private corporations, the engineers of the latter, doubtless in collaboration with those of the Federal Power Commission, will locate and design the dams, and the corporations will find their own money.

At the time of writing even the first of these three hurdles— that of ratification of the Santa Fé Compact—has not been cleared. The legislatures of six of the seven states of the Colorado Basin have given the agreement their approval by decisive votes; that of one—Arizona—has withheld complete ratification on a close division. As the Pact cannot be taken up by Congress until ratification by the states is unanimous, this action of Arizona—the result of the usual petty and sordid political squabble—deadlocks indefinitely the most desperately urgent relief measure that has come before the country for many years. Under the circumstances any discussion of the trend of Colorado River development based on the Compact assumes a somewhat academic character, or rather, it would do so were it not for the fact that it is unthinkable that the states of the Southwest will ever allow the fate of Imperial Valley to hang upon the glacial processes of the courts when direct and speedy action for relief can be inaugurated by the ratification of a treaty that all but a clique of selfish and short-sighted politicians agree is eminently fair to all concerned. Arizona must line up with her six sister states of the Basin in time, though she may have to flush her political stables with the whole flow of the Colorado to clear the way for action. On the assumption, therefore, that the states of the Colorado Basin will elect to facilitate action by agreement rather than to block it by litigation, I shall discuss very briefly the salient problems of flood-control, irrigation and power development as they will have to be approached when the way is finally cleared.

Perhaps the most weighty questions that will have to be decided by whatever body works out the plan for the Lower Basin will be those relating to the type and location of the first great dam. If a faulty type of dam is constructed, the consequences might well be disaster ten-fold more dire than that which the structure was primarily built to prevent. Similarly, a failure to locate the dam in the most favourable place to serve the triple purpose of flood-control, reclamation and power generation would entail losses that could not be fully rectified for generations. There are perfectly honest differences of opinion among the most highly qualified engineers as to both type and location, and variously ramified questions arising therefrom have been the subject of illuminative and constructive controversial discussion for several years.

The most carefully studied and comprehensively outlined plan for the development of the Lower Basin which has been put before the public is that prepared by the engineers of the U. S. Reclamation Service under the direction of Arthur Powell Davis. As a nephew of Major John Wesley Powell, first navigator of the Grand Canyon, it is peculiarly fitting that Arthur Davis should take a leading part in the final conquest of the

Colorado.   During more than forty years divided almost equally between the Geological Survey and the Reclamation Service—the last decade as the Director of the latter—he has brilliantly carried on the Powell tradition of setting face toward a goal and never turning back until it was attained.   The inauguration of work on a complete plan of harnessing and driving the Colorado before the close of Mr. Davis' Directorship would appropriately crown a career of public service rivalling even that of his illustrious uncle.[1]

The Reclamation Service recommends the construction of a masonry dam, ultimately six hundred feet in height, to be located either near the head of Boulder Canyon, a few miles below the mouth of the Virgin River, or in Black Canyon, which—save for a break of a few miles—is a southerly continuation of Boulder.   A number of reasons are advanced as to why either of these sites is preferable to any other, or to any combination of others, on the river.   It has, for instance, been suggested that the building of two dams of comparatively small size and cost—one at Flaming Gorge, on the Green, and one at the Dewey site, on the Grand—would be the most expeditious and least costly way of effecting flood-control.   Mr. Davis points out that, while the two sites mentioned are among the most favourable on the whole river from a technical standpoint, their use for flood-control would make them almost useless for power purposes, the one for which they are naturally best adapted.   He also shows that even for flood-control they would be far less effective than a dam located below the middle canyons, principally because the upper dams would not intercept the brief but torrential floods from fully three-quarters of the Colorado drainage area.   It is demonstrated, in short, that no combination or series of reservoirs on the upper tributaries could furnish as complete control as storage farther down; and, moreover, that to attempt to use reservoirs at these upper sites

[1] The unexpected resignation of Mr. Davis from the Directorship of the Reclamation Service will make this consummation impossible.   It cannot, however, affect the value of his twoscore years of service.

for flood-control would almost nullify them for power and irrigation.

Over a dam above Lee's Ferry, near the foot of Glen Canyon, Mr. Davis claims that the Boulder Canyon structure would have the advantage of holding "a little more water for a given height of dam." He also shows that the former would intercept the drainage from fifty thousand square miles of basin that the latter would miss, and that the transmission from Boulder Canyon to the main power market, the Pacific Coast, is rather less than half that imposed by a structure at Glen Canyon. He further shows that Boulder Canyon construction, being but forty miles from a main-line railway, would have an advantage in transportation charges over Glen Canyon, which is more than three times that distance from such a line. Again, for both flood-control and irrigation, a reservoir at Boulder Canyon would make possible a far more effective and economical handling of the water than one situated three hundred and fifty miles farther up the river. Finally, the native rock—the granite of Boulder Canyon and the rhyolite of Black Canyon— are far more favourable for dam foundations than the comparatively soft sandstones of Glen Canyon.

The dam that the engineers of the Reclamation Service recommend for the Boulder Canyon site would, if carried to its full height of six hundred feet, impound something like thirty million acre-feet of water—not quite two years' flow of the Colorado. Allowing the upper five million acre-feet for flood-control, there would still be available sufficient head to develop six hundred thousand firm horse-power of electrical energy. The cost of the dam proper is estimated at forty-eight million dollars, and that of the hydro-electric installation at about the same figure. There is no doubt that the sale of the power could be effected at a rate that would completely defray the round hundred million that it may be assumed would be spent before the dam and electrical installation are complete. This would obviate the necessity of making any charge against either flood-control or irrigation. Any new lands brought under water would, of course, have to stand the costs of their own diversions and distributions. But immunity from flood and an ample supply of water for all time would be theirs without direct contribution to the cost of the dam which conferred these boons.

In a recent letter Mr. Davis has outlined in considerable detail why the engineers of the Reclamation Service believe that the interlocking problems of the Lower Basin would be most effectually solved by a dam in Boulder or Black Canyon. He writes:

"The greatest financial asset to be established by the control of the Colorado is the development of water power. Heretofore this has been considered impracticable on account of the great distance of the sites on the Colorado from adequate markets. This difficulty is still the greatest to be overcome. . . . Any increase in the distance of transmission not only increases the cost of the transmission lines but involves heavy expense later for maintenance and perpetual loss of power in transmission. It is impossible to transmit power at all without losses, and these increase more rapidly than the distance. For this reason a power project at Glen Canyon is to-day practically out of the question. . . .

"The principal markets for power to be developed are the cities of the Pacific Coast, which are rapidly growing, and the towns and mining regions of Arizona. The Pacific Coast region is as a practical matter a market at least five times as important as the markets of Arizona.

"The site at Diamond Creek is much nearer the Arizona markets than the one in Glen Canyon and a few miles nearer these markets than the one in Boulder Canyon. It can only develop a small amount of firm power unless storage is provided, and in the natural state of the river will furnish water enough to develop sufficient power for the Arizona markets, but it would require about a sixty-mile longer transmission line to the Pacific Coast than would be required from Boulder Canyon, and this would so seriously handicap it, especially with the small amount of power available there, that it could not be considered feasible to-day nor in the near future to do this.

"The most eligible large power site on the Colorado River at the present time is at Boulder Canyon or its alternative location for a dam in Black Canyon. This would eventually be built to the elevation of 1,360 feet (above sea level), which is the elevation of the mouth of Diamond Creek. The present demands for power and for other purposes would hardly justify so high a dam just now, and so it is proposed to build a lower dam so designed that it can be carried to a greater height when the need arises in the future. This need may arise by the growth of a power market and is sure to come at some future time by the encroachment of impounded sediment upon the storage capacity. The proper regulation of floods in the lower Colorado demands a capacity of about 12,000,000 acre-feet. This would be depleted, however, by the accumulation of sediment at a rate which in round numbers may be taken to be as 100,000 acre-feet per annum. . . . It would be advisable, therefore, to build a reservoir considerably larger so as to postpone the date when additional storage would be required for silt storage, and I am therefore proposing a dam somewhere from 20,000,000 to 26,000,000 acre-feet capacity, depending upon the facility of financing and probable demands for power. . . . This will furnish complete control of floods, regulation for irrigation, and a large amount of power. It will be more than a century before additional storage will be needed on account of silt. At that time it can be carried to its full height unless for other reasons it is done sooner.

"As soon as this reservoir is completed the regulation of the river which it will accomplish will render valuable two smaller sites below —one at Bull's Head and one at Parker, both of which are of value for irrigation and both of which lie slightly nearer the markets of the Pacific Coast and Arizona than Boulder Canyon, and they should undoubtedly follow the first construction at Boulder Canyon. After they are built the next move where power is required would be to carry Boulder Canyon up to its ultimate height of 1,360 feet, backing the water to the mouth of Diamond Creek.

"It is important that as much power as practicable be ultimately developed at Boulder Canyon because no point above there is so near the markets of the Pacific Coast, and there is important economy in concentrating the development at one point because it costs no more to operate a large power house than a small one. . . . On account of the accessibility of Diamond Creek I have selected this as the logical upper limit of Boulder Canyon development, and Diamond Creek would ultimately follow the exhaustion of the market supply from Boulder Canyon.

"In the meantime it is probable that the development of the Dewey site on Grand River, and one or more of those on Green River, will so regulate the flow of the Colorado that the Diamond Creek site will have the advantage of the regulated river, which will probably treble the amount of firm power that can be developed there.

"The above facts ought to be convincing that from a financial standpoint the Boulder Canyon reservoir is the first one to build; and this conclusion is greatly emphasized when we take up the different subjects of flood control. . . . The greatest menace under which the Imperial Valley rests is the possibility of a concurrence of a flood on the Gila with one from the Colorado. The Gila floods generally come in the winter and early spring; smaller floods in the late summer. There is much difference in the Arizona climate and that of the upper Rocky Mountain regions, the floods from the high mountains occurring in times of melting snow and therefore in early summer. There are, however, about 50,000 square miles of drainage in northern and western Arizona and southern Utah which are similar in climate to the Gila. They drain about the same area as the Gila and may be regarded as subject to similar floods. The great menace, however, lies in the fact that they are likely to occur at the same time. It is of record that the greatest flood ever known at Yuma was caused by a coincidence of floods in the Colorado and Gila— the Gila discharging about 200,000 and the main Colorado about 40,000, made a total flood of 240,000 second-feet in January, 1916. Less than ten days later the Colorado furnished about 70,000, and had this coincided with the Gila flood it would have made a dangerous flood wave, much larger than any yet of record.

"A dam regulating the Colorado at Boulder Canyon would have reduced such a flood materially, while one at Glen Canyon, regulating the flow to 20,000 second-feet, would have increased it, because the flood-wave must have come in below Glen Canyon, which is fed from high regions frozen up at this season. The 50,000 square mile area, which has a climate similar to that of the Gila and is capable of furnishing a flood at the same time as the Gila, is not intercepted by a reservoir site located above Boulder Canyon, but is nearly all intercepted by that site."

Owing to the well-deserved confidence which the public has in the Reclamation Service, and, especially, to the great personal prestige of Director Davis, the Boulder Canyon project is the only plan for lower Colorado River development respecting which there is any considerable popular knowledge. Still further confidence in the plans of the Reclamation Service has been engendered by the fact that they have had the unqualified approval and backing of Secretary Hoover from the time he was appointed to the Chairmanship of the Colorado River Commission. With the run of Californians the endorsement of the man who fed Belgium carries great weight, which accounts for the fact that most of the Chambers of Commerce and other public bodies of that state have passed resolutions favouring Boulder Canyon.

Arizona shows somewhat less of a crystallization of sentiment in favour of a dam at Boulder Canyon than does California. This is doubtless due to the fact that the great industrial interests of the interior state feel that they would be better served by the carrying out of the Girand project for a power dam at Diamond Creek, with a great storage reservoir in the vicinity of Lee's Ferry, near the foot of Glen Canyon. In the irrigation areas—actual and potential—down the river, however, Boulder Canyon sentiment is predominant, just as in Imperial Valley.

I have set down, I think, a fair statement of the case of the Boulder Canyon project, and a fair estimate of the strong backing it has, technical, political and popular. The support of a dam at Lee's Ferry is technical rather than popular, yet it is of a character that it would be a mistake to ignore in locating a work which must stand for centuries. Several eminent engineers have gone on record as of the opinion that the exigencies of Colorado River development would be better served by storage at Lee's Ferry than at Boulder Canyon. Perhaps the most active of the proponents of this project is E.C. La Rue, one of the ablest hydraulic engineers of the Geological Survey. His "Colorado River and its Utilization" (Water Supply Paper 395), published in 1916, is still rated as the most authoritative and comprehensive work on that subject. Since that time Mr. La Rue has done much further investigation on the river, his studies extending from far above the mouth of the Green to Yuma, and missing no considerable sector of the drainage area save that of the Grand Canyon proper. This latter stretch he is covering in the summer and fall of 1923 as hydraulic engineer of the Geological Survey party that is completing the Colorado River survey in the course of a boat voyage through Marble and Grand Canyons. In actual first-hand knowledge of the water problems of the Colorado, therefore, he is unquestionably the leading authority in the country to-day. It is this fact, with his unquestioned sincerity and disinterest, that has given weight to La Rue's contentions and won him the support of engineers of national reputation.

Mr. La Rue holds that the natural conditions for dam construction at the Lee's Ferry site are so much more favourable than at any other, that the Reclamation Service has made a serious mistake in not investigating it fully before getting behind Boulder Canyon. It is his opinion that these natural advantages are more than sufficient to offset the greater remoteness of Lee's Ferry, so that the construction of any given type of dam can be effected for less cost at the latter site. This assumption is based on the estimate that bedrock at Lee's Ferry is not deeper than from fifty to eighty feet, as against the one hundred and thirty-five that the drills have shown it to lie at Boulder Canyon. As preliminary diamond drilling done by the Southern California Edison Company during the winter of 1922-3 appears to have shown that La Rue's estimates of the depth of bedrock at Lee's Ferry are conservative, there would seem to be reason in his contention that this site should be fully investigated before eliminating it as a possibility.

No less an authority than O. C. Merrill, Executive Secretary of the Federal Power Commission, has put on record views practically coinciding with those advanced by Mr. La Rue. In a recent Congressional Document [1] he is quoted as saying:

"If foundation conditions are not more unfavourable, this site (Lee's Ferry) should from the construction standpoint have distinct advantages over the Boulder Canyon site. The river forms a double loop at the dam site, one half of which is twenty-eight thousand feet round, but at its narrowest parts only three thousand and six hundred feet across at the water level and only two thousand feet at five hundred feet above water level. This condition provides better opportunity for handling water during construction than at Boulder Canyon, and also affords better opportunity for constructing outlet works and spillway independent of the dam by carrying the one through and the other over the narrow section which separates the two sides of the loop.

"The fact that this (the Lee's Ferry) reservoir must eventually be built in connection with power developments below, and that when built it is likely of itself to solve the flood problems of the main river, has naturally raised the question, 'Why build both Glen Canyon (Lee's Ferry) and Boulder Canyon, or, if both, why build the latter first?' The construction of Glen Canyon reservoir by eliminating flood conditions would make the construction of all dams in the river below far easier, cheaper and safer. Nothing which may be done at Boulder Canyon will obviate to any degree the eventual necessity of Glen Canyon reservoir or reduce the difficulties of other construction in the canyon above. On the other hand, if Glen Canyon is built, the greater part of Boulder Canyon storage— as storage—would become useless. It would seem, therefore, that the prior construction of this dam (Boulder Canyon) would be justified only on one or both of two grounds: Either that the imminence of the peril to the Imperial Valley justifies the cost of the Boulder Canyon Dam even if only temporarily required for flood control purposes; or that the cost is justified independently of storage, by the additional power that could thus be produced by a dam of the height proposed. . . . Which reservoir should be built first, and whether the full capacity of both is needed, are questions

[1] Hearings before the Committee on Irrigation of Arid Lands, House of Representatives, Sixty-seventh Congress, 2nd Session, on H. R. 11,449, by Mr. Swing, a Bill to Provide for the Protection and Development of the Lower Colorado River Basin.

about which there is considerable difference of opinion. I shall only say that there appears to be enough doubt to warrant a thorough study of the upper site before commitment is made to Boulder Canyon, and that in such study due consideration should be given to power development in the middle section, as well as to irrigation and flood control on the lower section. I have placed emphasis upon this question of the location of primary storage, whether at the head or the foot of the middle section, because it is a factor of great importance in the problems of power development and may determine the whole course of such development upon the river."

Mr. La Rue, admitting that the remoteness of the Lee's Ferry site makes power development at that point impracticable under the limitations of the present-day transmission, suggests the following as a compromise project that would combine the advantages of single great dams at Boulder Canyon and Lee's Ferry, and which he believes could be constructed in less time, and at less cost, than either: A dam at Lee's Ferry of a height to impound sufficient water for flood control only, supplemented by a power dam in the Grand Canyon at Diamond Creek. A dam at the upper site four hundred feet high and storing eight-million acre-feet would be ample to give flood control and equate the flow of the river. With the flow equalized, a two-hundred-foot dam at Diamond Creek would serve to make possible the development of two hundred thousand horse-power at that point. From Diamond Creek the transmission to the main power market of Southern California is not many miles greater than that from Boulder Canyon, while that to the mines of Arizona would be considerably shorter. Mr. La Rue further recommends that the feasibility of making the Lee's Ferry structure of rock-fill type be carefully investigated. Should a dam of this type—made by blowing in the side walls of the canyon—prove practicable, a great saving in cost would be effected.[1]

[1] Commenting on this plan, Director Davis writes: "The compromise you have mentioned involves the construction of two dams, one in Glen Canyon to store the water, and another at Diamond Creek to develop power.

ENGINEERS OF GEOLOGICAL SURVEY AND RECLAMATION SERVICE STUDYING LEE'S FERRY DAM SITE.

DIAMOND DRILLS AT WORK ON THE BOULDER CANYON DAM SITE.

Besides the topographical survey of the two alternative dam sites at Lee's Ferry, the investigations carried out at that point up to midsummer of 1923 are limited to some preliminary diamond drill work by the Southern California Edison Company and a study by a board of engineers sent in by the Reclamation Service to examine the proposed sites and lay out a plan for carrying on comprehensive drilling operations with a view to testing the depth, character and conformation of the bedrock. While no detailed report of the Edison investigations has been made public, it is understood bedrock conditions entirely favourable to the construction of a large dam were revealed. The preliminary report of the board of Reclamation Service engineers, on the other hand, compared the sites unfavourably with those of Boulder Canyon. This was mostly on grounds outlined above by Mr. Davis, but a new disadvantage of considerable weight was disclosed in the discovery that the sandstone of the canyon walls at Lee's Ferry is not well suited for either sand or concrete aggregate.

There is still so much to be said in favour of Lee's Ferry that one cannot but consider Mr. Merrill in good point when he wrote that "there is enough doubt to warrant a study of the upper site before commitment is made to Boulder Canyon." If the claims of the proponents of Lee's Ferry are borne out, the time and expense of preliminary studies at that point will be more than compensated for by the favourable natural conditions for construction. Arizona's deadlocking of action on the Compact will give ample time to make the necessary investigations without danger of imposing any delay upon ulti-

---

To develop an equal amount of power the dam at Diamond Creek would have to be nearly as high as the one at Boulder Canyon, and it would be much farther from the markets of the Pacific Coast, which are absolutely necessary to the feasibility of any project so large. We would then have two great dams on the Colorado River instead of one, to accomplish results not so good because farther from the market. This obviously is not so economical nor so wise. The Pacific Coast is unavoidably going to be a great center of population, and as a permanent policy it is imperative that the developments at Boulder Canyon, which is the nearest feasible development on the river to that market, be eventually the maximum amount."

mate action. Undue delay from any cause is, of course, the thing above all others to be guarded against. The risk to Imperial Valley is too great to leave any time for non-constructive criticism and fruitless controversy.

After the ratification of the Santa Fé Compact the most critical stage of Colorado River development will come when the matter of a Congressional appropriation is taken up. It is only to be expected, and only fair, that the states of the Upper Basin shall ask for almost if not quite as much financial help as do those of the Lower Basin. And with the states of the Colorado drainage area asking for some scores of millions, it is only to be expected, and only fair, that the splendidly conceived projects of the Columbia Basin should ask for Government help. One could mention several other reclamation and power projects in the West and South that may be counted upon to advance their claims if there is a disposition to grant any considerable appropriation to the Colorado River Basin states. To a Congress in which agriculture may be said to hold a clean-cut balance of power, the demand of a hundred million or so for the more or less direct purpose of bringing further land under cultivation at a time when the farmer is having trouble in marketing his crops at cost will not be too warmly received.

It is the fact that early flood-control of the Colorado is a matter of life and death to Imperial Valley that gives the Lower Basin project a distinct claim to an immediate hearing and immediate action. The fact that it can be conclusively shown that the sale of power will completely reimburse the Government for all of its expenditures on the Colorado gives also a decided strategical advantage over most of the projects whose claims may be urged by other sections. But the reclamation chords, grandiose as is the conjured vision of a million new homes on the irrigated farms of what is now a desert, will have to be played with a soft pedal to such a Congress as will sit in Washington for a number of years to come.

The point I would make is that absolutely the minimum appropriation needed to get the most imperatively demanded works under way should be asked for at this time. To ask for more will inevitably increase the chances of getting nothing at all. And it would be especially ill advised on the part of Imperial Valley to endeavour to put through a bill, such as was recently introduced in Congress, which would tie to an appropriation for a dam at Boulder Canyon another of twenty million dollars for an All-American canal. Fully as the Valley is entitled to have such a canal, should it be proved feasible from an engineering standpoint, early and complete flood-control is ten-fold more desirable. To risk the defeat, or at least the indefinite postponement, of the dam on the off-chance of getting the canal would be the height of folly. The All-American canal will come in its own good time once a comprehensive scheme of general development is under way. Indeed, the surest way to give it a set-back will be to endeavour to make it run the gauntlet of Congress on the back of a far more urgently needed project that will have a hard enough time staggering through on its own legs.

Because the most urgent problem of Colorado River development—flood control—is exclusively one of the Lower Basin, the Reclamation Service has not yet elaborated any comprehensive plan covering the projects of the Upper Basin. The upper Colorado or Grand, between the mouth of the Blue and that of the Green, has a fall of thirty-six hundred feet, with the possibility of developing perhaps 2,000,000 horse-power. The Green is capable of furnishing about one-third this amount of power, being inferior to the Grand in fall, volume and in the character of its power sites.

The most favourable point for power development in the Upper Basin is at the Kremling site, just above Gore Canyon on the Grand. Several hundred thousand horse-power could be developed here, within practicable transmitting distance of Denver and most of the mining camps of Colorado. Some power has been developed by private interests, but the work has been badly bungled.   The Dewey site, below the mouth of the Dolores River, is very favourable for a reservoir and, as it intercepts practically the entire flow of the Grand, has great power possibilities.   It is, however, rather too remote from any considerable power markets for present development.

There are many good reservoir sites on the Green, at all of which power can be developed.   Most of these are within reasonable transmission distance of Salt Lake City and the other intermountain markets.   That at Flaming Gorge is the logical first development on account of its proximity to the railroad. Brown's Park and Ouray would be the next in order, though the latter may be ruled out because it is in the way of a proposed railway line between Salt Lake and Denver, which is generally regarded as the more important enterprise of the two.

Unless the Government shows a disposition to handle all of the Colorado as one comprehensive scheme, sooner or later a considerable part of the power development will doubtless be turned over to private interests.   This is especially true of the Upper Basin, where there is little immediate need of development for flood control or irrigation, and where the power companies already in the field have shown a desire and the ability to undertake the work.   Mr. Davis believes that the ideal plan would call for concentration of management in the hands of the Government.   He writes:

"Personally I think the development of power on this whole watershed ought to be conducted by the Government on account of the conflicting interests and the dependence of one development upon another.   Unless all these power sites are ultimately under one management they would waste an immense amount of water for lack of coordination of the uses and the markets; but this is a bigger job than there is any prospect of Uncle Sam undertaking at present, and its agitation is therefore somewhat academic."

The extent to which private capital will participate in the development of the Colorado will undoubtedly depend very largely upon the promptness and decisiveness with which the

Government acts in getting under way with the first great project of the Lower Basin. Once the way is clear for Congressional action through the ratification of the Santa Fé Compact, any continued disposition on the part of that body to delay an appropriation for a dam will surely result in a strong and insistent demand that the Government either move or stand aside and make room for action on the part of a properly qualified private corporation. Those in the Southwest who are opposed to Government ownership or control on principle have contended all along that the Colorado River problems could be better solved by opening the way for private enterprise. There can be no question that the number of these will be greatly augmented the moment it becomes clear that Congress will not face squarely the issue of getting at least flood control under way. A private corporation is under the handicap of having to pay one or two percent more for its money than does the Government. A part of this difference is accounted for by the fact that the corporation bond is taxed and the Government bond is not, so that the saving in interest is more apparent than real. The higher efficiency of private as opposed to public management would probably make up the remainder of the difference in interest. That is to say, it would probably cost the public no more to have a private corporation build a dam on the Colorado than to have it built by the Government.

Under the present Federal statutory requirements, it should be understood, granting a power license to an individual or to a private corporation is in no sense an assignment of the rights of the people for exploitation. Neither titles to land nor any water rights in perpetuity pass to the licensee under the Federal Water Power Act. The licensee pays an annual rental, the amount of which is determined by the power capacity of the site in accordance with the formulæ that are laid down either by the Act or by the rules of the Commission thereunder. At the end of the period for which the license is granted provision is made for the return of the property to the United States at a value which represents the net investment and which cannot include any value whatever for water rights or lands.   The Act is administered by the Federal Power Commission, which consists of three members of the Cabinet, namely, the Secretaries of War, Agriculture and Interior.   There can be no question but that the rights of the public are as effectively safeguarded through its operation as under a project actually built and owned by the Government itself.

I mention these brief facts in order to make plain that the alternative to Federal financing and carrying out of the Colorado River projects will not—indeed, can not—result in the orgy of private exploitation that certain more or less socialistically inclined propagandists try to make out would take place. The development of the Colorado Basin is not necessarily in its last ditch in going to Congress for an appropriation.   From my recent trip through the states of the Southwest I am convinced that there exists to-day, along with the hope of financial assistance from the Government, a popular desire that the work on the Colorado shall also be carried out by the Government. It was equally plain, however, that the desire will pass the moment the hope is proved futile.   The decision is largely up to Congress.   The people of the Southwest, and especially those of the Imperial Valley, will not hesitate long as to which they will turn to for assistance between a Congress that prefers words to action and private interests of assured technical and financial standing that are prepared to spend thirty million dollars a year on the Colorado and start work at once.

.   .   .   .

As I write these concluding words the papers carry dispatches conveying two items of news likely to be of considerable importance in their bearing on the future of the Lower Basin of the Colorado.   One states that heavy snows and early thaws are expected to conspire to make the summer rise of the lower

Colorado especially dangerous, the other that a conference called by the Governor of Arizona has recommended that this state shall go ahead with Colorado River development independently of action by other states of the Basin. This means that as the menace of the uncontrolled Colorado becomes more imminent steps have been taken that will render the chances of relief from that menace more remote. The failure of Arizona to act in co-operation with the other states of the Basin inevitably means interminable litigation that may well paralyze the desperately demanded control work for many years. Should the half million acres of Imperial Valley become permanently submerged as a consequence of having to wait upon the Law's delays, the responsibility for what may well be the most destructive disaster of modern times will be placed squarely upon the shoulders of that misguided clique of selfish politicians into whose hands Arizona has delivered her destinies at the crucial moment of her history.

This situation, so potentially tragic, recalls to mind an allusion in the so-called prayer with which the late session of the Arizona Legislature was opened. The orotund supplication is illuminative as giving some hint of what this band of idealists is striving for, and how.

"O Thou Eternal Jehovah, on this inaugural day, as this grand old Roman assumes the gubernatorial responsibilities of this great commonwealth, we stand as hopeful, happy expectants of better days for Arizona. We pray that he may have wisdom to steer the ship of state over the breakers of extravagance and the deep seas of indebtedness which now confront him.

"During his tenure of office spare him the unjust, unreasonable criticism of disgruntled, mugwump Democrats, shrewd and designing Republican politicians and sensational headlines of newspapers. Grant that he may have the support and co-operation of all sections, from every hilltop high and valley low, from desert waste and city full, from these high and fertile valleys where the lowing herds come winding o'er the lea and the plowman homeward plods his weary way, from the golden west where the sun gilds the western hills and the beautiful Colorado winds its way like a silver thread on its way to the ocean; from the north, where the snow-capped mountains and waving pines kiss the skies and the aurora borealis shines at midnight like the noonday sun; from the east, where the quivering, glimmering rays of the coming sun prophesy the approach of the coming day and the stars pour their lustre on the mountain slopes; from the sunny south, where the notes of the nightingale are more melodious than the lays and lutes of Olympus and the song of the mocking-bird sweeter than the sound of the dulcimer that is heard in the shadow of death.

"Grant, O Lord, that the banner of peace and prosperity may wave over Arizona until every state in the Union shall point with pride to this, the youngest, fairest daughter and brightest star that shines in the galaxy of states, and that Arizona may be regarded as the playground of the angels."

In reprinting this modest appeal a Washington paper added the following postscript:

"Grant too that this lusty Roman may induce this state to ratify the Colorado River Compact so that protection from the floods may come to the people of the lower valley, and so that our giant river may no longer dissipate its energies as it idles its way to the sea but may be set to its God-given task of making deserts bloom and silent, tomb-like valleys echo with the clatter of busy industrial machinery."

As no item of the original supplication appears in way of being granted, probably no useful end would have been served by trying to get the amendment by. In the very session of the legislature which was opened by this prayer, that much-prayed-for old Roman and his willing lictors dragged the Colorado River Compact to its knees. Now they are trying to kill it for good.

Somehow one is reminded of that other old Roman—the one who fiddled while his capital was burning. As a matter of fact, there was probably not a lot that was inflammable (save specially tar-daubed Christian torches) in the ancient city by the yellow Tiber; probably not a tithe of what there is that is swampable in the valley by the yellowish Colorado. And Nero, if history is to be believed, was really a good deal of a virtuoso on the violin. His Christian torches at least went up in smoke to the accompaniment of music more or less comparable to the lays and lutes of Olympus, perhaps even to the sound of the dulcimer that is heard in the shadow of death. But disaster on the lower Colorado will be punctuated by no such musical interludes. If Imperial Valley swamps it will be as the result and to the accompaniment of the braying of asses.

Part III

AFTERWORD

AFTERWORD

THE GRAND CANYON NATIONAL PARK [1]

THE early Spanish explorers—possibly because they came in the time that geographical knowledge of the world was unfolding like a scroll to stir men's imaginations and men's souls—were more deeply impressed by the stupendous magnitude of the Grand Canyon of the Colorado than were the first Americans. Cárdenas spoke of the rocks in the great gorge, to whose verge he had been led by the Indians, as comparable in size to the Cathedral of Seville, while the gentle Garcés gazed in wonder at "the most profound caxones that ever onward continue."

The trapper, James Pattie, almost certainly the first American to see the great chasm, stressed only his relief at finally coming to a point where he was clear of "these horrid mountains." Lieutenant Ives, after writing the most brilliant descriptions ever penned of the gorges of the lower Colorado, found the desert plateau region above the Grand Canyon so inhospitable that he expressed a belief that his party would be the last ever to venture there.[2]

Major Powell was the first fully to appreciate the scenic wonders of the Grand Canyon, just as he was the first to traverse its depths. Lieutenant Wheeler, though regrettably matter-of-fact in the descriptions of his battles with the rapids of the lower canyon, donned the mantle of Elijah to good purpose when he wrote that this region would in time be visited by "the

[1] I am enabled to write these concluding words on a subject that should be very close to the heart of all outdoor-loving Americans through the courtesy of my publishers, at considerable inconvenience and expense, in holding open a place for it long after the galley proofs had been read and returned to them.

[2] See Pattie and Ives chapters.

441

denizens of all the world." The voluminous reports of both
Powell and Wheeler played an important part in bringing about
the movement which, after more than three decades, culminated
in the creation of the Grand Canyon National Park.

The National Park idea, which first took tangible shape in
the creation of the reserve of the Yellowstone in 1872, had a
slow growth in its earlier years. So little had that splendid
conception touched the popular imagination that the proposal
to set aside a similar park to include the most spectacular section of the Grand Canyon of the Colorado failed because the
public was not sufficiently interested to whip the politicians
into action. The first of the several bills designed to give this
region national park status was introduced in 1886 by Ben-
jamin Harrison, then Senator from Indiana. After twenty-two
years of inaction and apathy, Roosevelt cut a strand of the
Gordian knot by creating the area a national monument.
Various schemes for private enrichment at public expense prevented further action until 1919, when, thirty-three years after
the first measure was introduced, the present Grand Canyon
National Park was finally created.

At one time or another there were two or three projects for
railways through that section of the Grand Canyon region now
included in the Park. There were also numerous more or less le-
gitimate mining schemes. Finally, according to the 1923 edition
of "Rules and Regulations," "less than a year before it became
a park efforts were making in New York to raise money to
dam its water for power and irrigation."

Failing to enter the citadel by treachery, no further efforts
have been made to storm it by frontal attack. Of the score
and more plans for Colorado River Basin development that I
have had outlined to me in the course of the last two years, not
one contemplated construction calculated even so much as to
back the tail of a reservoir across the boundaries of the Grand
Canyon National Park.

I am not, thank heaven! to be numbered among those unchastened ones who experience no inhibitioning shame at the thought of trying to paint with finite words so supreme an expression of the Infinite as the Grand Canyon. None but a self-made man inordinately pleased with the work of his maker could attempt such a thing in all seriousness. Others have tried it, of course, but they would mostly have been writing back to the home papers by prearrangement. Henry Van Dyke, whose thoroughly sincere interpretative word-paintings of the great gorge stand head and shoulders above all the adjectival chromos that have ever been splashed by tongue or pen, is frank to admit that the tourist who exclaims "My God!" at his first awed sight of the abyss has just about compassed the alpha-to-omega of human expression. And Professor Van Dyke is our first authority on that sort of thing—perhaps just about the only living man who can be trusted to paint nature pictures with the English language without having the fumes of his colours go to his head and turn him into a whirling dervish.

"My God!" is, of course, somewhat conventional as an unconventionality, even as an expression of emotion. A certain type of person is impelled to use it rather freely for the very fact that it is so essentially "story-book." The deepest expression of feeling I myself have ever observed at the brink of the Grand Canyon was of a diametrically antithetical character. This was by a long, lanky Southerner—possibly a Texas cowboy or rancher—who drew up an awe-dropped jaw to mutter between clenched teeth: "Oh, you little old blank-of-a-blank!" He most certainly did not really intend to imply that the Grand Canyon was "little," any more than he intended to cast aspersion upon the lineage of its maternal ancestor. Yet I saw the glint of moisture on the lashes of a man who was possibly never before profoundly moved by anything above the latitude of the line of his close-cinched belt.

I have treasured that memory and shall always be fearful of marring the classic perfection of it by being drawn into something in the word-painting line myself. I am forbearing now, as I trust I shall be able to do in the future; but there is a short paragraph of what one might call characterization that I shall take the liberty of quoting.

"There is no doubt that the Grand Canyon is one of the world's greatest spectacles. It is impossible to compare it with the tremendous white spectacle of the Himalayas, or with the House of Everlasting Fire of the Hawaii National Park, or with the 17,000 feet of snow and glacier which rise abruptly between the observer's eyes and the summit of Mount McKinley, because it has nothing in common with any of these. But of its own kind there is nothing in the world which approaches it in form, size, and glowing color; it is much the greatest example of stream erosion. And in its power to rouse the emotion of the looker-on to stupefy or exhilarate, it has no equal of any kind anywhere, unless it be the starry firmament itself."

I like that paragraph immensely, principally, I think, because in its sanity, fairness and truthfulness it is in such refreshing contrast to the characteristic hysteria of the general run of so-called tourist literature. Some one in the National Park Service penned those lines, and the words I have used to commend them—sanity, fairness and truthfulness—may just as appropriately be applied to that bureau itself. At a time when that loosely-flung "Greatest on Earth!" is being tagged by a blatant minority upon everything from tooth-paste to scenery produced or discovered under the Stars and Stripes, it is indeed a relief to find one of the genuinely great things of creation so conservatively yet adequately characterized. Because the National Park Service has full confidence in the goods upon its shelves, it need not, and does not, resort to ballyhoo methods to bring them to the attention of the public. The dignity and sincerity of the publicity campaign of the Park Service stamp it as a thing apart from the flamboyant efforts of the common booster.

In writing last year of the men leading the fight of the National Park Service to save the Yellowstone from the encroachments of private interests working through their political puppets, I characterized them as "practical idealists." This term, used on the spur of the moment as the antithesis of the reiterated sneer of "impractical idealists," has been thoroughly vindicated by the fuller experience and knowledge of the Service that have come to me since. Like attracts like, and the example of Director Mather and his devoted lieutenants is developing an *esprit de corps* that is equalled in very few Government bureaus. From the Park Superintendents to the men of the farthest flung ranger patrol there is manifest a spirit for which I can think of no more apt comparison than that of a very conscientious trustee of a minor child. The child is the still annoyingly care-free and irresponsible American public (the same that the political spell-binder always calls "great" around election time), and the National Park Service as trustee is striving against what are at times discouragingly heavy odds to protect a fabulously rich natural legacy until he can be educated to know the value of his heritage and so be safe from frittering it away.

. . . .

The National Park Service took over a going concern when it extended its wing to cover the Grand Canyon—a very strongly going concern. The Santa Fé Railway already had a spur built to the very brink of the Rim and for many years had been making an earnest and increasingly successful effort to divert transcontinental travellers to the Canyon. The Santa Fé had brought Fred Harvey to run the hotels and camps, thereby making available to visitors one of the most consistently excellent systems of its kind ever developed. With a vision not generally conceded to the soulless corporation of popular fancy, the Santa Fé-Harvey combination was already planning to make El Tovar section of the Rim a Canyon gateway worthy of its incomparable setting. The readjustment incident to the advent of Federal control has been only a matter of bringing

frontiers of India. An interior motif carried out along Navajo
and Hopi lines has the same direct simplicity of appeal as the
red sandstone walls and the sage-green roofs which take their
shadings from the Tonto shale.

Notwithstanding the fact that it will be a good many years
before the travel to Phantom Ranch can possibly be expected
to pay a fair return upon the outlay, the sentimental satisfaction of having sketched in a bit of picture not unworthy of its
splendid natural frame brought completer if less tangible re-
ward, and doubtless prepared the way for facing squarely the
problem of an ideal plan for El Tovar section of the Rim. As
I write these lines a discussion of the tentative details of such
a plan is in progress between the three interested parties—the
Santa Fé, the Harveys and the National Park Service. This
has already gone to a point where it is evident that a full agreement can ultimately be reached. Director Mather has laid
down a broad, plainly demarked line to which any plan of permanent development shall conform in stating that it must be
compatible with the dignity of its surroundings. That is a
lofty mark at which to aim, but that the associated interests
concerned are ready to launch the shaft is evident from the
fact that they have called upon the firm of Graham, Anderson,
Probst and White, of Chicago, to prepare a plan for wiping out
all that is unfit to survive in the present Grand Canyon plant
and building anew from the ground up structures worthy and
capable of surviving the centuries. Phantom Ranch may be
considered as a microcosm of what is to be striven for on a
grand scale—something that fits as nearly as the wit and imagination of man can devise into the greater scheme of Nature;
something that "belongs."

The outstanding success of the commissioned architects in
handling such great works as the Columbian Exposition, the
city plans of Chicago and Manila and several important modern
railway terminals is earnest of their fitness to make the utmost
from the incomparable opportunity that has come to them. No

less fortunate is the presence at the Grand Canyon as Park Superintendent of Colonel W. W. Crosby, whose distinguished record as a civil and military engineer, no less than the fact that he has proven himself a man of the Mather and Albright enthusiasm for and devotion to the National Park idea, qualifies him as the ideal Governmental representative during the interval that the splendidly conceived plan is getting under way.

With the complete agreement between the Santa Fé-Harvey interests on the one hand and the National Park Service on the other a practical certainty, it would appear that the hardest hurdle yet to be cleared will be that of financing an expenditure which cannot but mount well into the millions before it is finished on a scale commensurate with even the needs of the present generation. It is believed, however, that the cost will not be greater than would be warranted by the returns from the increase in travel that the associated companies interested are justified in expecting.

The inauguration of a work of this character at the Grand Canyon will be a mile-stone in the history of the national park movement throughout the world no less important than that which marks the creation of the first of all national parks, that of the Yellowstone. As an example, a precedent, it is destined to open the way to developments of great significance, not the least of which may be the creation of a bureau of park planning as a branch of the National Park Service.

.   .   .   .

The appreciation of the minor child of the American public for his heritage of the National Parks has grown apace. Nearly three times as many of him visited the parks in 1922 as in 1918, and it is not improbable that even this steeply rising curve of increase will be maintained for a good many years. The child is learning to like the parks for a number of things besides their scenic attractiveness. Near the head of the list may be placed the fact that the areas inside of their borders have become the last and only spots in his broad land where he is safe from the more or less lawless greed of those with whom he needs must traffic when he fares forth upon his lawful occasions. No man or corporation that has not a record for clean, fair, decent dealings with the public has any chance of obtaining a park concession in the first place; in the second place, the park system of regulation is so comprehensive and drastic that no one can profiteer under it even if he has the desire. For this reason alone a project for the extension of the National Park boundaries until they were coterminous with those of Canada and Mexico and the shores of the Atlantic and the Pacific would be assured of active and enthusiastic support whenever it should be proposed.

Every good outdoor-loving American citizen, active or potential, will do well to set about learning what his National Parks can give him. A good way to start in would be to become a consistent reader of the annual report of the Director, as well as of all other publications issued by the National Park Service. That will fit him to acquire the park habit which, once it gets a footing, will stay with him for the rest of his days.

All that has ever been accomplished in preserving the National Parks for the public was effected in spite of the opposition of selfish private interests and their puppet political representatives; all that may ever eventuate to undermine the foundations of the monumental structure of to-day will be traceable to the same pernicious source. Public apathy was responsible for the slow growth of the park system in its earlier decades; public apathy will likewise be responsible if anything happens to check its vigorous growth of the present.

No American who has learned to know and love his parks but will entertain the same feeling toward the predatory politician who plots to plunder them as he does toward a thief in the night. One cannot very well use a gun on the political marauder, it is true, but it chances that this particular type of miscreant can be just about as painfully wounded by a well-dropped ballot as by a well-sped bullet. It should be the business of every park lover to learn where to plant his ballot to do the most execution. The open season for balloting the political plunderer into innocuousness comes round almost every November.